THE MAYOR OF CASTRO STREET

the Life & Times of

HARVEY MILK

RANDY SHILTS

ST. MARTIN'S PRESS
NEW YORK

Design by Manuela Paul

Library of Congress Cataloging-in-Publication Data

Shilts, Randy.
  The Mayor of Castro Street : the life and times of Harvey Milk /
by Randy Shilts.
    p.   cm.
  Includes bibliographical references and index.
  ISBN 0-312-01900-9 (pbk.) : $10.95
    1. Milk, Harvey.   2. Gay liberation movement—California—San
Francisco.   3. Politicians—California—San Francisco—Biography.
4. San Francisco (Calif.)—Politics and government.   5. San
Francisco (Calif.)—Biography.   I. Title.   88-1836
F869.S353M547 1988   979.4′61053′0924—dc19   [B]   CIP

Research for this book has previously appeared in *New West, Village Voice,
San Francisco Chronicle, San Francisco Examiner, Los Angeles Herald-Exam-
iner,* Criminal Justice Publications, National Public Radio, KSAN-FM news,
KTVU-TV's "Ten O'Clock News" and KQED-TV's "Newsroom," "A Closer
Look," and "Evening Edition" programs.
  The book is an expansion of "The Life and Death of Harvey Milk," first
published in *Christopher Street* magazine in March 1979.

For
Bud and Norma Shilts,
My mom and dad

*"If a bullet should enter
my brain, let that bullet
destroy every closet door."*

Contents

Appendix

Acknowledgments

More than anyone else, Scott Smith, Harvey's lover and the executor of the Milk estate, helped make this book a complete account of both Milk's personal and political life. He spent many hours unselfishly recounting his own memories with Harvey and putting me in contact with many other people important in Harvey's life. Like Scott, Joe Campbell also deserves special thanks for delving deeply into personal and sometimes painful memories about his relationship with Harvey. I'm also indebted to Harvey's friends Jim Rivaldo, Frank Robinson and Tom Randol for their help in the research phases. Political activist Michael Wong gave me the single most useful document for the book when he shared the detailed diary he kept of every interaction he had with Harvey for over five years. Jim Gordon of the Harvey Milk Archives, Bob Ross of the *Bay Area Reporter* and Charles Morris of *The Sentinel* also permitted me to intrude on them for many days, pouring over their files and back issues. I'm indebted to Allan Berube of the San Francisco Gay History Project for sharing his intriguing research about the effect that World War II had on the San Francisco gay community. My friend David Israels spent long hours as both sounding board and prodder. Many journalists shared their perceptions with me while I was researching the book; among the most useful undoubtedly were Francis Moriarty and Victor Zonana. This work would never have known a place on a bookshelf without the faith of my editor, Michael Denneny. Thanks also to my friends Dan Yoder, Ann Neuenschwander, Tom Lang, my brother Gary Shilts and, of course, Steve Newman for their personal support during the writing process.

Author's Note

There are times, rare times, when the forces of social change collide with a series of dramatic events to produce moments which are later called historic. Just such a time fell on San Francisco during the late 1970s. The tide of history that briefly swept the city included dramatic scenarios of assassinations, rioting, political intrigue and angry street demonstrations which routinely drew crowds numbering into the hundreds of thousands. But most significantly, San Francisco became the national vortex for the aspirations of a new movement which was only then coming of age—the gay movement.

History offers few people whose lives neatly parallel the social causes they come to represent, but from this turbulent era came such a man, Harvey Milk. The story of Harvey Milk is, to a large extent, the story of the gay movement in San Francisco, and, ultimately, the nation. This is the story of Harvey Milk, his life and times.

This book is a piece of journalism that employs standard, professional reportorial techniques in the gathering and verifying of all the information cited. In the course of this narrative I reconstruct scenes, recount conversations, and occasionally attribute observations to people with phrases such as "he thought" or "she felt." All such references are drawn from either the research interviews I conducted specifically for this book or from direct knowledge gained over the years working as a San Francisco reporter. In checking the accuracy of facts in this book, I have relied on the usual technique of using on-the-record interviews, or, when that was not possible, corroborating possible points of contention with at least three unnamed sources. That's a standard rule of reporting and the basic discipline of the book.

Most of the information about Harvey Milk's personal life came from approximately one hundred and forty interviews I conducted with people, ranging from septagenarians who have known three generations of the Milk family to the people with whom Milk played basketball on his high school junior varsity team and the men with whom he spent his last nights. The overall analyses of San Francisco city politics and the evolution of gay politics in the Bay Area was profoundly shaped by my five years of reporting in San Francisco, as both a television correspondant and a freelance writer. During that time, I knew Harvey Milk and covered the panoply of other figures in this book. I worked the City Hall beat under the administrations of both the late George Moscone and Dianne Feinstein. Most of the observations about the sociology of the Castro Street neighborhood come from the fact I've lived in the area since 1975. Because I'm an acknowledged gay journalist, I've also had access to interviews and anecdotes which generally elude other reporters. The lack of many lesbians in important roles in this book comes from a reality I could not alter as a journalist; Harvey did not have much contact with lesbians either socially or politically.

This book will not please ideologues looking for a political tract. Conversely some might complain that it is sympathetic to the gay point of view, because no traces of moral outrage against homosexuality are to be found on these pages. On this point I agree with historian John Boswell when he wrote, "What will strike some readers as a partisan point of view is chiefly the absence of negative attitudes on this subject ubiquitous in the modern West; after a long, loud noise, a sudden silence may seem deafening." I suspect others might fret that this book is indiscreet in its discussion of private topics not normally raised in the journalistic forum. I can only answer that I tried to tell the truth and, if not be objective, at least be fair; history is not served when reporters prize trepidation and propriety over the robust journalistic duty to tell the whole story.

Randy Shilts
July, 1981
San Francisco

Prologue

Eleven A.M., November 27, 1978. A huddle of disbelieving reporters crowds around a locked door in San Francisco City Hall. A few feet away, down a narrow hallway and behind another closed door, the lanky body of Supervisor Harvey B. Milk sprawls face down in a spreading pool of blood.

The outer door is opened and closed by the police and city supervisors; reporters knock elbows trying to get a glimpse of any detail. They don't know what they're looking for, but it's their job to look anyway. A television crew bursts on the scene, adding to the confusion. The mayor's been shot. No, Harvey Milk's been shot. They've both been shot? Are they dead? With the Jonestown mass suicide only nine days behind them, the newspeople ask the obvious question: Is this the work of the People's Temple hit squad?

The small door opens again. Inside, the cadre of young aides Milk had gathered together fall into one another's arms crying, their eyes dazed with confusion. "We've lost it," says one. "It's over."

Harvey had always told them it would end this way, with bullets in the brain. But only when they see the black rubber body bag, covered with a crisp, pleated sheet, being rolled to the waiting ambulance does Harvey's prophecy become the palpable reality that makes for bad dreams and bold headlines.

On the other side of City Hall, reporters mob another locked door. Behind it, a police officer picks the still-burning cigarette from between the fingers of Mayor George Moscone who, like Milk, was felled with shots in the chest and then coolly executed with two bullets pumped into the back of his head. Board of Supervisors President Dianne Feinstein must make the stunning announcement: "Mayor Moscone and Supervisor Harvey Milk have been shot . . . and killed." The gasps drown out her next words. Her voice breaks as she delivers the shocker: "Police have a suspect. Supervisor Dan White."

A few blocks away, Dan White and his wife are walking from St.

Mary's Cathedral to Northern Station. White turns himself in to a
former colleague and close friend. Within an hour, he puts his confession down on tape, telling how he crawled through the basement window, shot the mayor, reloaded his gun, and shot Harvey Milk because
Harvey had smirked at him. The all-American boy, former paratrooper, onetime firefighter, ex-cop, and the one politician who had
stood up to what he called the "splinter groups of radicals, social
deviates, and incorrigibles" is charged with two counts of first-degree
murder.

Hours later, forty thousand tiny flames quiver in the night breeze
as mourners carrying candles trudge somberly to City Hall. In three-
piece suits, black leather jackets, blue jeans, and neatly pressed dresses,
they gather under the cloudy autumn sky to remember the gangly ward
politician with the funny name, the thick black hair, the corny jokes and
the New York accent. The speakers apologize for talking less about the
powerful mayor, who was one of the best-known politicians in California, than about Harvey Milk, the unlikely populist who had lost three
of the four elections in which he was a candidate and served less than
eleven months in office once he was elected. The emphasis surprises few
in the largely homosexual crowd. The mayor had given them leadership, but Harvey Milk—the nation's first openly gay city official—had
given them a dream. "A true function of public officials is not just to
pass laws and approve appropriations, but to give hope," Harvey had
said repeatedly in his five-year political career. In death, Harvey Milk's
dream started casting a shadow far larger than anything he could have
fashioned in life; such is the nature of mortals and martyrs, dreams and
their shadows. Even as the mourners ponder the constant turbulence
of the recent troubled years in San Francisco, some start to speak of
a Harvey Milk legend.

A stocky, handsome man has driven fifty miles through the night
to join the mourners. He is confused by all this talk. Joe Campbell met
Harvey Milk in 1956. For seven years they were lovers. What do
politics have to do with homosexuality? he wonders. With the Harvey
he knew, homosexuality was something to conceal, to be vaguely
ashamed of, certainly nothing to walk down the street and crow about.
The lover he knew was infinitely more concerned with redecorating his
apartment than with changing the world.

Across the continent, a younger man watches pictures of the candlelight march on the late night news. Jack McKinley recalls the five
years he spent loving Harvey Milk in New York City during the 1960s.

That his stubbornly conventional former lover, a successful Wall Street financial analyst whose politics rarely strayed to the left of Barry Goldwater, would get shot to prove some political point seems unfathomable to him. But as McKinley looks at the mile-long procession of softly glimmering lights in San Francisco, he's sure of one thing. This is good theater and Harvey loved good theater.

Scott Smith barely feels alive as he walks down the marble steps of City Hall toward the sea of candles. He had met Harvey in New York when Harvey was a Broadway producer making the avant-garde scene as a forty-one-year-old hippy. They had moved to San Francisco together, established their camera shop, and lain in bed until the early morning hours arguing campaign strategy. "You're going to write about the life of Harvey Milk?" he asks some months later, almost sardonically. "It's all so strange. Nothing needs to be fictionalized. If somebody tried to write it as fiction, no one would believe it."

"Swing low, sweet chariot." The song drifts gently into the night, as forty thousand stand beneath the grand rotunda of City Hall where Harvey Milk had worked and died. At midnight, the crowd melts quietly away. Candles are left to shimmer on the bronze statue of Abraham Lincoln sitting in front of City Hall, the lights casting a multitude of tiny shadows. The mourners turn to walk back toward Castro Street, where it seems right for this night to end. After years of searching and drifting, Castro Street had become Harvey's hometown, and he had worked to make it a hometown for tens of thousands of homosexuals from around the world. The mayor of Castro Street, that was Harvey's unofficial title. And now the mayor of San Francisco and the mayor of Castro Street lie dead. What is left is the dream and its lengthening shadow.

THE MAYOR
OF CASTRO STREET

the Life & Times of

HARVEY MILK

PART I
The Years without Hope

one

The Men without Their Shirts

First came the feeling of being different. Somehow. It was like a radio. Before you hear it, even before you turn it on, a signal exists.

He was an ordinary sort, everybody agrees. Seemed to fit in well enough: an average student, a second-string high school athlete, and a wit that more than compensated for a plain, if not homely, face. Still, some noticed something different even then. Not peculiar or odd, just different.

Harvey Milk would strain, sweat, and wrestle to keep the difference a secret only a few could know. On the rare occasions when the cover did slip, he would realize the size of the stakes. They were high enough to keep him sweating and straining for many years, like so many others.

August 1947. A sweltering Sunday afternoon. Election years routinely forced the politicians to fend off charges that New York City had become a haven for prostitutes and perverts. The cadre of police moving lazily uptown through Central Park on that sultry afternoon were of little concern to the families lolling about the meadows. The husbands eyed their children briefly before laying back down

3

to sun their bare chests, their heads propped on rolled-up undershirts.

Minutes later, in the more isolated sections of the park, where men eyed each other instead of children, the police descended with methodical swiftness, as they had so many times before. By taking off their shirts, these men were technically guilty of indecent exposure—this *is* a public place.

Seventeen-year-old Harvey Milk trembled as police shunted him and the other homosexual men toward the paddy wagons. Across the meadow, Harvey saw the equally shirtless family men nodding grimly at the thought that their children had been romping so close to deviants. Young Milk was bewildered but not angry as he stepped into the dark paddy wagon. Anger had no place among homosexuals of those years, only fear. Not only fear of the police, but fear of himself and of his secret being revealed by an afternoon's routine police action. Harvey was lucky that day. Police often didn't bother to lock up their quarry. Just put a little fear of God in them.

Glimpy Milch, Harvey's other name. Glimpy was for his unlikely appearance, the big schnoz, flappy ears, and oversized feet that early on made him look like some character from a Walt Disney cartoon. Milch was the surname he always considered his. It was the name his grandfather Morris had when he emigrated from Lithuania, Harvey told friends later. Milk was merely the English translation.

The urbane, goateed Morris Milk earned Harvey's early admiration. Through peddling up and down Long Island, Morris acquired enough to open Milk's Dry Goods in Woodmere in 1882, a business that rapidly grew into the largest department store on the island. The Milk patriarch clearly knew how to get things done. Barely enough Jews lived in Woodmere for a minyan, the quorum of Jewish males necessary to hold a service, but Milk helped organize the area's first synagogue, Beth Israel. Years later, his widow even traveled to Palestine to choose the cornerstone and escort it back to Beth Israel's groundbreaking. When the local Rockaway Hunt Club did not let Jews join, Morris Milk and his fellow Jewish burghers simply started their own. But the second of Morris' six children, William, was not destined to be a pillar of the community. Bill worked some time at the store, then drifted out west to work as a cowboy, later enlisting in the navy to serve on a sub crew during World War I.

The spirited Minerva Karns did not know exactly what she would do with her life when the Great War broke out, but she knew it wouldn't be traditional. The lively Brooklyn girl wasn't about to sit around knitting while the guys saw all the excitement, so she trotted down to the navy enlistment office on October 10, 1918, and signed up as one of the first yeomanettes, the pioneers of the women's navy.

After the war, both Bill and Minerva returned to their disparate New York lives, not entirely settled. Minnie kept striking an independent course. She nearly lost her stenographer's job when she saw a Clara Bow movie and raced to the stylist to get one of the first bobbed hairstyles in Manhattan. Fortunately, half the steno pool bobbed their hair within two weeks. Bill was back working at his dad's store in Woodmere. By now he was distinctively forthright with an irritating penchant for a loud laugh at best; at worst, he was temperamental and tactless.

Measuring in at five foot two and 106 pounds, the brown-eyed Minnie was no match in size for her future gangly husband, but her sharp wit let her hold her own against Bill's tantrums during their courtship. From their marriage came two sons, Robert Milk and, four years later, Harvey Bernard Milk, born May 22, 1930, at Woodmere General Hospital.

Harvey was in an elegant tuxedo now, the orchestra assembled before him. He glanced up at the stage, tapped his wand, and from the handsome radio on the mantelpiece burst forth the live Saturday afternoon opera from the old Met. Standing on the hearth, closing his eyes, waving his hands with affected precision, eleven-year-old Harvey conducted the unseen orchestra.

The flair for theatricality was evident early. Harvey loved attention, and he got it. As a child, he and brother Bob would go to the Lone Ranger matinees in the Rockaways. The highlight of Harvey's day was not the serials, but the raffles, and the rare moments when he had the winning ticket and could mount the stage for his prize. The greater reward, of course, was the chance to bask briefly in the public eye.

Minnie was proud when Harvey came to her during the war years to ask for money. Not for soda pop or saddle shoes, Minnie boasted to the neighbors, but so he could go to the opera. Harvey already had his favorite composers by then—Mahler, Strauss, Wagner—and declared one day, with considerable pomposity, that he considered himself too sophisticated for Verdi.

Bidú Sayão sang that first Saturday matinee as Harvey peeked toward the stage from among the standees at the old Met. It was all he had imagined—and then some. Harvey had never heard the jokes about the old Met's standing section; about standees being the only New Yorkers who wore zippers on both the front and back of their pants, or the one about never being able to tell which sound was louder at the end of an opera, the bravos of the operaphiles or the sound of flies going up in the standing sections. But Harvey got the gist of what the jokes were driving at right off. Every week, Harvey took to asking Minnie for change to augment his allowance so he could go to the opera.

Harvey had always felt different. Now he was learning why. He also was learning that he had to keep that difference a secret. He knew it from the day Minnie sat him down for some serious counseling. If he was going to be trekking into New York City every week, there were some unpleasant facts of life he needed to learn. Minnie's eyes lost their usual twinkle when she told Harvey about people called homosexuals. He had heard the jokes about guys who put on dresses, but there was a second kind of homosexual, too. They hung around the train depot and did things to little boys, Minnie explained. She never said exactly what they did, but the way she talked about it made Harvey realize that what they did was so bad it wasn't even supposed to be talked about.

Am I going to grow up to be one of those men in dresses or end up hanging out at the Woodmere LIRR stop? Harvey worried about this during those first times at the old Met. Sometimes he pushed back the wandering hands. But the dark tinglings were too powerful to be long denied. Random groping led to brief trysts after the performances. The encounters taught him more valuable information: where he could meet other men who liked junior high athletes, how to walk down the streets just so, how to take a casual stroll through the gay sections of Central Park without getting busted.

Harvey dove headfirst into the newly discovered subculture. Rarely were there better years and a more fortuitous locale for a teenager discovering sexuality. The war had pressed sixteen million men together in the military. Pulled from traditional social constraints of families and hometowns, then thrust together in all-male environments, tens of thousands of men who may have once lived out their sex lives in fantasy discovered that many other men were secretly tuned to the same clandestine station. They soon learned how to find each other as they milled amid the thousands of soldiers in the major debarkation points of New York and San Francisco.

Since there weren't enough cots to bed on properly, many of these soldiers were forced to sleep in parks. If you happened to stumble out of the bushes and run into a cop, you were just another G.I. out to catch some shut-eye. Harvey soon heard all the stories, peering from the branches where he hid until the cop walked away. He learned all the tricks and, by his own account, was leading an active homosexual life by the age of fourteen.

Harvey still adored Minnie, but he realized increasingly that her expertise of making matzoh meal pancakes did not give her credentials as an authority on homosexuality. Though he had grave fears about the life he might end up leading—fears that sometimes troubled his sleep and tormented his days—his adolescent randiness drove him on. He'd protect Minnie, he decided, by keeping it a secret. Besides, he had only recently heard the words that described his condition. They weren't words that ever came up in conversation. As Harvey grew older, he learned how important it would be to keep his difference a secret not only from Minnie, but from everybody. Nobody knew in Woodmere or in Bayshore, where the family moved after V-E Day, 1945.

Harvey Milk, the linebacker in jersey number 60 for Bayshore High was no sissy. Bob, the son of the pharmacist—now there was a sissy. The guys hassled him in the locker room, so much he even broke down once and cried. There was another sissy too, Willy, the nelly black guy. He was swishy, but people got along with him. He had a great voice and could dance up a storm. Besides, his big brother was a prominent athlete who could stomp the shit out of anybody who gave Willy a hard time.

Bayshore High had its swishes, but they stuck to the glee club and drama club. They weren't on the football and basketball teams like Glimpy Milk. Nothing ever seemed funny about Harv, his high school friends all agree. Nothing except that big nose. "Better bring an extra high sled so your nose don't plow away the snow when you go down the hill," they joked one weekend when they went sledding at Beth Paige State Park. But Harvey could always snap back with an even funnier schnoz joke and keep everybody in stitches all afternoon. A real funny guy.

The only time anybody saw him mad was when Dick Brown, John Cochran, and Jim Gowan dumped horse manure on the homecoming parade and smeared more dung all over the principal's office. Harvey was furious when he heard of the prank. He kept shouting, "Why didn't you tell me? I wouldda been there."

Harvey's tall build made him an asset to the basketball team. He dabbled in track and wrestling, and made linebacker for the junior varsity football team. After the Friday night game, he'd be up in Attic's soda fountain with the other jocks, pressing jukebox buttons, hoofing the lindy, and making wisecracks when somebody played a serious song like the Mills Brothers' "Always." After Friday night, social life in tiny Bayshore pretty much dried up. Especially for Harvey who was, after all, a Jew and hung around pretty much with black guys who tended not to get all the party invitations. Covertly, however, Harvey kept up his own busy schedule.

The move from Woodmere to Bayshore was so damned inconvenient, Harvey thought at first. The trip to Manhattan took an hour longer on the Long Island Railroad. Harvey knew that admitting he liked opera would make him suspect with the other guys, so he never mentioned his weekly visits to the old Met. There was no doubt that, by now, Harvey had years on his buddies in street smarts. The only reason Harvey was stuck in Bayshore was because Morris Milk balked at turning his dry goods store over to Bill, selling out instead to the New York City conglomerate that owned Macy's. Bill packed up Minnie and Harvey—Bob was still in the service—and moved thirty miles up Long Island to set up Bayshore Furriers at Fourth and Main Streets.

The new location proved Harvey's luckiest break since his first trip to the standing section. Just a few blocks away was the train station where the LIRR deposited passengers for the ferry to a new vacation resort on a sandbar called Fire Island. Come summer, Harvey could catch glimpses of this other world so far from his middle-class Jewish life in Bayshore. Sophisticated writers, famous actors, and glamorous socialites walked by Bayshore Furriers on their way from the LIRR depot to the ferry landing. Ethel Merman sent shivers of excitement through the town when she stopped at the nearby Cortney Hotel for a drink one afternoon. Many of the visitors came in grand automobiles, catching the eyes of all the local boys since most families in Bayshore, including the Milks, were not rich enough to afford a car.

Harvey worked boxing groceries that the weekenders took over to the island. On some weekends, he'd skip the opera and catch the last ferry to Fire Island's Ocean Beach, striking up friendships with some of the older men he'd met in the store. Often, it wasn't even for sex. He had always felt so different, and here he could rub shoulders with other different people, a world away from his life as a j.v. linebacker.

Minnie didn't worry much if Harvey spent Saturday night away from home. She'd had her own maverick streak during her younger years and she wasn't about to deny the same independence to her headstrong son. And Harvey was a model child, not because he excelled, really, but because he had such tenacity. Though he would never have the quickest coordination, he plodded through years in school sports, never the star but always dependable. For some reason, he got it in his head he had to go on to college—and out of Bayshore—a year early, so even though Harvey was only a B student, he was pushing through school faster than just about anybody in his class.

Harvey sometimes felt the urge to bring the two strands of his life —the open and the secret—together, but he liked being popular and having his share of attention in athletics. He didn't want to be like that fat sissy Bob, getting beat up in the locker room, or Willy, sashaying down the halls while everybody made jokes behind his back. So Harvey, the plodder, learned to play the game.

On June 23, 1947, five weeks after his seventeenth birthday, Milk graduated from Bayshore High School. The legend beneath his picture in the yearbook reads: "Glimpy Milk—And they say WOMEN are never at a loss for words."

Eileen Mulcahy graduated a year after Harvey and now works in Bayshore High's audiovisual library. The imposing brick high school has a new wing now and the kids sneak a drag of marijuana instead of a Camel on lunch breaks, but Bayshore's maple-lined streets retain the small-town feel they had thirty-five years ago. John Cochran went on to become the district's state assemblyman. Jim Gowan sits on the state supreme court. The old-timers who work in the administrative offices, however, know that the school's most famous alumnus is Harvey Milk.

Eileen has methodically clipped all the newspaper stories about Harvey over the years and circulated them among her old classmates. "I've thought about this a lot," she says carefully, straining to be precise. "When we were young people, we didn't know there was such a thing as gayness. The worst thing you could do was call somebody a faggot. If Harvey knew this, he had to face it all by himself. It really is terrible to think about. It must have been traumatic for him."

Still, ordinary is the one word that best describes Milk—ordinary except for one point. "He was different, not in the sense that he was peculiar or out of it," says Mulcahy. "But in the sense that he was an individual at a time when people all tried to be alike."

Crusty Clifton LePlatney coached hundreds of teens through decades of football seasons at Bayshore High. Yes, he remembers Harvey Milk; he taught his physics class too. "Harvey was a nice ordinary fellow—not any different than any of the other kids. Just like the other kids in class, the other kids in sports, only more talkative," says the retired coach. "I was surprised, very surprised when I heard about his activities in San Francisco," he says, adding pointedly, "nothing like *that* was ever suspected."

Harvey never did seem to have any friends there, not really close friends. He hung around a lot with Dick Brown, the black basketball player from Williams Street, where Bayshore's four or five black families lived. Like a lot of the class of '47, Brown, now married and a father, has never lived more than five miles away from his hometown. "He kept his secret well—it makes you wonder how many other guys were funny too," Brown muses. "The one thing that gets me mad is, here I'm supposed to be one of his good buddies, but he never trusted me enough to tell me. I can't say how I would have reacted." Brown pauses in recollection. "I guess I would have ostracized him. What a cross to carry. You never know."

Nobody ever heard from Harvey after he graduated. "It was like he dropped off the face of the earth," Brown says. Nobody's ever heard from Bob, the fat sissy, either. The newspaper stories from San Francisco surprised Brown and Harvey's other Bayshore friends. They were especially surprised when they saw the pictures of Harvey in the dailies and he no longer had the nose everybody made cracks about.

Harvey himself never talked much about his childhood in Woodmere and Bayshore, except for two stories. First, the August afternoon a few weeks after his graduation when he was briefly picked up by police for indecent exposure. And then, there was the day his parents sat him down in 1943 to tell him about the brave Jews of Warsaw who were hopelessly outnumbered and surrounded by Nazi troops. But they fought on anyway, not because they thought they could win, but because when something *that* evil descends on the world, you have to fight. Even if it's hopeless.

By the time Harvey took his high school diploma, news of the Nazi Holocaust had shocked the world, especially the millions of American middle-class Jews who had grown to feel so secure. The Holocaust touched Milk doubly, in a way that he could not have imagined at that time.

Before Hitler's rise, Germany had an active gay liberation movement that pressed for legal demands and collected hundreds of thousands of signatures on petitions asking for homosexual equality. But in 1936, Reichsfuhrer SS Heinrich Himmler issued the following decree:

> Just as we today have gone back to the ancient German view on the question of marriages mixing different races, so too in our judgment of homosexuality—a symptom of degeneracy which could destroy our race—we must return to the guiding Nordic principle, extermination of degenerates.

About a year later, Himmler ordered that gays be rounded up and sent to Level 3 camps—the death camps. Gays wore pink triangles, so they would not be confused with Jews who wore yellow stars of David. Some estimates put the number of gays exterminated at over 220,000, the second largest category of Nazi genocide victims after Jews.

This attempt at genocide efficiently squashed the only gay political movement in the Western world. Harvey Milk, meanwhile, was seven years old then, playing in the aisles of grandfather Morris' dry goods store. It would be years before ideas of gay equality rumbled again, this time in the United States.

two

Gay Everyman

The winter of 1947 struck with unexpected fury. The campus of the New York State College for Teachers at Albany lay buried in mounting drifts of snow. The onslaught of returning veterans that year swelled enrollment so much that men were housed in slapped-up barracks. The guys in the C barracks felt lucky that they had the class clown, Harvey Milk, to entertain them. Harvey was assigned the bunk next to the barracks' bathroom, a site which competed only with his nose as a source for his cornucopia of jokes.

A certain camaraderie prevailed among the thousand students at Albany State then. These were the students smart enough to qualify for prestigious private schools, but not rich enough to afford them. So they attended Albany State, the only state school that offered a liberal arts teaching curriculum. They were at the poor man's Yale, they assured themselves; they were the intelligentsia of tomorrow. The young men of the new class of '51 spent their nights up late in their snowbound barracks, arguing Nietzsche, the Truman-Dewey race, and the escalating tensions in Korea.

The subject of homosexuality might flit by in an allusion, but this was the late forties and nobody talked much about it then. Howard Rosman, whose bunk was across the barracks from Harvey's, figured out that two of the other guys in the barracks were queers, but he never saw Milk have anything to do with them. Harvey certainly wasn't what most of the middle-class kids at Albany State thought queers were like. Harvey was just another math major with a minor in his favorite subject, history.

Milk's performance on Bayshore's j.v. team did not rate him a slot on any of the Albany State Great Danes teams, so he stuck to intramural basketball and football. He coached his fraternity basketball team to an intramural championship in his junior year. His major involvement with sports in college, however, was as sportswriter for the *State College News.*

Like the other Jews on campus, Milk could not expect to be invited to the cushier life of the live-in fraternities, so he joined Kappa Beta, the fledgling Jewish fraternity. His social life centered on Jewish activities. Though he rarely dated, he sometimes could be found at the Alpha Epsilon Phi sorority house, entertaining five or six girls at a time with his antics. He occasionally turned up at meetings of Hillel or the Intercollegiate Zionist Federation of America. A gregarious guy, but when the classmates thought back, they recalled something odd. He was always somehow detached.

I don't think you're going to find anybody who isn't Harvey's friend. Everybody likes him. He always has a joke, Doris Brody remembered thinking years later. She'd seen a lot of Harvey at the Alpha Epsilon Phi house and in her history classes. He seemed a paradox. Everybody's friend, but I don't think you'd find anybody who is a real close friend to him either, she thought.

Funny, because Harvey stuck his nose into so many issues. When freshman hazing got Milk's dander up, his writing jumped from the sports section to the editorial page as he railed against the practice. He sternly lectured the thirty-five members of his fraternity, Kappa Beta, that they should admit non-Jewish members. How could they deride the other frats for not admitting Jews when they discriminated themselves? he asked.

Though thoroughly conventional, he sometimes took a maverick path, escorting a black woman friend to a school dance if he felt like it. One of his better friends was a black basketball player who, like Milk, took up the somewhat suspicious pastime of jotting verses of poetry.

But that was about as suspicious as Milk ever got. Most of his grades were B's or C's as he plodded on. By his senior year, he was

State College News sports editor. That gave him the chance to travel with the basketball team, which lost all but four or five games in Division IV that year. "We have the pleasure without the pressure," quipped Milk about his team's unwillingness to win. On the way home from the games, Harvey could always be found in the back of the bus, the life of the party.

That was Harvey. Nobody knows what he did on those weekends away from campus. On a job application thirteen years later, Harvey told of a 1950 disorderly conduct arrest in Albany. No one got suspicious when he abruptly resigned his job as sports editor in the middle of his senior year. Everybody liked Harvey and when he was handed his diploma on a warm June day in 1951, he just left and nobody ever heard from him again.

The camaraderie of the class of '51 stuck, especially with the alumni of the Kappa Beta fraternity and Alpha Epsilon Phi sorority. Many kept in touch, sporadically updating addresses and gossip about other grads. Instead of ending up as the intelligentsia of tomorrow, they went on to teach in grade schools and junior colleges around the country.

Paul Buchman spent a lot of Tuesday and Thursday nights working with Harvey on the *State College News* sports section. He's fond of telling the story of how *Life* magazine surveyed the college graduating classes of his era, rating their subsequent contributions to American life on a scale of zero to four. The class of '51 was the only zero, Buchman says. "We weren't the lost generation, we were the blank generation. The class of '51 didn't have any unusual characteristics. We didn't have anything that stood out. We fell into a rut that had no character at all. Harvey and I were just like that—we were ordinary."

Doris Brody from Hillel ended up marrying Harvey's barracks-mate Howard Rosman and they settled back in Valley Stream, two LIRR stops south of Woodmere. "He was never thought of as a possible queer—that's what you called them then—he was a man's man," recalls Mrs. Doris Rosman. "In our day, of course, people were thought to be gay if they were effeminate—or if they announced it. Of course, nobody announced it in those days."

Another alumnus who kept in contact moved to the San Francisco Bay Area and supplied classmates with newspaper clippings about Harvey's budding political career. Christian Lievestro didn't have a hard time imagining what Harvey's life had been like at Albany State.

"Harvey was discreet—and sensible," says Lievestro, class of '50. "We didn't know about each other being gay. Of course nobody did in those days. You certainly never talked about it or let on because you were there to be a teacher, and it could destroy your chances at that." Gay life was a melange of "chance encounters" and "incidental things," he says. The braver gays joined the glee club where drunken parties might lead to that one desparate moment of gratification, followed by the days of regret, and, more saliently, fear that the secret would get out.

But Lievestro found that by the late 1970s, most of his Albany State contemporaries seemed downright proud of Harvey Milk. He was one of the few remarkable people from the class of '51. Some of Harvey's fraternity brothers even seem somewhat hurt that Milk never reached back. Sure they didn't end up Nobel laureates as they had once hoped, but they were from the liberal middle-class Jewish mold. They didn't call gays queers anymore. They wanted to pat Harvey on the back. He'd always been a winner.

Harvey had something special even back then; politicians later called it charisma. "Like I'm talking to you now. His face and his laugh come perfectly to mind, even though I haven't seen him in thirty years," says Doris Rosman. "In fact, I haven't seen anyone who has seen him since we graduated."

Harvey makes such a handsome sailor. Who to match him up with?

The question buzzed through the wedding reception as Harvey grabbed girl after girl to dance them through the celebration of Robert Milk's marriage. Robert and Audrey were a handsome couple, but Bob suffered in comparison to his tall, athletic younger brother, who looked positively dashing in his navy dress whites. The women marveled at his grace and humor. Everybody talked excitedly of how he actually put on those windowed helmets and thick wet suits like you see in the movies, to be dropped thousands of feet into the deep, silent ocean.

Minnie and Bill Milk, both in their mid-fifties, watched their sons proudly. Their eldest son was married, and tonight Harvey, who still worshipped Minnie, showed himself to be every inch a lady's man. The other relatives nodded approvingly and agreed. But, they added, Harvey better start thinking of a wife. He's only got another year in the navy and it's time he got his feet out of the water and on the ground. As Harvey methodically swung each girl across the dance floor, the relatives pondered the question: Who?

Other Albany State grads generally found the military to be a less than desirable aftermath to their comfortable liberal arts education, but Harvey saw the history of the world hinging on the outcome of the Korean War. He knew that he *could* make a difference.

At extended dinner-table arguments, he held that the communists were *this* far from grabbing all of Asia. They had to be stopped. Robert argued that the country had seen enough blood in World War II. Harvey, Bob thought, was just another flag-waver. Like his father, Harvey only got more stubborn in arguments. Harvey would join the navy, like his mom and dad.

Milk signed up just three months after graduation. His navy record shows a fast-paced advancement. Within eight months of enlistment, Milk landed a stint at Officers Candidate School in Newport, Rhode Island. The navy record Milk described on a job application showed that he rose rapidly through the ranks: communications officer, lieutenant junior grade, and served as chief petty officer of the U.S.S. *Kittiwake,* a San Diego–based aircraft carrier that cruised the Pacific. Harvey was always convinced he got the assignment because he coached his ship's wrestling team to a championship.

Harvey's first love in the navy was deep-sea diving. Before his stint was over, he was even teaching younger sailors how to master the unwieldly, old-fashioned diving suits on the ocean floor.

Harvey later told voters that despite all his accomplishments, the navy dishonorably discharged him after discovering his homosexuality. To be sure, exposure was a constant threat to his career. Like all branches of the service, the navy discharged thousands of gays on the most flimsy evidence. The fifties anti-gay pogroms drove untold numbers to lead lives of disgrace and sometimes to commit suicide. But the Harvey Milk of this era was no political activist, and according to available evidence, he played the more typical balancing act between discretion and his sex drive.

The latter frequently won out. Harvey's officer status allowed him the privilege of his own apartment off base in San Diego. He and his gay friends partied away their weekend passes there, cruising the main strip near the base for hitchhiking sailors. The huge numbers of military men leaving for Korea strained San Diego's standard housing. Thousands slept on the concrete floors of the local YMCAs. "Hey, sailor, do you want to sleep on a concrete floor or a bed?" asked Harvey Milk, the patriot, after a perusal of the available material. The guests often would not know that Milk's apartment had only one bed until they walked in the door.

For all the promise Milk showed as officer material, his enthusiasm for the service rapidly dimmed. When he ran into his old Bayshore High basketball buddy Dick Brown in Manhattan, Milk seemed far less the gung-ho sailor of the early days. In Tokyo he ran into a Kappa Beta alumnus, Max Fallek, and complained about all the bullshit. Why did he have to take orders from so many demonstrable assholes?

This, of course, didn't stop the manly young sailor from drawing every ounce of theatricality from his natty dress whites. At his brother's wedding reception, he properly charmed all the eligible young ladies and then announced he had to leave early to get back to his ship. As the band blared "Anchor's Aweigh," Milk cocked his head, tipped his hat and, with a stiff military salute, marched out the door in tempo. Harvey always had a sense of staging, Bob thought.

Harvey knew by then that his future was not with the navy. He was too headstrong for the bullshit. For the first time in his life, he had also spent a considerable amount of time whooping it up with other gays. He knew a better life waited in the civilian world. Harvey lasted his three years and eleven months, getting the usual month cut off his enlistment because of his model behavior.

The flirtation with danger. All the experts in the 1950s insisted that this indeed represented a key characteristic of the homosexual species. They obviously loved flirting with danger. They must love it, since, after all, being a homosexual meant facing so much danger.

In the fifties going to a gay bar in just about any city in the United States meant grappling with the possibility of a raid by police. Just serving a homosexual a drink in states like New York and California represented a crime for which a bar could be shut down. Raids engendered a host of messy ramifications, since police rarely let such an arrest pass without calling the victim's employer to solemnly explain their employee was in a business frequented by homosexuals. The fear of bar raids pushed many gays into cruising parks, making themselves easy prey for plainclothesmen out to chalk up arrests for soliciting for deviant purposes. In California that meant permanent registration with the police as a sex offender.

More savvy homosexuals took to socializing at home with large private parties. These parties, too, were sometimes raided. Few of the charges from parks, bars, and parties ever stuck, of course. But what the hell? The queers were kept in line. A number of policemen's families could also count on steak dinners from the practice, since there were always enough men with pocket money to persuade an officer that the court docket need not be cluttered by minor offenses.

Suicides were a common postscript to the raids and subsequent exposure as a homosexual. The suicides, like the enticement to danger, only served to prove that homosexuals were a self-destructive, unstable lot, a cancer on the social body. These certainly were not the kind of people who should be permitted responsible positions in society, much less a license to socialize freely. You could not legislate against the existence of homosexuality, but you could legislate against the practice. You could send police to places where homosexuals "recruited" the young, or places where "community morals" were flaunted. You could do this, and it was routinely done.

Harvey Milk, for one, did not like to live dangerously. At a raid, he'd be the guy slipping out the back door, not arguing with the police. Like most men of his generation, Milk assiduously stuck to the double life he had carefully followed since his high school days. To family, friends, and colleagues, he was Harvey Milk the joker. In college and in the navy, he was always an ordinary guy. Maybe a little stubborn when he argued politics, or when he argued anything. But other than that, Harvey was a funny, friendly, guy.

Yet, during those early years, Harvey was wrestling against a strong urge to bring all facets of his life together. Though his life bore all the trappings of a gay everyman, he could never settle into the double life homosexuals were supposed to lead and for his first forty years, he was something of a drifter. It was as if Harvey spent his first four decades trying to figure out what he wanted to do when he grew up. All the while, he delicately walked the tightrope that kept him above the danger, that thin line stretched between the poles of sexual desire and conventionality.

It was August 1955 when Harvey got out of the navy, but the world had changed little since the day he had been arrested in Central Park in August 1947. Being homosexual was still dangerous business. Harvey would not flirt with danger. He soon found a lover.

The hot July sun darted on Joe Campbell's mischievous dark eyes, entrancing Harvey Milk, who lay near Campbell and his friends at the gay section of Riis Park Beach in Queens. With his thick dark hair combed back, except for the waterfall curl on his forehead, the nineteen-year-old Campbell looked a lot like James Dean, only more handsome, and Harvey couldn't take his eyes off him.

Campbell had first started wending his way toward the gay subculture in 1945 amid the tattered seats of the Southland Theater on Chicago's south side. Sometimes, he looked up to the theater's ceiling, where stars twinkled down and clouds drifted lazily by, and he pretended he was in a fantasy world, some kingdom beyond care. Not in the Southland Theater, ducking under old men's coats for a quarter.

That was nine-year-old Joe Campbell's introduction to gay life. Under the coats for a quarter, staring up at the theater's ceiling at the projected images of stars and clouds, wishing himself into a magic kingdom.

The guys started beating him up because he liked playing with girls. Joe always envied the girls, who could play house and be the people who were taken care of, protected. The guys' favorite trick was to take Joe, whack him around some, and then stick him headfirst in a garbage can. Joe learned he could get attention, even affection and a quarter, from the men who sat nervously in the Southland Theater. That's what being homosexual meant—getting attention without getting beat up.

Even without the daily fights, Joe was fated to a hard childhood. His father had died in 1937 when he was a year old, leaving his wife, Theotha Campbell, to bring up the five children alone. Theo was strong, so she managed; her staunchly fundamentalist family in Tennessee reminded her that her name, after all, meant "from God." Theo moved often. Joe, the youngest, lived in a half dozen cities in as many years after his sexual awakening in Chicago. When Joe was fourteen, the family finally settled in Jamaica, Long Island.

Joe walked down to a neighborhood park one night and stumbled on a group of teenage boys who called themselves funny names like Miss Thing and Lady Burma. They easily welcomed Joe into their clique and soon receded further into the park where, under the eaves of an aging bandstand, Lady Burma modeled a rayon taffeta gown with a plunging backline. He had just lifted it from Woolworth's that day.

That was the first time Joe realized there were other boys like him. He wasn't just some isolated kid who had happened to find a couple of horny men with quarters to spare. Joe's new friends took the adolescent to Greenwich Village and showed him that there were, in fact, many more men like themselves. Not all of them wore taffeta gowns, either. Many of them were at first reluctant to approach a boy who looked barely past puberty, but Joe had dark, intense eyes that bespoke vulnerable sensuality and a firm, muscular build that gained better definition as each month brought him nearer manhood. He soon became popular.

By the time he was fifteen, Joe had dropped out of P.S. 170 in Queens and taken a job as a Western Union delivery boy. He learned about the hustling scene where boys his age could earn far more than a quarter for their efforts. He was taken in by a bar owner and discovered, for the first time, what the good life could be like. Being a homosexual meant being a member of a small exclusive club, something you had over everybody else, finally.

When Joe Campbell went to Riis Beach one hot July day in late summer in 1956, he didn't notice the tall, handsome man with the finely sculpted nose on the blanket next to him, as he and his friends talked excitedly about meeting at a bus depot before hitting a Jamaica gay bar that night. Joe did not remember seeing the athletic older man at the bus depot either, or on the bus. He does remember their first dance, the warm moist spot that spread near the man's zipper, the embarrassed apology, the next morning when the man virtually ordered Joe to have sex with him, and the quick decision that Joe Campbell was the lover he was looking for. A few weeks later, Joe left home and moved into Harvey Milk's apartment in suburban Rego Park.

Joe, nineteen, had at last found someone to take care of and protect him. Harvey Milk, twenty-six, found someone who needed him. "It was a selection basically," Joe Campbell said later. "Harvey selected me and I was in the market to be selected." That was how Joe and Harvey started what would be the longest relationship in either of their lives.

Harvey taught math and history at Hewlitt High School near Woodmere, coaching basketball every day after school. Joe painted gold leaf on the ornate furniture with which gays of the 1950s liked to decorate their apartments. Even after they were living together, Harvey courted Joe with gushy love poems and impromptu gifts. Notes were addressed and signed with "-san" suffixes to both names. They spoke baby talk to each other, adding strings of nonsense syllables like "-uminimuns" to every word, as they cooed away their evenings in front of the television.

They quickly settled into a safe middle-class marriage. Harvey accepted nothing short of complete monogamy. Their outings were to the opera, ballet, and museums—not gay bars. Harvey was accepted into Joe's family. "We had a Jewish man here in this house once, standing right where you're standing," explained Joe's grandmother hospitably when the lovers took a trip to the Campbell family hometown of Veto, Alabama. "Of course," she added, "he was invited in by my father. That must have been, well, fifty years ago."

The topic of homosexuality of course never arose during visits to either Joe's or Harvey's families. Joe Campbell still thought that Bill Milk seemed uncomfortable around him. But Minnie was concerned that the young man looked skinny, so she cheerfully made sure Joe kept eating when the new couple visited the elder Milks' household.

For all the stability Milk gained in his domestic life, he remained unsure about what to do professionally. He quickly tired of teaching. Besides, that was a risky career that could easily be destroyed by even a rumor of homosexuality. He had never liked New York's cold weather, so, by June 1957, Harvey told Joe they would be moving to Dallas. Joe spent that summer working as a Good Humor man. Harvey hawked fruits and vegetables for a cousin's business. They saved up enough money to buy a push-button Plymouth Savoy in September and they were on their way.

"Y'know here in Dallas, you won't find a Baptist firm hiring even a Methodist," businessmen counseled Harvey as he started applying for jobs. "Either change your name to something like Miller or go to work for a Jewish firm."

The advice startled Harvey, but he did wrangle a job as an assistant credit manager—at a Jewish-owned department store. He lost the post when his boss's son graduated from college and needed a job. The best employment Harvey found after that was selling used sewing machines to families who couldn't afford them. That way, the buyer made a couple payments, defaulted, and the machine was repossessed to sell again.

The scam disgusted Milk. He complained that it was the only job they'd let a Jew have in Dallas. Joe told him he had a persecution complex. After Minnie's first heart attack, Harvey talked more about going back to New York. Finally, at a performance of *Swan Lake*, Harvey announced his decision: They were going back east.

Harvey got a job as an actuarial statistician at the Great American Insurance Company. Joe went back to gilding furniture. Between Harvey's $140 weekly salary and Joe's $90, they could rent a comfortable apartment at Ninety-sixth Street and Central Park West. Joe decorated the apartment in late-fifties splendor. Harvey bought a pet toucan he named Bill and got on with adoring Joe, who seemed to get more handsome every year.

One morning Joe woke up to find a cup of hot chocolate, a glass of orange juice, and a sweet pastry sitting on the apartment windowsill, with a note: "Someone is waiting for you outside." Across the street in Central Park stood a snowman. "Hello" was spelled out in the snow at his feet. Joe finally had his fantasy kingdom. Both knew it was going to last forever.

On their second anniversary in 1958, Harvey wrote one of his typical love notes:

To my Joesan,
To me you are my warrior—
You are my knight—
You are my day—
May the many many days and years pass pleasantly, happy and reward-
ing, for we have many years to spend together—the first two have swept
by and with each I have found I love you 365 days more and 365 times
harderuminiumuns.
Your dollbabysan,
Harveysan.

If there was oppression of homosexuals, it wasn't of any concern to Joe or Harvey. They had a beautiful apartment, a box at the opera, season tickets for the ballet, and regular trips to the beaches of Puerto Rico. Who was oppressed?

Joe's mother died suddenly after that second anniversary. Soon after, doctors told Minnie Milk she had only a few years to live. Not one to waste a minute of it, Minnie insisted that she and Bill move to Manhattan so she'd at least have something interesting to look at out her window. She started taking up all the interests she'd been putting off, began guitar and singing lessons and got active in senior citizens' groups.

For Christmas, Minnie knitted Joe and Harvey matching afghans and crocheted booties. The pair did everything as a couple; they were treated as a couple; but Harvey insisted it would kill his mother if he ever brought up the fact he was gay.

Milk still had his unpredictable moments. At a Manhattan restaurant in the late fifties, a patron muttered "faggot" one night when Joe and Harvey walked by. Milk reached over a divider, grabbed the offender's collar, started shouting epithets of his own, and shook the man until his chair trembled. Joe was embarrassed. And surprised.

Harvey was far more militant on any matter relating to Jews. Joe invited a German friend to dinner one night and Milk quickly turned the conversation to the Holocaust. What did the guest think about Buchenwald? When Joe's friend said he didn't know about the death camps until after the war, Harvey flew into a rampage: "How could you have lived in Germany and *not* known what was going on?" he shouted. "How could you *not* have been aware of the carnage? Huh? Were you deaf? Dumb? Blind? Huh?" Joe was now convinced Harvey had a persecution complex. Harvey told Joe he was anti-Semitic.

Harvey reserved virtually all his affection for Joe, however, having few friends beyond an older man he worked with at Great American, Harvey's surrogate father figure. Harvey had Joe's teeth capped, took endless rolls of photos of Joe's finely tuned body, and showered him with small gifts. Harvey confided that a plastic surgeon had developed a certain fondness for him shortly after Milk's release from the navy. He'd fixed Harvey's nose, but Milk turned down the suggestion that his oversized ears be tucked in, thereby saving the feature that political cartoonists would later find so useful.

Life for Harvey and Joe fell into predictable patterns. Every Saturday, the pair took laundry to the Chinese cleaners and ran errands. Every Sunday, they slept late, ate Harvey's matzoh meal pancakes, and lay in bed, reading the *Times*.

It would always be that way. Joe thought so even after he withdrew from Harvey sexually, not understanding Harvey's voracious sexual appetite. Joe had always considered sex little more than an easy way to get attention. Harvey, meanwhile, threw himself into the act like he was some marathon runner in the last days of training for the big race. He could never get enough. Joe felt he was a device for Harvey's pleasure and pulled back. Harvey pleaded and begged, shouted and threw tantrums.

Dissatisfaction faced Milk on all fronts by late 1962. His job was boring and there was nothing Harvey hated more than being bored. He had to make a break. He decided to quit and get a new job. Joe was ironing shirts one afternoon when Harvey walked in the room.

"Have you thought about moving out?" he asked with characteristic tact.

"Yeah," Joe said, "but I don't want to."

"Maybe you better think about it some more."

Joe moved out a few weeks later. That was how Harvey's longest relationship ended. Harvey regretted the decision immediately. He sent long notes imploring Joe to come back: "Now that I can no longer see or hear you, I have no desire to fight for a job, no desire to make it good, no desire for anything."

Joe knew Harvey would make it; he'd just select somebody else.

"What did Helen Keller's parents do to punish her?"

"Rearrange the furniture. You told me that one yesterday." Craig Rodwell looked at the alarm clock next to his phone. Sure enough, it was 9:30 exactly.

"No," giggled Harvey, pausing dramatically.

"Okay, okay. What did they do?"

"They made her read the waffle iron."

With boyfriends like Harvey, who needs an alarm clock? thought Craig as he pulled himself from bed. The relationship certainly had its advantages, especially for a boy who had run away from the Rogers Park neighborhood of Chicago at seventeen to savor big-city homosexual life in Manhattan. Besides the frequent love notes, there were Harvey's personally guided Sunday tours of the museums, Saturday nights at Milk's box at the opera and cozy evenings in his Upper West Side apartment where Harvey struggled for just the right texture in the sauce for the chicken and broccoli. Every morning at precisely 9:30 A.M., Rodwell got his wake-up call so he wouldn't be late for his ballet classes. The calls always opened with one of Harvey's sick jokes.

Harvey's good humor faded only once in those early romantic days of his relationship with Craig. Harvey mentioned watching Joe Campbell move out of the apartment a few months before, pulling his possessions out of the building's front door while Harvey watched from their apartment window several stories above. "I wanted to jump out the window to follow him," Harvey told Craig. But Harvey didn't dwell on the past and Craig spent most of his time being utterly enchanted by his new boyfriend.

For twenty-two-year-old Rodwell, meat loaf had previously been the most exotic item of his cuisine and Chicago Cubs games were the closest he ever got to cultural events. The affair with Harvey came straight from a Hollywood romance, with Milk cast as the ardent, cultured, witty, and, by Rodwell's standards, rich suitor. In all, Harvey seemed a Prince Charming.

Though Milk was only ten years Rodwell's senior, he genuinely enjoyed the role of teacher and charmer. It would be to such boyish-looking men in their late teens and early twenties that Milk would be attracted for the rest of his life. But this relationship would be different, haunted—and ultimately doomed—by strange new ideas that tied homosexuality to politics, ideas that both repelled and attracted the thirty-two-year-old Milk.

A soft September breeze blew in from Lake Michigan. The cherry tops of Chicago police cars converged on the corner of Clark and Schiller, dazing fourteen-year-old Craig Rodwell. He spent two or three nights a week on this strip. Always the same. He'd walk aimlessly around the block until he caught the eye of a passerby or a man slowly driving his car down the street. Tonight he had picked up a forty-year-old Italian dishwasher who had taken him to a nearby fleabag hotel. Afterward, they had washed—the first time Craig had ever seen scented soap—and the older man was politely walking Craig to the elevated train stop.

Then the police cars swept upon them. The older man insisted he was Craig's uncle, but a fatherly patrolman took the frightened four-teen-year-old aside and sternly ordered, "Tell me the truth right now." Craig did. The older man got a four-year sentence for his "crime against nature." Craig got two years' probation.

Craig had spent most of his childhood in a private boys' school playing doctor and, later, necking among boys. It seemed natural, even romantic. Only when thrust into the Chicago public schools did he learn that the nature of his sexual longing was taboo. The contradictions tore at his conscience. Here he and the many Jewish kids at the liberal high school were cheering on the blacks who demanded to go to white public schools in Little Rock. Even if you were different, you were equal, his civics teacher told the class. Craig was different too, but instead of being equal, he was called a faggot. He saw a gentle Italian man go to prison for four years, his life destroyed. It made him angry. Anger bred defiance.

He kept cruising the streets and struggled to graduate from high school a year early. By August 1958 Rodwell, seventeen, was on his way to the one place where he heard other queers lived, Greenwich Village. He set up housekeeping with a buddy he had met in his first weeks at the YMCA, Collin, a teenager taking refuge from Helena, Arkansas. He soon learned that gay life in New York was no less risky than Chicago.

One night of cruising at the popular Washington Square park in the Village brought Rodwell face-to-face with a police officer. "Keep moving, faggot," the officer tersely ordered.

"This is harassment of homosexuals," objected Rodwell, with less discretion than valor. That night in jail police filed by Rodwell's cell to examine this defiant homosexual like some exotic curiosity. "Whats'a matter, lose your purse?" one asked. "Whats'a matter, lose your dress?"

"Whats'a matter," Rodwell shot back, "never seen a faggot before?"

Charges, of course, were dismissed. They generally were in such cases, since the purpose of arrests was not the enforcement of any particular law but the broader social goal of keeping homosexuals in their place. The ongoing scrapes with the police did, however, give Rodwell some radical notions that kept him sparring with the tall, urbane man he met months later cruising Central Park West.

"Yes, Harvey, you've got a great job, a nice apartment, all the kitchenware a queen could ever dream of," Craig argued. "Everything but the chance to be openly who you are, like a normal human being."

"I can't let it out—it would kill my parents," Milk insisted adamantly.

"Excuses, they're all excuses," retorted Rodwell, pointing out that the United States would be in far shorter supply of living mothers if that were the case.

"When you get older, you'll understand," snapped Harvey, using the line with which he usually concluded such arguments.

The mushy romantic moments dominated many more days of the relationship than the arguments, but the debates kept arising. Harvey seemed intrigued with Rodwell's ideas, though he frequently shuddered when Craig suggested such things as holding hands in public. In more abstract conversations, Craig argued that if only homosexuals banded together and pushed for equal treatment, as blacks were doing with their march on Washington, things could change.

Rodwell became active in the Mattachine Society, New York City's only gay group of that time. Chapters had been popping up since 1950, named after the Italian *Matachinos,* the court jesters who, behind a mask, could speak truth to otherwise obdurate rulers. Rodwell decided he'd help bolster attendance at meetings, so he and his Arkansas roommate hand-wrote notices of upcoming Mattachine events and dropped them in at the Greenwich Village apartments that bore two male names on the mailbox. The unsolicited leafleting infuriated Milk.

"You shouldn't do that to people," Milk shouted. "Getting those in mailboxes will make people paranoid that everyone knows about them being gay."

"You're just thinking about how *you* would react if it showed up in your mailbox and you thought somebody might suspect you were gay," Rodwell later remembered arguing back.

Harvey loved to argue and, like his father, he was pigheaded. This proved especially true in politics. A staunch conservative, Milk was then looking forward to Barry Goldwater's getting the 1964 Republican presidential nomination. That could get the true conservative message out to the nation, he thought. His fiercest argument with Rodwell was not about gay equality, but President Kennedy's move against the steel companies. The raw use of federal power in the economy made Harvey's blood boil. Rodwell ended the argument by calling Harvey a fascist and stomping out of the apartment.

Craig should have seen the end coming. Harvey was too set in his ways. It came soon after Rodwell made a Labor Day trip to the gay cruising section of Riis Park. About twice a year, police swept down on the gay section, enforcing an archaic law that demanded male swimmers be clad in suits that extended from the navel to over the thigh.

"This is harassment of homosexuals," Rodwell shouted. He was promptly arrested for both indecent exposure and inciting a riot. In court, the judge glanced down at the young man and dismissed the incitement charge. What about the other offense? Craig started to explain how the police routinely used the charge to harass homosexuals. Homosexuals? At the mention of the offensive word, the judge slammed down his gavel. Nothing more need be said. Rodwell went to jail for three days.

During Craig's disappearance Harvey kept nervously calling Collin to see when his young paramour would resurface. Rodwell still recalls the curious look that crept across Milk's face when he saw his head—the police had shaved it. Craig explained about jail and the angry judge.

"Harvey never wanted to talk about it much, but I could see he was terrified by what I had done," Rodwell recalled. "Here he had this carefully constructed life. Everything was in its place. He was terrified that someone might find out he was gay because he was going with me, and I was branded."

The early morning wake-up calls became less frequent: every other day, then twice and then once a week. Then no more. Harvey Milk shifted his attentions to other young men with less troublesome ideas; he had carefully compartmentalized his life for years and he wasn't about to change now. Craig Rodwell was alone and confused.

Dazed, being lured into a sweet, comfortable sleep. So relaxed. But he had to get the note. The note. He had to put it where Collin would find it. For two weeks, Craig Rodwell had carefully planned that moment. He quit school, gave his two-week notice on the job, bought a bottle of turenol and then waited for Thursday night, when Collin went to Times Square to catch his usual diet of bargain 1930s movies.

Collin had left an hour ago. Everything went fine. But the note. Craig had taken half the bottle, fifteen pills, and then remembered he had left the note on a chair. The note instructed Collin to call Craig's aunt, so his mother would not have to hear the news from the police. God, Craig hated the police. Collin might not see the note on the chair, so Craig had to put it on the living room table. Jesus, he was tired. He'd finish the pills when he got back from the chair. He had to get the note over to the table.

A boring double bill, Collin thought, so he left the theater early. He found Craig stretched out between a chair and the living room couch. Craig remembered waking up hours later in Bellevue Hospital where a police officer stood over him, waiting to take a report. The sight of a cop infuriated him so much he bolted upright in bed, breaking the restraints. Months of sedatives and shock therapy followed. Rodwell groped for a purpose and it finally occurred to him. He would do something for the gay movement.

Harvey visited Craig once in the hospital. Rodwell next saw Milk where the pair had first met, cruising Central Park West. Ever the pragmatist, Harvey suggested an afternoon tryst. "I was still so madly in love with him," says Rodwell. "I got such a thrill out of saying no."

"Yes, I used to sell insurance with Harvey Milk, back almost twenty-five years ago." The septuagenarian's voice is tired and worn now, but the crankiness subsides for a moment as he falls back on his old memories. He was one of the few people with whom Milk had both a professional and personal friendship from the 1950s through the 1960s, the kind of gay father figure that many young homosexual professionals seek out early in their careers.

"I was sick once, in the hospital for two weeks. Harvey came in every single day with all the paperwork I needed. Kept me up to date at work in the hospital and then nursed me when I got home. He was a kind man, so gentle."

But he doesn't have anything to say about the Harvey Milk people read about in the newspapers. That was a different person. What does politics have to do with homosexuality? The old man is afraid that by talking he might be exposed. It's not that he has any family left. No friends to shock either. As far as exposing his lover, well, they were together for twenty-three years and he passed on a few months back. He's retired, so there's no job to lose. It's just that their *condition* wasn't anything he ever talked about his whole life, so why start now? All homosexuals his age wanted to do was live undetected, be grateful if they passed, and then die, he explains. That should be easy to understand.

"Excuse me," the old man says. "I'm just from a different generation." But it's also the generation Harvey Milk came from, he stresses. Once, a long time ago.

Harvey was one of the lucky ones of his generation. At least he had lovers, knew other gay men, and could pursue sex and romance. These alternatives were available only to gays who lived in a handful of major American cities. Most homosexuals simply lived without. But even the lucky ones like Harvey paid the price of vigilance for their liberty. The constant fear of the loose phrase, the wrong pronoun, the chance moment, the misspoken word that might give it all away.

three

Judy Garland's Dead

"I came to New York so I could suck cock."

John Galen McKinley delighted in telling Harvey that this was the sole explanation of why at sixteen he decided to quit high school, jump a Greyhound bus, and leave rural Hagerstown, Maryland, for the gay scene in Greenwich Village he'd heard rumors of.

Milk's friends immediately noted the physical resemblance McKinley bore to Joe Campbell. The mix of Scottish, Cherokee, and French-Canadian blood in Jack's background yielded deep sultry eyes, thick dark hair, and a compact build. Lodging came easy in New York, first with Tom O'Horgan, an entertainer who had made a small mark in the lounge circuit by telling jokes as he strummed a harp. By 1963, O'Horgan had gone bohemian and was trying his hand at experimental theater. McKinley had lived with O'Horgan for only a few weeks when he came in one day to announce that a handsome businessman twice his age was vying for his affection.

O'Horgan dismissed the news, thinking Jack was trying to make him jealous. He was relieved when the suitor materialized, since he was already worried that the sixteen-year-old McKinley was looking for some kind of father figure. If Jack was indeed dangling the new boyfriend merely to tempt O'Horgan's devotion, Jack had vastly underestimated his new pursuer's tenacity.

Within a few weeks, McKinley moved into Harvey Milk's Upper West Side apartment. They bought a dog they named Trick, a cat they called Trade, and settled into a middle-class domestic marriage. At thirty-three, Milk was launching a new life, though he could hardly have imagined the unlikely direction toward which his new lover would pull him.

Only months before, the insurance job had become so unbearable that one payday Milk collected his check, walked out at lunch, cashed it and never went back. Harvey never bothered with niceties like two weeks' notice once he made up his mind to do something. He finagled a job as a researcher in the information center of Bache & Company, a Wall Street investment firm. The job allowed him to use his sharp memory, his knack for math, and, most significantly, his uncanny intuitions about social and business trends that could influence investment futures. He rose rapidly. Within a year he was the information center supervisor. Soon he was issuing a daily report that provided updated tips for Bache's offices throughout the country.

Milk's success intrigued Monty Gordon, the man who had hired him. Gordon had spent years watching the men who took the entry-level jobs in the information center. He could instinctively pick out who would make it on Wall Street and who wouldn't. Harvey had covered up the years of drifting on his job application, concealing his jumps from teaching to Dallas by saying he had worked years at his dad's store. Nevertheless, from the first day Monty Gordon met Milk, he had one assessment—Harvey was a drifter, not cut from the Wall Street mold. He might wear three-piece suits, but Milk seemed somehow unsettled, as if he still didn't know what he actually wanted to do with his life. You could always depend on Harvey, Gordon thought; he'd always get the job done with flair and a personal touch, and his advice was literally making millions—for other people. But as for Harvey himself, Gordon sensed that he was uncertain, still not committed to any course. It was a race between talent and wanderlust, and Monty Gordon was betting against talent.

Milk kept his sexuality a closely guarded secret at work. Only one person managed to break the barriers between Harvey's personal and professional life and it wasn't by Milk's own choice. Jim Bruton, a Bache vice-president, met Milk when Harvey approached him for authorization to open an investment account as a guardian for a younger man who was his ward. Bruton, a perceptive and urbane man, could barely contain his smile as he looked Milk sternly in the eye.

"What's this guardian crap?" he asked. "What you're really talking about is opening an account for the boy you've got living with you. Right?"

Milk broke out laughing, and tore up the forms he had carefully filled out. "Okay, I guess we'll start this over."

Bruton and Milk struck a warm friendship. Bruton was surprised to learn that his gregarious colleague had few close friends, lavishing virtually all his affection on his lover, Jack McKinley. Through the office grapevine, he also learned that however bright Milk was on business trends, he was downright callow when it came to cultivating professional relationships. In conferences, Milk would stubbornly stick to his own idiosyncratic ideas about economic trends, arguing bitterly with older executives who took their bearings from more orthodox business wisdom. Milk frequently ended up being right and didn't refrain from saying I told you so.

Bruton privately agreed that his friend was often smarter than his superiors, but he spent hours blasting Milk for his lack of tact. "That's not how you play the game if you want to get ahead," Bruton insisted. Milk, however, heeded only his own advice.

Milk and Gordon became the Laurel and Hardy act of the Bache offices at 51 Wall Street and Milk's humor came to compensate for his poor marks in office politics. Harvey's ability to deliver Henny Youngman one-liners was the perfect foil to Gordon's drier wit. The company promoted Harvey rapidly over the years, frequently breaking its own salary policies to reward him with large annual raises.

Harvey used his income to share the good life with Jack. Like a patient father, Harvey intoduced Jack to opera, ballet, museums, and, of course, the reams of love notes and romantic poems he churned out. To Jack, it was love out of a Leslie Gore song. For all the flippancy that marked his sassy character, Jack fundamentally needed someone to take care of him and he had found the perfect protector in Harvey Milk.

Harvey took a new apartment in Greenwich Village. The flat had the bonus of overlooking the townhouse where opera star Leontyne Price lived. Milk spent hours at the window trying to catch a glimpse of the diva. He would occasionally play her records at high volume and after every aria applaud loudly, shouting "Bravo" out his open window.

Tom O'Horgan, meanwhile, had started producing experimental plays in his Lower East Side loft and at Ellen Steuart's fledgling Café La Mama. Harvey jumped at the chance to take a firsthand role in theater after so many years of watching ballets and operas. The bright McKinley showed a talent for tending to the technical aspects of theater and learned the basics of stage managing in O'Horgan's plays. The three became an indivisible trio: the teenaged high school dropout, the avant-garde director, and the Wall Street businessman. Harvey occasionally slipped O'Horgan a loan as he encouraged him to be more ambitious and take on a major production. While McKinley was learning his career and O'Horgan was setting his sights for his future, Harvey Milk, the only established professional in the bunch, was rubbing shoulders with an artistic community whose bohemian lives were thoroughly different from his own rigid conventionality.

Nothing brought out the incongruities of Harvey's new peer group more than political discussions. A hard-boiled conservative in the laissez-faire capitalist mold, Harvey and Jack spent much of the fall of 1964 rising early so they could distribute Barry Goldwater leaflets in New York City subways. Harvey even managed to talk Joe Campbell, his first lover, into campaigning for the Arizona Republican. Jack began to doggedly mimic Milk's stubborn arguments for Goldwater, much to the dismay of their theater friends, who considered such views only slightly more contemporary than the pterodactyl.

Joe Campbell also found himself at the center of a network of avant-garde friends who clustered at Joe's hangout, Kelly's Bar. As New York's best-known hustler bar, Kelly's had become the watering hole of Manhattan's new trashy chic set. Campbell traveled on the fringes of the Andy Warhol crowd, where he was dubbed the "Sugar Plum Fairy," the name rock 'n' roller Lou Reed later called Campbell in Reed's paeon to the New York hustling scene, "Walk on the Wild Side."

Harvey could never completely abandon his protector role with any of his former lovers, and he occasionally dropped by Kelly's to see Campbell. Campbell's trendy friends were amazed that Joe had spent nearly seven years with Milk. The staid businessman didn't seem enough—attractive enough, rich enough, and certainly not chic enough—to warrant the attentions of the dazzling Sugar Plum Fairy.

Campbell was amused at Milk's attempt to juggle his stolid bourgeois values with the new peer group Harvey was finding among the least traditional folk in New York. "Here Harvey is trying to lead the perfect middle-class life with the perfect monogamous marriage and the upwardly mobile Wall Street career," Campbell thought, "But he can't get away from the fact that he's a faggot and a Jew. He'll always be Minnie's boy."

Harvey worried incessantly that Campbell might seduce Jack. At one point, he even presented Joe with a statement that solemnly swore that Joe would never go to bed with Harvey's newest ingenue. He refused to sign, but Joe's new romantic interest allayed Harvey's fear. Joe fell head over heels for a younger man he met at Kelly's, Oliver "Bill" Sipple. The pair soon left New York to set up housekeeping in Fort Lauderdale.

Then Joe crashed his motorcycle. Billy couldn't get a job. Within months, they were broke and Harvey had to fly down to loan them enough money to pull through the next few difficult months.

The final heart attack struck when Minnie was preparing a Thanksgiving turkey for a Lower East Side mission. Harvey ordered a traditional white Jewish shroud for Minnie's funeral—and then had her body cremated, spreading her ashes on the Atlantic Ocean. The cremation infuriated the more orthodox Robert Milk. Harvey later told friends that upon learning of the cremation, Bob had accusingly shouted, "You burned my mother."

Harvey had never been particularly close to either his brother or father, so the fracas at Minnie's death did little more than finalize a split between Harvey and the male members of his family. Harvey never had much to do with his family after that.

A sunny July afternoon in 1964, just the kind of day that made Jim Bruton glad he'd invested in his East Hampton house. Jim and Harvey spent the afternoon in an exhausting volleyball game. Despite Milk's athletic prowess, his team had lost, largely because of the vigor of a strong, handsome opponent in his mid-fifties.

"You'll end up just like him if you keep exercising," Bruton told Milk. "You've kept your body in shape so far. You've got a quick mind. Keep it all in shape and you'll be as attractive as he is twenty years from now."

"No, he's over fifty," Harvey said matter-of-factly. "I'll never make it that far."

Jim thought Harvey was gearing up for one of his sick jokes. "The only way you'll go before you're fifty is if you finally get somebody at the office so mad that they'll push you out a window on Wall Street," he joked.

"No, really," Harvey insisted. "Something will happen before then."

Jim knew Harvey had a tendency to be melodramatic, but this talk was taking it a little far, he thought.

"Harvey, we all have that kind of feeling now and then. It's nothing to take that seriously."

"I've known it since I was a kid," Milk persisted. "I'll never make it to fifty. There's just something sinister down the road. I don't know what it is, but it's there."

That's how Bruton recalled the conversation years later. Harvey was almost nonchalant about a conviction Bruton considered morbid. Milk never dwelled on the point, but it occasionally came up during the years of their friendship. After a whirlwind week of going to opera, ballet, and theater performances, the pair retired to the Russian Tea Room next to Carnegie Hall one night where a somewhat dazed Bruton mentioned they had partied four of the last seven nights.

"Harvey, while you're doing this, you're not putting any money away," Jim warned. "You're blowing your future. You should invest your money in a house or something."

"What for?" Milk asked. "I'll never live to enjoy it."

Bruton looked at his friend incredulously.

"I've got to live fast," Harvey said. "I know I'm not going to live long."

Maybe it was these forbodings that kept Milk's own compass set strictly on the present with little regard for either the past or future. Harvey sometimes told the story of how he had bought Minnie a handsome set of porcelain dinnerware on one of his many leaves in Japan. He returned home to find that Minnie had given the new dishes a place of honor in her china cabinet while she kept on using the plain dinner sets that had withstood decades of use in the Milk family. Harvey shouted that he had bought his porcelain for Minnie to use, and not to save in some cabinet. Milk promptly ran through the kitchen collecting every old dish in the house and then proceeded to smash them. "Now," he humphed, "You *have* to use them."

Jack McKinley was a paradox, Harvey complained. At times, he was the bright, vivacious charmer Harvey had fallen in love with. But from the start, he had also been given to moody fits of depression.

The psychiatrist had a word for the contradictions: manic-depressive.

Friends first attributed the problems to his background. Jack had, after all, been the youngest of a large, impoverished brood, raised on the strict backwater fundamentalism common among the poor families of rural Appalachia. The way Jack told it, the sin of Sodom was, to his family, only slightly less heinous than matricide. It was hardly a prescription for good mental health. But Jack's problems did not fade as the years separated him from his unhappy youth. They got worse.

He started using the drugs that were coming in to vogue in the mid-sixties—marijuana, speed, and LSD. He took to drinking. He returned from binges to tell Harvey tales of sexual promiscuity. Harvey soon stopped getting jealous. That would get Jack even further depressed and he'd drink more. Early on, Jack discovered he had one trump card that was guaranteed to light the short fuse of Harvey's temper—the suicide threat.

One night at the couple's Greenwich Village flat, Harvey heard a clatter in the garage. He arrived just in time to cut McKinley down from the rafter. After a particularly bitter fight, McKinley and Milk were walking through the narrow Village streets and the youth simply threw himself in front of a taxi. He missed death by inches.

Harvey tried sending him to a psychiatrist. After a month of visits, however, Jack bored of the mental gymnastics and increased his drinking. Harvey thought Jack might improve his self-image if he resumed his aborted education. Jack, however, was glad to have bypassed high school and would have nothing to do with such tedium.

A tragic turn in Joe Campbell's life gave Milk the chance to try to shock McKinley out of his suicide threats. Campbell's love for Billy Sipple had a passion Joe had never felt for Harvey. One afternoon, he returned to their Fort Lauderdale apartment to find that Billy had summarily left him. Campbell moved back to New York and promptly tried to kill himself.

Doctors had to perform a tracheotomy to save his life. Tubes coursed in and out of various parts of his body when Harvey took Jack to see the slumbering twenty-nine-year-old. "That's what happens when you don't succeed," Harvey explained tersely.

Harvey kept a long vigil over Campbell, insisting someone should be there when he awoke. As Campbell slept, Harvey ruminated about suicide, a phenomenon that would haunt his life and loves for decades. He wrote Campbell a letter, concluding with his basic assessment of existence:

*Life is rotten—hard—bitter and so forth—but life is life and the best
that we have—no one should take another's—no one should let another
take his—*

*people in worse situations than you have come back strong—have
been against worse odds and won—only because they felt that somewhere there was some reason for living—they are not sure, but they had
hope.*

Love As Always,
H.

When Joe awoke, Harvey had blunter advice. "If you're going to
commit suicide, you should go deep in a forest, cover yourself up with
leaves and needles, then take all the pills you want." Leaving a messy
aftermath was simply bad theater. Harvey also mentioned his amazement that Joe would try to kill himself over the young unschooled Billy
Sipple, and not for Harvey who had always done so much for him. The
sight of Joe Campbell lying in that hospital bed breathing through a
tube in his throat would return to Harvey's mind a decade later in San
Francisco when Billy Sipple made his rendezvous with history.

Harvey thought Jack might improve if he left Manhattan's fast
lane for a slower paced life, so in 1967 Milk accepted a transfer to work
for Bache in Dallas. Jack lasted all of a few weeks in Texas. He quickly
packed and moved back to Greenwich Village where his friend, Tom
O'Horgan, had attracted enough acclaim to be asked to take over a
faltering production about the budding counterculture.

In McKinley's absence, Harvey took to courting a handsome,
blond twenty-one-year-old named Joe Turner. There was the usual fare
of love notes, candlelight dinners, and evenings at the ballet. Harvey
talked excitedly about the incredible success O'Horgan was having with
his first Broadway play, *Hair.*

McKinley, now the *Hair* stage manager, returned to visit Harvey
in Dallas. He was no longer the cute young boy Harvey had known.
His thick dark hair tumbled around his shoulders. He was wearing an
unlikely outfit of beads, bells, fringed boots, and a transparent shirt with
puffy medieval sleeves. Hippies were taking over New York, but Dallas
had never seen the likes of it. Joe Turner, for one, thought Jack looked
like an erotic dream of Genghis Khan.

The old problems persisted, despite the new image. Turner visited
Harvey one night during Jack's stay to find Milk uncharacteristically

subdued. Jack had taken a knife and locked himself in the bathroom, swearing he would kill himself, Milk explained. As Turner left, Harvey assured him, "Don't worry. He's done this before."

Harvey asked for a transfer back to New York in 1968, growing dissatisfied with his life in Texas. He soon resigned from Bache. His boss, Monty Gordon, was not surprised. After five years with the firm, Milk was still a drifter, Gordon thought, still unsure of what he wanted to do when he grew up.

The times clearly were eroding Milk's conservatism. With both McKinley and O'Horgan preoccupied with *Hair,* Milk found himself surrounded by some of the most outrageous flower children on the continent. Harvey started assimilating the new countercultural values, which spurned materialism, eschewed conformity, and mocked orthodoxy. With each month, Milk's hair became a little longer. With each political argument, his views became more flexible. With each new apartment, he discarded more of the tasteful furniture, stylish decor, and middle-class comforts he had cherished since first settling down with Joe Campbell in 1956.

McKinley got the job as stage director for the San Francisco production of *Hair.* Harvey followed and took a job as a financial analyst on Montgomery Street, the heart of the city's financial district. When friends asked how Harvey could continue to put up with Jack's drinking and periodic suicide threats, Harvey would make a bawdy comment about Jack's finely curved buns. Indeed, the sexual bond was one of the few connections the pair had. Their house was adorned with large blowups of this unclad aspect of Jack's anatomy.

Though Harvey quickly came to love the more laid-back pace of San Francisco, his relationship with McKinley deteriorated steadily. One night, McKinley stormed out of a performance of the campy Cockettes when he saw Harvey flirting with another young man. Milk ended up taking that man home, only to be awakened by a soggy, mud-covered McKinley who claimed he had thrown himself off a pier near Fisherman's Wharf. Rather than falling to a lover's death, Jack landed in four feet of water and the oozy floor of San Francisco Bay. Frustrated, Jack started wildly throwing punches at Milk and could only be restrained when Harvey literally tied him up and threw him in a closet.

The next morning, Harvey unbound Jack. McKinley marched to the kitchen table where his competition was munching on a piece of toast. "You've been fucked and fed," McKinley shouted. "Now leave."

By then, Harvey had had enough. Though Jack had little formal education, his quick wit and easy charm had earned him success as a Broadway stage manager. He was no longer a helpless sixteen-year-old who needed a protector. Tom O'Horgan offered Jack the job as stage manager of his new play, a rock opera based on the life of Jesus Christ. Jack moved back to New York. Harvey moved in with a group of "Hair" cast members and stayed in San Francisco; that, he said, was where his future lay.

"I would love to be mayor of San Francisco."

Harvey's new roommate, Tom Eure, knew Milk had a weird sense of humor, but he had a queasy feeling that Harvey wasn't joking when he made that observation over breakfast one morning. The newspapers were full of talk about the 1969 municipal elections. "Yes," Harvey stated conclusively. "I want to be mayor."

Harvey's new found liberalism was rankled by San Francisco politics. Downtown business interests controlled City Hall, he complained. Gays had no voice in city government at all. No matter how liberal that new candidate Dianne Feinstein sounded, Milk wasn't convinced she would do much to substantively change the problems. Eighteen years earlier, Harvey had decided *he* could help stop the communist tide in Korea; now, he could save San Francisco too.

Harvey even called a number of wealthy friends together for a dinner to discuss their possible campaign contributions. They all kept straight faces as they gently persuaded Milk that success would be, well, improbable. Harvey's political fantasies drifted elsewhere. Ironically enough, by the time the board elected in 1969 sought reelection four years later, Harvey would be making his debut in city politics.

By 1969, after a successful run as the Sugar Plum Fairy in the hustling scene, Joe Campbell had also moved to the Bay Area. Joe was now thirty-three and felt burned out. The feeling that he was in some exclusive club faded as the gay milieu became more assertive and open. He had a hard time understanding these younger homosexuals, since he had increasingly come to regard his homosexuality as an inconvenience. It was the reason he had gotten beat up all the time as a kid. Though useful in his youth, his sexuality was now more a complication to social acceptance, so he grew his hair long, moved to a farm in Marin County and, to use the term fashionable then, dropped out.

Harvey's hair was beginning to inch toward his ears as well, but he was too much the New Yorker to go the mellowed-out route. Milk was falling more into the urban hippie frame of mind, going to anti-war marches and spending his time with his flower children friends from the *Hair* cast. Every weekday morning, however, he would don his three-piece suit and wingtips to join the business world.

By the early months of 1970, the country was as bitterly polarized as it had been since the Civil War. Families divided not over mere political issues of liberal and conservative, but on profound questions of values, materialism, patriotism, war and peace. Harvey had lived forty years trying to corral his nonconformist instincts into everything a Jewish boy from Long Island was supposed to do, from leading an upwardly mobile career to settling into insular middle-class marriages. Nothing was more emblematic of the split in Milk's life than the dichotomy between his home, where he lived with *Hair* cast members, and his job, working among the most establishment of institutions.

The break came the day the United States announced the invasion of Cambodia, April 29, 1970. Spontaneous demonstrations broke out on college campuses and in major cities across the country. The escalation infuriated Milk. He blamed the nation's major corporations for fostering the conflict, because war was good for business. During his lunch hour, Milk joined protestors at the Pacific Stock Exchange. In a burst of characteristic theatricality, he jumped in front of the crowd and angrily burned his BankAmericard, denouncing big business. This gesture got a thunderous ovation, since it came from a member of the three-piece-suit species that generally had no use for such statements. A few minutes later, Harvey was on the phone to his friend Jim Bruton at Bache in New York. Jim was hardly surprised at the news. For years he'd seen Milk getting bored with the establishment life. Jim had long thought Harvey was in a constant hurry to go somewhere, though he didn't know where he was going. Severing his ties with the business world would at least force the issue, but Bruton couldn't resist goading his old friend.

"Now, what the hell did you do that for?" he asked.

"That's what I felt about it," said Milk. "I'm sick of putting up with the crap."

Milk talked briefly of opening a Jewish delicatessen in San Francisco. But Bruton figured that Harvey wasn't really worried where his money would come from. As Jack McKinley was fond of saying about Harvey, "She didn't know what she'd do next, but she knew she'd do something." Harvey seemed much more concerned with the unpleasantness of getting fired for the first time.

"I'm just sitting here waiting for somebody to say something," he said.

The ultimatum came that afternoon. Cut your hair or quit. Milk refused to do either and was fired. Tom O'Horgan summoned his old friend to Los Angeles to help him put together a film about Lenny Bruce, a dead comic who had once roamed the night club circuit with O'Horgan. Even as he watched Harvey pack, roommate Tom Eure thought to himself, "He'll be back. He loves San Francisco too much to stay away. He fits in too well."

The film project fell through. Harvey drove back to New York along Route 66 through the Southwest. He was pale and shaken when he appeared at Jim Bruton's door days later.

"It was just like out of *Easy Rider,*" he told Jim. A bunch of rednecks taunted Milk's hippie appearance at a Texas truck stop. Not one to suffer in silence, Milk snapped back and, he said, almost got his head blown off as the locals chased him out of town.

"I thought that was it—the end I've always seen coming," Harvey told Jim. "I thought it was all over."

"How did you get out of it?" Bruton asked.

"I ran like hell."

Judy Garland lies delicately on the satin bed, looking angelic in a high-necked gray chiffon gown, her hands folded over a prayer book.

The lines stretched for blocks around the East Side funeral home where her body lay in a glass-enclosed coffin. Thousands stood for four hours to catch a last glimpse. Many were homosexuals, swarming around the funeral home like so many shirtless ones for that last moment of reverence to the woman who seemed the metaphor for their existence: put-upon and therefore self-destructive, a victim with a nebulous vision of Oz over the rainbow.

The next night, some of the still-disconsolate made their way to the Stonewall Bar at 53 Christopher Street in Greenwich Village. Police arrived for a raid at 2 A.M. The ostensible charge was selling liquor without a license. The Stonewall had been peddling booze for three years only a few blocks from precinct headquarters, so the real offense was probably failure to pay off the police that week. No difference. This was to be a typical raid, the kind that had been going on in New York City for decades, the kind that had been coming down in every major American city for decades.

The crowd moved out of the Stonewall and lingered on the street outside. A few drag queens campily entertained them. More men came from the other bars to see what was happening at Sheridan Square, under the bright, full moon of June 28, 1969.

When the police began to come out with the arrested bartenders, a few people tossed coins at them. Then beer cans. Then rocks. Someone shouted, "Christopher Street belongs to the queens." A full-scale riot erupted. The outnumbered police officers barricaded themselves in the Stonewall for protection.

Craig Rodwell and his lover were wandering home from a bridge game when police sirens and clamoring crowds drew them toward Christopher Street. Rodwell was amazed at what he saw. The crowd was bombarding the Stonewall with bricks. Some were trying to batter down the doors to get at the police who cowered inside. Rodwell started leading chants: "Police and Mafia out of the bars" and "Christopher Street belongs to the queens." Craig hadn't had so much fun since he was a kid cheering the Chicago Cubs.

Buses ferried in the city's tactical police force to disperse the crowd. Gay rioters played cat and mouse with patrolmen through the night on the twisted narrow streets of the Village.

When the bars closed the next night, over two thousand restless gays gathered again outside the Stonewall. Again, helmeted police returned, brandishing nightsticks and finally forming a flying wedge to break up the rioters.

This undoubtedly was the first American riot with a schedule determined by when the bars closed and staffed by soldiers who retreated to cruise the nearby docks when the serious business was over. Craig Rodwell saw it as the opportunity for which he had long waited. By the third night of rioting, he had printed up fliers decrying both the organized crime control of gay bars and police harassment of gays. Other fliers appeared when the riots reached their fourth and final day. Newly radicalized gays soon formed the first Gay Liberation Front and talked optimistically about new ideas like gay power and even gay revolution.

For gays like Rodwell, the burst of gay militance couldn't have come at a more fortuitous time. Ever since his suicide attempt, Rodwell had devoted his energies to trying to create the gay movement he had discussed with Harvey in 1962. He had tried working with the Mattachine Society, but quit when he met resistance to a resolution he had penned, stating that Mattachine's position should be that homosexuality was equal to, on a par with, and no different in kind from heterosexuality. That Mattachine even hesitated to approve such a statement nauseated Rodwell.

Few alternatives, however, existed then. Rodwell worked two summers as a Fire Island bartender to save enough money to open the Oscar Wilde Memorial Bookstore on Mercer Street in 1967 (later moved to Christopher Street). The first openly gay business in New York, the bookstore published its own newsletter, *The Hymnal,* prodding gays to do things like register to vote and pressure political candidates. Harvey Milk even dropped by the store occasionally and briefly contributed a column on investment tips—written, of course, under a pseudonym.

Once the social change movements of the 1960s hit, it seemed only a matter of time before gays would leap into the kind of militant movement Rodwell and a handful of early gay activists envisioned. For years civics classes talked about all men being created equal; it was not until the 1960s that blacks and women militantly pushed society to bring theory into practice. Traditional Christian values always talked of the curse of materialism; it was not until the flower children that a generation rejected materialism on a mass scale. "Peace on earth, good will toward men" had long been religious watchwords; it was not until the Vietnam War that millions of Americans took to the streets to make that phrase more than a Christmas card slogan.

Society had long demanded that homosexuals exist with the greatest incongruity of all—to live without regard for the powerful urges of sexuality. The disharmony between body and soul had twisted the lives of generations of gays. Without the ability to express this most powerful of biological impulses, many turned against themselves in bitter, self-destructive lives. Social institutions compounded and enforced the despair on many fronts—police raids, military purges, and the omnipresent discrimination. Now all this would be challenged as gays demanded the right to live in harmony with their bodies. The birth of gay liberation on a sultry June night in Greenwich Village seemed a natural outgrowth of the Age of Aquarius. Judy Garland was dead.

"Do you mind critics calling you cheap, decadent, sensationalistic, gimicky, vulgar, overinflated, megalomaniacal?"

Reporters love asking such tantalizingly combative questions. But Tom O'Horgan, as mild mannered as ever, had little desire to start a row. "I don't read reviews much," he answered calmly, if not honestly.

That such a question could legitimately be asked gave a fair indication of the critical disdain in which O'Horgan was held by late 1971. That the question comprised the cover blurb of the Sunday *New York Times Magazine,* superimposed over a picture of the long-haired director, indicated the meteoric rise O'Horgan had experienced in the late 1960s. Within the space of three years, he had directed three of the most successful—and wildly controversial—plays on Broadway: *Hair, Jesus Christ Superstar* and *Lenny.*

O'Horgan's bohemian coterie shared the success. Jack McKinley —who now went by his middle name, Galen—served competently as stage manager for many of O'Horgan's productions. The *Times* story, however, spent an inordinate amount of space discussing another member of the idiosyncratic director's entourage: "About O'Horgan's age, Harvey Milk is a sad-eyed man—another aging hippie with long, long hair, wearing faded jeans and pretty beads; he seems instinctively attuned to all of O'Horgan's needs."

Craig Rodwell read the story with disbelief that Sunday morning. " 'Long, long hair. Faded jeans. Pretty beads!' " he thought. "Is this the same Harvey Milk?"

As usual, when Harvey did something, he did it all the way. Though friends of the conventional Wall Street Milk could not imagine Harvey the hippie, friends of the new Milk had a hard time imagining how he could ever have been straightlaced. He once tried explaining his employment history to author Eve Merriam. She wasn't sure if he were telling the truth. Still, she noticed that Milk took childish delight in his transformation. Every time he talked of his background, she saw a man impishly amused at what had happened to Harvey Milk, the nice, middle-class Jewish boy from Long Island.

Harvey moved among the vanguard of New York's counterculture. When it came to romance, however, he was set in his ways and he quickly found a new lover to fit his new life-style. Harvey met Joseph Scott Smith at the Christopher Street Subway stop on his forty-first birthday, the same week *Lenny* opened on Broadway. Smith's Equity pseudonym was Joe Scott, but Harvey would never call him Joe. Probably, friends thought, because of the reminder of his first lover, Joe Campbell. With long blond hair, piercing blue eyes, and a firm build, the twenty-two-year-old Smith proved the perfect lover for the transformed Milk.

Smith had only recently moved from Jackson, Mississippi. Like many men his age, Smith skipped a stint in Vietnam by checking the little box on the final page of his draft medical form—the box next to the word homosexual. The deferment put Scott in league with Jackson's small countercultural scene, since hippies were the only locals who were unshaken by Smith and his handful of openly gay friends.

Hip life in Jackson, however, was less than scintillating. There are only so many times you can take LSD, listen to the same Moody Blues songs, and stare at the three-dimensional cover of the Rolling Stones' *Satanic Majesties Request* album before a lusty young man yearns for greater things. When two gay friends announced they were quitting the magnolias for Greenwich Village, Smith cast his lot with them.

Harvey was twenty years older than Smith, but his appearance and entourage were very au courant. The onslaught of invitations to opening nights and backstage parties was enough to charm any boy fresh from Mississippi. Harvey wasted no time mapping out their future. Once he finished work on O'Horgan's new play, *Inner City,* they would move to San Francisco.

Tom made Harvey associate producer of *Inner City* in the hope that Milk's background in finance could make him a serious Broadway producer. Like any good boss, Milk promptly got his boyfriend Scott on the payroll, where he worked under the stage manager, Galen McKinley. The play was based on the controversial *Inner City Mother Goose* by Eve Merriam. The book was then the second most banned work in America. An Orange County teacher was fired for simply loaning his copy to a student. The play enumerated the injustices of urban life and seemed well-suited for Harvey's new left-leaning politics.

The critics had little use for the iconoclastic O'Horgan, however, and panned the play. Audiences were wildly enthusiastic but small. Keeping the play afloat required hyperactive fund raising by Milk. He hit up his old friends at Bache, many of whom did not even recognize their former colleague when he turned up at 51 Wall Street.

The play's two other co-producers, meanwhile, were horrified that O'Horgan was using some aging hippie as his representative to the project. Fights between Milk and the play manager escalated rapidly. The management was horrified at the blatant marijuana smoking of the cast. The play was probably one of the only Broadway productions to have to issue a policy statement that pot could be smoked only in the second- and third-floor dressing rooms since the gallery had begun to stink of weed. Every week, the stage manager would plead that the play was broke and issue a notice giving Equity actors warning that they would soon be fired. Every week, Milk would delight the cast by tearing down the notice, swearing he would raise the money to keep the play open.

The play's three-month run lasted into 1972, but events conspired to drive it to an early end. Richard Nixon was about to be reelected president. The country was tiring of incessant gripes about injustice. The counterculture was losing steam. Social conscience became passé. Broadway audiences didn't want to see plays about blacks in ghettos. They wanted musicals with lots of nice dancing.

Feeling he could do no more, Harvey left the production and moved to San Francisco. Scott Smith had to stay behind until the play closed. Smith's mailbox was soon crammed with daily letters from Harvey explaining in detail why Smith *had* to join him in San Francisco as soon as *Inner City* folded. On the back of a Dots candy box, Milk assured Scott that San Francisco had many movie theaters they could enjoy. Another handmade card insisted Scott should move because his shoulder-length blond hair would dry faster in the California sun.

Once reunited, Milk and Smith picked up a mutt from the pound, named it The Kid, climbed into Milk's 1967 green Dodge Charger and spent nearly a year driving through California. They lived meagerly off their unemployment checks, usually tossing their sleeping bags under the redwoods of the state park to which they were closest. When the unemployment checks stopped coming, they returned to San Francisco, lived on their income tax refunds, and frittered away their afternoons on massive jigsaw puzzles.

Harvey's old roommate Tom Eure had never seen anybody throw himself into jigsaw puzzles with such passion as Harvey. Day after day. Night after night. Harvey stood over the puzzles, trying to get the complex, confusing pieces to fit together. Somehow.

"Harvey, what are you going to do for money?" Jim Bruton asked when he visited Harvey and Scott in San Francisco. "Aren't you almost out?"

"Yes."

"How are you going to get more?"

"I don't know," said Harvey. He didn't think the subject needed to be discussed any more.

"What are you going to do for a living?" Bruton persisted.

"It doesn't matter."

"And you know what?" Bruton observed years later when he recounted the conversation. "I think he was happier than at any time I had ever seen him in his entire life."

four

Sodom by the Sea

If this little book should see the light after its 100 years of entombment, I would like its readers to know that the author was a lover of her own sex and devoted the best years of her life in striving for the political equal and social and moral elevation of women.

—Laura De Force Gordon, May, 1879 (Found in time capsule at San Francisco's Washington Square Park, April 22, 1979, on the flyleaf of Gordon's book "Great Geysers of California.)

"United we stand. Divided they catch us one by one."

A warm breeze rustled through The Black Cat bar in San Francisco's North Beach neighborhood on a soft October night in 1951. Hazel the piano player had just announced last call and Jose, in his usual sequined gown, stepped forward to deliver his nightly oration.

"Remember, there's nothing wrong with being gay. The crime is getting caught," he shouted. "Let's all stand up and form a circle." The crowd slowly went into a formation. "For one moment, I want you to stand and be proud of who you are."

With an evangelist's fervor, Jose led the chorus:

God save us nelly queens
God save us nelly queens
God save us queens. . . .

Moments later, the sergeant at the old Hall of Justice across the street motioned to the prisoners of the gay tier. "There's your leader," he laughed, pointing out the window.

Below, Jose had moved his sing-along to The Black Cat's front door, where they could look up to their friends who had been unfortunate enough to be caught in that week's sweep of gays. Small figures on a sidewalk, singing up to their friends behind the bars: *"God save us queens."*

Decades later, grown men would break into tears when they remembered those nights in the 1950s, singing to their friends in jail. No one else could possibly have cared about the queens, in those lonely days, they explain, except maybe God.

Generations before people like Harvey Milk went west to build a political movement that would one day capture the nation's attention, a homosexual underground thrived in San Francisco. The early settlers dubbed the cosmopolitan city "Baghdad by the Bay," but ministers throughout the West quickly gave the town another nickname, "Sodom by the Sea."

From the start San Francisco attracted an unlikely conglomeration of adventurers, vagabonds, bohemians, and assorted misfits. The city was a wild town that could challenge the world's rowdiest ports. Among the whorehouses of the early Barbary Coast were the forerunners of gay bars, small elite restaurants with all-male staffs and very private booths.

Necessity, if nothing else, forced a see-no-evil attitude toward homosexuality. Between 1848 and 1858, San Francisco leaped from being a backwater hamlet of one thousand to become a major metropolis of fifty thousand—and virtually all the gold-seeking newcomers were men. The late twentieth-century homophile vogue of denoting sexual inclinations by colored handkerchiefs, for example, dates back to those Forty-niner days when raucous miners used hankies to separate male and female roles for their all-male square dances.

The scandal sheets of a more Victorian America fretted about the city's unnatural vices in the 1880s. In England, Oscar Wilde noted, "It's an odd thing, but anyone who disappears is said to be last seen in San

Francisco," an observation that undoubtedly said as much about Wilde's company as it did about the city's magnetism.

The Spanish-American War infused new excitement into the city's gay scene when San Francisco became home port to the thousands of men bound for the Philippines. Helpful young soldiers learned they could make extra money if they escorted admiring older men around the Presidio military base—and earn more if they proved serviceable.

The earthquake shattered San Francisco's bawdier side when church leaders came forward to warn that the shaker obviously represented God's wrath on Sodom West. A clean-up campaign swept away the Barbary Coast. Prohibition later closed any *sub rosa* gay bars that may have survived. Resourceful gays staked out Market Street, the city's main thoroughfare, as a cruising zone and there shopped among the always numerous sailors for satisfaction.

Dangers abounded. Some plucky navy men would dress in their tightest blues and memorize license numbers of cars that sputtered slowly by. From motor vehicle records, the voter registrar, or the city directory, the military men could trace the cruiser's address. Before the week was out, many a hapless victim would receive an extortionist's invoice, casually mentioning that if payment were not promptly received, both family and employer could expect revealing mail.

Gays who escaped blackmailers had to run the gauntlet with "Lilly Law," as police were known among gays in the 1930s. Police knew that one Market Street theater was a popular pit stop for wandering gay men, so authorities routinely assigned seats there to the most comely police cadets. Once a gay man sidled into the next seat, the cadets would wriggle their legs suggestively. After the preliminaries of fellatio, the plainclothesman would suggest that the pair meet outside for more fun. In the darkness of the theater, the gay cruiser would not know the policeman had painted mercurochrome on his penis. The artistry, however, was obvious to vice squaders who stood in the lobby, arresting any man who emerged with telltale red lips.

The wealthy managed to stay above such trouble in this era. Templeton Crocker, the scion of the city's prominent banking family, reportedly headed local gay royalty, throwing lavish parties and surrounding himself with pretty young men. Other famous characters fluttered in and out of the tea dances and private parties where each guest was carefully vouched for. A homosexual septuagenarian fondly recalled decades later how in his youth, no less than the Catholic archbishop had "gently laid hands" on him.

Parties, street cruising, and theater blow-jobs, however, could hardly be described as the norm for San Francisco gays before World War II. These players were the lucky ones. Most gays of that time did not even have words to describe the longings they felt, much less any awareness that others like them existed. The ones who did understand their malady generally stuck to propriety, becoming the archetypal bachelor uncles and spinster aunts, the secret of their moral depravity gnawing at them until death.

A movement for homosexual equality had grown in Germany since the 1880s, arguing for legal reforms and greater public awareness about homosexuality. That ended when Hitler methodically exterminated its leaders and rounded their followers into Level 3 concentration camps. Ironically enough, America's move to squash Hitler began the historical processes that would turn San Francisco from a town that only tolerated homosexuality to the international gay Mecca.

The sheer scope of the war's social effects were staggering. Some sixteen million men joined the armed services during the war. It marked a social dislocation unprecedented in American history. Men were uprooted from generations-old family centers, pulled outside the ken of their peers' values, shunted anonymously through big cities in almost exclusively same-sex environments—all of them streaming toward points of debarkation from which they might never return.

When Allan Berube of the San Francisco Gay History Project interviewed dozens of such soldiers later, he found most had similar stories. For the first time in their lives, they heard a new word—a word that not only defined the difference that had lurked secretly within, but also indicated that others like themselves existed. If the word didn't come from fellow G.I.s, the soldiers learned it from gay cruisers who frequented the parks, depots, and YMCAs used as makeshift sleep sites for servicemen. Many a California gay had his salad days in San Francisco then, since the city was the major point of debarkation for the Pacific theater.

The military speeded San Francisco's growth into a gay center. The second world war marked the first conflict in which the armed services tried to systematically identify and then exclude homosexuals. In the process of examining the nearly 36 million men eligible for service, thousands were found to be homosexual and classified as such by the draft boards. The tens of thousands more who escaped this early classification faced a tougher fate in the service. Purge after purge of gays in various branches condemned thousands to the "blue discharge," named for the blue paper upon which homosexual discharges were written. The discharge was stamped with a large H and guaranteed the bearer the status of *persona non grata,* especially during the patriotic war years. The Department of Defense still refuses to say how many thousands were subjected to this ignonomy. The action, however, created an entire class of social outcasts who were public homosexuals. Some committed suicide, but most tried to start quiet new lives. Returning home was an improbable option, with all the messy questions it would raise. Most of the men discharged from the Pacific theater were processed out in San Francisco, and that's where they stayed. By the end of World War II, the military establishment had given San Francisco a disproportionately large number of identified gays.

The massive purges of gays from the military and government during the McCarthy era—spurred by the Wisconsin senator who apparently was homosexual himself—increased the number of gay refugees in the Bay Area. A full contingent of former State Department employees moved en masse to nearby Sausalito, say gay old-timers, after anti-gay hysteria swept the foreign service.

It was in these turbulent years that the modern gay bar started. Unlike the clandestine gay speakeasies and parties of the past, these were public institutions—the first places where homosexuals could publicly assemble. Their patrons had less to lose than their predecessors. Many had already been publicly identified as gays by the military. Once plucked from the isolation of generations past, it was only a matter of time before this new San Francisco minority would begin its slow and irresistible movement toward civil rights.

Aunt Maria threw the long sequined gown on the parlor couch. "I've brought something for Jose to play with," she told her sister, Delores. Jose raced into the sitting room, fingered the beads adorning the soft lamé, and then ran to his mother's full-length mirror. Jose Sarria had always been an unpredictable child and his family humored his fondness for dressing up in his mother's and aunt's gowns and high heels, forsaking the pursuit of baseball for his fantasies of duchesses and royal balls.

Jose and his sister fell in with the bohemian crowd of North Beach in the late 1940s. They frequently wandered into The Black Cat bar where writers like Bill Saroyan, John Steinbeck, and, more recently, Allen Ginsberg were known to imbibe. One night the pair spotted a handsome waiter, Jimmy Moore, and promptly placed a bet over who could get him in bed first. Jose invited Jimmy to an Independence Day family picnic. Toward the end of the outing, Jose's mother decided she had at last found the perfect mate for her son. She asked Jimmy to move in with the family. Jose won the bet.

A dutiful husband, Jose would fill in for Jimmy when he got sick, adding his own colorful presence to The Black Cat as he traipsed through the bar in red high heels. Jose recognized the piano player's background music one afternoon as the theme from *Carmen* and in his strong tenor started belting out arias as he delivered cocktails among the tables. Within a few months, Jose was regularly drawing Sunday afternoon crowds as he put on camp productions of his one-man operas.

The sight of Jose's plump figure stuffed into a tight red dress campily singing *Tosca* proved irresistible to the growing number of San Francisco gays, and homosexuals soon crowded out the bar's North Beach patrons. They were, Jose thought, a dispirited bunch. Jose had spent his life bucking every norm. He'd be damned if he was going to see far more conventional men wallow in self-contempt while he was having a good time. That's when the preaching, as Sarria called it, began.

Jose saw hundreds of men getting arrested every month on specious charges, then meekly pleading guilty to whatever police alleged in the vain hope that they could somehow preserve their anonymity. In the course of his one-man version of *Carmen* he launched into a prayerful monologue. "When you are on your knees, praying to God in your own way, if you get tapped on the shoulder by a big blue star, remember, you swallow first." Jose always got a big laugh when he affected a big swallow here. "And then you say—I'm not guilty and I want a trial by jury."

The weekly operas provided the first gay news service. "A blue fungus has hit the parks," he told his fans during a heavy crackdown on park sex. "It does not appear until about 2 A.M. It twinkles like a star. Until this fungus dies, it's best to stay out of our parks at 2 A.M."

Jose pioneered two battle cries: "There's nothing wrong with being gay—the crime is getting caught," and "United we stand, divided they catch us one by one." At the end of every night at The Black Cat, he would order the patrons to stand in a circle, join hands, and sing "God Save the Queens," sometimes flocking them outside to do a final stanza to friends across the street in jail. "For one moment," Jose said, "be proud of who you are."

Jose's activity made him an urban guerrilla to San Francisco's heavily Irish Catholic Police Department and especially to the two-man vice team of Murphy and Gallagher. The Alcohol Beverage Control Commission (ABC) took steps to close Jose's den of insurgency.

The first salvo came in 1948 when the ABC tried to close The Black Cat because they had evidence that the establishment actually served liquor to homosexuals, a criminal act in those days. The court-room was packed with gays in neat suits and ties the day the case finally got to trial.

"Can you point out the homosexuals in this room?" the bar's lawyer asked the judge.

The judge allowed that he couldn't.

The lawyer argued that if a wise judge with years of worldly experience could not pick out a homosexual, how could a mere bar-tender? The logic held, though The Black Cat ultimately had to go all the way to the California Supreme Court to get a court ruling affirming the right of homosexuals to peacefully assemble.

The fact that a homosexual case had dared go to court and then actually won infuriated the ABC and the vice squad. They launched what would be a fifteen-year war on The Black Cat. Feisty Jose, how-ever, proved equal to the challenge.

The city's thirty-five gay bars set up a network, calling each other at the first sight of a man who might be a plainclothes cop or ABC investigator. When the hapless agent came into The Black Cat, Jose would take to the stage, graciously introduce the gentleman, and ask everyone to give him a round of applause.

The police took to enforcing an archaic ordinance that forbade anyone from posing as a member of the opposite sex. Jose responded by simply getting the city's drag queens to pin to their dresses little slips of paper saying, "I am a boy." Once in court, police could hardly claim that a man with such a sign was seriously posing as a member of the opposite sex.

Court dockets, meanwhile, became clogged with gays who fol-lowed Jose's advice, pleaded guilty, and demanded a trial by jury. Never eager for overtime, the city's judges started insisting that before bring-ing a case to trial, the police and district attorney's office have evidence against the accused—a troublesome detail that had long been avoided in gay prosecutions.

Even as Jose and his Black Cat battled on, the police and ABC carried out their vendetta against the newly emerging minority. Those were the days when the Catholic archbishop reportedly had veto power

over the mayor's selection of police and fire chiefs. The police department, where much of the power structure rested on which parish controlled key positions, acted accordingly.

Paddy wagons routinely rolled up to the doors of gay bars and
police bused all the patrons to jail, generally for being "inmates of a
disorderly house." Charges were dismissed most times, but usually after
the city's newspapers printed not only the arrested person's name, but
his address and place of employment. Police also followed up these
arrests with calls to the victim's employer and family, even if charges
were dropped within hours. This forced gay bars to observe the most
circumspect standards. No touching or holding hands. Gays dancing
together was itself an offense that could warrant a bar's closure. The
few daring bars that did allow dancing kept a bouncer keenly observing
everyone nearing the bar. If a person looked slightly suspicious, the
bar's lights flicked on and off and couples raced to change partners,
lesbians pairing up with gay men. Only through elaborate payoffs to
police officers did the bars continue to operate.

One evening a year, like a chapter from a Cinderella story, the
police would bestow a free night upon the homosexuals. Halloween had
been staked out years before as the homosexual high holiday; gays did,
after all, live most of their lives behind masks. The chief of police
routinely escorted Jose to the center of North Beach that night, opening
the car door politely for the elegantly gowned drag queen and giving
the traditional send-off for the night's activity. "This is your night—you
run it."

Jose then held court at The Black Cat. For that one night the
police let homosexuals roam the city freely, even if they wore dresses.
But when the hours shifted from October 31 to November 1, the iron
fist of Lilly Law would fall again. Few had any hope that it would ever
change.

"Sex Deviates Establish National Headquarters in San Francisco."

The headline in the *San Francisco Progress,* a small neighborhood
paper, shocked the 1959 mayor's race as had few other charges. The
city's gays knew all too well that the administration of Republican
Mayor George Christopher was not coddling perverts, but City Assessor Russ Woolden was having a tough time stoking up his own campaign for mayor. Woolden's accusation that Christopher had permitted
two gay groups to exist in San Francisco marked the first time that
homosexuality had appeared as a local campaign issue since the post-
earthquake clean up. It was also the first time many gays themselves

learned that there were actually two local organizations serving their interests.

The first generation of American gay activists, born out of the traumas of World War II, had been trying to start various gay groups in the city since 1948. Only when police chased a Chicago advertising salesman, Hal Call, out of the Windy City in 1952, did San Francisco gets its first permanent gay activist. Call founded a local chapter of the Mattachine Society. The idea of even joining a homosexual group was so risky that the Mattachine chapters started as secret societies, becoming open organizations only as the 1950s wore on.

Police raids made going to gay bars so risky that four lesbian couples, led by lovers Del Martin and Phyllis Lyon, got together in 1955 to form the Daughters of Bilitis (DOB), the nation's first lesbian organization. The secret organization had purely social goals. They wanted a place where they could hold hands and dance, so the DOB's function was to organize parties at various members' houses.

Only when Del and Phyllis kept getting unusual phone calls did it strike them that there was something political about lesbianism. They heard many stories from women, whose in-laws were plotting to take away their children because for one stark moment the mask had dropped, women in jail as "inmates of a disorderly house" with all their friends too fearful to bail them out, women driven from their jobs and near suicide. The DOB started "public discussion nights" in 1959 where they could invite the public to hear gay complaints. Of course, only gays attended, but the term "public" provided a cover of respectability, and they were among the first gatherings of gays outside bars.

The two groups were publishing their own newsletters by the mid-fifties. The publications approached the subject of homosexual rights with utmost caution, insisting they were neither communist nor out to recruit new deviates. They used terms like sex variant, invert, and homophile rather than such loaded words as homosexual. The *Mattachine Review* regularly ran such tentatively titled stories as "Handicap or a Talent?", "Rehabilitation or Punishment?", "Disease or a Way of Life?"

These groups' memberships never soared beyond several hundred. Their impact was largely on gays themselves, not the heterosexual society they professed to educate. For the first time, gays could imagine that there might one day be a world where they could have meetings, discuss relevant issues, and petition their government, just like regular people. It took Assessor Russ Woolden to bring these groups into public debate by denouncing Mayor George Christopher's alleged leniency to gays in a campaign flyer.

> I am convinced that the true purpose of the Mattachine Society is to subvert public morals and change our entire social structure to the point that homosexual activities will be regarded as normal and harmless. Do not be misled. Organized homosexuality in San Francisco is a menace that must be faced today.
> TOMORROW MAY BE TOO LATE.

A flyer hand-delivered to the city's conservative neighborhoods also alerted citizens that their daughters were threatened too by the insidious activities of the Daughters of Bilitis.

Both the morning *Chronicle* and the *Examiner* ignored Woolden's broadside. They were relieved to finally have a Republican in City Hall. After the *Progress* headline, however, the papers turned on Woolden with a vengeance. The *Chronicle* wrote that Woolden's charges "degrade the good name of San Francisco." The *Examiner* noted that homosexuality was a problem in most of the nation's big cities and that "The San Francisco Police Department deals with it firmly, as it should be dealt with."

Woolden went to a bitter defeat, but to ensure that city government would never again hear charges of embracing gays, the police came down even harder on gay bars. By 1961, the harassment proved too much for Jose Sarria. He abandoned his red gown and high heels, donned a suit and tie, and stomped into City Hall to file his petition to run for the board of supervisors, the eleven-member body that serves as both city council and county commission for San Francisco's city-county consolidated government.

Jose had no problem raising money for a filing fee, but he faced a major obstacle in getting twenty-five signatures necessary to put his name on the ballot. In a city that already had the reputation as one of the freest gay centers in the world, it was still difficult to find twenty-five people who would sign their name to a paper endorsing an acknowledged gay. Jose got his signatures, however, and filed his candidacy. He did no campaigning; he simply spread the word among friends. Every vote would be a protest against police harassment of gays, he said.

On election night, political pundits were amazed when the drag queen entertainer polled an amazing seven thousand votes, not enough to win, but far more than many better-known political names. The fact that the first openly gay candidate for public office in American history could tally such a total stirred the imaginations of the handful of activists who then dared consider political action as a future option. Votes. Few had thought of themselves as equal human beings and citizens, so few had bothered to consider that no matter what police or judges could deprive them of, they could still vote.

The police and ABC were not impressed. Pressure continued on gay bars in general—and The Black Cat in particular. Cat employees frequently had to go without their paychecks, since every extra dollar went for lawyers' fees. The bar owner was a heterosexual who fought the authorities as a matter of principle. Toward the end of 1963, he took Jose aside. "I've got a family to support," he told Jose. "This has been going on fifteen years. They can afford to keep doing it fifteen more years. I can't."

Jose tried to get other gay bars to raise money for The Black Cat's defense, fretting that the demise of The Cat would embolden authorities to push harder agianst other gay bars. No one offered any help. The bar hung on until Halloween, 1963, when after that one precious night of freedom The Black Cat closed its doors for good.

A week after The Black Cat's last day, San Francisco voters elected a handsome Italian liberal, George Moscone, to the San Francisco board of supervisors. At thirty-three, he was the second youngest man to serve on the board in the city's history. Of course, this electoral victory had nothing to do with queers' problems in North Beach. It would be twelve years before such issues would help bring George Moscone to the forefront of city politics.

A wave of repression followed The Black Cat's demise. Police and the ABC closed five bars within a week. Of the thirty gay bars open on Halloween, 1963, only eighteen survived a year later—and fifteen of them faced hearings for revocation of their liquor license. One dramatic raid on a Tenderloin bar, the Tay-Bush Inn, prodded gays into action. The police loaded seven paddy wagons full of gays to jail—103 in all —though authorities bitterly complained in newspapers the next day that amid the confusion, another 139 intended arrestees slipped away. Wrote a bemused reporter covering the raid, "It was vaguely reminiscent of loading sheep from a corral."

"The majority of the males affected swishy-hipped walks, limp-wristed gestures, high-pitched voices and wore tight pants," the prose-

cuting attorney later told the court. "The women," he added meaningfully, "were mannish." The bar lost its license because, of the 242
present, police claimed that at least five or six were dancing in same-sex
couples.

The night after the raid, six men who had been marginally involved in gay organizing efforts met in a living room and formed the
Society for Individual Rights (SIR). The group called "candidates'
nights" for the 1964 elections, but few politicians had the courage to
attend, so activists took a chapter from the black civil rights movement
and decided to mobilize liberal San Francisco church leaders for their
cause. A new organization resulted from the alliance, the Council on
Religion and the Homosexual (CRH).

The CRH excited the handful of gay groups already in existence.
In an unprecedented show of unanimity, all the city's gay groups—
Mattachine, DOB, SIR, and the few others—banded together to hold
a New Year's Eve benefit on the last night of 1964. A delegation of
ministers went to police with the plans. "If you're not going to enforce
God's laws, we will," snapped a police inspector.

The night of the benefit Del Martin and Phyllis Lyon were working the doors. They were startled to see that an inordinate number of
the lesbians and gay men in attendance seemed dazed and shaken. A
step outside showed them why. The police had bathed the hall's entrance with floodlights and were busy taking both still photos and films
of everyone who entered. Paddy wagons waited ominously nearby while
nearly fifty uniformed and plainclothes officers filtered through the
crowd. Over five hundred gays walked this gauntlet, upset at its proportions but not particularly surprised, given the years of similar police
harassment.

The heterosexual ministers had come expecting an evening of
dancing. They were stunned at the sight. They had heard the gays'
stories of police problems, but most had never seen such intense police
presence in their lives, much less one aimed at harmless men and
women in formal evening wear.

Police officials shocked the ministers even more when a number of
officers demanded to go inside. A trio of lawyers was waiting for just
such a request and they quickly explained that under California statutes, the event was a private party and unless the police bought tickets,
they had to stay out. The police promptly threw the three lawyers in
the paddy wagon and arrested a pregnant housewife who happened to
be standing near them. This, of course, was business as usual for police

who were only enforcing an unwritten department rule that dealt with any gathering of more than one hundred homosexuals as an armed insurrection.

For the first time, however, heterosexuals saw what it meant to be gay in San Francisco. The ministers held an angry press conference the next morning, likening the SFPD to the Gestapo and demanding an investigation. Even the Catholic archbishop was reportedly up in arms. For this, if no other reason, City Hall had to respond.

Two officers from the police community relations unit, including a young unorthodox cop named Richard Hongisto, were assigned to smooth relations with the city's gays. Harassment decreased. By the end of the year Jack Morrison, the first incumbent supervisor ever to seek the gay vote, was at a SIR meeting flanked by ambitious aspirants. The dailies, of course, were shocked by the appearance, but the supervisor won reelection nevertheless. By 1966 two brash, liberal San Francisco assemblymen, Willie Brown and John Burton, were also wooing votes at SIR meetings. Their end of the deal: to introduce a bill repealing the 1872 statute proscribing felony punishments for any gays convicted of the "crime against nature."

SIR ensured its role as the central institution of the gay community when it undertook a radical activity unimaginable in San Francisco a few years before—holding dances. Without an ABC liquor license to lose, the dances were immune to raids, and SIR membership swelled to over 1,200 by 1967, making it the largest gay group in the United States and lending even more credence to the notion that gays were a significant political constituency.

Proof of that claim came in 1969 in the form of a charming, attractive, thirty-five-year-old housewife from the city's wealthy Pacific Heights neighborhood. Dianne Feinstein's appearance on a roster of what were otherwise familiar political faces excited city liberals more than the emergence of any politician since now-State Senator George Moscone's debut six years earlier. Though the darling of environmental groups and limousine liberals, Feinstein's stint on the state women's parole board gave her law-and-order credentials that attracted conservatives. Moreover, Feinstein's ties with segments of the downtown establishment assured her a hefty campaign chest. She became the first supervisorial candidate in city history to run television advertising.

That such a charismatic and promising candidate would come to the SIR center to court gay voters was almost beyond belief. Feinstein quickly garnered gay money, volunteers, and votes at a level unparalleled since Jose's 1961 candidacy. When Feinstein ultimately beat out all other candidates in the citywide at-large elections—a status that gave her the powerful board presidency—she credited her substantial margin of victory to gay voters.

That same year, gays in New York City rioted at the Stonewall. A series of radical, gay liberation-style groups emerged in the Bay Area, but the brunt of San Francisco gay activism fell into methodical, work-within-the-system politics that put California's gay movement years ahead of its New York counterpart.

SIR activists played a key role in encouraging Police Community Relations cop Richard Hongisto to run for sheriff in the 1971 municipal elections. The flamboyant Hongisto pulled together a previously un-heard-of coalition of gays, blacks, and anti-war activists. His symbol was the anti-nuclear symbol blazened on a lavender background. Hongisto won an impressive city-wide victory. Conservatives were in a state of shock—the sheriff's office had long been a right-wing domain. With Hongisto, gays won a politician who not only publicly thanked them for his election, but one who became a forceful pro-gay spokesman, bringing gays into all levels of the sheriff's department.

The story of gay political clout spiraled into a self-fulfilling prophecy. The more politicians talked about it, the more others came to court gay favor, making gay claims to political power all the more credible. Power, of course, breeds power brokers. By the early 1970s, three dominant figures presented themselves as gay community power brokers, the people elected officials should deal with if they wanted to avoid the scruffy radicals who carried picket signs.

As political chairman for SIR, Jim Foster was often the first gay activist that many San Francisco politicians had ever met. He understood the need for reform intimately: Like so many others, he had come to San Francisco in 1959 after being dishonorably discharged from the army because of his homosexuality.

David Goodstein appeared in 1971 when he rallied gay lawyers together to start civil rights challenges of anti-gay statutes. An independently wealthy man, Goodstein had originally come to San Francisco to be vice-president of a major bank, but lost his job as soon as the bank learned of his homosexuality. Goodstein's power came not only from his work among gay lawyers, but from his money. He could afford to give generous campaign contributions, which guaranteed access to politicians' offices.

Rick Stokes came on the scene as a crusading gay rights lawyer.

In his earlier years, he had been committed to an institution and subjected to electro shock therapy because of his homosexuality. He struggled through law school so he would have the weapons to mount a legal assault on anti-gay laws. A wise business investment in the city's most popular bathhouse, meanwhile, assured him the income to take on the fights.

Men like Jim Foster, David Goodstein, and Rick Stokes were deemed the young Turks of the San Francisco gay movement of the early seventies. Their peers constantly reminded them that they could make far more money if they dropped this troublesome homosexual cause and used their considerable talents in business. They, however, had confidence that they were the political wave of the future. Since they were often the first gay leaders politicians had ever heard of they developed connections that later activists like Harvey Milk could only envy.

The great corporate and tourist center, that was to be San Francisco's future. The city had once been known as a blue-collar town, a typical ethnic big city with a bustling port and a heavy industrial base. But in the 1960s, it all started changing, almost imperceptibly. The port started withering. Manufacturing moved to the suburbs. The city government did little to stem the flow and instead insisted that San Francisco needed to strike a new path. It would be a headquarters for major corporations. The city could also put a greater emphasis on tourism.

The city's blacks, Latins, and working class began to feel the pinch. Blue-collar workers followed their union jobs out of San Francisco. Amid great promises of urban renewal, the city bulldozed giant tracts of the black Filmore neighborhood. The new housing that was to renew the decimated area was never built, so there were that many fewer blacks in the city. The office workers who would fill the new corporate skyscrapers certainly were not about to live in San Francisco, so 1.6 billion dollars was sunk into the ultramodern Bay Area Rapid Transit system, which daily sped the workers from the suburbs. By coincidence, a main line of the subway cut down Mission Street, the center of the Latin neighborhood. The years of digging there drove many businesses into bankruptcy.

The election of the charismatic Joe Alioto as mayor in 1967 only accelerated these changes. Real estate developers and unions both contributed heavily to his campaign. In return, he made sure the massive high-rises kept reaching above the once-quaint San Francisco skyline.

Wealthy hotel owners were ecstatic about the new emphasis on tourism, so they supported Alioto and like-minded members of the board of supervisors.

The city's neighborhoods, meanwhile, were dying, as workers fled to suburbia and City Hall focused its attentions on downtown and tourism. Alioto adeptly kept minorities in line by handing out a minority training program here or a new public mall there. But the change to a white-collar city bred one result that even the wisest hotel owner or real estate developer could not have predicted. The growth in service-oriented corporate jobs came as the success of SIR and gay politicking were dramatically inflating San Francisco's already considerable reputation as a gay center. Gays began trekking westward in greater numbers, and since homosexuals reflect the overall make-up of society, this newly mobile group was largely white and middle-class, with at least a few years of college education. It would have been harder to find a segment of the population more suited to fill the thousands of new jobs in the skyscraper corporate headquarters and tourist industries.

The gay population soared. In any other plan, such white-collar workers could have been counted on to vote conservatively and not worry too much about what was happening to blacks, Latins, and inner city neighborhoods. But gays were a sorely disenfranchised group who could not afford the luxury of voting their pocketbook or ideology. They had to vote on survival issues, and survival was no small task for San Francisco gays. Though charming and affable, Alioto ruled the city with an iron hand. He even refused to appear on his City Hall balcony since critics were quick to note that in such poses he bore a striking resemblance to Benito Mussolini. The comparison certainly held true for gays. Alioto was, above all, an Italian Catholic politician with his sights set on higher office. To shore up his Catholic constituents in San Francisco, he dearly wanted to bring a cardinal's hat to the city. And you didn't get red hats by allowing perverts to run wild.

Police bore down heavily on gays who, afraid of bar raids, took to finding sex in public parks. By 1971, police were arresting an average of about 2,800 gay men a year on public sex charges; the same year, only sixty-three such arrests were made in all of New York City. The number of men harassed in the crackdown was many times this official arrest statistic, since it was common knowledge that a $30 payoff to the police usually let the transgressor escape with only a stern warning.

Many of the arrests were thrown out of court once information surfaced about the common police tactics of entrapment. But sentences meted out for gay offenses were sometimes higher than those given out for rape, armed robbery, and even manslaughter. According to one gay newspaper, 110 men were sentenced to fifteen years to life for the crime of "sodomy and oral copulation"—in 1971 alone.

Supervisor Feinstein easily galvanized gay support for her run against Alioto for mayor in 1971. She had kept a moderate voice as a supervisor, however, and could not get enough liberal or conservative votes to win. Gays were still smarting over the 1971 police crackdown after the elections. Many felt the hit-and-miss endorsements at SIR candidates' nights weren't doing the job. Embattled liberal Democrats around town were organizing into Democratic clubs, however, so Jim Foster organized his SIR political committee into the Alice B. Toklas Memorial Democratic Club.

Foster, the club's president, knew the group needed a bold stroke to establish itself on the political horizon. The chance came in early 1972 during the presidential campaign of Senator George McGovern. McGovern had issued a seven-point gay rights plank that satisfied virtually every demand the fledgling gay movement was making, from upgrading dishonorable discharges to banning discrimination against gays. The California primary shaped up as a crucial battle for McGovern. To get his name at the top of the ballot—a slot worth several percentage points—the South Dakota senator needed to be the first candidate to get all of his nominating petitions into Secretary of State Jerry Brown's office.

The city's more staid Democratic clubs decided to hold chic wine and cheese parties at midnight on the first possible day they could circulate petitions. "Nobody in their right mind is going to get out of bed at midnight to sign some goddamn petition," Jim Foster argued. So, when the key night came, Foster divided his Toklas club members into two groups. The first cadre went into gay bars before midnight, furiously registering new Democrats. At twelve, the second group recruited all the newly registered Democrats to sign McGovern petitions.

Before the bars closed that night, the gay Democrats had gathered over one-third the Northern California signatures McGovern needed to get on the ballot. Gay fund raisers, meanwhile, made gays a key part of the McGovern campaign money efforts. With such results, liberals quickly welcomed the new club into the Democratic fold. Most of the city's major liberals supported Stokes when he made a run for a seat on the local community college board of directors in November 1972. Milk would later criticize the candidacy, noting that for all the heavyweight liberal endorsements, Stokes seemed to downplay his homosexuality in campaign literature, but Stokes polled an impressive 45,000 votes—not enough to win, but a showing that surprised political analysts.

By the end of the year, the board of supervisors passed an ordinance prohibiting discrimination against gays by city contractors. Supervisors were timid at first. "Does this mean that contractors have to hire men who wear dresses?" the bill's sponsor, Dianne Feinstein, asked Del Martin when Martin first suggested the law. Virtually all the board members were Democrats with an eye for higher office, so only one supervisor, future mayoral hopeful John Barbagelata, opposed the measure.

"What the hell is this propaganda?"

Jim Foster was about to take the podium at the Democratic National Convention in Miami Beach. An NBC newscaster was among the Alabama delegates, asking about the Humphrey backers' attempts to delay speeches for the proposed gay civil rights plank to the party platform. "As far as I'm concerned, they could take them off the convention and I'd be very happy," said delegate Fred Folsom.

The political pundits couldn't believe what McGovern was about to let happen. They knew nothing about the petitions in the California primary or McGovern's private piedge to give gay rights a full floor debate. They were stunned that McGovern was going to let two speeches for gay rights air on national television the same night he was to appear to accept the Democratic nomination. Just another example of McGovern's bumbling, they decided.

"We do not come to you pleading your understanding or begging your tolerance," Foster began. "We come to you affirming our pride in our life-style, affirming the validity to seek and maintain meaningful emotional relationships and affirming our right to participate in the life of this country on an equal basis with every citizen."

In even, forceful sentences, Foster ticked off the encyclopedia of injustices against gays. He condemned the "brutal and ruthless" purges of gays in the armed forces. He noted the $12 million which the Civil Service Commission spent each year investigating suspected homosexual employees. According to government regulations, a homosexual was not even permitted to push a broom down the halls of the Smithsonian Institute or hang pictures in the National Gallery.

If police enforced laws against heterosexual bars with the vigor they employed against gays, Foster said, "there would not be jails in the United States big enough to hold all the prisoners." All this bred a terrifying fear, he said, leading to "the most devastating fear of all—the fear of self-acceptance."

Foster knew the plank would never pass, but he relished the irony of the occasion. He had been disgraced by the American military he had sought to serve, and then harassed in hundreds of smaller ways in almost every aspect of his life. Tonight, he was debating public policy before the Democratic convention and a national television audience. Things were changing faster than he had ever imagined possible.

"These are not conservative or radical issues, these are human issues," he concluded. "Regardless of whether this convention passes this plank or not, there are millions of gay brothers and sisters who will say to the Democratic Party, 'We are here. We will not be still. We will not go away until the ultimate goal of gay liberation is realized, the goal that all people live in the peace, freedom, and dignity of who we are.' "

Castro Street? Sounds like a Cuban tourist resort.

Harvey kept joking as usual, but by the end of 1972, both he and Scott knew they had to get serious. Their income tax refunds were running out. They needed to find a cheap place to live. They heard that apartments were cheap over on Castro Street, the main strip in an old Irish neighborhood gone to seed. Two gay bars there were doing booming business catering to gay hippies like themselves.

They moved into a Castro Street apartment and tried to figure out what to do for money. Harvey had the brainstorm when he dropped off a roll of film at a neighborhood pharmacy, only to have the pictures come back ruined. They would open a camera store, he told Scott enthusiastically.

Scott reminded Harvey that neither of them knew much about film or cameras. Harvey, however, was already taken with the idea of having his own little neighborhood shop, just like his grandfather Morris and his parents. If it flopped, the worst that could happen is that they'd have to work downtown. The pair took their last $1,000, spent $500 on buying up supplies and the rest on the first payment on a five-year lease for a Victorian storefront on Castro Street. They moved in upstairs. The store's 2,500 square feet gave them plenty of room to work their jigsaw puzzles too. On March 3, 1973, Harvey put the hand-carved shingle in the window: "Yes, We Are Very Open."

"Harvey spent most of his life looking for a stage," observed Tom O'Horgan years later. "On Castro Street, he finally found it."

PART II
The Mayor of Castro Street

five

Politics as Theater

Michael Wong impatiently sipped his Seven-Up as he waited for the other members of San Francisco Tomorrow, the city's major environmental group, to show up for the year's most important meeting. His friend Joan Irwin munched her Kentucky Fried Chicken dinner and talked casually of the many candidates expected to vie that night for the group's endorsement in the supervisorial elections. Well before any other members arrived, however, a tall hippie with a pony tail and mustache sauntered into the room.

"My name is Harvey Milk and I'm running for supervisor," he said.

Irwin and Wong knew who he was, the crazy guy Jim Foster kept worrying about. When Milk started discussing issues, however, both Wong and Irwin warmed to the candidate. He was talking their kind of politics. He would stop the helter-skelter airport expansion, he insisted, and try to block an expensive downtown development project that was tearing out large tracts of low-income housing in favor of more high-rises. As a supervisor, he would even work to municipalize the electric company and, of course, abolish the vice squad. Irwin ended Milk's liberal litany with one question.

"Harvey, how do you really expect to

69

win without any money? I mean, the incumbents have *so* much money."

"Well," Harvey quickly replied, "I figured that since I am openly gay, some father who is nuts and upset over the Texas homosexual killings will come out and shoot me." Milk paused briefly, as if he had calculated this possible denouement on an actuarial table. "I figure that I'll be lucky and survive and I'll get a lot of sympathy votes, as well as the liberal and gay votes."

A finger-lickin' good drumstick dropped from Irwin's mouth into her lap. Wong choked on his Seven-Up.

"Harvey," Irwin asked after a moment of silence. "Don't you think you're going a little too far with that?"

"Well, I'm not out to get killed," Milk assured her, "but who knows about the crazies that run around?"

Crazies indeed, Wong and Irwin thought. Now they knew what Jim Foster meant when he said Harvey was unpredictable, even dangerous to the serious gay political movement that had been building in the city in recent years.

Milk went on to deliver a theatrical hellfire and brimstone populist speech that stole the show from the more seasoned politicos who sought the club's endorsement. Milk probably could have had the club's endorsement by acclamation—except that when it came time to vote, Irwin and Wong repeated what Milk had told them before the meeting started. Wong also noted that the established gay leadership was fretting that Milk's penchant for off-the-wall comments would give the local gay movement a black eye. Harvey lost the endorsement.

The night typified Harvey's first foray into electoral politics in the 1973 elections for the board of supervisors. He was among the most issue-conscious candidates in the campaign, delighting liberals with his programs to wrest control of the city from real estate developers, tourist barons, and downtown corporate interests. He had no intention of just being a gay candidate. His fiery oration rambled at times, but still enraptured audiences. His wit and showmanship gave him all the markings of a true San Francisco character, the kind of idiosyncratic enragé that the city had long embraced as among its chief natural resources. That, however, did not mean the city was going to elect him to run the government.

Harvey became bored of working jigsaw puzzles as the spring days of 1973 lengthened into summer, and Harvey hated being bored.

Dianne Feinstein and four other board members were up for reelection, but Harvey had not thought much about going into politics, until a pompous bureaucrat, a dedicated teacher, and an absentminded attorney general all got him so mad that he *had* to do something.

A chubby state bureaucrat appeared at Castro Camera shortly after the business opened to sternly warn Milk that he could not legally run his business until he paid the state a $100 deposit against sales taxes. The pronouncement rekindled all of Milk's old resentments about government interference in the economy. "You mean to tell me that if I don't have one hundred dollars, I can't run a business in free-enterprise America?" Harvey shouted. "You mean I have to be wealthy to operate a business in the state of California?"

The ruffled official was not about to be pushed around by some hippie camera shop owner in some run-down neighborhood, so he started shouting right back. Customers who had been waiting for film quietly exited, prompting Milk to rant further, "I'm paying your fucking salary and you're driving my customers away."

The bullheaded Milk stormed around state offices for weeks, upbraiding officials and finally bargaining the deposit down to thirty dollars. Peace might have returned to Castro Camera except that a few weeks later, a young high school teacher wandered in to ask if she could borrow a slide projector. The schools were so low on funds, that it took over a month to requisition one and she had lessons to teach from it now, she said.

Harvey went into another tirade. The city had enough money to finance endless expansion of the airports to fatten the wallets of tourist trade moguls, enough money for long freeways to service manpower needs of downtown corporations—even enough money to send arrogant bureaucrats to drive away his customers. But here was a dedicated teacher—the kind of teacher *he* would be if he had used his Albany State credentials, he thought—without the equipment to do her job.

The final impetus came with former Attorney General John Mitchell's performance at the Senate Watergate hearings. Milk kept the portable television set in the camera store every day to watch the hearings. Customers frequently came in to find the wild-eyed, ponytailed, over-aged hippie screaming at John Mitchell: "You lying son of a bitch, you lying son of a bitch." One friend had to physically restrain Harvey from kicking in the screen when Mitchell started droning through his "I don't recall" responses to questions about whether he was indeed trying to undermine the democratic processes during the 1972 elections.

That was it. The country was going to hell in a handbasket. Liars and crooks at its helm. Bureaucrats could run roughshod over small businessmen. Teachers weren't being allowed to do their jobs. From all over the city, meanwhile, came stories that the 1973 elections had started to engender the traditional pre-election cleanup. Harvey figured he could win with gay and hippie votes alone. Just before the filing deadline, Harvey decided on his eleventh-hour candidacy.

In early August, an old hippie friend of Scott Smith's from New York, Tom Rando, silk-screened the campaign posters: "Milk Has Something For Everybody." He painted the word "soap" on the side of a crate and, with a handful of supporters, walked up to a small plaza on Castro Street where Harvey Milk stood on the soap box and announced his intent to run.

"I am forty-three years old now and I can do one of two things," Milk told a gay interviewer shortly after the announcement. "I can concentrate on making a lot of money while I enjoy perhaps another ten years of active gay life. Then, after fifty-three, I can just coast. Call the whole thing good. Or I can get involved and do something about the things that are wrong in this society. I've got to fight not just for me but for my lover and his next lover eventually. It's got to be better for them than it was for me."

Harvey was now a politician.

Politics? Why politics?
Joe Campbell stood in Castro Camera and tried to figure out what Harvey was trying to accomplish with all this politics crap. Nothing about Harvey jelled with his first lover, the man he had met seventeen years ago at Riis Beach, except that he seemed as horny as ever. Why politics? Why, for that matter, a camera store? Harvey didn't know anything about cameras, he thought. Why not sell greeting cards or pets?

Harvey wanted Joe to work in his campaign, so Joe had driven down from nearby Marin County to see Harvey in his new store. Milk told him enthusiastically about his campaign as an openly gay candidate for supervisor. Joe didn't know what Harvey was getting at with all his talk about oppression, discrimination, and liberation. Joe never felt oppressed. Sure he'd been beaten up as a kid, but he had come to learn that was to be expected if you joined a group held in contempt by society. He'd moved to his farm in Marin to get away from all that homosexual bull.

I can't think of one homosexual who would not prefer to be a heterosexual if they had the choice, Joe thought. Here was Harvey, talking about being gay in newspapers, living in a gay neighborhood, and trying to be some gay messiah. Joe couldn't believe that he really meant all that gay liberation stuff; Harvey was just running to get attention, Joe thought. No, he was not going to work on the campaign.

Joe's apathy exasperated Milk. Harvey was convinced that Joe was among those so oppressed they didn't even know they were oppressed. Joe acted as if it were his own fault that he got beat up, not society's. Society, that was the problem, he railed. Somebody had to change society; I'll be the one to do it, he insisted.

The more the two talked, the more they realized they had drifted apart. Harvey thought Joe was too wrapped up in himself to care about society. Joe thought Harvey was still suffering from his persecution complex. He just talked about gays now instead of the Holocaust. The only thing Harvey said that made sense to Joe was when Campbell asked Milk why he had established his store at a run-down place like Castro Street. "I like to sit in the window and watch the cute boys walk by," Harvey said. That sounded like the old Harvey.

"Why should I endorse you, Harvey?"

Jim Foster had heard about the fast-talking, long-haired political novice through the grapevine. He didn't take the candidacy any more seriously than Joe Campbell did.

"You should endorse me because I've been active in the gay movement and the Democratic Party," Harvey said.

"There's an old saying in the Democratic Party," Foster explained. "You don't get to dance unless you put up the chairs. I've never seen you put up the chairs."

Milk didn't argue, but he was clearly taken back by Foster's candor. Foster had enjoyed playing the role of Mr. Gay San Francisco ever since his convention speech had gained him local prominence a year before. It rankled him that some hippie would come out of nowhere, having put in no work in any local gay organization, and decide that *he* would be the gay spokesperson. He, not Harvey Milk, had been the one working to build San Francisco gay power for ten years. He decided to get the goat of this unskilled newcomer.

"There's another old saying in the gay movement," Foster continued. "We're like the Catholic Church. We take converts, but we don't make them Pope the same day."

Harvey now thought Foster was patronizing him. Foster didn't care. He and his allies, respectable professionals like David Goodstein and Rick Stokes, had worked out a plan. They had to claim their power gradually. Stokes's community college board campaign was a good first step. It did not reach for too high an office. Stokes had not stressed his homosexuality in any aspect of the campaign, except, of course, to gay voters. Stokes, therefore, got the support of "our straight liberal friends."

Our liberal friends. In recent years, they had become the key constituency that gay moderates courted throughout the country. Starting in the early 1970s, gay moderates had been shaping the gay liberation movement into the gay rights movement. All we want are equal civil rights, simple legal reform, the moderates stressed. You get that, they figured, by showing liberals that you're decent respectable people, just the same as they are except for a few bedroom gymnastics. Liberals clearly were much more comfortable with this approach. The word liberation made them uneasy. By keeping the topic of gay sexuality a private, bedroom matter, liberals also did not have to confront the reality of gay sexuality, something that still made them uncomfortable.

We have to be realistic, gay moderates insisted. Liberals held many of the trump cards and gays couldn't afford to alienate them. Besides, Foster worried, a brazen attempt to seize something as powerful as a supervisorial seat might bring the iron fist of the Alioto administration down even harder on gays.

"No," Foster told Harvey, "It's not time yet for a gay supervisor."

"When is it ever going to be time?" Harvey stormed after he left the meeting. He was convinced gay moderates had lost sight of the forest for the trees. In pushing for this or that legal reform, they had lost their grasp of the larger goal of changing the overall way that society viewed and treated gays.

Harvey had a simple prescription. Gay candidates for public office are the best tool for advancing the gay movement, he reasoned. They create newsworthy leaders who can both articulate grievances and serve as role models for younger gays. His candidacy was good for the gay movement. To be against his candidacy was to be against the gay movement. Harvey began saying this to gay groups: Jim Foster and his allies were against the gay movement. They were more concerned with coddling their liberal friends—and securing their own personal power

—than with changing society, he said. The liberals would never give gays power, Milk argued. "You're never given power, you have to take it," he repeated over and over again.

"Masturbation can be fun, but it does not take the place of the real thing," Milk fumed in a column for the *Bay Area Reporter.* "It is about time that the gay community stopped playing with itself and get down to the real thing. There are people who are satisfied with crumbs because that is all they think they can get when, in reality, if they demand the real thing, they will find that they indeed can get it."

Harvey's angry outbursts at Foster and the gay moderates only solidified their opposition to him. The gay Alice Toklas Democratic Club did not even come near endorsing him. Many Toklas members resented Milk's candidacy. They had spent years doing shit work in the gay movement and this interloper decides that after living in the city a few months, he can take over. "Come back when you pay your dues," many told Milk. That, in turn, infuriated Milk further.

Drag queens, however, did not share the moderates' disdain of Harvey. They had no investment in respectability. Jose Sarria proudly put his name at the top of Milk's endorsement list. He pushed his cohorts to do the same, harrumphing that he had been years ahead of his time. The drag queens needed to look no further than their "I am a boy" signs to see the reason for a campaign for gay power in the city. A number of other gay bar owners, similarly angered at the police, signed up for Harvey. Milk's link to his other major constituency came with the support of Dennis Peron, a marijuana dealer Harvey had tricked with at a San Francisco bathhouse in 1970. Peron had become the local guru to the city's considerable population of potheads. If nothing else, Peron's appearance guaranteed what he called "the brown rice vote."

With the fervor of a convert, Milk staked out the turf of the populist Democrat, the champion of the little guy against the big institutions, be it big business or big government. Few familiar with Milk would ever accuse him of blaming the problems of the world on pat talk of dialectics or economics. Drawing from his Republican roots, Milk could talk a convincing fiscal conservative line. He called for the city to put revenues in high-interest accounts. He excoriated the poorly managed public transit system, insisting he would pass a law to force all its bureaucrats to take buses to work every day.

Milk thrust himself into the core of the city's progressive elements as well, when he decried the push to make San Francisco a major tourist and corporate center. He strongly backed a ballot proposition that would replace the city-wide, at-large board with district elections. The current city-wide board, he argued, favored moneyed interests, since only candidates who could get financial backing from downtown business could afford the costly city-wide campaign. A district board would be more beholden to the dying neighborhoods.

"I want a city that is not trying to become a great bank book, a major money center," Milk told an endorsement session of the long-shoreman's union. "It's true there are no statistics to quote, no miles of highway to brag about, no statistics of giant buildings built under your administration. What you have instead is a city that breathes, one that is alive and where the people are more important than highways."

As for the notion that his fiscal conservatism was inconsistent with his civil libertarian stands against the vice squad and marijuana prohibition, Milk waxed, "It takes no compromising to give people their rights. It takes no money to respect the individual. It takes no political deal to give people freedom. It takes no survey to remove repression."

Few candidates could match Milk's eloquent speeches. Unfortunately, not many people listened. It would only be years after Harvey's death, for example, that Dianne Feinstein realized that the hippie at candidates' nights with her in 1973 was the same man with whom she later served on the board; Harvey wasn't the kind of candidate pundits call serious. Ally and adversary agreed that his pony tail was Milk's major liability. Harvey conceded that his shaggy appearance hurt his appeal, but he feared that getting it shorn in mid-campaign would look like he sold out principle for expediency. "I entered the campaign with it, I'll end it that way too," he said stubbornly.

Michael Wong wanted desperately to be San Francisco's first elected Chinese supervisor. In grade school, teachers prodded Michael to be more polite, like the other Chinese-American children. Wong noticed his demeanor was no more impolite than what passed as standard behavior for WASP kids. Trying to be equal, he figured, meant being uppity. Michael decided he liked being uppity, even if the significant Chinese-American community was the least uppity minority of the city's population. If the lack of representation of gays at any level in city government was an injustice, the gross underrepresentation of Chinese-Americans proved one of San Francisco's grossest travesties. Only power would solve this problem. The twenty-two-year-old Wong was among the new generation of liberal Democrats who would try to change things. Wong wisely foresaw that gays would hold the future balance of power in the city's increasingly polarized politics. He carefully built bridges to the city's established gay leaders. He heeded their advice on matters pertaining to the gay community, his future constituents.

"It would be disastrous for the gay community if Harvey Milk ever received credibility," Jim Foster told him. "Maybe if we just ignore him, he'll go away," hoped Jo Daly, a leading Toklas lesbian. Rick Stokes assured Wong that Milk "had no support in the gay community . . . he's running on his own." Eager to shore up his links with gay leaders for his own political future, Wong helped torpedo endorsements for Milk from the environmentalists in San Francisco Tomorrow and later sank any chance of an endorsement from San Francisco Young Democrats, Harvey's likeliest constituency, by citing the objections of the entrenched gay moderates. And Michael Wong was just one among many politicos who had ambitions that included gay votes and, therefore, the gay leaders. The cards were stacked against Harvey. He'd earned the emnity of the moderates, who actively campaigned against him. His appearance turned off many more voters. Harvey Milk, in 1973, was running against Harvey Milk.

The complex political machinations would have buried a less tenacious novice. Like any good Broadway producer, however, Harvey knew the success of any show ultimately lay with the reviewers. The candidate courted the press. He had a major San Francisco peculiarity going for him. Though the two daily papers maintained a conservative posture on their editorial pages, both based their news format less on traditional journalistic considerations than on what they felt people liked to read. Early on, the newspapers realized that their readers lapped up stories about gays. While other American newspaper editors snickered about San Francisco's idiosyncratic press and roundly ignored the fledgling gay movement, San Francisco's dailies braved charges of sensationalism and jumped to cover the gay community. Gays were good copy. In 1973, therefore, Harvey Milk was also good copy.

Harvey manipulated every obstacle into a press advantage. The Golden Gate Democratic Club, for example, never bothered to hear the presentations of minor candidates like Milk before starting to vote on endorsements. Milk frantically sought out another aggravated—and

appropriately newsworthy—candidate who felt slighted by the tradition. Days later, the papers ran the doleful story of how snotty liberals
had aced out candidates Harvey Milk and Alfred Seniora from getting
their fair say. This was no average pair, Harvey reminded reporters:
Milk was a gay Jewish hippie Democrat and Seniora was a heterosexual
Arab Republican. Injustice bands together the most anomalous of adversaries, Milk declared, knowing full well it was the unlikely pairing,
not the injustice, that would entice editors to assign the story. Milk
ladled out a series of quotable comments. Snorted Harvey, "They care
as much about democracy as John Mitchell cares about justice."

The staid Democrats retorted that neither the gay hippie nor the
Arab grocer deserved serious consideration. Harvey Milk couldn't even
get the backing of other gays; ask anybody in the Toklas club. As he
read the angry responses, Milk only chuckled. "Sticks and stones may
break my bones, but just spell my name right," he told Scott. "And it's
hard to misspell Milk."

Seniora provided the copy for Harvey's next press release too.
Seniora had been very impressed with Harvey's campaign flyer, which
listed Milk's stands of twenty-five major city issues; in fact, he was so
impressed that he reprinted the fliers, replacing Milk's name with his
own. The trick would have infuriated most candidates, but Harvey
didn't get mad; he just issued a press release. The fact that an Arab,
Republican businessman could use the same campaign flier as a gay
Jewish Democrat hippie showed that Harvey Milk had a unique ability
to "bridge ideologies" with his campaign and that the "need for a new
direction in our leadership is far more important than Milk's homosexuality."

By the end of the campaign, Harvey and Scott Smith worked out
an intricate map that they used on their frequent press release runs. The
map sketched out precisely which obscure alleys and legal U-turns were
needed to make an efficient circuit to every television station and newspaper in San Francisco. Various press releases announced the formation
of Street Artists for Milk and the Performing Artists for Milk, chaired
by Equity member Scott Smith. A dishonorably discharged sailor, Tom
Randol, chaired the Veterans for Milk Committee, and the press release
sorrowfully told a story about how Harvey Milk had been booted out
of the navy for being gay. He had not suffered this disgrace, he told a
later campaign manager, but he knew the story would make good copy.

If anyone said something to Harvey about his fondness for such
stunts, he would gesture wildly as he launched into a lecture. "Symbols,

symbols, symbols," he insisted. Sure, he had not been kicked out of the military, but he had a dozen friends who had had their lives muddled by anti-gay purges in the services. The point of the story was to let people know that service personnel routinely *do* get kicked out. Besides, he once confided, "Maybe people will read it, feel sorry for me, and then vote for me."

Politics as theater.

It became one of Harvey's favorite topics of conversation. A continent away, Harvey's friends from Broadway were reveling in Harvey's stories about his candidacy. Eve Merriam, author of *Inner City,* sent Harvey his first campaign contribution, her own "buck for luck." Harvey had always been involved in political plays like *Hair, Jesus Christ Superstar,* and *Lenny,* she thought, but he never could find a niche in theater since he wasn't interested in acting or producing. "Politics seemed the next logical step," she later observed. "If he couldn't do politics in theater, it made sense that he would try to do theater in politics."

"Harvey, why on earth are you doing *that?*" asked his old friend Jim Bruton.

"Somebody has to do it," Harvey snapped back. "It might as well be me."

Jim came to San Francisco to pitch in with the campaign. He could tell Harvey was finally realizing that purpose he had talked about so many years ago on a beach in East Hampton.

Harvey knew better, but he hoped he might actually win one of the five seats up for grabs on election day. He assembled a dozen friends in a Chinese restaurant after the polls closed to await election results. Bigger names like Dianne Feinstein and John Barbagelata carried the day. Harvey came in tenth in a field of thirty-two candidates, polling seventeen thousand votes.

That was an impressive tally, pundits noted, especially for a candidate who had everything going against him—long hair, homosexuality, and gay moderates' antipathy—not to mention the fact he spent only $4,500 on the entire campaign, a pittance compared to most candidates. The political analysts had been looking toward the Milk campaign as a clinical study of whether a gay vote actually did exist. Harvey's seventeen thousand votes showed that it clearly did.

Harvey beat out all challengers in the heavily gay neighborhoods around Castro and Polk Streets. He was the top vote-getter in the precincts around San Francisco State University and swept the "brown rice belt" of hippie voters. Milk was hoping for broader appeal, but even he was surprised at the intensity of support he got from the constituencies that swung his way. On a precinct-by-precinct basis, Harvey either won big or lost big; that's how people responded to him.

The effort to establish district election of supervisors also failed. But two facts were not lost on Milk. First, the highest vote totals for district elections came not from traditionally liberal areas but from the city's gay neighborhoods. A look at the voter returns from the district that would have been carved around Castro Street showed why. Had the district elections plan been in effect for the 1973 race, Harvey Milk would have been elected a member of the board of supervisors from the Castro district.

Milk's concession speech lashed out at gay moderates who had supported liberal friends over a gay person. Liberals' toleration, he said, was "a crumb thrown to keep us happy, to let us feel that we are getting something when in reality we should be getting our freedom.

"I have tasted freedom. I will not give up that which I have tasted. I have a lot more to drink. For that reason, the political numbers game will be played. I know the rules of their game now and how to play it. All human beings have power," he concluded. "You are just one person, but you have power. That makes power so significant."

Two weeks after the election, Milk cut his hair. Milk also swore two oaths to himself: he would never smoke marijuana or go to a San Francisco bathhouse again. "I decided this was all too important to have it get wrecked because of smoking a joint or being in a raid at some bathhouse," he told a reporter years later.

Michael Wong barely recognized Harvey when he ran into Milk at a political event. Michael was relieved that Harvey did not appear to know how he had subverted the political endorsements. Harvey was as affable as ever. "I cut it all off to get more votes," Harvey said. "You have to play the game, you know."

SIX

The Early Invaders

Everybody's worried the neighborhood isn't like the old days. Hell, Allan Baird thought, it's more like the old days now than it's been for a good fifteen years.

The son of two Scottish immigrants, Baird was born just seven blocks from the central Castro shopping strip in 1932. That's the farthest from Castro Street he ever lived. The gentle slopes surrounding the street seemed to cut the neighborhood off from the rest of San Francisco, lending the cozy, working-class area all the trappings of a small, insular town. As Baird started the two-block walk from his house —where his wife Helen had lived forty years—to Castro Camera, he looked at the neighborhood that was changing so much. There on the corner of Eighteenth and Castro, he hawked newspapers as a kid during World War II. Across the street, the Walking Book, in his wide-shouldered double-breasted suits and white fedora hat, used to take the morning bets, cutting seriously into Jack MacCormack's booking operation in the back of the nearby cigar store. The Little Man's Store used to be down the street; it had done a booming business in bootleg gin during Prohibition.

The city maps had always called the area Eureka Valley, but to most of the people who lived there, it was just Most

Holy Redeemer Parish. The Catholic Church dominated every facet of
the neighborhood's life from the schooling of children to the family
picnics and weekly bingo games. Wives stayed at home to take care of
their large broods; families stayed here generation after generation;
God was in His heaven, and, most Castro residents would agree, He
was probably Irish. And now it was all changing.

The coming of the downtown skyscrapers heralded the end. This
had always been a working-class neighborhood of longshoremen, steve-
dores, factory workers, and cops. But the blue-collar workers had to
move to where the new factories were. By the 1950s, the kids no longer
wanted to live in a big city anyway. Some of the old people stayed, but
the later generations moved to subdivisions near San Jose, buying into
the ranchhouses of the new American dream. The small-town ambience
faded fast. Stores went out of business. Houses stood vacant. Then,
came the whispers.

Maybe it was Mrs. O'Malley talking to Mrs. O'Shea over the cod
at the open-air fish market. It could have been Mrs. Maloney fretting
to Mrs. Asmussen, who was a good friend even though she *was* a
Lutheran. The word went out. A former police officer, not a good
Castro boy, but—the housewife flicked her wrist, raised her eyebrows,
and, after a meaningful pause—a funny one, bought The Gem bar. And
he's probably going to make it over for *his* crowd. Real estate agents
were already writing obituaries for the Haight-Ashbury neighborhood
over the hill. The hippies came in and wham, there went the neighborhood. Now the gays were going to do that too, right here in Most Holy
Redeemer Parish.

Baird never saw anything like the panic that followed the establishment of the first gay bar on Castro Street in the late 1960s. The stolid
Irish families sold their Victorians at dirt-cheap prices, fearing greater
loss if they waited. By 1973, the numbers of gays moving into the
neighborhood amounted to an invasion. That's what the old-timers
called the new men of Castro Street—invaders. Now it was 1973 and
Baird figured at least half the people moving in were gay, while more
and more of the old-timers sold out.

A hard-working German family used to live where Harvey Milk's
Castro Camera was now. Baird remembered playing in the back lot as
he stepped inside the shop's door. He'd heard that Harvey Milk was
the man to talk to if you wanted to work with the gays. The other guys
at the Teamsters hall might think I'm crazy, Baird thought, but it's
worth a try.

"I'm Allan Baird, a representative of the Teamsters and director of the Coors beer boycott in California." Allan began formally.

"I know who you are," Harvey smiled. Allan realized he didn't need to be formal.

"I know you're the spokesperson for the gay community here and I think I can use your help."

The beer drivers' local was striking the six major beer distributors who adamantly refused to sign the proposed union contract. "These guys are like me," explained Baird, who had trucked newspapers before working his way into the Teamsters hierarchy. "They can't be out of work long." So far Baird had enlisted a group representing over four hundred Arab grocers and the federation of Chinese grocers who would boycott scab drivers. If gay bars chipped in, they could win it.

"I'll do what I can," said Harvey, pausing to add one condition. "You've got to promise me one thing. You've got to help bring gays into the Teamsters union. We buy a lot of the beer that your union delivers. It's only fair that we get a share of the jobs."

Baird liked Milk's straightforwardness. After years in the give-and-take of union politics, the beefy teamster thought he could spot a bullshitter. Harvey Milk was no bullshitter. Baird grew more impressed when he later learned Milk was in the middle of his campaign for supervisor. Any other politician would have asked for an endorsement, he thought. Milk just asked for jobs.

The project gave Milk a chance to test out his new theories about achieving gay power through economic clout. He enlisted his friend, gay publisher Bob Ross, to help connect him to bar owners and started buttonholing support for the boycott. Baird was amazed at Milk's ability to get press attention for the effort; Milk enjoyed the symbolism of tying gays to the conservative Teamsters union.

The boycott worked. Gays provided the coup de grace shot to the already strained distributors. Five of the six beer firms signed the pact. Only Coors refused to settle. Harvey used the refusal as a basis to launch a more highly publicized boycott of Coors beer in gay bars. Baird was surprised not only at Milk's success, but by the fact that Harvey was as outraged at Coors discrimination against Chicanos as by the fabled Coors antipathy to gays. This guy's got a national philosophy, Baird thought.

At a Colorado meeting with arch-conservative William Coors, Baird warned the executive about the success of the gay boycott and about the persuasive gay leader who had just made an impressive showing in the local supervisorial race. These guys are getting more powerful, Baird warned, and they'll be on the unions' side. Coors acted astonished by the talk. He didn't come out and say it, but Baird felt he could tell what Coors was thinking by the sneer on his face: Community. What the hell is a *gay* community?

Baird kept his end of the bargain. Gays started driving for Falstalf, Lucky Lager, Budweiser, and soon all the distributors, except, of course, Coors. The biggest recruiting problem came not from biased employers, but from gays who found it hard to believe that there would be companies who were openly *not* discriminating against them.

"Those guys in the gay community are real powerful. I don't think you understand their power yet," Baird told Teamsters officials. "They can turn something on and off just like that."

The officials liked Baird's work, but some worried that Allan might be turning queer himself. "He *does* live just a few blocks off Eighteenth and Castro," one speculated. "Just how close *are* he and this Harvey Milk anyway?"

Back in the neighborhood, the growing friendship between Allan Baird and Harvey Milk caused no small consternation. The wizened old housewives had known Allan for years, as well as his wife Helen, since her parents had run the Greek restaurant next to the Castro Theater in the 1920s. "Is your husband a fag?" one neighbor bluntly asked her.

The massive gay influx clearly was driving people to extremes. Baird saw gays as the new generation of residents and small businessmen who would revitalize a neighborhood that had been going to pot since the white flight of the 1950s. Most of his neighbors, however, were convinced the gays would come in, wreck the district, and then just go away, the way the flower children had destroyed the Haight.

Where were all these gays coming from, any way? they asked.

Fortunately, older men found him cute.

That would be good for free drinks and a few dinners in those first difficult months.

Cleve Jones knew he was different long before the guys at Tempe High School in suburban Phoenix realized it. Once they did, Cleve had to learn how to bend over at just the right moment, affecting the right posture of pain, while still avoiding the full force of the punch that ground him into the locker room's tiled walls. When simple brutality grew tedious, Jones's classmates took to dunking his head in the toilet. Cleve became insecure. The slight Jones faked a lung ailment to escape from two years of gym classes. Even a five-minute oral report for

English class would have him dry heaving in the bathroom for an hour. Cleve, everyone knew, was the class sissy.

Vaguely aware that his effeminacy stemmed from an infirmity he did not understand, Cleve slipped into the library of his father, a psychology professor at Arizona State University. Jones reached carefully into the shelves and looked under "H" in his dad's compendium of psychological disorders. He found homosexuality cross-referenced to a chapter discussing genital deformities and hormonal imbalances. The experts told him why he got beat up in gym class. Homosexuals, they said, were "injustice collectors," as if injustices fell randomly from the sky and were magnetized toward a genetically predetermined human subspecies. In another generation, Jones might have then resigned himself to be another hapless miscreant doomed to liaisons in the Phoenix Greyhound depot.

During his sophomore year at Tempe High, however, Cleve read a small item in the back pages of the *Arizona Republic.* In New York City, homosexuals had rioted a few weeks before. Now they were actually forming organizations. Just think. Organizations for homosexuals. Cleve started reading the back pages more carefully and picked up more snippets. In San Francisco, homosexuals were influencing elections, coalescing into gay neighborhoods and even holding parades. From the age of fifteen on, Cleve Jones decided he had only one goal —to move to San Francisco and march in a Gay Freedom Day Parade. The beatings continued, of course, but Jones was courageous enough to scrawl the metaphor of his adolescent defiance on his notebook: "Jesus Christ had limp wrists. Nails do that to you."

Jones hitchhiked to San Francisco in 1973, just weeks after his eighteenth birthday. That first night he ended up wandering the streets of the seedy Tenderloin district and was lucky enough to trick with Joey, a seventeen-year-old hustler from Mexico. As they climbed the stairs to Joey's room in the Grand Hotel, they walked through a hallway where a transvestite had killed himself that morning; his blood still stained the wall. A half dozen other seventeen- and eighteen-year-old hustlers shared the room; they let Cleve sleep on the floor in his sleeping bag until he got settled. Jones found a job as a bicycle delivery boy downtown and learned how to get free drinks and dinners from older men who liked his boyish looks. Every night, Cleve, Joey, and the rest of the gang rendezvoused at Bob's Burgers on Polk Street. Those hustlers who had had a generous trick that day treated the less fortunate to a cheeseburger and fries.

Cleve next got a job as a houseboy in the Haight-Ashbury neighborhood. The once-legendary neighborhood had fallen into decay by 1973. The hard-core flower children had left for communes in Oregon and not very many people talked about creating the New Age any more. Jones and his young Haight friends started drifting over the hill to the run-down street where there were bars full of young gay and hippie men like himself. Those were exhilarating times to be gay on Castro Street. It was like being in a club without paying dues. The fellow émigrés tended to come from the counterculture, so Cleve shared not only a common sexuality, but the same general tastes in music, politics, and social values. Being gay in the Castro of 1973 meant being opposed to the Vietnam War, smoking marijuana, and having a more than casual interest in Hermann Hesse, Mick Jagger, Walt Whitman, and John Lennon.

The materialism of the early homosexual gentry was *passé*. These new gays were not going to devote their lives to acquiring tasteful end tables and spot-lighted impressionist paintings. Orange crates and Jimi Hendrix posters did just fine. No expensive colognes, just petulia oil. The carefully tailored suits of the gay upper crust or the flamboyant silk scarves and sheer shirts of the glitterati were nowhere to be seen. Instead came a new homosexual fashion born out of the J.C. Funky secondhand clothing shore. This august institution sold army fatigues and used blue jeans for $2 a pair, flannel shirts for $1.50, and hooded sweatshirts for $1.75. The prices were ideally suited for the customers' rejection of the work ethic. The fashions proved functional for the city's Mediterranean climate. Fashion designers later called it the layered look; the Castro men just called it cheap.

The new gay fashion matched a new gay attitude. The clothing spoke of strength and working-class machismo, not the gentle bourgeoise effetism of generations past. The politically conscious men of the Castro did not mince or step delicately down the street; they strutted defiantly. A sour look from a crusty Irish widow was the most valuable form of flattery.

The smart gay money had been buying up the neighborhood's Victorians for several years, renting long-vacant flats to groups of guys who could each afford to chip in $40 or $50 for their share of the monthly rent. The cheap leases and inexpensive wardrobes kept working time to a minimum and street life blossomed. Men with mustaches, miniskirts, and high-heeled pumps could be occasionally seen picking through the vegetable bins at the produce market. Campy street entertainment from artists like the Cockettes—featuring a black drag queen named Sylvester—flourished regularly on the streetcorners where the guys assembled to cruise and smoke joints.

The excitement sparked the imaginations of young men like Cleve Jones, who could tell the Castro neighborhood was going to go somewhere, even if he didn't know just where. Hanging out on the street one day, Jones stumbled into a camera store where he met a long-haired merchant who had a fondness for helping the young gay refugees who were pouring into the neighborhood. Maybe it was because the aging hippie foresaw that the lively young men might later be useful in campaigns; maybe it was just because he liked lively young men. It didn't matter, because in 1973, Harvey Milk was just a small camera shop owner and Cleve Jones was just another eighteen-year-old drifter far more interested in manning the dance floors than the barricades. But things were changing and all because boys like Cleve Jones got beat up and called sissy in high schools around the country and because a man like Harvey Milk was gaining a sense of how an unusual permutation of power, politics, and personality might rewrite the script by which gays had acted out their lives for so long.

"Some people call me the unofficial mayor of Castro Street."
Harvey first tried the title out during his unsuccessful run for supervisor. Once he threw himself into the Coors beer boycott and a host of other local issues, he always brought the title up to any reporter who happened by Castro Camera. Nobody was ever sure who the "some people" who allegedly made up the nickname were, but the appellation made good copy, so nobody groused.

Business was slow the first months, so Milk left Scott Smith to tend the store alone on many days and went off to meet his neighbors. He methodically walked door to door on the two-block central business strip of Castro Street, introducing himself to gay and straight merchants alike. At forty-three, Harvey was one of the older gay merchants and he sometimes was the first gay businessman who tried to make contact with the neighborhood's old-timers. He soon became an ex-officio liaison between the established Castro businessmen and the new gay merchants who were moving into the once boarded-up storefronts. What surprised many of the businessmen was that Milk never tried to drum up business with his visits; he just stopped by to chat.

When Harvey was in, Castro Camera became less a business establishment than a vest-pocket City Hall from which Harvey held court. The barest minimum of space was devoted to the skimpy camera supplies. An old overstuffed maroon couch was stretched in front of the store's large bay window, next to the old barber chair where The Kid sat much of the day, lapping at the hand of any customer who had a penchant for mutts. Harvey could often be found on his frumpy couch when new Castro residents came to find where to look for apartments, what to do with a lover who had an alcohol problem, or how to find that first job. Local merchants discovered that Harvey was the man to go to if police took too long to answer a suspected burglary or if the sewer overflowed; Harvey always knew whom to call at City Hall, or the reporter to buzz with the proper story of moral indignation if nothing was done. The store's large picture windows displayed announcements of upcoming demonstrations, environmental protests, commission hearings on Castro issues, or neighborhood meetings. Petitions for a host of causes, from whale-saving to gay rights, cluttered the beat-up counter. At night, Harvey took the addresses from every check cashed at the store that day and put it on his political mailing list.

Harvey loved circuses and holidays, especially Christmas, and the store's picture window sprang to life every December with ornate holiday displays. On Christmas Eve, the window would be packed with unopened presents under a fully decorated tree; the next morning, bows, ribbons, torn wrapping paper, and empty boxes lay haphazardly about the window, to be joined by bottles of Alka-Seltzer and Anacin a week later on New Year's Day.

More than one young boyish-looking patron would also be surprised when they came to pick up their photos and Harvey would giggle, "I see you have a new boyfriend." Scott had worked out a system of marking the envelopes of incoming film from men who were particularly noteworthy, while Harvey thumbed through the daily delivery of processed photos to check for names of men he'd always wanted to see in less formal surroundings. If a customer seemed indignant at the prying, both Scott and Harvey would plead they were only spot-checking photos as part of their quality control. Neither Harvey nor Scott any longer put much faith in Harvey's once-dear devotion to fidelity. Promiscuity was practically an article of faith among the new gays of Castro Street, stemming both from the free-love hippie days and the adoption of aggressive male images. This proved particularly fortuitous for Harvey, whose sexual appetite never waned.

By now, of course, Harvey had found a political rationale for his accentuated horniness. As a representative of the SIR publicity committee, Harvey talked to a human sexuality class at Napa State University shortly after his forty-fourth birthday in 1974. He surprised the students by saying that intensified sexuality was one of the benefits of not being able to hold hands or express affection publicly. "What happens is," he explained, "You get inside that room and the door closes. The intensity of the relationship increases to make up for it. The sexuality of many homosexuals is one of a very intense moment. In essence, sometimes I say thank you because the repression of my outside activities has heightened my inside activities."

The old Irish businesses resisted the rapid shift in the Castro area. The first skirmish came when two gay men tried to open up an antique store. The established burghers associated with the Eureka Valley Merchants Association (EVMA) were taken aback; an antique store just doors down from The Family Store where the kids go to buy their Most Holy Redeemer uniforms? The EVMA pushed the police to deny the store a resale license. The antique store won the fight, but the fracas soured relations between the old and new merchants. The EVMA would have nothing to do with the gay invaders.

Milk took a page from his grandfather's problems with the Rockaway Hunt Club. He assembled the younger gay merchants in the back room of a pizza parlor and resurrected a short-lived merchants group that had been organized by hippies a few years before. Harvey was dutifully elected president of the Castro Village Association (CVA), if for no other reason than nobody else wanted the job.

Harvey quickly picked up a new slogan. While he had spent 1973 preaching that gays should vote gay, 1974 was the year he insisted gays should buy gay. At various appearances at SIR meetings and any public forum he could muster, Milk enthusiastically talked about when blacks refused to be shunted to the back of municipal buses and the policy had changed not because whites came to understand the moral problems of discrimination, but because a year-long boycott was driving the bus company into the red. "Blacks won the right to ride buses for the wrong reason," he argued, "but they won. When you want to win, it doesn't make a difference whether you win for the wrong reason. It's better than not winning at all."

Milk took to promoting his new theories through the CVA with all the flair he had once demonstrated in pushing Broadway shows. He read in the newspaper one morning that Polk Street, a heavily gay area, was planning a street fair. Castro Street was not going to be outdone, he decided, so Milk cajoled the other CVA members to organize a

Castro Street Fair. Over five thousand came to the first fair in August 1974. The street hadn't seen a crowd like that since the festival celebrating California's centennial fifteen years earlier. An Italian liquor store owner who had decried the gay onslaught rushed to Castro Camera the next day to tell Milk breathlessly he had sold three times the booze on that one Sunday than on any other single day in his decades of business. It was as if he just figured out that homosexuals liked ice-cold cans of Bud like anybody else. He signed up as a CVA member.

The fair earned CVA citywide attention and a growing membership. Harvey decided it needed the respectability of having established institutions as members. The street's two banks were ideal new members: one was a branch of the gigantic Bank of America, the other a branch of the Irish locally owned Hibernia Bank. Executives at both branches rejected Milk's suggestion that they join. Most of the CVA members avoided Bank of America because of its bad-guy image as the world's largest bank, so Hibernia held most of the area's gay money. Harvey carefully wrote a letter to the Hibernia branch explaining that the CVA annual dues were $20 a year and that his research showed that Hibernia's central offices budgeted money for that branch's neighborhood involvement. "We strongly urge you to send the $20 to join our group," Harvey wrote. Instead of signing the letter with the CVA members' names, Milk had each business affix their bank deposit stamps to the bottom of the request.

Rarely have the words "for deposit only" produced such quick results. Hibernia's $20 dues came in the return mail. Harvey took his newly revised list of CVA members to the Bank of America branch manager, mentioning he would hate to have it get around that B of A was anti-gay. The branch signed on.

By the end of 1974, politicians began coming to CVA meetings. Membership swelled. The political possibilities titillated Harvey, who rarely looked further than the next election. He pushed his friends into being voter registrars. Customers in Castro Camera were rarely greeted with a pitch to buy film; instead, the first question was, "Are you registered to vote?" If the unwary patron said no, Harvey would issue a harsh and incredulous, "Why not?" Registering voters was no mere passion with Harvey, it became an obsession; Harvey considered his most important accomplishment of 1974 to be the registration of 2,350 new voters for the governor's race. Surrendering the right to vote was, to Milk, like surrendering the chance to make a difference in the world. Each person *can* make a difference, he stormed. That was the precept that fueled everything he did and formed the basis of his realpolitik philosophy. All of Milk's alderman activities, meanwhile, confirmed this and taught him more about the workings of the City Hall. The more he learned, the angrier he got at the distance that had grown between the downtown-oriented city government and the picturesque neighborhoods that were withering from neglect and, sometimes, abuse.

"I asked you where you got those bruises."

The police badge shimmered in the darkness of the paddy wagon. Minutes before, the two young men had been standing inside Hamburger Mary's, a popular gay hippie restaurant. Two police officers had simply walked in, beat them to the floor with their billy clubs, and hauled them into a paddy wagon where they pummeled them more.

"I asked you where you got the bruises," the officer repeated.

"I don't know."

The officer delivered another blow to his prostrated victim's stomach. "I didn't hear that."

"I said I don't know."

At the police station, an officer ordered the pair to strip down and they were beaten further. "He got a funny look each time he hit me," one of the victims said when he recounted his story to a gay paper. "It was like all his frustrations were coming out. He would call me 'fag' or 'queer' and get this weird look on his face and then hit me."

The two were charged with drunk and disorderly conduct and, of course, resisting arrest. Their stories held up under polygraph tests and the charges were dismissed. As usual, no disciplinary actions were taken against the police officers.

The hard-working Irish families of Most Holy Redeemer parish had long supplied the San Francisco Police Department with a high proportion of its tough Irish cops, so there were few officers who did not have a parent, aunt, or cousin muttering about the gay invaders. Police had held little fondness for the Haight-Ashbury degenerates in the first place, but the idea that long-haired, dope-smoking, anti-war fags could get so uppity as to try to take over a neighborhood, their neighborhood, was galling. Allan Baird noticed a police cruiser or a hawkish motorcycle cop became a fixture on the corner a block from his home at Nineteenth and Castro. Police had never viewed the quiet residential intersection as a high-priority target before, but suddenly

Baird started noticing that cars with pairs of white, long-haired males were routinely being pulled over. "Going down to the Midnight Sun?" the policeman would ask politely. If either man showed any glimmer of recognition for the name of the gay bar, the officer slapped the driver with a ticket and ran a warrant check to see if any outstanding tickets could land his prey in jail. On weekend nights, cadres of officers ran sorties into the district, sometimes rounding up groups of four or five gays, dragging them to a nearby park, handcuffing them and then beating them senseless with their nightsticks. According to an account in one gay newspaper, the police managed to hospitalize three men on one foray alone, one with his skull split open. The trio were charged with "trespassing in a park" and resisting arrest; the charges, of course, were later dismissed.

The confrontations peaked at bar closing time in the early morning hours of Labor Day, 1974. Tensions had already run high with police that weekend. In two days alone, police sweeps of the local park had put nineteen gay men in jail. Still, the sidewalk outside the popular Toad Hall bar bustled with men out to make their last-minute choices when a police car pulled up next to a patron walking down Castro Street. "Off the street, faggot," the officer shouted.

When the young man just glanced back and slowly walked away, two officers leaped from the car, threw him to the pavement, and started beating him with their billy clubs. Like clockwork, a paddy wagon rolled up to the curb and the cops hurled their unsuspecting victim in the back. Police reinforcements suddenly appeared from all directions, most keeping their badge numbers well hidden. Dozens of gay men were knocked down and beaten. Fourteen were herded into paddy wagons and taken to jail. The heinous charges that brought about the massive police action—obstructing a sidewalk.

Harvey Milk dubbed the victims the Castro 14 and headquartered their defense fund in his store. Rick Stokes filed a $1.375 million lawsuit against the police. Tensions boiled over at a neighborhood hearing of the police community relations board when Milk horrified staid gay moderates by calling the police "pigs." Galvanized at last by a brazen issue, gay radicals joined the chorus as well and police officials got a crash course in future shock. Castro gays weren't a bunch of Judy Garland fans who would take a beating and sulk back to their lace-lined apartments just because Joe Alioto wanted to get a red hat for the city's Catholics.

Police brutality in the Castro area dropped markedly after the incident, but Milk used the fracas to underscore the need for building a tight neighborhood political base. "I pay my taxes for police to protect me, not persecute me," he wrote in his column for the *Bay Area Reporter*. Milk's temper flared further when the Board of Supervisors frustrated his attempts to raise a defense fund by passing an ordinance requiring all such organizations to register and obtain permits—from the San Francisco Police Department. Milk typically ended his tirades with a pitch for gays to register to vote and "no longer hide, but join together and use Gay Power." The Castro 14 furor sealed the neighborhood's reputation as *the* new homosexual hot spot. What in 1973 was a seedy, out-of-the-way hamlet was, by the beginning of 1975, coming alive with new business activity that was gaining the grudging appreciation from even the stodgiest of old neighborhood merchants. It was ironic that two of the men who shared the most similar view of what the Castro could become were as different as the beer-bellied teamster Allan Baird and the militant gay, Harvey Milk.

"This is for gays only."

Allan Baird couldn't believe what he was hearing. He and Helen had taken Helen's mom out for a night on the town for her birthday. Since his mother-in-law had lived in the neighborhood fifty years, Allan thought it would be fun to take her for a drink at the central institution of the new Castro, the Toad Hall bar. The bouncer wouldn't let the trio in.

"Wait a minute," Baird argued. "I worked in the Coors boycott. I'm a personal friend of Harvey Milk's."

"Sorry," the doorman repeated. "This is a gay bar."

"This is discrimination," Baird shot back. "*I'm* not part of the problem. You shouldn't be doing things like this."

Allan and Helen ran into Harvey a few days after the incident. The three went to the Elephant Walk bar for a drink. The Elephant Walk had drawn awe from gays around California since it was one of the first gay bars to actually have large plate-glass windows looking out on the street. Harvey liked the symbolism of the bright open bar, after gays had spent so many years in dark, windowless toilets. Allan and Helen liked the bar since it was one of the few places on Castro Street that drew an even mix of gay and straight patrons.

"It's important that a place like this exists," Allan said, after telling Harvey about the problem at Toad Hall.

"You're right," said Harvey. "We need more of it. No gay person or straight person should feel self-conscious about going anywhere. That's what Castro Street should be all about."

Allan liked the way Harvey talked about Castro Street. For all the complaints his neighbors came up with, Allan thought Castro Street was getting more like it used to be when he was a kid; for the first time in years, it seemed like a small town again where everybody knew each other and said hi on the street. Now Castro Street could also show that gays and straights could live together and get along just fine. He'd learned it could be done from Harvey; he was convinced his neighbors could learn too. That's why the incident at Toad Hall bothered him so much. It boded poorly for his vision.

During the 1973 campaign, Allan gave Harvey a pen-and-pencil set. "You'll need it once you get to City Hall to sign bills," he told Milk. Harvey now confided he was going to run for supervisor again. The problems with the police and the unresponsiveness of City Hall to the predicaments of the neighborhoods hadn't changed any in two years, he said. Allan was excited about Harvey's second try for office, because Harvey seemed to care not only about Castro Street but about all San Francisco. The guy even had a national perspective on things. Allan pledged to introduce Milk to more union leaders. "Don't worry," he said. "You'll get to use that pen yet."

seven

The First Skirmish

"Whaddaya mean you're thinkin' of endorsin' this Harvey Milk guy? For Chrissakes, I'm supposed to go back to work and tell the guys we endorsed some goddamn fruit for a supervisor. Ya gotta be kiddin'."

Jim Elliot had been a union man since 1949. His talk was thick with the hard, gutteral brogue that marked the native San Franciscan's Chicago-like accent. His fingernails were rarely without the black residue from his years of fixing lawn mowers and tractors at Golden Gate Park. The idea that he might have to go back to the 2,300 mechanics in his machinist local and try to foist some fruit as their candidate for supervisor seemed downright mortifying. But here he was at the San Francisco Labor Council's endorsement meeting, hearing serious talk from good union men like himself about why they should endorse Harvey Milk for supervisor.

"Who the fuck is this fruit that we should even think about endorsin' him?" Elliot asked.

"Hey. Harvey Milk's the guy who's been gettin' Coors beer out of gay bars," a Teamster quickly retorted.

The very words "Coors beer" was enough to make any good union member

95

shut up and listen. Here's this fruit who got Coors beer out of gay bars, Elliot thought. How many bars have the big macho labor guys gotten Coors out of? Still, Elliot was among the union stalwarts who successfully thwarted Milk's endorsement by the Labor Council that day, but the support Milk was gaining from union regulars made him follow the candidate's career more closely. "It kinda makes you think," he told his wife when he got home.

Campaigning in a staunchly middle-class neighborhood, Milk makes the rounds of coffee shops, dutifully tagged by a *Chronicle* reporter assigned to make sense of this unlikely politician who calls himself the mayor of Castro Street.

In a coffee shop, a middle class man and woman recognize Milk. "What are you doing here? Why aren't you over in . . ." She seems embarrassed to mention Milk's neighborhood. But she says, "I hope you make it." Her companion shakes Milk's hands and observes that "we need to see some new faces at City Hall."

Another surprised coffee shop customer has never heard Milk's name before and jokingly asks if Harvey is running for dairy queen. Harvey laughs the question off, didactically telling the reporter, "If I turned around every time somebody called me a faggot, I'd be walking backwards and I don't want to walk backwards."

Harvey Milk, at last, was a serious candidate. He was taking on six incumbent supervisors who were all seeking reelection. His real opponents, however, were downtown business interests. "As a small businessman, I intend to fight for the needs of small businesses rather than solely for the interests of downtown," he said when he announced his campaign in March 1975. He accused the incumbents of having "distorted priorities" and promised that his "priorities would be reoriented to the people and not to the downtown interests."

Milk outlined a four-point program to revitalize city neighborhoods. He wanted the 300,000 commuters who daily came from suburbia to work in corporate high-rises—and used expensive city services—to start paying a "fair share" tax to finance the fire and safety services that so drained city coffers. He sharply criticized City Hall's assessment policies, which drastically underassessed the hotels and skyscrapers of powerful campaign contributors, leaving small homeowners to pick up the tax bill.

Harvey's strongest tactical allies came from unions. Mayoral hopeful Supervisor John Barbagelata had thrust labor against the wall by putting a number of anti-union initiatives on the city ballot, rolling back municipal employee pensions and pay scales. The propositions horrified the once-powerful unions, but they were convenient vehicles for dozens of hellfire and brimstone speeches by incumbents who were fanning public outrage over a recent police strike.

Harvey was one of only two supervisorial candidates in the entire city to back labor 100 percent. Allan Baird introduced him to labor leaders, advertising the fact that Milk was committing virtual political suicide by backing the union cause. Milk had discarded the bohemian flavor of his first campaign for three-piece suits he bought secondhand from a Castro district dry cleaner. Milk's no-nonsense straightforwardness impressed the union men.

"I know the guy's a fruit, but he shoots straight with us. Let's support him." Cigar-chomping union boss George Evankovich was not a man to take alliances lightly, so Stan Smith, the new secretary-treasurer of the San Francisco Building and Construction Trades Council, had to take his advice seriously. Evankovich had organized workers since he was an unschooled sixteen-year-old miner in Butte, Montana's silver pits. His enthusiasm earned him an investigation by the House Un-American Activities Committee during the McCarthy era. After braving the front lines of civil rights marches for his heavily black local, he wasn't going to lose much sleep if the boys down at the Labor Council didn't like the endorsement.

Stan Smith had just taken over the 22,000-member Trades Council, which was the umbrella group for the city's thirty-five hard-hat unions. He was wary about going out on a limb, but both Baird and Evankovich recounted Milk's good deeds for labor, from the Coors boycott to his current pro-labor stands. "The guy's our friend," Evankovich concluded. "You don't screw your friends."

Evankovich arranged a lunch with Smith and Milk. Harvey's humor quickly won the leader's support. Besides, Smith was no stranger to the city's gays. As a teenager, he and his high school buddies used to hang out at gay bars—those taverns were the only saloons desirous enough for young customers to overlook drinking age laws. Evankovich, for one, thought the true test for Milk would come when he had to rub shoulders with the guys he needed to walk precincts and do the grass roots "Jimmy Higgins" work.

"That guy has charisma," Evankovich told his labor buddies, as he saw Harvey campaigning. "A lot of our guys think gays are little leprechauns tip-toeing to florist shops, but Harvey can sit on a steel beam and talk to some ironworker who is a mean sonuvabitch and probably beats his wife when he has a few too many beers, but who would sit there and talk to Harvey like they knew each other for years."

The announcement that the giant Building and Construction Trades Council joined the Laborers Union and Baird's Beer Truck Drivers local in endorsing Harvey Milk had the hard-hat hiring halls buzzing. The council was supporting only two candidates—a gay and a feminist. Bullheaded labor leaders like Evankovich weren't going to let Milk's virtues go unextolled. Evankovich set up a meeting with Leon Broschura, head of the firemen's union. Broschura was impressed that Milk had done his homework on the fire department's needs, and by the fact that Milk's face appeared at every major candidates' night in the city. The guy might not win this time, Broschura thought, but he's somebody you're going to have to reckon with in city politics. While firefighters' unions in New York City and Chicago led the fights to squash gay civil rights laws in their cities, the San Francisco Fire Fighters local endorsed Milk's effort to be the nation's first openly gay city official.

Harvey relished the symbolism of gaining the endorsements from the city's three most macho unions—teamsters, firemen, and hard hats. When the city's Union Labor Party held its endorsement night, Harvey walked away with the highest tally of any supervisorial candidate. Publicly, Milk waxed on about how he was bringing diverse peoples together; privately, he enjoyed seeing the shock on his gay volunteers' faces when groups of beefy firemen and teamsters trooped into the camera shop to fold fliers and stamp envelopes.

Harvey's labor supporters pleaded with the old-line labor leaders who ran the Labor Council to give him the backing of all the council members. "He ain't gonna win and besides, we don't need those gays," an official told Evankovich. The younger Broschura implored the council for Milk. "You guys got to move with the times," he said. "When the horses come down to the finish lines one of these days, he's going to be among the winners." But the leadership wouldn't budge.

A mammoth hook and ladder truck appeared in front of Castro Camera after Milk lost the council endorsement. Harvey's new friends were going to cheer him up. "C'mon out Harv'—we got somethin' to show ya," the driver shouted. On the end of the truck, two fireman had chalked a slogan on the back of their black rubber coats: "Make Mine Milk."

The 1975 municipal elections proved a watershed year for San Francisco city politics. The social conflicts that had been building during the Alioto administration erupted into the mayoral race. San Francisco faced a profound turning point.

By city charter Mayor Alioto could not seek a third term, so he stepped aside to resume his multimillion-dollar law practice. The conservative Democratic coalition that had kept him in office crumbled.

Blacks yearned for change. Their Filmore neighborhood had once been one of the most thriving black cultural centers west of New Orleans. Leveled by urban renewal, its people sank into despair. By 1975, the most influential man in the area was a charismatic minister who preached his own mixture of populist Christian theology and Marxist politics out of a converted synagogue he called the Peoples Temple. The blacks who flocked there had lost their neighborhood; they were not needed in the sparkling glass and steel skyscrapers in downtown; their hopes lay in the sermons of the Reverend Jim Jones. He, in turn, could order hundreds of volunteers to work tirelessly for the candidates of his choosing.

The Latino Mission district's businesses had never recovered from the digging up of the central shopping strip for the Bay Area Rapid Transit. Younger Chinese-Americans wanted better conditions for the tens of thousands crowded into Chinatown, one of the nation's most appalling ghettos.

The city's more conservative voters in the sprawling west side residential neighborhoods also wanted change. They already had had to suffer through the tide of hippies in the late 1960s; now they were seeing the Castro neighborhood being swiftly taken over by gays. Property taxes spiraled, though the homeowners saw few additional services for the added money. The revenues, they complained, were going to support minorities in the east side of the city. The police strike had left them madder; the pushy city unions seemed to be getting out of hand.

Altogether, the city was ready for what one newspaper called "a bloodless civil war."

Supervisor Dianne Feinstein hoped the studied moderation she'd followed in her six years in city politics would give her the broadest base of any candidate. Most pundits gave her a strong chance of grabbing a first-place showing in the election. Liberal neighborhood activists had long ago soured on Feinstein, accusing her of indecisiveness at best, or at worst of being a puppet of the downtown business interests that so generously filled her campaign chests. She retained some of her gay support from wealthy upper-crust gays and managed to simultaneously assuage fears of middle-class voters by noting her strong support for tough law enforcement. Another major asset came from the Hearst Corporation, owner of the afternoon *Examiner,* which regarded Feinstein with a reverence generally reserved for virgin mothers. Any story that might have any possible tangential relationship to city government, —and many that didn't—usually carried a Feinstein quote.

Observers rated Supervisor John Barbagelata as having only an outside chance at capturing the mayoralty. The fifty-six-year-old realtor came from solid Italian stock, the last angry man of the city's west side. The feisty maverick entered politics in the late 1960s because of his outrage at the degeneracy of Haight Street. He quickly emerged as the board's foremost conservative, the sole vote against Feinstein's 1972 gay rights ordinance and the friend of real estate developers. Unlike Feinstein, Barbagelata was a true social conservative, the voice of the frustrated silent majority. "Gay people don't have what I have," he characteristically told one newspaper, "somebody to cook your meals, somebody to love, somebody to share your burdens and frustrations with."

George Moscone emerged as the clear liberal choice. Moscone was part of a new breed of ethnic politicians who had been emerging in San Francisco since the late 1960s, more concerned with abortion and marijuana reform than with getting a cardinal's cap. They eschewed the Catholic conservatism of old-line ethnic politicos like Joe Alioto and were among the first figures to reach effectively to black, Chinese, Latino, and gay voters. Once considered something of a radical, Moscone had worked his way from the Board of Supervisors to the California senate where, after one year, he became senate majority leader. Most analysts were aghast that Moscone would give up the powerful post to run for San Francisco mayor. To such questions, Moscone simply explained that ever since he'd played boccie ball in the parks of his childhood Italian neighborhood, he'd wanted to be the mayor of the municipality that he'd always described with the four-word appellation, "the world's greatest city." Besides, he confided to Jim Foster, "Sacramento is boring as hell."

Moscone entered the campaign as the strident proponent of neighborhood power, decrying the "Manhattanization" developers had wrought with their skyscrapers and corporate headquarters. He turned his back on well-heeled campaign contributors by refusing to accept any campaign gift over $100. Never had the city's hard-core left and neighborhood activists been offered a candidate who so eagerly articulated their vision of the city's future; they united in a coalition few thought could be built.

The city's other major races saw a similar emergence of liberal candidates. Sheriff Richard Hongisto was gliding toward easy reelection despite his controversial term. In the district attorney's race, the incumbent, who so enthusiastically prosecuted gays, waged an uphill campaign against two liberal candidates, both of whom courted gay voters.

Michael Wong looked around the camera shop, stunned. In all the papers, he had read so much about the scores of volunteers Harvey Milk had working in his low-budget campaign. Harvey's campaign now had a near-legendary quality, derived from Milk's list of unexpected endorsements. Commuters on various mornings would frequently encounter his block-long stretches of human billboards, lines of smiling faces holding up "Harvey Milk for *Supervisor*" signs. The human billboards were good theater, Harvey decided. Wong had gotten to know Milk from working on Senator Fred Harris' presidential campaign. He was, by 1975, impressed enough with the candidate's resourcefulness to surrender his earlier misgivings and come down to the Castro Camera headquarters to join the cadre of volunteers he'd heard so much about. The camera shop, however, was empty. Wong leaned over the counter to Scott Smith.

"Where are the volunteers?"

"There are none," Scott whispered, as if worried someone might overhear. "The ones we have are out leafleting."

Wong was shocked and took the matter to Harvey. "The press wanted to say we had volunteers," Milk reasoned. "Who wants to dispute that?"

"But Harvey," Wong pleaded. "You should have told us that you needed help. We would've come down. A lot of Harris people would have."

"I know that. A lot of them helped me get the human billboards out," assured the candidate, adding, "besides, I couldn't take the chance of letting the press or the Toklas people get wind that we had less than a great campaign going. This way, the media is happy and I'll get elected because of it."

"I knew then," Wong wrote in his diary, "that Harvey was a great media manipulator."

Milk did indeed keep the media happy with his flamboyant campaigning, always ready to give reporters an outrageous joke or a quotable jab. Harvey seemed ubiquitous in the campaign, especially considering he had less money than any major supervisorial candidate in the race. The campaign's strength lay not in the mythical legion of volunteers, but with a small cadre of supporters who worked protracted hours. A group of politicos from more disparate origins would be hard to find, even in San Francisco.

Harvey quickly nicknamed Wong "my little yellow lotus blossom." Wong, not familiar with the homosexual penchant for campy nicknames, took to telling Milk that he was "a credit to your proclivity." Wong recruited other volunteers from the Fred Harris campaign. Deputy Attorney General Arlo Smith, the highest civil service officer in the San Francisco branch of the attorney general's office, often spent evenings stuffing envelopes. He sometimes ran into another Milk volunteer who had an intimate knowledge of the criminal justice system, Dennis Peron.

Peron was now running a marijuana supermarket from his bustling apartment a block down the street from Castro Camera. True to the most karmic of 1969 values, the long-haired Peron held that he was providing a valuable community service, and offered free joints to anyone who walked in his door. He then fed his thousands of dollars in profits into an organic restaurant catering to an odd assortment of hip gays and left-over flower children. At Harvey's urging, Peron had organized his ninety-five employees into a Democratic Club. Their Island Restaurant was always available to Milk for campaign dinners and fund raisers.

Harvey recruited more volunteers from the many disaffected who were moving to Castro Street. A pensive Harvard graduate, Jim Rivaldo, wandered into Castro Camera one day and mentioned his uncle used to be a New York assemblyman; Harvey put him to work handing out fliers. A mild-mannered thirty-nine-year-old, Frank Robinson, started coming into the shop to pet The Kid. Frank started spending more time at Castro Camera because it reminded him of the days he had spent as a kid hanging out at his neighborhood alderman headquarters in Chicago. After several visits, the man mentioned he was the co-author of *The Glass Inferno,* the book upon which the film *Towering Inferno* was based; Harvey put Robinson to work writing his speeches and campaign fliers.

Scott Smith had his hands full as Harvey's campaign manager.

Somebody had to take care of the store, so Harvey and Scott almost casually turned over the shop to a youthful twenty-year-old art student who had drifted to San Francisco from upstate New York. Danny Nicoletta had the right combination of hippie idealism and naiveté to guarantee trust—and the slight build Harvey found so attractive in young men. That Harvey often turned over major responsibilities so casually worried some friends. The entrenched gay leaders, they noted, got their power by entrusting important decisions only to proven allies with experience and track records. Milk insisted that his campaigns could train a new corps of activists. A committed novice from the streets was worth a dozen old-timers, he said.

"I'm very disappointed in you, Michael," Jim Foster told Michael Wong when he learned Wong was working in the Milk campaign. An angry Duke Smith, a close ally of the Foster-Goodstein clique, chided Wong further. "All of you will realize what a nut he is if, God forbid, he should ever get elected."

The antipathy gay moderates had held in the 1973 election turned into open hostility in 1975 when it looked like Harvey Milk actually had a shot at capturing a supervisorial seat. To all politicos who would listen —and many, impressed by the burgeoning numbers of gays, did—the Toklas activists fretted about the bad image that the maverick camera store owner would give all the city's gays. The fact that Milk had taken the politically suicidal route of bucking the anti-labor tide by chumming up with rednecks like teamsters and hard hats was in itself proof of Milk's naiveté, if not outright insanity. Once again, the Toklas club and most of the gay leadership shunned Milk's candidacy, backing incumbents. As was the case in virtually all of Milk's campaigns, Harvey drew little support from lesbians, who distrusted his alliances with drag queens and also noted that Harvey had few, if any, close lesbian friends. A few people, like Jim Foster, publicly endorsed Milk but privately derided enthusiastic supporters like Wong.

The gay moderates' extolling of liberal friends' virtues made Milk's blood boil, and he compared the Toklas club to the homosexual groupies who had once idolized Judy Garland. For all the liberal friends, gays still had not received a single city commission appointment or gotten a comprehensive civil rights law that banned discrimination beyond the handful of city contractors. "To hear those who are already working for a particular candidate praise that person, one would think that the gay community has already achieved gay rights," Milk wrote. "But we haven't. There is no reason why any gay should go to any candidate. Let them come to us. The time of being political groupies has ended. The time to become strong has begun."

Milk's battles with moderate gays were no less virulent than his fights with the radical left-wing gays who had coalesced in the wake of the Castro 14 controversy. The radicals' chief organization, Bay Area Gay Liberation (BAGL), reflected the more Marxist gay groups that had flourished in the post-Stonewall days of New York, but had rarely gotten off the ground in San Francisco, where political energies were directed toward reformist Democratic Party politics. Once established, however, BAGL meetings spent endless hours splitting hairs over issues of the politically correct, worrying not so much about gays' disenfranchisement, but about such abstruse issues as "looksism," the penchant of gay men to want to go home with men to whom they were physically attracted. Milk first raised these activists' ire when they started to organize a contingent to march with Cesar Chavez' farm workers. Influenced by the strong anti-gay teachings of the Catholic Church, Chavez and his United Farm Workers union had long refused to take a stand in support of gay rights. Milk argued that gays should not man the picket lines for Chavez until he was willing to issue at least a one-sentence statement in support of gays. The stance earned Milk the hoots, jeers, and long enmity of the gay radicals.

Besides, they confided to each other, Milk *was* a small businessman. Some took to scolding Scott Smith, saying if Castro Camera really cared about the people, they would give away free film and offer developing services gratis. That Milk even involved himself in electoral politics was further evidence that Harvey was part of the System, which, they were convinced, was going to crumble any day.

Harvey saw little more than traditional homosexual defeatism in the views of both the reformers and radicals. One side would pay any price to be accepted by liberal friends, even if it meant having no gay public officials themselves. The other showed the same deference to the heterosexual radical left, prostrating themselves before the causes of Chicanos and socialism, even if those causes rejected gays as much as the political establishment.

A fine frozen Alaskan salmon arrived midway in the campaign, a birthday gift from Milk's old Wall Street friend Jim Bruton, who was now working in Anchorage. The salmon gave Milk the chance to fix a gargantuan feast, a delight that had become rarer as the campaign gobbled up all his time and money. Harvey could not mask his air of melancholy when he called Jim to thank him for the gift.

"Here I am, out campaigning sixteen hours a day," he complained. "And what for? A bunch of people who don't want to stand up for themselves, who don't even seem to know that *they're* the ones who are going to have to stand up if we're ever going to win this thing."

"Don't worry, Harvey, you're so goddamned bullheaded you're going to end up winning even if it takes you until you're ninety years old," Jim said.

Milk's tone changed slightly. "You've got to remember," he said quietly. "I don't have until I'm ninety. I don't have that much time. I've got to get it done sooner."

If gay moderates needed to prove the power of liberal friends, they had to point no further than the California legislative session in which the powerful legislators of San Francisco's Democratic machine— mindful of the 1975 mayoral race—produced results of national significance. Assemblyman Willie Brown, a close ally of George Moscone's, had pushed for years to strike down the 1872 statute which prescribed felony penalties for "crimes against nature." The bill was defeated repeatedly in the legislature. Governor Ronald Reagan had indicated he would veto the reform even if it did pass.

By 1975, Reagan was no longer governor and the new Governor Jerry Brown had privately assured gay leaders he would sign a repeal, though, fearful of stirring up questions about his perennial bachelorhood, he would not publicly campaign for it. Rick Stokes's tireless lobbying among lawyers' groups had won the reform an impressive list of endorsements, many from conservative law enforcement organizations. The most important factor boding for passage, however, was that Senate Majority Leader George Moscone was running for mayor of San Francisco. The city's legislative delegation could have pushed the bill to passage years before, some gay lobbyists thought, but it was not necessary. The gay leaders were not a demanding lot. The politicians got the support of the gay moderates whether they produced or not, and there was no reason to give gays such an important victory until the gay gratitude could be exploited for a cause dearer to the politicians' hearts. The election of Moscone was just such a cause.

Moscone shepherded the measure through committees, jawboned reluctant moderate Democrats from rural California, and pulled in every outstanding I.O.U. in the capitol. The bill passed the assembly.

The day the measure came up for its final senate vote, a gallery packed with reporters and anxious gay activists sat aghast when the chamber came to a 20–20 tie vote. With a dramatic flourish, Senator Moscone asked that the senate president invoke a little-used rule that allowed the president to literally lock the senate chamber's doors, so that no legislator could leave the room. In Denver, meanwhile, Lieutenant Governor Mervyn Dymally boarded a jet for Sacramento. For the first time in decades, a California lieutenant governor entered the ornate state senate chambers to cast a tie-breaking vote. Saying his vote would take California "one step farther from 1984," Dymally voted to abolish the law that had for over a century made homosexuals de facto felons in California.

The demise of the anti-sodomy statutes had far-reaching implications for gays' legal status around the country. California had long been a leader in criminal justice law; the fact that the nation's largest state legalized all sex between consenting adults gave the libertarian posture new credibility. By the end of the year, fifteen more state legislatures took up the issue. Four struck down sodomy laws, some of which dated back to the Colonial era. These legislative successes gave gays more clout in court when they argued for an end to the myriad forms of anti-gay discrimination, especially state-imposed bias against gays in licensing and civil service jobs.

The biggest political plum, however, fell in the lap of mayoral candidate Moscone. The gay bandwagon of support for the state senator even worried activists like Milk, who thought gays should hold out on their endorsements until the last moment, so they could cut better deals from desperate candidates. The arguments were to no avail. Moscone clinched virtually all the major gay support, earning a constituency that would remain in his camp for the rest of his life. The gay swing for Moscone was pushed further when, in the waning days of the Alioto administration, gays were reminded of the political consequences that any continuation of the status quo would bring. A reporter offhandedly asked the police chief's public relations man what he thought about having gay cops on the force. "We feel they are emotionally unstable and unsuited for police work," Captain William O'Connor huffed.

Was the captain aware of any gay police officers?

"No," he said. "But I'd sure like to have a list of them."

The ensuing flap pushed even moderates' tempers to their limit and gave Senator Moscone the chance to talk of how he would wipe away any vestiges of anti-gay prejudices. "I will only be satisfied," he said, "if in four—or hopefully eight—years, I can not only change the face of San Francisco, but change the soul of San Francisco, and, with its extraordinary international authority, become a catalyst for conversion for the rest of the country, if not the world."

The marijuana supermarket closed its doors for the 1975 election night. Downstairs in the Island restaurant, Harvey's diverse throng of supporters drank their non-Coors beer and cheered as Senator Moscone surged into an early lead in the mayor's race. Few got depressed when Supervisor Feinstein disappointed all the prognosticators and fell into a third-place finish behind Moscone and Supervisor John Barbagelata, the mecurial conservative who, according to the pundits, never had a chance. Moscone would have to face Barbagelata in a runoff four weeks later.

The good news for gays came from all quarters. Sheriff Hongisto surged to a better than 3–1 victory over his conservative opponent. In the district attorney's race, the two liberal gay allies, Joe Freitas and Carol Ruth Silver, left the anti-gay incumbent in the dust. When the final returns on the tight race came in, D.A.-elect Freitas promised to end the prosecution of victimless crimes that had haunted San Francisco gays for decades.

The liberal voting trend, however, did not extend to the races for supervisor. Harvey made an initial strong showing, but as more returns trickled in, it became obvious that all six incumbents would be ree-lected, with Harvey finishing the race in seventh place, just one slot away from victory. The finish startled many political observers, how-ever, since few believed a gay candidate could really be a serious con-tender. In his concession speech, Harvey left no doubt that he would try again. "We established a great amount of contacts," he said. "We will build upon those basics in the next two years."

Most of the speech, however, was a paean to his lover Scott Smith, who had worked so hard as Milk's campaign manager. "When people thank me for what I'm doing, they really are thanking Scott, the man I love," Harvey told the crowd. "He's the one who puts up with me. The world may one day be a little bit better because Scott was there."

A roar rose from the crowd when a beaming George Moscone swept into the restaurant on a surprise visit. Harvey Milk may have lost the supervisorial race, but the liberal political establishment was now ready to embrace him. Moscone quickly sought out Milk. Dennis Peron did his best to look nonchalant as he eavesdropped on the two politicians.

"Y'know you're going to have to make some appointments of gay people to commissions if you get elected mayor." Harvey grinned.

"I think we should set up an appointment to talk in my office." Moscone smiled back.

Both knew who the first gay commissioner would be. Harvey introduced Moscone as "the next mayor of San Francisco." Moscone designated Castro Camera as one of his neighborhood campaign headquarters.

It was not until Jim Rivaldo grabbed a handful of magic markers and started charting Harvey's precinct totals that the depth of Milk's support became apparent. Milk was no also-ran who finished in seventh place because of soft support. Instead, Rivaldo found that Milk had beat out all incumbents in one-ninth of the city's precincts, losing his seat only because of his poor showing on the conservative west side of town. Harvey carried the Castro and the Haight by landslide proportions and swept aside all contenders in the brown rice belt. The better heeled liberals of Pacific Heights also backed the maverick in high numbers. Rivaldo's neatly color-coded map showed that Milk had a solid constituency in the city, hard support even if it wasn't wide enough yet to win a citywide election. The map delighted Harvey, who wasted no time in calling a host of the city's politicians to casually invite them to drop by Castro Camera because he had something they might want to see.

The city's Italian community shuddered at the thought that two Italians should be competing for mayor. "You should've gotten together and worked it out among yourselves," one elderly Italian lectured Moscone. But the days of the old ethnic voting lines were over. The contest between Moscone and Barbagelata represented an even more profound dichotomy than liberal or conservative, since it concerned questions of the traditional versus alternative life-styles, the franchised against the disenfranchised. No politician in the city had succeeded in tying together the have-not votes of blacks, Latins, liberals, and gays. There just weren't enough of them to swing an election. The massive gay migration to San Francisco in the early 1970s, however, was shifting the balance, and Moscone courted the émigrés with an enthusiasm local politicians once reserved for the Chamber of Commerce.

It didn't hurt Moscone when Barbagelata polarized the race further by insisting he was "unaware" that discrimination against gays existed and that he would continue to oppose the law banning anti-gay bias among city contractors because the city might be forced to accept higher bids from nondiscriminating companies over the low bids of biased employers. At a breakfast meeting with twenty-five gay leaders, Barbagelata added that he had nothing against gays personally, but worried about "public displays" such as the annual Gay Freedom Day Parade. When asked if he similarly opposed public displays of other minorities such as the flamboyant activities surrounding the Chinese New Year's Parade, he sharply retorted that at least Chinese were "traditional." Some of the more conservative gay leaders would have forgiven much of this, except for one point—Barbagelata could not bring himself to utter the word gay. Instead he referred to his guests as "you people." Moscone got nearly unanimous gay support.

In the runoff, Moscone squeaked to a narrow victory, edging out Barbagelata by a bare 4,400 votes. A jubilant Moscone publicly thanked Harvey Milk in his victory speech that night, adding that the unofficial mayor of Castro Street would soon have an official role in his administration. Moscone dropped another bombshell days later when asked by reporters whom he would appoint to the board if any vacancies arose. Moscone judiciously weighed the question and said he would feel obliged to appoint the man who had the next highest number of votes in the 1975 race. He didn't need to add that the candidate was Harvey Milk.

The euphoric aftermath of the 1975 elections had liberal neighborhood activists counting blessings they could barely have imagined a few years before. Liberals occupied the city's top three posts: the mayor, district attorney, and sheriff. The direction of San Francisco was finally turned away from moneyed corporate interests to the neighborhoods. Harvey Milk would soon be the first acknowledged gay commissioner in the United States. But the euphoria belied the election's more troubling implications. Moscone had won, but by one of the slimmest margins in San Francisco history, in this the most liberal city in the country. Feinstein's humiliating defeat showed that the city's new political spectrum had little room for moderates, as the city had become polarized between the more extreme left and right—and the sides were almost evenly matched. The election, therefore, was not the decisive battle, between the old and new San Francisco, but merely an early skirmish.

For Harvey, the future path was clear. He had staked out his turf as the most influential gay politician. He was an insider at last. He could count on the support of the liberal establishment in the next supervisorial elections in 1977. All he had to do was settle down and play ball with the big boys. The trouble was, Harvey never could learn how to play ball.

eight

Gay Main Street

"Something's happening here."

The realization had been germinating for months. The politics and vote tallies were the least of it. Every time he reviewed the monthly balance sheets to see his soaring receipts, every time another realtor made an astronomical offer on his building, every time he ran into another friend from Fresno, awestricken at the rows of handsome men lining the street, Steve Lowell couldn't escape the obvious conclusion: Something's happening here.

Lowell certainly hadn't expected it turn to out this way when he and Donn Tatum opened Paperback Traffic on Castro Street back in 1972. They were just out to do something for the people. The store fit in well with what the idealistic young couple wanted to do with their lives. They could recycle old paperbacks, frustrate high-profit corporations with their dirt-cheap prices, and even live in the back of the store, like the mellowed-out proprietors of some mom and pop grocery.

The pair had their political consciousness up too. Steve got his schooling in the turbulent days after the Stonewall riots when Gay Liberation Fronts swept into the nation's campuses. Within six months of Stonewall, Steve had joined the Boston GLF, helped seize a Harvard building, and learned to talk convincingly of the new order about to be established. Both were charter members of the Castro Village Association and had voted for Harvey Milk for its president. Donn even succeeded Milk as CVA president when Harvey resigned to run for supervisor in 1975.

Neither hoped or planned to end up as a successful businessman, but by early 1976 it was clear they didn't have a choice. Between 1973 and 1975, their business gross tripled and the early months of 1976 saw this rate of business growth increase further. The heavy demand forced the couple to open a second shop across the street. In 1974, they bought a deserted six-unit Victorian a few doors down from Castro Camera. Only one unit was occupied; the other five had been vacant for years and were filled with refuse. Now five shops, a restaurant and their bookstore did a bustling business there. Within a year, they found they could sell the building for many times what they had paid for it; the edifice was less a good investment than a gold mine. Similar stories came from all corners of Castro Street.

Allan Baird watched the gay onslaught transform the old neighborhood bars. Mart's Place, where Allan had once served beers to crusty Scandanavians, was now the Pendulum, catering to white gays who liked black men. The old German merchant marine hangout became the place for the over-forty Castro crowd. Candy counters, smoke shops, and even an old bank branch became gay bars too. Dee's Dress Shop used to sell maternity smocks for expectant mothers. Now it was the All-American Boy, specializing in tight straight-legged Levis and specially logoed jock straps. The family florist store became Leather Forever. The cigar store–bookie operation now housed a fashionable hair stylist. The old pool hall sold Mandarin food. Many more boarded-up storefronts and residential units became bars, boutiques, and restaurants in the business explosion.

The texture of the new Castro immigrants was changing as well. The counterculture had faded. Many former flower children had tired of street life and geared their ambitions toward careers. At Paperback Traffic, this meant that sales of once-popular titles like *Be Here Now* and *Siddhartha* fell off, and patrons started demanding the latest hardbound best-sellers. The low demand for second-hand paperbacks barely justified continuing that line of business. By then publishers were churning out gay books, so it was not unusual for the store to be ordering fifty or one hundred books a throw, an unheard-of volume a few years back. The astounding success of the store, and many others like it, forced the laid-back former hippies to pick up business acumen. Merchants like Lowell and Tatum cut off their shoulder-length hair, started worrying about once-obscure issues like cash flow and overhead, and took to finding their inner peace through formal meditation instead of the hopes for the imminent New Age.

This did not mean that business merchants and immigrants alike did not sense that something vital was indeed growing in the Castro. Something clearly *was* happening. In 1975 and 1976, however, it was just hard to tell what that something was. All that was clear was that wave after wave of gay men were descending on Castro Street. They were not counterculturals who had moved to San Francisco to be hippies and then found the Castro. They were people from all backgrounds who had come to Castro Street to be gay , and they had a lot to sort out.

Hit the cue ball just so and it's gonna be number six in the corner pocket. Smartest thing Toad Hall ever did was put in the pool table. What would the National Merit Scholarship people think if they saw me now? Or the other guys at the Port Arthur Methodist Youth Fellowship? Or the Methodist minister from Clover, South Carolina, and his daughter Fran? My wife.

Harry Britt leaned over the table, peering at the intransigent six ball that stood between himself and the next guy up, a stud in cowboy boots, plaid shirt, and button-fly Levis, with the bottom button provocatively unhitched. That guy's hot. No doubt about it. Not that Harry tricked around a lot. But there he was at Toad Hall, almost every day for the three years between 1975 and 1977, even on Chistmas Eve when nobody went to gay bars. What would they all think now?

Harry had spent all his life being good. He was president of the Port Arthur Methodist Youth Fellowship (MYF) and then regional MYF president. He liked the MYF because it was the one environment where men did not expect him to live up to the macho ideal that so intimidated him. Harry was on the debating squad, served in student government, and won the only National Merit Scholarship in his part of West Texas, the first year they were given out. He went off to Duke University because it looked like all the colleges he had seen in the movies. He was fraternity president. Still his life had no focus, no direction. He sped through college in a little over three years, and he couldn't decide on a major. His life didn't seem to fit together. Somehow.

Then came Fran, the daughter of his Methodist minister. He married Fran; that's what he knew he was supposed to do. He even became a Methodist minister, holding parishes in Port Arthur, then Chicago. He compounded his acts of goodness there by living down the street from Martin Luther King, working in the civil rights movement, pleading for integration of his Community United Methodist Church on West Fiftieth Street. Harry Britt had spent his entire life being good, like many others; the secret still burned deep within him. He had worked so hard to justify his existence; he had known all that time that he was vile in the eyes of God, of himself, always lusting after the handsome young guy across the aisle. By the time he was a thirty-year-old preacher in Chicago, he had bloated out to 270 pounds and was smoking four packs of Old Gold Straights a day.

But then an assassin pumped a bullet into King's neck and the parishioners at Community United Methodist were horrified, not so much at the murder, but over the fear that rampaging black rioters would cross over Ashland Avenue and burn their houses. Fear overcame moral indignation. Harry spent hours riding the elevated trains in Chicago's South Side just to be around blacks. He knew he had to pull out of all of it, his marriage, his church, his entire past life.

He kept telling himself he didn't come to San Francisco to be gay. He came because of Esalen and the human potential groups who could provide him with a guru. His life had never had direction, maybe a guru could provide it. He watched Jim Foster address the Democratic convention on TV in 1972. That marked the first time Harry Britt ever saw a human being stand up and say he was gay. Harry knew he was too, but still he wrestled hard against the truth for another two years, until in 1974 he answered an ad in the *Berkeley Barb.* "I'm coming out and scared," Bob's classified read. Harry answered the ad and the pair cautiously sidled into their first gay bars. Harry needed only a few months before he shifted into the intense gay life of the Castro. Finally, he got to do something he never thought would happen in his lifetime —he made love to a man.

He'd been on Castro Street ever since. For Harry Britt, being gay in the Castro in 1975 meant buying a sun lamp, losing one hundred pounds, joining a gym to pump up his sagging pectorals, and changing from glasses to contact lenses. His Texas twang and lean Castro look made him a hit at the pool tables. Since he'd taken a night auditor's job at the Hilton, he had all day to shoot pool at Toad Hall, walk through the Twin Peaks bar for a draft and then saunter past the stores, window-shopping both the wares and the salesmen. Harry was less concerned with whoring around to make up for lost time than with trying to fully integrate himself for the first time. After living over thirty years under the assumption he'd never experience a moment of passion, much less love, just seeing such a panoply of available partners was enough to set a guy's head spinning.

Harry had done his political number too, walking precincts for Harvey Milk's 1975 campaign, even standing in a human billboard one chilly morning. But that was mainly because Harry thought Scott Smith was a gorgeous hunk whom he'd like to land in the sack some time. Harry did not come to Castro Street for politics, he just wanted to cruise, like the other guys he kept running into on the street who came from the same west Texas MYF camps.

Thousands of them. The police chief estimated that in 1976, about 140,000 gays lived in San Francisco, over one in five citizens. About eighty gay men a week arrived to put down roots in the city, according to the conservative police estimate. They fueled the expanding gay business base in the Castro, but that was the most superficial gauge of their significance; they were creating a new counterculture. San Francisco had for decades been the birthing ground for America's new social tides: the beatniks came from North Beach in the 1950s; hippies created the flower generation in Haight-Ashbury during the 1960s; the new social phenomenon of the 1970s was the gay counterculture and it was being born on the streets of the Castro neighborhood where, on every sunny Saturday afternoon, hundreds of guys like Harry Britt, Cleve Jones, Harvey Milk, and Scott Smith cruised the strip.

The young men from Port Arthur, Tulsa, and Davenport were crowding in on the early hip invaders, and men of the new gay subculture followed their predecessors more in style than substance. Their common ground, of course, was their male gender and their sexuality. The casual practicality that dictated the Castro's earlier fashions slipped into rigid macho conformity. The men didn't buy plaid shirts from J.C. Funky's for $1.50, but the expensive Pendleton variety from All-American Boy, tightly fit to show just the right tuft of chest hair. No more used jeans, but brand-new straight-legged models, pulled tight at the ass and suggestively stretched around the crotch. The fashion models were derived from the most virile male images of the society—cowboys, construction workers, and military men. Cowboy hats and Western Fryes became common. Engineer boots, keys dangling from the belt, and a shiny hard hat lent the contractor's look. Fatigues, army jackets, olive caps, and leather bomber jackets also became de rigueur.

The mating rituals became carefully honed as the hundreds of young men cruised the strip. Eye contact first, maybe a slight nod, and, if all goes well, the right strut over to the intended with an appropriately cool grunt of greeting. Getting that far was three-quarters of the battle and a few sentences more were all that was necessary to complete arrangements for a tryst. But if the first stare was too longing, if the nod came off at all prissy, if the salutation's tone was not aloof or masculine enough, then you could blow the whole thing *that* easy. Before long, the posturing became a caricature of the heterosexual ideal, as if this new generation of gays were out to deliver one big "fuck you" to society. Tell 'em they're femmy queers who need wrist-splints and lisp lessons and they'll end up looking like a bunch of cowboys, loggers, and M.P.s. Whaddaya think of that?

"Harvey, they're coming here to be free and they all look alike."

Haight Street camera shop owner Rick Nichols moved to the Castro in the early days. Nichols was irritated that the emerging macho conformity both amused and delighted his friend Milk. They were on the tattered maroon couch, going over the familiar argument.

"They have to find a family here," Milk snapped back. "They need support—they've never had it before. This is the first chance they've ever had to be free."

"Why are they going about it like *this?*" Nichols asked. "All they're doing is fitting into another mold, finding a new conformity."

"They've been through hell, give these guys a break. This is just a necessary stage they're going through, once they've done their Castro bit, they'll go on to . . ." Harvey paused, not able to think of what exactly they would go *to,* but he dismissed the problem with a characteristically grand flourish of his hands. "They'll go on to something else."

Nichols thought the new gay denizens were on the wrong track. The point of gay liberation was not to make it so gay men could be macho too, but to make macho passé altogether. "They're not being free," he said, "they're just being lazy."

Nichols was never sure whether Harvey was as interested in the sociological implications of the burgeoning gay counterculture as he was in the vast numbers of handsome young men. The romance with Scott was slowly fading. They remained business partners and confidants, but the couple also took ample advantage of the available material, especially the young waifs Harvey had always found so appealing. Though Harvey was in his mid-forties, his sexual appetite showed no signs of diminishing.

Scott and Harvey casually lived above the camera store. Between the campaigning, community organizing, and scores of commission hearings Milk addictively attended, he had never gotten the chance to unpack all the boxes of his New York possessions. As the years wore on, every available table and counter became buried in the reams of fliers, news clippings, and official reports, which Harvey could never bring himself to throw away. But the kitchen remained in working order and several times a month Harvey's friends would troop to Castro Street for a multicoursed feast. Other than the circus and an occasional ballet or opera performance, cooking remained the only luxury the peripatetic campaigner permitted himself.

For all the money made by Castro Street merchants—in no small part because Milk tirelessly promoted the neighborhood as America's gay Main Street—Harvey concerned himself little with the mundane matters of business. Milk's lack of interest in his commercial health exasperated bookstore owner Donn Tatum.

"Harvey, you should get more stock. Look at all this space," Tatum waved his hand around the cavernous store, most of which was filled with campaign paraphernalia. "You could start selling used cameras. You should see all the business stores in downtown do in used cameras."

Harvey dismissed the pleas with a wave of his hand.

"If I did that, I'd have to put bars on the windows and worry about burglars," he said.

Milk sometimes mentioned that his lease expired in 1978 and that if neighborhood patterns held steady, his rent would probably double or triple. "At that point, I may have to rethink our policy of being a specialty shop," he'd say—and then he'd be off campaigning more.

Milk's laissez-faire attitude about his own success did not prevent him from needling old-time merchants who had originally been so fearful about the gay influx. "How much is that building worth now?" Harvey asked a neighboring realtor, knowing full well the value had gone up 250 percent between 1972 and 1975. When the old realtor mumbled that it was probably worth more, not sure just how much though, Harvey did his best not to say "I told you so," and put on his backslapping politico's manner. "That's good to hear, real good."

Another store owner had complained that the early gays were

destroying the "family character" of the Castro. Harvey tried to affect genuine concern when he asked, "By the way, you're not having any problems—your business *is* all right?" The merchant would be damned if he was going to concede that business had tripled since a gay bar had replaced the competition across the street, but he would grumble, "No, we're doing just fine." Harvey would nod his head with relief, as if a great burden was lifted from his shoulders. "Just checking."

The Italian delicatessen owner once talked of how gays were disrupting the "neighborhood balance." By 1976, he had hired homosexual clerks and was courting the new gay business. The old man who owned the windowshade shop—and was originally horrified at the gay invasion—discovered new-found appreciation for decor-minded gays when his business soared. The young manager of Cliff's Variety Store, Ernie Astin—the fourth generation of his family to run the emporium —had no problems with gays, and he became the only straight charter member of the revitalized CVA. In constant contact with gay merchants, Astin realized that gays were renovating hundreds of the area's old Victorians, so he bolstered his store's stock of building supplies. The area's two established hardware store owners snubbed both the CVA and gay clientele and were out of touch with the new buying trends. They both went out of business when Cliff gobbled up the lion's share of business in renovation hardware.

The CVA's membership jumped to nearly sixty members in one year, about half of whom were straight. Membership rolls increased another 50 percent in 1976, dwarfing the old EVMA. The 1975 Castro Street Fair drew twenty-five thousand, making it the best attended neighborhood fair in the city. About 100,000 came to bask in the August sunshine for the 1976 fair. Still, the downtown-based Council of District Merchants adamantly refused to let the CVA—by now, the best-known merchants group in the city—join and be enfranchised as an official district merchants organization.

The trend that most caught the eye of San Francisco was the massive facelift gays gave to a neighborhood that had been degenerating into an eyesore. The endless rows of Victorians had been little more than tract housing when they were built in the 1880s; to the Irish who stayed in the neighborhoods until the 1970s, they were just "old houses." Unburdened by a homebody wife and 2.2 children, the gay immigrants started an unprecedented wave of private urban renewal. Block after block of high Italianate Edwardian homes burst forth in polychromatic splendor. News that a pair of men had bought the home next door would once have set shudders up Mrs. Gallagher's housecoat, but by 1976 the same revelation sent her to the phone to euphorically report, "Guess what—gays have moved in next door!"

The Irish who had sold out in the panic of the late sixties now kicked themselves as they saw housing prices as much as double in six months, and increase another 50 percent six months later. Between 1973 and 1976, prices of many of the solid old homes quintupled. The phenomenon engendered a new kind of blockbusting. Many of the old ethnic pensioners found they couldn't afford *not* to sell their homes at the astronomical sums they were being offered, so they moved out and the neighborhood became even more gay. Real estate speculation created similar conditions in all parts of San Francisco, but in no area was the explosion as marked as in the Castro where thousands were willing to pay any price to live at last in a neighborhood where they would not be different.

The dream that Harvey and Allan Baird shared of an integrated neighborhood was taking a drubbing by 1976. The traditionalists who remembered the days when the district was called a parish had been far too stubborn to live side by side with people whom the church, the law, and the city government had always said were to be disdained and disparaged. Maybe a more educated, genteel neighborhood could have absorbed the influx and become a mix of gay and straight like Greenwich Village, but that would not be the fate of the Castro. Exacerbating the rapid change were the massive numbers of gays moving in. The high schools of America had been filled with class sissies like Cleve Jones who had suffered too much to stay in their hometowns. There had been too many wrongs; the lure of their own neighborhood was too great; their numbers would elbow out the old-timers who did not understand.

The Alioto administration had roundly ignored the homosexual immigration, but the political potential was not lost on a wily politician like George Moscone. George became a regular at the cocktail parties of the Alice Toklas Club. Gays who, months before, could not even get an appointment with Mayor Alioto, were being charmed by Mayor Moscone at every major gay event.

"Hey, Michelle," Moscone shouted to a prominent drag entertainer at his first major post-election gay speech. "How come you didn't wear a gown at the swearing-in ceremony like you promised?"

"When you escort me down the marble stairway, I'll wear a gown to City Hall," Michelle shot back.

"I'll do that when you dress and look like Jeanette MacDonald," Moscone quipped, adding, "And I know you're going to answer me, 'And when I look like Nelson Eddy, right?' "

The changes ran deeper than jokes and personal appearances. The most meaningful gesture for gays, and the move that remained the most controversial of his administration, came with the appointment of Charles Gain as chief of police. Calling himself a "sociological cop," the soft-spoken, pensive Gain had worked his way up through the Oakland Police Department, serving as its chief during the tense years of racial strife there. Gain's conciliatory posture with blacks earned him applause as one of the most liberal law-enforcement officials in the country, and an early vote of no confidence from the city's heavily white police force.

Gain acted swiftly to shake up the old-boy Irish network that had made San Francisco's nepotic department the laughing stock of California police agencies. Police veterans gasped when Gain took the oversized American flag out of the Hall of Justice lobby, saying such super-patriotism alienated many of San Francisco's cosmopolitan citizens. Even worse, Gain issued an edict that had most cops muttering invectives: From now on, Gain ordered, police officers were not allowed to drink on duty. Police rank and file were also stung when Gain ordered that the traditional black and white SFPD cars be repainted a powder blue and labelled "Police Services," reflecting a softer, more humanistic posture. Police old-timers thought the new color scheme was sissified.

The biggest shocker concerned the policies Gain demanded of his officers in dealing with gays. He had come to Oakland as a child from Texas, he explained to gay reporters, and he could never forget how the other neighborhood kids made fun of his Southwestern drawl. He knew what it was like to be different and he wasn't going to let his officers treat gays with any less respect than other San Franciscans just because they happened to be different. A reporter from a gay paper asked what Gain would do if a gay police officer came out. "I certainly think that a gay policeman could be up front about it under me," Gain replied. "If I had a gay policeman who came out, I would support him one hundred percent." After the quote broke in gay papers, the two dailies called Gain to see if such an unlikely statement could possibly be true. Gain repeated his stance, stressing that not only would he support gay cops, but that he hoped they stepped forward since it only made sense that a police force should reflect the city it served and gays certainly

deserved to be represented. The story made headlines locally and nationally.

Within days, the graffiti appeared in bathrooms throughout the
Hall of Justice: "Gain Is a Fruit." Veterans joked that you didn't get
ahead by the reports you issued over Gain's desk but the service you
could perform under it. The great mass of the SFPD, from the captains
and assistant chiefs to the lowest beat cop, never forgave Charles Gain
for the remark he made about gay cops in the first weeks of his tenure.

"President Ford should be coming out through that door."

Bill Sipple hadn't planned to spend the afternoon in front of the
St. Francis Hotel when he went to take his afternoon stroll on September 22, 1975. He was surprised to see a crowd of several thousand at
the St. Francis and decided to stick around to see the President when
he left the luncheon of the World Affairs Council. Since he was living
off his SSI disability payments, he didn't have much else to do anyway.
Sipple was no longer the handsome kid who looked like the quarterback
of Hometown High's football team, the way he looked a decade ago
when Joe Campbell so passionately loved him. He had spread out to
224 pounds and looked far older than his thirty-three years. He'd kept
his Midwestern conservatism, edging to the front of the crowd to get
away from the "damned demonstrators" who were protesting Ford's
visit. Sipple took little notice of the gray-haired woman in the blue
raincoat next to him.

The crowd started applauding when the President emerged from
the hotel. The flash of a chrome-plated revolver caught Sipple's eye.
The woman in the blue raincoat was aiming at the President. Sipple
lunged. The gun went off as he wrestled the woman to the street. Ford
ducked momentarily and then was shoved into the waiting limousine.
The bullet had missed him by only a few feet; Billy Sipple had saved
the President's life.

The police grabbed the woman and carried her battering ram style
into the hotel. Authorities questioned Sipple for three hours. He was
so nervous he could barely light his cigarette. He begged the police and
Secret Service not to release his name. He didn't want anybody to know
who he was or where he lived. He just wanted to be left alone. The
officers were incredulous. The guy was a certifiable hero and he wanted
to keep it a secret.

"How did you guys get here, anyway?" Sipple asked reporters who
appeared at his door a few hours later. Because of the recent capture

of Patty Hearst, the national media already were crawling over San Francisco. Coming just three weeks after "Squeaky" Fromme's attempt on Ford's life in Sacramento, the Sara Jane Moore assassination attempt was a major story. Sipple, however, insisted he wanted to avoid the limelight. He had done what anybody would have done. The papers carried a story of the humble hero, the disabled ex-Marine who, by accident, had his moment in history.

"Harvey, whether he wants to come out is *his* decision," pleaded Frank Robinson. Harvey wanted to leak an item to the press saying Sipple was gay. Robinson was amazed that Milk would take such an important decision in his own hands.

"It's too good an opportunity," Harvey persisted. "For once we can show that gays do heroic things. That guy saved the President's life. It shows that we do good things, not just all that ca-ca about molesting children and hanging out in bathrooms."

"Harvey, it's still not right. It's his life we're talking about," Frank argued. "That decision should be up to him."

Two days later, the item appeared in Herb Caen's *Chronicle* gossip column:

> One of the heroes of the day, Oliver "Bill" Sipple, the ex-Marine who grabbed Sara Jane Moore's arm just as her gun was fired and thereby may have saved the President's life, was the center of midnight attention at the Red Lantern, a Golden Gate Ave. bar he favors. The Rev. Ray Broshears, head of the Helping Hands center and Gay Politico Harvey Milk, who claim to be among Sipple's close friends, describe themselves as "proud—maybe this will help break the stereotype." Sipple is among the workers in Milk's campaign for supe.

The story made the front pages of newspapers across the country. The *Chicago Sun-Times* headlined Sipple as a "Homosexual Hero" while the *Denver Post* labeled Sipple a "Gay Vet." Most papers avoided saying Sipple was gay, since the acknowledgment did not come from Sipple himself. Instead, they referred to later talk of Sipple's activities in a gay social organization and Milk's 1975 campaign.

A drained and angry Sipple faced reporters days later. He had just gotten off the phone with his mother, a staunch Baptist. "I want you to know that my mother told me today that she can't walk out her front door, or even go to church, because of the pressures she feels because of the press stories concerning my sexual orientation," said Sipple. "My sexual orientation has nothing to do with saving the President's life."

Sipple's mom went into seclusion and would not talk to her son. Sipple went into despair and blamed the newspapers.

Sipple's mom wasn't the only curiosity, Milk soon discovered. President Ford had been expected to publicly thank Sipple. Ford thanked the Secret Service who had pushed him into the limousine after the bullet rang out, but once stories surfaced about Sipple's gay connections, Ford would say nothing to Sipple. Just months before, Ford had actually sent a note of apology to a carload of kids who had rammed his car; now, he refused to thank the guy who had probably kept his skull from getting blown apart by an assassin's bullet because it looked like he might be gay. The board of supervisors similarly did not pass a resolution honoring Sipple, even though such measures were routinely doled out for the slightest achievement. Harvey shot off an angry telegram to Ford and lectured reporters that the lack of gratitude was an even better story than the thwarted murder attempt. Harvey talked to his labor friend Stan Smith and Smith organized a luncheon at which Sipple was awarded a plaque on behalf of the Building and Construction Trades Council. Weeks later, a brief note of thanks came from the White House. Sipple autographed a copy of it: "To Harvey, a good friend. Oliver W. Sipple."

Bill ran into Joe Campbell after the assassination attempt. Joe barely recognized the man he had once tried to commit suicide over. Bill showed Joe his room full of plaques and honorary certificates. Joe still wasn't sure, however, if Bill really remembered exactly who Joe was.

Sipple later sued the *Chronicle, Post,* and *Sun-Times* for invasion of privacy. A San Francisco Superior Court judge threw the case out with a summary judgment, citing obvious First Amendment grounds. Sipple was represented in court by John Wahl, personal attorney of the man who leaked the news in the first place, Harvey Milk.

Sipple's attempt at legal remedy bucked the national trend of the gay movement in the mid-seventies. Homosexuals were still something of a curiosity to the public, but the taboo that had long kept a lid of media silence on the subject was lifting. Newspapers were full of stories about improbable people who turned out to be gay. Elaine Noble, an acknowledged lesbian, started the parade when she was elected to the Massachusetts House of Represnetatives in 1974. Minnesota State Senator Allan Spear was so inspired by Noble's example that he sat down with a *Minneapolis Star* reporter a few weeks later and told her that he was gay too. The story headlined the next day's paper. The series of coming outs hit high gear nationally after Technical Sergeant Leonard Matlovich went up to his commanding officer in March 1975.

"I have a letter I want you to read," Matlovich said. "I think you'd better sit down."

"I'll stand."

"I think you'd better sit down."

"I'll stand," the captain maintained, taking the letter. He couldn't believe what he read. Matlovich, a decorated military man, stated he was a homosexual; he was inviting a legal challenge to the regulations forbidding gays from serving in all branches of the military. The captain sat down.

"What does this mean?"

"It means *Brown* vs. *the Board of Education,*" Matlovich said.

The captain tried to give the letter back to Matlovich. "A similar letter is being delivered to the Secretary of the Air Force," the thirty-two-year-old sergeant said. "So I think you'd better give it to the colonel." A letter wasn't really being delivered in Washington, but Matlovich thought that comment would ensure delivery. By August, Matlovich's face landed on the cover of *Time* magazine over the headline: "The Gay Drive for Acceptance." A television network soon began filming a docu-drama on the case.

Former Green Bay Packer linebacker Dave Kopay startled the sports world four months later when he openly discussed his homosexuality with the *Washington Star* for their series on homosexuality in sports. Kopay was the first professional athlete to come out publicly; his memoirs hit *The New York Times* best-seller list. Other celebrities followed the ritual of sexual confessionals. Pop super star Elton John said he would "only draw the line at goats." Even Tab Hunter told *Washington Post* reporter Sally Quinn about living with his male "friend and secretary."

The revelations had little immediate political impact, but they underscored the extent to which the social pressures for staying in the closet had crumbled during the early 1970s. After all, disclosing homosexuality used to mean disgrace, despair, and, to some, even suicide. Now it meant book contracts, documentaries, the TV talk show circuit, and newsmagazine cover photos. The risks involved with coming out were drastically decreasing. Even more significantly, youngsters who had never even heard the term homosexuality were now seeing a diverse range of public figures talking freely about being gay on television news shows and front pages.

The new openness touched all walks of American life. The ruling by the American Psychiatric Association that homosexuality no longer represented a disease shattered the old psychiatric justification for summarily banning gays from government jobs so, in July 1975 the United States Civil Service Commission struck down their sweeping policy of refusing gays any civil service job in the country. The same year, ten cities and three counties enacted gay civil rights ordinances. Congress took up the federal gay rights bill for the second time in gays' ongoing efforts to amend the 1964 Civil Rights Act to prohibit discrimination on the basis of "sexual orientation." The measure mustered twenty-three co-sponsors; gay lobbyists confidently predicted that by the 1981 session, a comprehensive national gay rights bill would move to the President's desk.

The optimism seemed well founded to the gay moderates. They congratulated themselves on the gentlemanly tactics that were winning so much more success than the obnoxious outbursts of scruffy gay liberationists who kept demanding that *everybody* should come out of the closet. The optimism came in part because no organized opposition to the gay rights drive had yet emerged. Some individual opponents certainly existed, often because politicians were still skittish about discussing a topic polite people had previously kept out of decent conversation. But the gay rights drive had more the markings of a chic social cause than a burning controversy. The lack of organized opposition left the gay reformers in the dangerous situation of believing their own propaganda—that the success of the gay rights movement was both imminent and inevitable. It was only a matter of waiting patiently until our liberal friends came along; they could not be rushed.

Harvey Milk and the handful of activists who still clung to the gay liberationist credo held more apocalyptic visions of the future. Milk thought the gay reformers were like so many southern ladies from a Tennessee Williams play, always depending on the kindness of heterosexuals. In a pinch, Milk thought, the liberals would always act solely to save themselves; they would always urge gays to wait and be patient; the time would *never* be right. The answer, Milk thought, lay in seizing power for gays. Power, not polite lobbying, would win the gay cause.

Every day of waiting would only increase the suffering wrought by a society that, Milk believed, still fundamentally hated homosexuals and still prodded gays to hate themselves.

Jim Bruton, on one of his visits from Anchorage, and Harvey were talking in the back of Castro Camera one night after the store had closed when the phone rang. As soon as Harvey heard the voice, he rolled his eyes impatiently at Jim.

"It's Jack McKinley," he said.

He paused and listened further.

"He says he's going to kill himself." Jim knew it wasn't the first time Jack had called San Francisco with such a threat. Once he had even claimed to have cancer of the anus, probably figuring that disfigurement of that part of his anatomy would upset Harvey's aesthetic sense.

"Tell him not to make a mess," Jim suggested.

"Jim said not to make a mess," Harvey deadpanned.

Jack hung up.

nine

Harvey Milk vs. The Machine

We feel that San Francisco is alive and reaching out for world conquest, a city reincarnated and ambitious for the future.

—From review of the newly dedicated San Francisco City Hall, The Architect, *October 1916*

The phoenix rising from the flames.

The image fluttered gracefully, in the center of the golden-bordered San Francisco flag, above the classical pillared portico of San Francisco City Hall.

Harvey realized again how much he loved San Francisco's grand City Hall as he arrived at its wide granite steps that brisk January morning in 1976. With a rotunda higher than the nation's capitol, flanked by wide colonnades of Doric columns, the grandiose edifice was meant to symbolize San Francisco's resurrection after the massive earthquake and fire of 1906. The French Renaissance structure was considered one of America's most majestic public buildings when it was dedicated in 1916, the centerpiece of a stunning network of ornate Beaux Artes structures that surrounded the Civic Center plaza.

Harvey glanced at the Grecian friezes on the pediment over the entrance and

127

walked through the oversized doors, with their golden grilles, through the lobby and the sun-bathed expanse of marble beneath the massive rotunda, ringed by Corinthian columns and lighted from the clerestory under the copper dome. Harvey always paused here, looking at the engraved medallions high above him depicting Liberty, Equality, Learning, and Strength. A giant terraced staircase of California marble lapped gently into the center of the magnificent hall. Harvey never took an elevator when he came to the mayor's office, always choosing to walk up this grand staircase, slowly making his entrance.

Milk turned and walked toward the mayor's office. On the pendentive over the mayor's wing of City Hall was the golden city clock under a granite carving of Father Time, flanked by History and the representation of future generations passing the Torch of Progress. In low relief behind them were background figures eerily symbolizing the fleeting hours of the day.

The fleeting hours. By early 1976, the imposing and idealistic City Hall was the stage for what was nothing short of a coup in city government. No event better symbolized the unfolding political drama than the swearing-in of the city's Board of Permit Appeals for the Moscone administration. That's why Harvey had come, to be sworn in as a member of this powerful commission, which was the court of last appeal for any matter dealing with a permit issued by the city. To be sworn in before the assembled television cameras in the mayor's ornate office were a black woman, a woman neighborhood activist, a Filipino, and, of course, the first acknowledged gay city commissioner in the country. In fact, only one white male heterosexual sat on the board—and he, conservatives grumbled, was a scion of the cursed Hallinan family of lawyers, which had been representing radical causes in San Francisco since the 1930s.

Newspaper columnists started complaining that the only way to get on a Moscone commission was to be a member of a minority. At the swearing-in, Milk sarcastically allayed the fear by insisting he would be a magnanimous commissioner "so the bigots will be surprised." Of course, new ambitions were percolating in Milk's mind, even on that day—ambitions that would make Milk's tenure one of the shortest commissionerships in city history—but the focus of the day was on the unprecedented diversity emerging in city government. The bloodless civil war of the 1975 elections had overthrown the moribund mayoralty of the past and nothing was more emblematic of this than the newly constituted city commissions.

"Jesus Christ, Harvey, you've got to be kidding. You were just sworn in last week."

Every friend and advisor told Harvey the same thing: Don't do it. Don't even think about doing it. Jim Rivaldo told him it would be a big mistake. Frank Robinson said it would make Harvey look opportunistic. Scott Smith dreaded the idea of launching another campaign when the last race was still only two months behind them.

But Harvey had Jim Rivaldo's neatly color-coded maps of the 1975 supervisorial race and the evidence was incontrovertible. It would have been impossible to find a better legislative district for Harvey than the 16th Assembly District. With Assemblyman John Foran leaving the seat behind to take over George Moscone's state senate seat, Harvey was lured by the tantalizing possibility of being a California assemblyman. Just two months before, Harvey had garnered 17,000 votes in the 16th A.D.; Foran had won the seat in 1974 with only 16,500 votes. The seat was his for the taking, he figured.

There were other reasons even his closest confidantes did not know, reasons he cited only to Scott in the long talks about politics and strategy they had in bed until the early morning hours. An old diving injury from the Navy was acting up. Pain had frequently wracked his shoulders during the hectic handshaking of the last campaign. His endurance might not hold out until the 1977 supervisorial elections. And in a few months, he would be forty-six, that much closer to his deadline.

Politicos floated rumors that Assembly Speaker Leo McCarthy's top lieutenant, Art Agnos, might go after the seat, but that was of little concern to Milk. His supervisorial campaign had given him extremely high name recognition. He could easily roll over Art Somebody, leap frog the small-time arena of municipal politics and forge a highly visible role as California's first openly gay legislator. Harvey's agenda called for getting the public platform that comes with public office; it didn't matter which public office he had. The race would be a cakewalk; it seemed too good to be true. And it was.

The deal—probably just a few comments dropped over lunch. The right inflection when Assembly Speaker Leo McCarthy talked about whether he'd ever want to run for Congress. The pregnant pause after Senate Majority Leader George Moscone wondered aloud if another liberal would oppose him for the mayoralty. People who know don't talk about such things publicly; that's why they are the people who know. By the closing days of 1974, however, over a year and a half before the 1976 assembly race, the deal deciding that election was struck.

The agreement had all the trappings of a medieval marriage between two warring dynasties. On one hand was the McCarthy clan, the more conservative of the two Democratic power structures in San Francisco. McCarthy first won public office in 1963 when he and George Moscone were elected freshman supervisors. McCarthy had since worked up to the speakership of the California assembly, a position of power second only to that of the governor himself. In 1974, he helped his old law partner, John Foran, win the seat in the neighboring 16th A.D.

On the other side was the more liberal Burton-Moscone axis, a group which had been estranged from McCarthy since the bruising primary battle between Moscone and McCarthy for Moscone's first senate term in 1966. Moscone had done well for himself, becoming senate majority leader in a year. His ally, Congressman Phil Burton, meanwhile, was in 1974 working on his plan to become majority leader of the United States House of Representatives, the second most powerful post in that body. Toward securing his power base, Phil Burton helped his younger brother John rise from the state assembly to become San Francisco's other congressman. Still another Burton brother presided over the community college board. Closely allied with this axis was Assemblyman Willie Brown, the dapper black politician who was Moscone's closest political friend—and a McCarthy enemy after he emerged as McCarthy's chief opponent in the battle for assembly speaker.

By late 1974, both factions needed to patch things up. Earlier that year, Moscone's attempt to run for governor had fizzled. He decided to run for mayor, but McCarthy could destroy his chances by running his own moderate Democrat. Phil Burton wanted to shore up his congressional backyard as he pushed for House majority leader. His likeliest Democratic opposition would come from the McCarthy camp. Ever since his attempt to be Speaker, Willie Brown had been pushed in the assembly basement by the vengeful victor so he needed a committee chairmanship to regain his clout. Brown, after all, made a good chunk of money as a lawyer for special interests who needed legislative connections. The more powerful he was, the more money he made.

The McCarthy forces had much to gain from a rapprochement as well. A Moscone move to City Hall would open up a senate seat which, if under proper control, could increase McCarthy's already considerable power. McCarthy still worried that Willie Brown might make another try for the speakership. And there was one more matter. If, say, Assemblyman John Foran moved into Moscone's senate seat, he would leave behind an assembly seat. McCarthy wanted that too, filled by his top aide, Art Agnos.

There was talk that it was all decided over a luncheon meeting between Phil Burton, McCarthy, and Moscone, but that was only talk. What was certain was that the deal was struck with something in it for everybody. Moscone got to be mayor. Willie Brown moved up from the basement to be chair of the Assembly Revenue and Tax Committee. Phil and John Burton did not have to worry about being challenged in congressional primaries by a McCarthy candidate. McCarthy, meanwhile, got his closest aide made into an assemblyman, while his former law partner became a state senator and he had no more fears about being again challenged by Willie Brown. Just about every politico and government reporter in town figured the machinations out—everybody, that is, except Harvey Milk.

Art Agnos put together a list of key community leaders in the district he needed to contact before formally announcing his candidacy. He had never heard of Harvey Milk before culling the names, but he politely stopped by Castro Camera to try to wrap up an endorsement just the same. Harvey showed Agnos his neatly color-coded map, mentioned he felt he might have a chance in the district, but that he probably would not run, even though he had not made his final decision yet. The way Agnos later told the story, Agnos was probably not as far as the corner of Castro Street before Harvey was on the phone.

"Well, Leo, your boy Art Agnos was just here."

Leo McCarthy was not amused. He knew Agnos was making the rounds, so he probably had stopped to see this Harvey What's-His-Name, but the speaker did not like to have Agnos referred to his "his boy" and he didn't like the tenor of Milk's conversation. Jim Foster and David Goodstein certainly treated him with proper respect. What was the matter with this Milk guy?

"Tell you what," Milk said. "I'll stay out of the race if you get Burton to back me for supervisor next year."

The speaker turned down Milk's offer and hung up as soon as possible. The story quickly spread through political circles. The respectable gay leaders solemnly assured politicians that this was indeed what they had come to expect from Harvey Milk. Agnos and McCarthy considered the call crude. That's not how political deals are struck, Agnos thought. You never come out and say it. It was as if Milk thought that Moscone, McCarthy, and Representative Burton had sat down with a big map and indelicately carved up the power. Deal-making, of course, required the art of leaving little pauses, darting meaningful glances, and dropping hypothetical questions that aren't really questions at all. As far as Agnos was concerned, he just happened to be at the right place when all the pieces happened to, well, fall together. "It was serendipity," he later said.

Agnos felt he had far more expertise than Milk to represent so diverse a district. He had labored for years as a social worker in China-town, the black Hunter's Point area and the Latino Mission district. He knew more about these neighborhoods than this camera store owner who hadn't set his sights much further than Castro Street. He'd also spent years at the right hand of the assembly's most powerful member. It was patently obvious that he would be the most effective assembly-man, he thought. Milk's lack of diplomacy in calling McCarthy further proved that he'd never make it in the assembly.

"Who's Art Agnos?"

Harvey kept repeating the question rhetorically to any reporter who would listen as he spent February launching trial balloons, hinting coyly that he might run if no other viable candidate stood forth to challenge this guy nobody had ever heard of. The Democratic establishment was aghast. Milk had been paid off with his commissionership. What more did he want? He could even be supervisor in 1977, maybe. All he had to do was wait. Mayor Moscone issued a statement saying he would fire Harvey from the Board of Permit Appeals the moment he filed papers to run.

Harvey started calling activists to see how much support he could expect if he ran. He quickly discovered that even if John Q. Public did not know Agnos' name, three key politicians did: Moscone, the city's most powerful man; Leo McCarthy, the state's second most powerful leader; and Phil Burton, who was working on being Congress' second most powerful figure. Virtually every politico of any importance—from the lowliest sanitation commissioner to the governor—was beholden to one of these men. They had all been lined up long ago to support Agnos —months before the general public even knew the seat would be open. Jim Foster, Rick Stokes, and David Goodstein had long ago committed themselves to Agnos. Their payoff was repeal of the sodomy statute. That everything had been sewn up so long in advance offended Milk's basic belief that politics was a matter of one-on-one, meet-the-people handshakes. He became more convinced he should run.

Harvey Milk vs. The Machine.
The bold headline in the liberal weekly newspaper titillated Harvey right down to his publicist's soul. He had only let out a few hints that he might, just maybe, consider running. The press was having a field day. The specter of machine politics surrounding Agnos' candidacy horrified Michael Wong's populist sensibilities and he called Harvey to see if Milk would champion the anti-machine cause.

"Like the way the media is covering all this?" Harvey asked.

"Resign," Wong insisted. "Show that you will not be a pawn."

"No, no, no," Harvey said. "I would get more out of being fired than if I resigned. No, Mike, I'm gonna let him fire me. Then people will be outraged."

Milk's five weeks stewardship on the Board of Permit Appeals saw him gleefully playing cat and mouse with the Democratic establishment to the delight of the media and the horror of supporters who thought Harvey was crazy to buck every politician in town. The newspapers, however, had never had much use for people like Moscone and Burton, so they goaded Milk on. *The Examiner* editorialized that Moscone's threat to fire Milk represented "Chicago-style politics" and took to calling the mayor "Boss Moscone." When the mayor insisted he wanted commissioners who would devote their efforts to commissions, not campaigning, another newspaper wrote that Moscone "ought to build a stadium for us to laugh in." Holding public office had not stopped Moscone from campaigning for both governor and mayor. It didn't help Moscone's case when he insisted that he *had* to support Agnos for the assembly seat because he had promised to do so a year and a half earlier—a defense that only raised more questions about the deal. Stories also revealed that John Foran had only moved into Moscone's old senate district the weekend before the filing deadline. The secretary of state, a Democrat with ambitions of her own, certified Foran's eligibility for candidacy, but the entire chicanery provided more fuel for the columnists' charges that the political musical chairs was bossism at its worst.

All this press and Harvey hadn't even announced he was going to run. With the battlelines so clearly drawn, however, the temptation provided irresistible, "I think representatives should be elected by the people—not appointed," Milk said in his announcement speech at the San Francisco Press Club. "I think a representative should earn his or her seat. I don't think the seat should be awarded on the basis of service to the machine. Machines operate on oil and grease; they're dirty, dehumanizing, and too often unresponsive to any needs but those of the operator."

Within hours of Milk's statement, Mayor Moscone had an announcement of his own. Harvey was off the Board of Permit Appeals; Rick Stokes took his place. He also appointed two more members of the old guard, veterans Del Martin and Phyllis Lyon, to the Human Rights Commission and Commission on the Status of Women.

Harvey's campaign slogan soon appeared on buttons and posters all around San Francisco: Harvey Milk vs. The Machine.

Politicians have an aversion to deodorant, thought John Ryckman when he met Harvey Milk. And this one's no exception.

One of the adoring little old ladies who were always whispering advice in Harvey's ear insisted that Ryckman would be the perfect campaign manager. Ryckman had decades of experience in Democratic Party politics. He'd been in his nice stable relationship for years. Besides, he knew all the rich Pacific Heights people who had lots of money to spread around the campaign. Ryckman never doubted that all this made him the perfect campaign manager for Milk; the question was whether Milk was the candidate for him.

Ryckman instantly felt uneasy about the hyperactive politician at their first meeting. Instead of boyishness, Ryckman saw something of a spoiled child, demanding nearly superhuman efforts from his employees, friends, and campaign workers. He ran off at the mouth with long trains of hyperbole. His temper flared easily—especially at his lover Scott—and he seemed inordinately preoccupied with minutiae, using only bottled distilled water for his ritual morning cup of coffee which, of course, had to be of an exotic blend mixed especially for his tastes.

The candidate seemed totally disorganized. His supporter roster consisted of a boxful of matchbook covers, bar napkins, and scraps of paper. Milk's business was in a shambles, no small consideration for a manager who had only handled campaigns with money. Harvey's ragtag corps of volunteers from Castro Street showed few signs of affluence. I'd have to be crazy to get involved with this campaign, Ryckman thought.

But Ryckman had liked lost causes ever since he had been a volunteer in Young Californians for Stevenson in 1952. The fact that the alleged new breed of San Francisco liberals would do something like sew up an election over a year in advance irritated his old-fashioned Democratic spine. And in the back of his mind, he could never forget the pained look on his lover's face when he talked about the awful hours of interrogation and trial during the proceedings that had resulted in a dishonorable discharge from the Navy. Steve never became the man he could have been because of that disgrace. Maybe if this uncouth, pushy New York Jew could do something to take a swipe at it all, well, maybe, it might be worth a few months. That's how Harvey Milk got his first professional campaign manager.

Ryckman knew he had made the right decision a few days later when a half-giggling store employee told him a new campaign volunteer had arrived at the Castro Camera headquarters. At the counter stood a pert young girl in her Most Holy Redeemer uniform, a wool hat, and school bag. Ryckman thought she might be a midget, but no, she was a sixth grader who had carefully printed out the volunteer card:

Name: Medora Payne
Age: 11
Occupation: School kid
What like to do: precinct work, fund raising

Medora's appearance marked the only time Ryckman ever called a prospective volunteer's parents to get permission. "She just loves Harvey," Mrs. Payne explained. "She's been wanting to get involved in his campaigns for so long, we couldn't keep her away if we wanted to." The precocious young Medora became a fixture at the camera store, bringing in her best girl friend from Most Holy Redeemer and bossing around any volunteers who might be indolent enough to lay back when there was so much work to be done.

Michael Wong was horrified when he came to Castro Camera to see how the spacious area behind the camera supplies should be organized into a campaign headquarters. Paint spilled from the '75 campaign's handmade posters stained most of the floor. Campaign signs, old brochures, and a thick coating of dust covered every square foot.

"Harvey is this how *you* people live—in pig pens?" Wong demanded.

"No, my little yellow lotus blossom," Harvey grinned back. "We were waiting for our houseboy to arrive. There's the broom."

The opening weeks of the campaign dissolved Ryckman's early misgivings about the peripatetic Milk. If Harvey shouted too loudly at Scott and his closest friends, he could also purr softly into the ear of any reporter who happened by—and usually come out of it with some good press. Milk demanded too much of those around him, but his demands of others paled in comparison to what he demanded of himself. Every morning at five-thirty, Milk rose to pump hands at bus stops, hit the coffee shops, attend an afternoon political luncheon, hit more bus stops, lecture at early evening candidates' nights, take in at least one bingo game and return to the headquarters at midnight to help volunteers lick stamps and seal envelopes. Harvey could bring a new twist to each day's campaiging. The arrival of the film *All the President's Men* inspired Milk to work the long lines of moviegoers each night, talking auspiciously of the dangers of too much power concentrated in too few hands. What intrigued Ryckman most about his new candidate, however, were the endless lines of Irish widows, stodgy merchants, and troubled teenagers who were always coming in to see Harvey and ask his help to solve this or that problem. Other candidates would have had flak-catchers screen out such nuisances since they were hardly the people with whom campaigns were won or lost, but Harvey always had time, sometimes putting important politicians and campaign donors on hold while he reassured a worried mother that he'd work on getting a stoplight installed near the neighborhood grade school. That, to Harvey Milk, was what politics was all about.

Milk frequently jawboned his volunteers straight off Castro Street if enough hands were not on board to get a task done, or if the volunteer was cute enough to warrant attention. Everybody got a task. Joggers were conscripted to run in marathons, wearing their "Harvey Milk vs. The Machine" T shirts. If a volunteer had nothing more than good penmanship, the worker went straight to the piles of personalized thank you notes Milk habitually sent out. Even eleven-year-old Medora organized a fund raiser geared for Milk's growing preteen constituency, and she proudly plunked the $39.28 she raised on the Castro Camera counter, dutifully reminding Ryckman to make sure it was properly reported on the campaign contribution forms.

The campaign, however, marked the first time Ryckman had to allow the business of serious politics take a backseat to practical joking. A close look at the issue of campaign posters, for example, revealed that

Milk sometimes threw out the standard "Milk for Assembly" logo in favor of the more direct tag of "Ministry of Propaganda." Someone bought a Mr. Machine toy robot for the camera store and Ryckman walked in to find his candidate entertaining Medora by holding mock debates with the obdurate wind-up toy. Soon, everyone was calling Wong the "little yellow lotus blossom." Wong got even by dubbing Ryckman, "Ms. Ryckperson." Ryckman tried to escape the Marx Brothers ambience by cordoning off his work space in the rear of the camera shop with some ancient swagged-back velvet curtains he ferreted from an old trunk. He noticed only several days later that Danny Nicoletta had put a sign over this office entrance announcing: Fortunes Told, 10¢—With Lipstick, 50¢. Amid the continual pranks, more than one Teamster volunteer shook his head with amazement as he walked in the headquarters to find an eleven-year-old bossing around a new Milk worker three times her age and clad in full leathers, while the candidate loudly insisted that Michael Wong should really be doing the laundry instead of the direct mail campaign.

The early months of campaigning inspired an optimism Harvey had never known in his previous ill-fated efforts. Ryckman connected Milk to what he called the NYJ—New York Jew—network in San Francisco, and though the machine had scared most contributors away from Milk, the few Harvey did gain made this the best financed campaign of his career. Milk's uncanny ability to grab the limelight continued to get the campaign favorable press coverage. At one fund raiser at the end of a long and bitter city strike, Harvey even managed to get his lone supporter on the board of supervisors, Quentin Kopp—a rabidly anti-labor spokesman—and a Teamsters official to shake hands with Harvey smiling on. Of course, Harvey made sure the handshake didn't occur until a news photographer was standing by.

It was too much to expect the Toklas club to even come near endorsing Milk, whom they had opposed in the two previous campaigns, but a cadre of Milk supporters there managed to deny Agnos the endorsement by a one-vote margin. The local California Democratic Council's endorsement was a cinch for Agnos, except that the vote took place in a grade school right next door to marijuana marketeer Dennis Peron's restaurant. Peron enlisted all ninety-five of his employees to vote that day, since Harvey had long ago formed them into their own Democratic club, and Agnos lost that endorsement. The odd thing that Harvey's friend Frank Robinson noticed was that the political victories that stirred Milk most came not from powerful political organizations but from the bus stops he worked every morning.

"Everything could be going against him, but he would come back to the headquarters jubilant because he had persuaded one old lady to vote for him," Robinson recalled later. "It was as if every person he won over represented an important victory. Here he was, a gay and a Jew —a street radical at heart—and he was able to convince some little old lady that he was a decent human being worth voting for. Those moments meant more to him than anything else in the world."

The only victories that rivaled his conversions at bus stops occurred when Milk brought a gay person into the political fold. Slowly, they straggled in, many to become the political leaders of the future. Tall, blond Dick Pabich wandered into the headquarters one day willing to do something, anything. At twenty, he was too young to know the times of Vietnam protests and civil rights marches. He had spent his college years at the University of Wisconsin as a glitter queen, affecting the then fashionable androgyny of David Bowie and Lou Reed. But the ongoing parties of his chic set, first in Madison, then in San Francisco, engendered only ennui as the fad passed. Harvey showed particular interest in Pabich—only later did Dick learn that the candidate liked thin, young, blond men—and sent him out doing what Milk considered the most valuable chore of any campaign, registering voters. Within a few weeks, Pabich found himself making decisions with Harvey's inner circle, amazed at how casually this unorthodox politician delegated responsibility.

An early poll showed that though half the voters were undecided, the half who had made up their mind favored Milk over Agnos by a two-to-one margin. Harvey knew for sure that he was making a major impact on the district the day he got a phone call from one of the most politically influential preachers in California. He was interested in helping Harvey canvass the precincts in the heavily black Hunters Point neighborhood. Harvey pulled Michael Wong aside after he got the call.

"Guess who is coming down here this weekend to work Hunters Point?" Milk asked Wong.

"Who?"

"That was the Reverend Jim Jones on the telephone. He apologized for not knowing I was running and said that he did not mean to back Art Agnos as much as he was doing." Harvey could barely hold back his giggle. "He told me that he will make it up to me by sending us some volunteers."

"He's helping Agnos and now backing you?" Wong asked incredulously. Jones was known for being politically savvy, so the notion of jumping candidates in mid-election seemed very improbable.

"Of course not," Milk retorted impatiently, as if Michael should have known better. "Jones *is* backing Agnos and giving him a lot of workers, but he wants to cover his ass, so he'll send us some volunteers too." Most politicians would do anything to get at the Peoples Temple volunteers who, for some reason, seemed so devoted to their leader. Jones' duplicity, however, only irritated Milk.

"Well, fuck him," Milk decided. "I'll take his workers, but," warning Wong for future reference, "that's the game Jim Jones plays."

A few days later, Jones's confidante Sharon Amos called Harvey's friend Tory Hartmann and asked her to drop off a whopping 30,000 brochures at the Temple. Hartmann and Tom Randol loaded up Randol's pickup and took the fliers to the converted synagogue in the middle of the desolate Filmore district, which had been devastated by urban renewal a decade before. The pair started unloading the boxes when a gruff guard emerged from the locked door.

"What do you want?" he barked.

"We're just dropping off these brochures," Hartmann assured him, trying her best to keep a chipper tone.

"Just put them down right there," said the guard, gesturing to a spot well outside the locked compound.

"No, that's all right," said Tory as she unloaded. "We'll carry them inside."

The guard went inside, deliberated with superiors, and finally admitted Hartmann and Randol. As they carried the boxes in, they saw the door of each room was guarded by men who stood at attention, staring dead ahead like the soldiers at Buckingham Palace. This is a church? Hartmann thought.

Both Tom and Tory were relieved when they sped back toward the Castro. Tory later confided her anxieties to Harvey, who dropped his normally jocular tone to give her some deadly serious advice.

"Make sure you're always nice to the Peoples Temple," he admonished her. "If they ask you to do something, do it, and then send them a note thanking them for asking you to do it. They're weird and they're dangerous, and you never want to be on their bad side."

Tory was involved in a number of Democratic Party causes and kept tabs on the party nationally through her friendship with San Mateo's Congressman Leo Ryan. She began mentioning her experience with Jones to a number of her other political friends. Hartmann was worried. Jones was, after all, a major political force on the scene now that Mayor Moscone had made him chairman of the Housing Authority, an incredibly powerful position for a man who oriented his work toward the same poor who used public housing. District Attorney Joe Freitas, meanwhile, had made Jones's top lieutenant, Tim Stoen, an assistant district attorney and even assigned him to investigate allegations of voter fraud—quite a choice assignment considering Peoples Temple itself was the brunt of many of these charges. Tory's political contacts, however, only reassured her of what a marvelous new fixture Jim Jones was on the political scene. He could turn out so many volunteers, just like that. It seemed they'd do anything for him. "Nobody wanted to listen to me," Hartmann said later. "It was like I was telling a joke but there wasn't any punchline."

"Harvey's a friend. You don't screw your friends."

It was a rule labor leader George Evankovich stuck by, but it fell on deaf ears at the San Francisco Labor Council, which wanted nothing to do with the fruit candidate. A few union leaders kept their unions with Harvey—the Laborers, Fire Fighters, Teamsters, and the massive Building and Construction Trades Council—but most pulled into line for Agnos. Nobody knew much about Agnos, that was true, but they had to keep in good with Burton and McCarthy. They couldn't risk the wrath of the Democratic Party's cartel that was behind Agnos.

That's the way it worked with virtually every special interest group in the city. Milk stood by stunned, as group after group endorsed Agnos, even though many of the leaders privately conceded they hadn't heard his name until just months before.

"I'll tell you why I can't stand Harvey Milk."

His face blushing, his arms waving about his roly-poly figure, David Goodstein was having one of his tantrums again. Even his reverence for Werner Erhard and his erhard seminars training (est) couldn't keep Goodstein from controlling his temper. Goodstein's employees at the *Advocate* offices in San Mateo didn't even have to casually stroll to the coffee machine to eavesdrop on this one. His voice resounded through the partitions of the nation's largest gay paper. Goodstein had purchased the biweekly only two years before and his penchant for mixing journalism with his idiosyncratic theories of gay activism had by now earned him the nickname "Citizen Goodstein." That this nobody camera shop owner was tangling with "our liberal friends" in-furiated him.

"Harvey Milk's goddamn crazy. He can't be trusted. He'll embar-rass the shit out of us." Goodstein's normally sociable terrier, Minnie, huddled in a corner while her master's tirade continued. "He's just an opportunist."

When Goodstein learned that his old Pacific Heights friend Anne Eliaser had donated money to Milk, he quickly got on the phone. "Why are you doing this off-the-wall thing?" he fumed. "Harvey is a crazy man."

Eliaser found herself in the curious position of being a heterosexual trying to explain to the nation's major gay publisher why it was time gays themselves, not just their liberal friends, hold public office.

Jim Foster was angry at the whole tenor of Harvey's anti-machine theme. Sure it's a machine, Foster thought, a machine that finally got that fascist Joe Alioto out of office; a machine that got a district attor-ney who stopped prosecuting gays like they were Jews in the Spanish Inquisition, a machine that made it legal for gays to have sex in Califor-nia for the first time in 102 years; a machine that had made the first gay commission appointments in the nation's history; a machine that was carrying gay civil rights legislation in Congress. It's a machine all right, Foster thought, remembering back on the years of bar raids and police harassment he had experienced over a decade before Harvey Milk even moved here. But it's *our* machine for a change, a machine on *our* side.

Rick Stokes had more pragmatic concerns. He had specific gay civil rights legislation he wanted passed in Sacramento. Even if Milk did win—a very doubtful possibility, he thought—Milk would have the instant enmity of the all-powerful Speaker McCarthy. An assemblyman sitting on the sanitation committee could do little good for changing the laws for lesbian custody cases, or anti-gay job bias, Stokes thought, while Assemblyman Agnos would immediately sit at the right hand of McCarthy from which he could judge the quick and the dead among legislative proposals.

Virtually every major gay leader endorsed Agnos, usually with a vitriolic denunciation of Milk. They even imported State Representa-tive Elaine Noble, the openly gay legislator from Massachusetts, to come all the way from Boston to tell San Francisco gays why they did not need an openly gay legislator from California. Milk shouted carpet-bagger, and the corps of Castro Street workers for Milk were generally speechless at the sight of the nation's foremost lesbian leader opposing Milk, a man with whom she had neither talked nor met. "It's easy to explain," an *Advocate* editor said at a Noble fund raiser for Agnos. "She wants to run for U.S. Senate in 1978 and she'll need all these gay leaders to raise money for her out here." Milk's Castro volunteers may have been committed, but they certainly had little to offer Noble's campaign chest, so the gays with the Agnos campaign, with the prospect of money for Noble in the future, got the advantage of running full-page ads in gay papers heralding Noble's endorsement.

With characteristic hyperbole, Milk compared the gay establishment to Nazi collaborators, insisting that gays' priority should be electing the first gay candidate in California, not a liberal friend. "Since these self-appointed 'leaders' lack the courage to run for public office themselves, they then MUST try to destroy anyone who does run for office unless that person is blessed by them," he wrote. "You don't dictate to us by going to four or five 'gay leaders' and making a deal," he told one reporter. "These leaders can't deliver. They are not going to deliver the votes of the people on the streets."

Art Agnos, meanwhile, learned the hazards of campaigning in the San Francisco of the 1970s. At a Sunday afternoon campaign stop at a spaghetti feed in a Folsom Street bar, Agnos was stumping for votes when a leather-clad patron shook Agnos' hand with his right paw and grabbed the candidate's crotch with his left. The affable Agnos smiled at the masher. "Do I measure up to Harvey?" he asked. The crowd hooted. "Ya sure do, buddy," the leather man answered. Agnos got an ovation; he figured he walked out with every vote in the bar.

Even as the campaign grew more bitter, Art Agnos had to concede, Harvey Milk was a quick study. Though unschooled in the niceties of diplomacy, Harvey was an effective speaker who kept his sense of humor while the pair stumped together through endless candidates' nights. It wasn't unusual for even the most bitter opponents to review each others' performances; after all, they heard their campaign speeches more than anybody else. Agnos later remembered putting his arm around Harvey's shoulder as the two emerged from a particularly fierce debate and walked toward the parking lot.

"How do you feel having the machine around you?" he joked.

"Best machine I've ever had handle me," Harvey quipped.

Agnos wondered how seriously Harvey took all this machine business.

"Y'know Harv', your speech is too much of a downer," Agnos

suggested. "You talk about how you're gonna throw the bums out, but how are you gonna fix things—other than beat me? You shouldn't leave your audience on a down."

Shortly after that, Agnos noted that Harvey started ending his speeches on an up note, a tone that became especially eloquent when Milk talked to gay audiences. He talked about the time when the only homosexuals he heard of were drag queens and child molesters; it was time to change that. "A gay official is needed not only for our protection, but to set an example for younger gays that says the system works," Harvey implored. "We've got to give them hope."

At meetings with fewer gays, Milk would change the words to black, Chicano, or whatever group he was wooing, but as the campaign progressed, he increasingly ended every speech with this call for hope. Frank Robinson soon refined it into a polished appeal that sounded as if it came straight from the orations of Hubert Humphrey. Harvey's friends began calling the pitch Harvey's "hope speech."

A quick study, Agnos thought—maybe too quick. Agnos couldn't help but be impressed, and two or three weeks before election day he was also getting worried. He called Leo McCarthy. He was sure he was trailing Milk, he told the speaker. He didn't know how much, but he was scared. Leo laughed off the fears. Just campaign jitters, he told Agnos. But Art remembered the color-coded map Harvey was so proud of and took a poll. The results showed 25 percent for Milk, 16 percent for Agnos and the rest undecided. Leo didn't laugh at Art's fears any more; he was about to lose an assembly seat. McCarthy started pulling every string he could to get money for Agnos' campaign. Just about every politician and industry in the state had to deal with the California Assembly in some way, so astonishing sums poured in from special interest committees all across California. The Friends of Leo McCarthy, the speaker's own reserve fund, donated $11,000. A nebulous "Association for Better Citizenship" gave $4,000. Campaign committees from two neighboring assemblymen chipped in another $4,500. In the last two weeks of the campaign alone, Agnos collected an amazing $22,580—about the same amount Milk spent on his entire campaign.

Agnos focused on the weak points in Milk's campaign. The district was one of the most liberal in the state, but to belie fears that his homosexuality might brand him a crazy radical, Harvey had made his business experience a major campaign theme. He would cast a cold businessman's eye on the state budget, cut fat and red tape. The only two public officials to openly endorse Harvey, meanwhile, were moderate State Senator Milton Marks, the only Republican legislator from the city, and Supervisor Quentin Kopp, the board's most conservative member who endorsed Harvey because he was planning to take on Moscone for mayor in the 1979 elections. Putting it all together, Milk was running as the more conservative candidate. Agnos was also surprised to find Harvey had downplayed campaigning in the district's heavily black and Latino areas, assuming they would be too homophobic to support him. That left Agnos virgin territory.

Agnos dug into Milk's weaknesses, using the expertise he had learned in the speaker's office: direct mail campaigning. Every other day for the rest of the campaign, a new district-wide mailer hit the post office accenting Agnos' work in liberal social programs, especially to the city's minorities. One brochure juxtaposed a year-by-year rundown of Agnos and Milk's past activities. Art's side was graced with the many bills he had drafted as a legislative aide. On Milk's side there were few accomplishments of any note; those that did merit attention were often pointedly preceded with the blunt phrase "first up-front gay." The barrage of mailers was unprecedented in city politicking.

As Harvey felt the momentum slip from his campaign, his fights with Scott grew more frequent and bitter. "You fucked it up," he would shout at Scott when his lover made the slightest error. "You've ruined everything." From there, Milk would launch into one of his tantrums, while Smith, whose Mississippi background bred a less abrasive demeanor, sat quietly absorbing the abuse, knowing he was the only person Harvey could shout at so vehemently and still count on loving the next morning.

That, however, was when Scott became sure the passion had ebbed from their relationship. Maybe it had been happening for years and they hadn't noticed it between the campaigns and the extracurricular flings, but it was gone now. Outside the Castro Camera window, scores of handsome young men strode by casually every day, all day, and twenty-eight-year-old Scott was always trapped inside, constantly stuck in a store that barely showed a profit, constantly campaigning for a forty-six-year-old lover who grew more harried with each race, and the races never ended. Scott had fallen in love with a man who excelled in gourmet dinners, slept under Redwoods, rarely missed a Broadway opening, fell into trances during Mahler operas, and never let a circus go by. Now it was all politics. Scott agreed with the politics, and had devoted three years of his life to helping Harvey, but Harvey still wasn't the carefree, footloose hippie he had fallen in love with at a subway stop in Greenwich Village in 1971. Somewhere during the campaign, Scott stopped sleeping with Harvey and moved into his own bedroom.

One night, Michael Wong went upstairs to Harvey and Scott's apartment to fix a can of soup, the only dinner he could fit in between his nine-to-five job and the six hours he spent every night at the headquarters. He found Scott slumped in a chair, exhausted from the long hours of campaigning and simultaneously running the business. Wong saw pictures of Harvey in what looked like theatrical costumes. It surprised Mike. Like most of Milk's friends, Wong had no idea Harvey had had anything to do with Broadway. Harvey always seemed too tied up in the present to discuss the past.

"Did Harvey use to be in plays or something?" he casually asked Scott as he made his soup.

Scott was nodding out at the kitchen table and didn't answer.

"So, Scott, do you and Harvey intend to move to Sacramento?" Smith shook his head no.

"Can I ask you a personal question, Scott?"

"Sure."

"Do you think you and Harvey are going to last?"

Scott quietly answered in one word. "No."

Scott excused himself and went off to bed. Wong looked around the apartment, which reflected the dishevelment of Harvey's personal life. Piles of studies, commission reports, and unopened bills covered the tables. Boxes filled the corners. He paused to think how Harvey's friends knew so little of the man's personal life; it was as if he didn't allow himself a personal life.

The store suffered again through the campaign. Every extra cent went to putting out the next leaflet or buying the next roll of stamps. Poverty was nothing new to Milk. "I just eat a lot of eggs," Milk lectured Tom Randol. "When you can't eat the best, eat eggs." It was only late in the campaign that a Pacific Heights matron confided to John Ryckman why Harvey's suits always looked so threadbare. He bought them from a charity secondhand store she ran; he hadn't paid more than $10 for a suit in years. "And the guy never complained once," Ryckman said later, shaking his head. "It was always the campaign, beating the machine."

The news of the death of Harvey's father could not have come at a worse time, just when the campaign came into the home stretch. Milk had always been closer to his mother, but the death forced him to return home and see the brother from whom he had been estranged so many years. The fact that Harvey could convert senior citizens on bus stops but never his own brother frustrated him. Both were too bullheaded to change. There was the preliminary argument about cremation.

"You burned my mother, you're not going to have my father," Robert told Harvey, according to Harvey's later account to friends.

Tory Hartmann later recalled the sadness in Harvey's eyes when he returned from the funeral with the story about the good relationship he had struck up with his nephew. The way Harvey told it, he overheard his nephew say to Robert, "Uncle Harvey's a real open-minded guy. Why can't you be more like him?"

"You better be glad I'm not anything like him."

The first serious death threat came in a twelve-page letter signed by a man claiming to be from the Black Muslim Temple 26. "Harvey Milk will have a dream journey and nightmare to hell, a night of horror," it warned in childlike handwriting. "You will be stabbed and have your genitals, cock, balls, prick cut off."

In later years, Milk grew callous to the many threats, but this first graphic letter frightened him. Bomb threats soon after forced him to hold staff meetings far in the back of the store. The "dark destiny" was no longer a figment of a melodramatic imagination.

"You know I will probably be killed one of these days," he mentioned to Tory Hartmann one evening. Hartmann was startled by Harvey's casual tone. He acted as if that were as integral a part of his campaigning as, say, getting the firefighters' endorsement. All part of the same game.

The final days of the campaign were among the most desperate and discouraging Milk would ever face. A month before election day, his poll showed he was eleven points ahead of Agnos, but the lead was shrinking with every Agnos borchure that hit the mailboxes. The newspapers that had goaded Harvey into running turned their backs on him. The *Examiner* and the *Chronicle* certainly could not endorse a Moscone-Burton-McCarthy candidate like Agnos and, of course, they deplored the machine politics, but they were not about to endorse Harvey Milk either. The *Bay Guardian,* an alternative newspaper, had penned the "Harvey Milk vs. The Machine" slogan and then endorsed Agnos. Only the conservative *Progress* endorsed Milk. One major politician says the editor did it only to jab at Moscone, leaking news of the endorsement to politicos saying, "Yeah, we endorsed the fag." Liberals who claimed to support gays kept insisting they might like Harvey but Agnos could get more *done* in Sacramento. In it all, Harvey saw prejudice. Of course, they thought a queer couldn't get things done in Sacramento; it wasn't time yet for homosexuals to hold office. As far as they were concerned, it never would be time either, Harvey thought.

The cruelest blow came with an unexpected district-wide blitz of mailers featuring the endorsement of California Governor Jerry Brown. In February, Brown had promised a Democratic con-fab he would not endorse any candidate in any California primary, relieving party activists of all hues, since Brown was then riding on the apex of his California popularity in his first presidential bid and could swing thousands of voters. Brown had stuck to his pledge in every race—except one. Leo McCarthy happened to be his national campaign chairman and the man who could devastate Brown's legislative program in Sacramento. On the last weekend, a postcard from Brown arrived at the mailbox of every Democrat in the district. The sting dug deeper at a Brown for President campaign rally in Union Square, where Milk supporters—many of whom also worked for Brown—had buoyed Milk posters above the crowd with helium balloons. Assemblyman Willie Brown took the podium to say the governor would not even set foot on the stage if Milk's signs were not removed.

Harvey's friends thought such tactics stunk of the lowest machine politics, and they were ready to respond in kind. An intimate advisor came to Castro Camera one day with a tape recording of a male prostitute propositioning a major elected official who was part of the complex game of political musical chairs that had been played to clear the assembly seat for Agnos. The politician enthusiastically accepted the hustler's wares, even though he had only been a recent and lukewarm supporter of gay rights. The tape could embarrass the entire machine and perhaps give Milk the edge, Harvey's friend suggested. Others counseled Milk to start dropping comments about George Moscone's reputation as a notorious womanizer with exotic sexual tastes. Milk, however, refused to use such tactics.

Late in the campaign, Allan Baird brought Tom Hayden by Castro Camera to help Hayden's challenge to incumbent Democratic U.S.

Senator John Tunney. Milk eagerly took Hayden in and out of shops
on Castro Street to help the once-famed radical glad-hand merchants.
A bevvy of television cameras soon arrived on the scene to record the
two mavericks campaigning together. Baird thought it would be good
P.R. for Harvey if Hayden wore a Milk button while he bandied reporters' questions. "I don't wear buttons," Hayden snapped. When the
cameras were gone, so was Hayden. Baird thought Harvey had been
used.

Milk tenaciously pushed on until the end. He held his first expensive campaign fund raiser, a $45-a-plate dinner—but ended it nontradi-
tionally when he had to ask the twenty-three attendees to follow him
back to Castro Camera after the meal to help him stuff envelopes. Jim
Rivaldo loaned Milk his life savings. During the 1975 campaign he had
washed dishes to pay his rent while working for Harvey; now he had
to nickle and dime his expenses from the Castro Camera till. I graduated from Harvard for this? he asked himself. John Ryckman nudged his
lover into loaning $2,000 to Harvey's campaign for last-minute radio
commercials. Harvey begged his brother for an eleventh-hour loan, but
Robert Milk would have none of it.

Stunned, their mouths hanging half open, Leo McCarthy and Art
Agnos sat in the basement of City Hall where the election results were
first announced. The early returns showed Milk leading Agnos. Un-
thinkable.

At Dennis Peron's Island restaurant, the marijuana trading upstairs was closed down for the night and the victory party's crowd
swelled as the first optimistic results poured in. "Harvey, it looks like
you're winning," Peron said, trying to shake the shocked expression
from Milk's face. "I know," Milk admitted. "It's just that I'm not used
to it."

The assessment proved premature. As the tallies came in from the
outlying black and Latino neighborhoods, Agnos gained ground. The
race remained nip and tuck for hours, but substantial leads in the
Castro could not overcome Agnos' minority strength. Harvey looked
down at his suit and shook his head. "I guess I'll have to be in this
monkey suit for the next one and a half years—until the next election,"
he told Peron.

It was late in the night when Harvey took the podium to concede
defeat. "We gave them a good fight. We showed them that they can't

take us for granted, that we're always going to have some say." Harvey's voice was cracking. "Maybe not this time, but remember that every election we get closer. And what's important is that we keep on working, getting people to vote, getting out there in campaigns. Because if we do that, if we can keep on doing that, there's no way they can stop us and what we stand for."

The final tally didn't come in until 1:30 A.M. Harvey had lost by 3,600 of the 33,000 votes cast. "I guess you could call me a gay Harold Stassen," he joked to a reporter.

John Ryckman was back in the headquarters cleaning out his desk the next morning. He hadn't broken down all night. This is what I do for my job, he kept telling himself, I'm not going to cry. The camera shop door slammed and a small, blond eleven-year-old figure trod slowly to his desk. Medora tried to say something, but it didn't come out and she threw herself into his arms, sobbing. And John Ryckman had to cry too.

Hard bitter days followed for Harvey. He took his first vacation in three years to visit an old Dallas boyfriend who lived in Nevada City. Within weeks of his return, the bickering began again with Scott and by August, Scott had moved out. The couple began the difficult process of finding out where their sex ended and their love began, and how to continue to be both former lovers and business partners.

The entrenched gay leaders were jubilant at Milk's loss. "When votes start changing against a candidate, it usually signals the beginning of the end of that candidate's political career," wrote gay publisher Charles Morris, who planned a political career of his own. "Two defeats for the price of one," another gay reporter called Milk's loss of both the election and his commissioner's seat.

The Democratic establishment drew the gay moderates deeper into the fold after the defeat. Clearly, the gay reformers, not Harvey Milk or those newcomers on Castro Street, were the people to deal with. Since the politicos did not take homosexuals seriously enough to examine closely the precinct maps, they did not note that despite the united opposition of the entire gay leadership, Harvey Milk had carried the gay precincts by margins of 60 to 70 percent. The gay leaders had not delivered. Events about to unfold a continent away in Dade County would tremendously recast the shape and tenor of San Francisco gay politicking, but for the rest of 1976, the gay reformers were happily writing Harvey Milk's political obituary.

Some political observers were far less eager to write Milk off and were genuinely shocked that the unorthodox maverick had come so close to beating the quintessential insider. The winner had every conceivable advantage—certainly more than any other nonincumbent primary challenger in the state that year—and still he had only narrowly defeated a camera store owner. Some news stories focused less on Agnos' victory than on the fact that Milk had come so close to winning. Before long, Milk's spirits returned. He confided to Wong, "Mike, if losing like this means all the publicity I'm getting, I think Agnos wishes he had lost."

The Alice B. Toklas Democratic Club would never support Harvey for anything, a number of Milk's supporters agreed in a post mortem meeting shortly after the election. They even doubted that the club would ever support a gay candidate as along as there was an adequate supply of liberal friends willing to attend their cocktail parties, make annual appearances at Toklas dinners and assure members that there were heterosexuals who thought some gays were just fine after all. Harvey needed a Democratic club to support him. The younger, more militant gays from Castro Street also needed an apparatus to rigorously press demands for the gay community, even if it did make "our liberal friends" nervous. Harvey, Jim Rivaldo, Dick Pabich, and Harry Britt were among the early members; Chris Perry was elected presdient. The San Francisco Gay Democratic Club set forth a basic manifesto:

> No decisions which affect our lives should be made without the gay voice being heard. We want our fair share of city services. We want openly gay people appointed and elected to city offices—people who reflect the diversity of our community. We want the schools of San Francisco to provide full exposure to and positive appreciation of gay lifestyles. We are asking no more than we deserve: We will not settle for less.

"What am I doin' here with a bunch of fruits and kooks?"
Jim Elliot looked at the unlikely group sitting around him in the cluttered back room of Castro Camera. There were solid union men like himself, good men like Stan Smith and George Evankovich. And then the kooks: the environmentalists and neighborhood activists who kept trying to put union men out of jobs with their rhetoric about limited growth and high-rise controls. If that weren't enough to worry the

be'jesus out of him, there's all these fruits with Harvey Milk; at least *he* seemed like a regular guy. Still, he couldn't help wondering aloud, "What am I doin' here with a bunch of fruits and kooks?"

Feelings were mutual on all sides and Harvey could probably have never pulled off this meeting except all present had one interest in common—they hated, positively loathed, the current board of supervisors. Labor was still licking its wounds from the wave of anti-union ballot propositions that the board kept putting before voters and voters kept approving. The radical neighborhood activists still thought downtown interests and real estate developers owned the board. Under the current system, gays worried that they'd never be able to get their admission ticket to the democratic process—their own elected official.

Harvey was the only neighborhood activist, however, who had built ties to labor and now he was pushing both sides to join and kick the bums out. Plans for district elections of supervisors, led by a motley assortment of leftover sixties radicals, had failed in both 1972 and 1973, largely because proponents considered fund raising a pass-the-coffee-can affair and never garnered the funds to assert a strong campaign. Labor, however, had money. Plenty of it. The massive gay immigration since 1973 had also vastly increased the pool of available votes.

Both sides felt each other out cautiously at the meeting. Even Jim Elliot had to admit that without Harvey Milk they probably would never be in the same room. In a few weeks, larger meetings with more labor leaders and neighborhood organizers had struck a deal. As Evankovich put it bluntly, "We were out for revenge on the board." Between labor money and the neighborhood organizations' ability to get legions of volunteers and mount a grass-roots effort, they easily qualified the proposal for the November 1976 ballot.

The novel alliance between neighborhoods, gays, and unions created no small fuss in political circles. Jim Elliot picked up his newspaper one afternoon to read the one quote that summarized the improbable coalition, his quip about "fruits and kooks." He felt like shit. Sure they were fruits, but he'd gotten to know some of them at Castro Camera and they were nice guys, he thought. That night, he screwed up his courage, knowing what he had to do.

Gays were throwing a fund raiser for district elections at a gay bar on Castro Street. Elliot figured he'd probably get punched out if he showed up, or at least yelled at, but he had to go there and let the guys know he really didn't mean it to sound the way it came out in the papers. He'd never walked into a gay bar in his life. Timidly, the machinist slid in the door and saw a drag queen leading a raucous auction. He ran into some of the gay men he had met earlier; they just patted him on the back and bought him a drink as if nothing had happened. In a gesture of conciliation, he bid on a cake.

"I'll bid four dollars on it," shouted Elliot, then, spotting the plain-speaking man from Texas he'd gotten to know at Castro Camera, he added, "And I want the cake to go to Harry Britt."

"Four dollars, sold."

"By the way," Elliot asked as he moved up to give the money. "What kinda cake is that?"

The auctioneer wrinkled his nose. "Why, a fruitcake, of course."

The crowd roared and Jim Elliot, the guy who fixed tractors and lawn mowers at Golden Gate Park, knew everything was all right.

George Moscone campaigned vigorously around the city for the district elections. Though the old-line leftists who had long pushed for district elections had little use for gays, Harvey and a nearly united front of gay activists organized efforts to get gay precincts behind the new plan.

On election day, San Francisco voters threw the bums out. District elections passed, forcing the entire board to run in the new districts in November 1977. The city split along east-west, liberal-conservative lines and, once again, without the massive tallies from the voter-rich Castro, the coup might not have succeeded.

"I think I'm going to run Medora Payne," John Ryckman teased Harvey soon after. "She can be the first openly child supervisor."

"Better not," Harvey shot back. "She'd probably end up beating me."

Harvey had a new color-coded map to show anyone who dropped by Castro Camera. The results of the 1976 assembly race were shaded into each precinct and Jim Rivaldo had drawn a thick black line around the perimeters of the new District 5, the district around Castro Street. "The map says it all," Harvey offered cheerfully. It did. Milk had carried most of District 5's 16 A.D. precincts handily, with margins approaching 70 percent in many precincts. "You tell me who is going to win in this district," Harvey said confidently.

The ward politician finally had his ward.

ten

Orange Tuesday

Each student had neatly chalked his name below the office they sought. There was only one problem, and the fifth grade teacher strode purposefully to the blackboard to take care of it. Grabbing the eraser, she quickly wiped away the offending name of little Johnny Briggs. He was the son of Jessie Rae Briggs, that Okie waitress at Whitey's truck stop outside town, the one whose husband had run off to be a Pentacostal minister. Just more white trash from the Dust Bowl, come here in their mattress-covered station wagons like they owned Orange County. No, Johnny Briggs can't run for class vice-president; his mom's divorced.

As a California assemblyman and later a state senator, John Vern Briggs frequently told the story of this first attempt for public office in the early 1940s. The memory never seemed far from his political libido. Even after his impressive track record as a staunch defender of the Orange County conservative faith, John Briggs was always the outsider, taken seriously by neither his Democrat nor Republican colleagues, having the allegiance of only his constituents, who had faithfully elected him to five terms in the assembly and now his first term in the senate. He kept his message to them simple. The way

153

Republicans could win was to hammer away at the Democrats as the party of the three G's—gays, grass, and Godlessness.

Finally, on this sultry June day in 1977, John Briggs had found understanding peers in the bustling North Miami office of Save Our Children (From Homosexuality), Inc. The busy housewives shook their back-combed, frosted hairdos in shock as he regaled them with stories of the "San Francisco influence" in California politics. "The land of fruits and nuts," chirped one volunteer. The election on the repeal of the Dade County gay rights law—or the "sin and immorality law," as it was branded by opponents—would be the next day and pundits predicted a close race. California State Senator John Briggs knew better, however, and saw the election less as a contest over one law than the unleashing of a new potent force in American politics. He knew he was at the starting gate.

The first warm night of summer, Tuesday, June 21. It was 8 P.M. and husky thirty-one-year-old Robert Hillsborough was getting ready for his date with Jerry Taylor. An affable, soft-spoken man, known as Mr. Greenjeans to the children at the playground where he worked as a city gardener, Hillsborough wanted only two things when he moved to California from Oregon: to live and work in San Francisco, and to be in love, settling down with another man into a quiet domestic life.

If Robert Hillsborough had any political ideas he kept them to himself. Like so many gays, he had registered to vote at Harvey Milk's camera store, but now that he had a job, most of his thoughts were on getting a boyfriend. Hillsborough's determination for an old-fashioned marriage had somewhat intimidated Jerry Taylor, who had moved out of Robert's apartment only two weeks earlier. Tonight was their first date since Jerry had moved out. Robert gave himself one last going over in the mirror, brushed his hair, stroked his beard, decided he looked his macho best, and went to pick up Jerry.

At about the same time, San Francisco Sheriff's Deputy Al Asmussen was kissing his mother good-bye in the comfortable suburban home they had shared since Al's dad died. He had already quietly slipped into the garage and put his blue jeans, plaid shirt, and construction boots in the trunk, as he had so many other Tuesday nights. Now it was off to his weekly Young Republican meeting in San Francisco. No, he didn't want his mom to stay up late and wait. As usual, he would be out late drinking with his YR buddies.

A warm Tuesday night in San Francisco. Robert Hillsborough and

Al Asmussen shared a tenuous connection with the Castro: Hillsborough had moved to the neighboring Mission neighborhood five blocks east of Castro Street and freely took part in the Castro's social life; Asmussen was born and raised in the Castro, part of the stolid ethnic community that had long churned out lawmen for the police and sheriff's departments. Other than that, they shared little, except that both were dynamic young men and that before the night was over, both would be dead.

The year of the gay. That was the way 1977 was supposed to turn out. The year started on an upbeat when the Dade County Commission voted 5–3 in January to enact a broad gay civil rights ordinance banning discrimination against gays in employment, housing, and public accommodations. The ordinance marked the first time any southern city had passed a gay rights law. Now some forty cities had guaranteed rights for homosexuals, including such major metropolitan areas as St. Paul, Detroit, Minneapolis, and Seattle. Of course, a few Bible thumpers were on hand to talk about immorality and Revelations' warnings of the Final Days, but their presence was predictable and most activists expected them to go back to their tents once the voting was over.

Momentum for gay rights picked up. By late spring, gay-related bills had surfaced in twenty-eight state legislatures. Wyoming decriminalized gay sexual acts in late February, making it the nineteenth state to legalize sex between consenting adults. Five other legislatures were considering similar reforms. Lawmakers in eleven state houses had introduced statewide gay rights bills; gay activists were privately placing bets on which state would be the first to enact a rights law—a long-awaited breakthrough for the gay movement—while national gay leaders picked up even more sponsors on the national gay bill.

The homosexual cause got a further boost in early 1977 when a dozen gay leaders met at the White House with presidential aide Midge Costanza, the first time a gay delegation was ever officially received at the executive mansion. The meeting produced more style than substance, and gay insiders whispered privately that the invitation came only because a nationally prominent gay leader was having an affair with a White House staffer. To a movement seeking a place on the agenda of the nation's social issues, however, the White House meeting marked a significant event all the same. The year, it seemed, surely would show that the gay movement had reached the juggernaut status; nothing could stop this idea whose time had come.

"Homosexuals cannot reproduce so they must recruit."

Gay activists snickered over the assertion made by Anita Bryant the day she announced she would lead a campaign against the Dade County gay rights ordinance. Bryant's background as a former Miss America runner-up, a mediocre pop singer, and an orange juice promoter hardly gave her credentials as an authority on homosexuality, they thought. Unfortunately, gay activists had little knowledge about how the media works. Bryant was pretty; she had a penchant for making outrageous comments; if baited too far, she did marvelously telegenic things like break into the chorus of "Battle Hymn of the Republic." That was all she needed. As far as the media and her backers were concerned, she was an authority on homosexuality. She became a national media star and her statements were equally balanced, as journalistic ethics demand, against those of psychologists and sociologists who had long ago decried the "recruiting" theories. The fight was on—on a battleground few expected, to be sure, but five weeks after the Dade County ordinance passed, Bryant's Save Our Children group collected 65,000 signatures on petitions calling for the law's repeal, more than six times what she needed to put the measure on the June ballot.

Like feudal barons, the two wealthiest gay leaders, David Goodstein of the *Advocate* and Jack Campbell, an owner of the nation's largest gay bathhouse chain, divided the turf for the gay rights battle, said gay leaders in both San Francisco and Miami. Both would put their considerable resources behind the gay effort if each got to name one of the two co-equal leaders to head the fight. Campbell wanted the prestige of a victory to bolster his own political ambitions in Miami. Goodstein wanted to use his role in the victory to build a rival to the National Gay Task Force, with which he had long been feuding. Goodstein sent Jim Foster to Dade County to oversee his end of the deal. Foster's strategy reflected the tactics gay moderates had long used in San Francisco, currying favor with liberal friends, raising a substantial campaign chest, and garnering a wide range of labor and political endorsements. They worked furiously to discourage volunteers—hundreds from San Francisco alone were itching to come to be new "Freedom Riders"—fearing the street-level, Harvey Milk-style campaign which they had opposed so often in San Francisco. Instead of grass-roots volunteers, they brought liberal politicians, like Sheriff Hongisto and Assemblyman Willie Brown, to campaign. That San Francisco's gay moderates worked so hard for Dade County's gay rights law was no small irony.

In all their years in San Francisco, they had never pushed the board of supervisors to enact a measure nearly as sweeping; they were fighting in Miami for something they had never even tried to get in San Francisco. And ironically, some of the Miami gay activists who had gotten the law enacted in the first place felt they had been frozen out by the moneyed gay interests.

The gay moderates' strategy backfired disastrously. The appearance of Foster, Hongisto, and Willie Brown had anti-gay rights campaigners complaining about carpetbaggers. The cultivating of liberal leaders, at the expense of grass-roots work, did not filter down to the alleged followers. On June 7—Orange Tuesday, as it was later called—Dade County voters repealed their gay rights law by a better than two-to-one margin.

"Tonight, the laws of God and the cultural values of man have been vindicated," Anita Bryant said in even tones at her victory press conference. "The people of Dade County—the normal majority—have said, 'Enough, enough, enough.' "

In the back of the press conference, State Senator John Briggs, who had just flown in the day before, was overjoyed. "We won, we won." He candidly recounted the statistics that made the win so personally intriguing. He was a candidate for the Republican gubernatorial nomination, he explained, noting that in the last governor's race only half the voters had bothered to go to the polls to elect Jerry Brown. "And today you got half the voters of Dade County at the polls just to vote for this," he said. The arithmetic was downright stirring.

"I knew we were going to win the minute this old lady came to me and told me she voted for repeal." Briggs relished the chance to affect a vaudevillian Jewish accent. "She said, 'I voted vor repeal becuss I haf grandchildren.' " The parody was nothing less than an inspiration to the state senator. A lot of the people voting in the Republican gubernatorial race have children and grandchildren too, he added. California didn't have a gay rights law to repeal on a statewide level, so when he got back to Sacramento, Briggs said he would get right to the heart of the matter: He would introduce a measure in the state senate to ban homosexuals from teaching in public schools. If that law didn't make it out of the legislature, he would simply take the issue directly to the people with a statewide ballot initiative.

Briggs later learned that the reporter to whom he had so excitedly poured this all out was a homosexual. But that did not dampen the relationship. In fact, it seemed highly doubtful from the start that John

Briggs ever really had anything personal against gays. He was just running for governor. "It's politics," he confided to the reporter later, "just politics."

Love rekindled on a warm San Francisco night. It was just like starting over for Robert Hillsborough and Jerry Taylor. They had spent a hot night at the disco; Jerry remembered the reasons he had moved in with Bob in the first place. They decided to spend the night together at Robert's place and stopped at the Whizburger stand in the Mission to pick up some cheeseburgers and fries on the way back.

The usual number of Latino teenagers sauntered around the parking lot. Gays had been slowly filtering into the neighborhood, just east of Castro Street, so the sight of two young white men together in a pickup brought the usual comments about faggots and fruits. Once safely ensconced in Robert's car, Jerry Taylor shouted "fuck off" as they pulled from the lot. A few of the kids pounded on the hood, shouting more epithets, but the couple made their escape and headed toward Hillsborough's apartment. Neither saw the car that quietly followed them.

Dressed nattily in slacks, blazer, and tie, Al Asmussen was his old self when he made one of his irregular appearances at the monthly meeting of the San Francisco Young Republicans. Few men seemed as married to their jobs as this thirty-four-year-old deputy. He rarely was without his handcuffs, gun, and tales of excitement. None of his friends imagined that his job entailed nothing more glamorous than "till tapping," standing by a business' cash register to make sure sometimes-reluctant merchants followed court-ordered liens of funds; Al instead dropped hints that he was embroiled in vague investigations with shady implications. Since Sheriff Hongisto's trip to Dade County, more controversy had come down on the department. The right-wing San Francisco Deputy Sheriffs Association, always looking for a reason to snipe at the liberal Hongisto, voted its support of Anita Bryant. Asmussen, the YR chapter's former president, regaled his Young Republican cohorts that night with warnings about his boss's radical beliefs. At one point in the conversation, he even pulled out his Smith & Wesson to show his friends, passing it around the room.

At about the same time Hillsborough and Taylor were pulling out of the Whizburgers parking lot, the YR meeting broke up. As usual, Asmussen turned down the invitation to go drinking with some of the guys, saying he had to go home and give some medication to his mother. He left and, somewhere, slipped into his tight blue jeans and plaid shirt. He cruised over to gay bars in the South of Market area.

"We are your children. We are your children."
Their chants echoed through the streets of the Castro neighborhood as news of Bryant's stunning victory galvanized San Francisco gays. In Miami, homosexuals were disconsolately singing "We Shall Overcome" in a grand hotel's ballroom; in San Francisco, they were taking to the streets. A crowd of 200 grew to 500, then 1,000 and then 3,000 on Castro Street, shouting, "We are your children," and "Two, four, six, eight, separate the church and state."

Over the next two years, such shouting mobs would become a common occurrence in the city, but police were dumbfounded at the first spontaneous eruption of long-buried anger. They feared a riot and called on the one person who they knew had credibility with the militant crowd, Harvey Milk. "Keep 'em moving," Harvey shouted, "We've got to keep 'em moving." Harvey led the throng through the Castro. They stopped briefly to chant their hostile mantras on the steps of the Most Holy Redeemer Church before moving out of the Castro, down Market Street, past the grand City Hall, and up the steep streets of Nob Hill. For three hours, Harvey led the crowd over a five-mile course, worried that any pause might see that first rock hurled through a window or at a cop and then, the inevitable. Finally at midnight, the tired demonstrators assembled at Union Square for a rally. Harvey took up his bullhorn. "This is the power of the gay community," he exhorted. "Anita's going to create a national gay force."

A startled prostitute, working a nearby corner, shook her head in shock. "All those guys are faggots?" she asked a reporter. "This is crazy. All these men are taking my business away!"

After the rally, the crowd made a silent march back to Castro Street, where a thousand of the still-angry protestors decided to simply sit down in the middle of Market and Castro, blocking one of the city's busiest intersections. The police wanted to move in with a show of force, but, talking over a police loudspeaker, Milk cleared the street with the promise of still another demonstration the next night. Even Harvey's most adamant detractors conceded that only his presence had averted a riot that night. The photo of Milk with the bullhorn made the front page.

The next night, five thousand marched in Greenwich Village, four hundred in Denver, and another crowd surged from Castro Street past City Hall and through the city's wealthy neighborhoods. Thousands more took to the streets on Thursday and Friday nights, shocked and angry, as if for the first time they realized that somebody out there really didn't like them. It had been easy to forget that most of them had not been attracted to Castro Street, they had been driven there; the forces that had driven them to seek sanctuary were finally getting organized. On Friday night, after a City Hall rally, one thousand sat stubbornly at Castro and Market, unable to think of any other way to vent their growing rage. And three thousand marched again on Saturday night. The next morning, as Catholic worshipers went to St. Mary's Cathedral, they faced five hundred silent demonstrators lining the long wide plaza to the church entrance, standing in vigil to protest the Dade County archbishop's support of Anita Bryant's campaign.

A day later Assemblyman Art Agnos shelved his gay civil rights bill pending in the California legislature. The support, he said, had evaporated with Bryant's unexpectedly overwhelming triumph. The next day, a politician of whom few Californians outside Orange County had ever heard, State Senator John Briggs, stood on the wide granite steps of San Francisco City Hall to announce his campaign to remove all gay school teachers from California classrooms. According to some reports, his staff had taken the precaution of calling gay groups so they knew that Senator Briggs would appear. The confrontation between the pugnacious senator and the angry gay demonstrators ensured lead-story coverage around the state, as Briggs insisted San Francisco should be granted "captured nation status" because of the gay influx there.

The gay movement experienced an explosion unprecedented since the first days of gay liberation fronts following the Stonewall riots. Gays who had come to San Francisco just to disco amid the hot pectorals of humpy men became politicized and fell into new organizations with names like Save Our Human Rights and Coalition for Human Rights. No longer was the gay movement the realm of offbeat liberation fairies —as David Goodstein had long called militant gay activists—but a necessary response to a clear and present danger. These young gays might have taken their locker-room beatings at home, because they knew they could always go to San Francisco one day, but once in San Francisco, there was no place else to turn. They wanted more than mild assurances of "tolerance," the word liberals most frequently used toward gays; they wanted more than social cachét and press coverage.

Ten days after Orange Tuesday, the leaders of the militant San

Francisco Gay Democratic Club moved to take decisive action. Vice President Walter Mondale came to Golden Gate Park to address a local Democratic fund raiser on the subject of human rights. Surrounded by pickets, Milk lectured the Democrats entering the event with his trusty bullhorn from a flatbed truck. Dozens of S.F. Gay members, meanwhile, filtered inside the crowd for what was planned to be a silent protest. When Mondale started discussing the finer points of human rights policy in Latin America, dozens of demonstrators silently held up signs asking for a statement on human rights in the United States. A man with little use for such trivial causes as homosexuals, Vice President Mondale clearly was miffed at the sight of gays at *his* rally, and he turned awkwardly to get support from the Democratic leaders who shared the stage.

"When are you going to speak out on gay rights?" a demonstrator shouted.

With that, a furious Mondale spun on his heel and walked off the stage and out of the rally. The state Democratic chairman turned red when he went to the podium. "Are you glad you disturbed the meeting?" he shouted. "Well, you're not going to win your fight."

The Democratic leaders turned to Jim Foster. Why couldn't he keep his troops under control? Foster knew this new generation of gays were not *his* troops; he didn't even try to exert control. Harvey was particularly ecstatic at Foster's humiliation. "You should've seen the bastard squirm," he told Michael Wong. "You would've loved it. Those stupid elected officials were so embarrassed that these usually docile queens were now loud and demanding. I loved it. Maybe now, they'll realize that Foster and the whole group are frauds. They got what they deserved."

The liberal establishment was aghast. What happened to all the polite homosexuals these politicians had seen every election year at courteous candidates' nights and chic cocktail parties? "Their conduct is not only unacceptable in that it violates the right of all to be heard," George Moscone announced, "but it is also deeply counterproductive." Counterproductive proved the key word. The Mondale demonstration, the endless marches, and all the new angry rhetoric; toleration is one thing, liberals warned, but all this could lead to a backlash. They had no paucity of evidence to buttress their contention that a backlash could indeed fall on San Francisco.

Random beatings of gays increased sharply in the Castro after Bryant's win. Not robberies or muggings, just violent attacks. Gays started carrying police whistles and organized street patrols. Harvey and Tom Randol heard a whistle one night and rushed to a beating. While Randol tended the victim, Harvey chased down the attacker.

"Don't beat me," the youth pleaded when Milk tackled him.

"No, I'm not going to beat you," Harvey taunted. "I'm going to take you down to Toad Hall and tell everybody what you tried to do and just let them take care of you."

Harvey dragged the punk to the victim who, as afraid of the police as he was of the attacker, said he wouldn't press charges. Milk reluctantly let the kid go, warning, "Tell all your friends we're down here waiting for them."

Conservatives had organized their own political backlash against the city's liberal direction in the form of successful petition drives to put two measures on a special election ballot in August. One measure simply repealed the hard-fought district elections scheme and would keep the election of supervisors on a citywide basis. Supervisor Dianne Feinstein soon emerged as this propostion's spokesperson. The second, more sweeping measure, not only repealed district elections but in effect recalled Mayor Moscone, District Attorney Joe Freitas, and Sheriff Richard Hongisto. Proponents of this initiative made no small issue of the close connections all three politicians had to the increasingly raucous gays while promoting the proposition in the conservative west side. Were these officials letting homosexuals take over San Francisco?

Liberals also warned that anyone who needed proof of a backlash need go no further than the heavily Irish Catholic working-class neighborhood two miles south of Castro Street, where a police officer-cum-firefighter was making waves as an unorthodox supervisorial candidate out to restore traditional values to San Francisco government. "I am not going to be forced out of San Francisco by splinter groups of radicals, social deviates and incorrigibles," the candidate wrote in his campaign literature. "You must realize there are thousands upon thousands of frustrated angry people such as yourselves waiting to unleash a fury that can and will eradicate the malignancies which blight our beautiful city."

The candidate's slogan: "Unite and Fight—For Dan White!"

"Faggot, faggot, faggot."

No sooner had Robert Hillsborough and Jerry Taylor climbed from their car on that warm night of June 21 than the four attackers were upon them. The slight, thin Taylor scrambled over an eight-foot fence and hid behind garbage cans, convinced the huskier Hillsborough could handle himself.

Then came the screams: "Faggot, faggot, faggot." A Latino youth, later identified as John Cordova, was kneeling over the prostrate body of Robert Hillsborough, stabbing him passionately, thrusting the fishing knife again and again into the gardener's chest, then into his face. Blood stained his hand, spurted into the streets and still he sank his blade into the fallen man; fifteen times he lashed out, sinking the steel into flesh, shouting "Faggot, faggot, faggot."

About two hours later, Police Sergeant George Kowalski answered a panicked phone call from the heavily gay Polk Street area. The caller was standing nervously by the pay phone on a street corner when Kowalski found him. He had picked up this guy at a South of Market bar, he told Kowalski, and they were starting to make out at his apartment, but he could swear he felt a gun under this guy's coat during the first hugs. Fearing his trick was one of the homophobes preying on gays, he had slipped from the apartment to call the police.

Kowalski and the caller cautiously approached the apartment where Al Asmussen sat. Asmussen became agitated and hyperactive when Kowalski asked to check his deputy identification. Kowalski assured Asmussen he would file no report; everything was over as far as he was concerned. But Asmussen still became visibly distraught and hurriedly left the apartment.

At about 3 A.M., a cab driver called police to tell of a car that was idling in the middle of a deserted city intersection, right off the freeway heading for the suburbs. The driver was slumped over the wheel, like he was drunk and passed out. That's how the police found Deputy Sheriff Al Asmussen, his Smith & Wesson near his right hand. A homicide inspector was briefly called off the Hillsborough murder to check into the case. He didn't need to do much sleuthing to see this was no homicide, and he went back to work on the Mission district killing. According to the coroner's report, Al Asmussen had died of "severe laceration to the brain due to a gunshot wound of the mouth."

The news of the Hillsborough murder leaped to the front pages. Mayor Moscone ordered the city's flags flown at half-mast and angrily blamed the killing on the anti-gay campaigns of Anita Bryant and John Briggs. From San Diego came a slight, seventy-eight-year-old widow, Bob Hillsborough's mother. "I didn't think much about Anita Bryant's campaign at first," said Helen Hillsborough. "Now that my son's murder has happened, I think about the Bryant campaign a lot. Anyone who wants to carry on this kind of thing must be sick. My son's blood is on her hands."

The weeks of spontaneous demonstrations had already made police fear a potential riot at the 1977 annual Gay Freedom Day Parade, scheduled for just five days after the murder, so they raced to solve the crime before the expected throngs took to the streets on Sunday. Though loud in their condemnations of the killing, the city's liberal politicians started backing away from the gay community. Last-minute problems arose with parade details, for example, problems only the mayor could resolve. Suddenly, however, parade officials found that Moscone simply refused to talk to them. Fearing that association with the gay parade might later prove a liability, many of the city's leading liberal politicians started phoning gay leaders to insist that last-minute obligations had arisen to prevent their attendance at the event.

The day before the parade, a relieved police spokesman made the announcement. They had arrested four youths—two Latinos, two whites—for the Hillsborough slaying. Two had pegged John Cordova, a nineteen-year-old car mechanic from a heavily Latino suburb, as the slayer.

Nearly 250,000 assembled the next day along the wide Market Street boulevard, more people than had come together in the city for nearly a decade. It would have been difficult for politicians like George Moscone or Joe Freitas to find a more receptive crowd, especially since they faced recall, but they and the many other liberal friends were nowhere to be seen as the quarter million solemnly marched toward the grand City Hall rotunda. Television stations had to rent helicopters to get a high enough vantage point to film the entire parade. Contingents came from as far away as Denver and Alaska. Vast crowds lined the streets. Hour after hour, the demonstrators poured into the Civic Center plaza. The largest group carried uniform placards: Save Our Human Rights. One row of picketers stretched the breadth of a street holding aloft large portraits of Adolf Hitler, Joseph Stalin, Idi Amin, a burning cross—and the smiling face of Anita Bryant.

As the thousands passed the wide stairs of the majestic City Hall, one marcher dropped a flower over the headline announcing Robert Hillsborough's murder. Several more followed, the flowers falling for a man few had ever heard of a week ago. A small mound grew and, by the end of the day, thousands upon thousands of blossoms rested silently at the golden-grilled doors of City Hall, all in remembrance of a mild-mannered gardener who had been falling in love all over again just a few days before, on the first warm night of the summer.

Harvey had long planned to announce his candidacy for the board during the week of festivities that surrounded Gay Freedom Day. The announcement was hardly necessary, since Milk had made no secret he would seek a slot on the board, whether through district or citywide elections. Coming the day after the Hillsborough murder hit the papers, his announcement was buried amid the deluge of other gay news. Harvey didn't need the extra publicity, however, since virtually every new story about the rapidly changing developments featured some quotable quip from the one gay leader who seemed to echo the sentiments of the young militant gays who, in a few short weeks, had burst to the forefront of the San Francisco gay community. Harvey and Frank Robinson honed the announcement speech just the same, since it would become the standard pitch for the rest of the campaign.

> I'll never forget what it was like coming out. . . . I'll never forget the looks on the faces of those who have lost hope, whether it be young gays, or seniors, or blacks looking for that almost-impossible-to-find job, or Latinos trying to explain their problems and aspirations in a tongue that's foreign to them.
>
> No it's not my election I want, it's yours. It will mean that a green light is lit that says to all who feel lost and disenfranchised that you can now go forward.
>
> It means hope and we—no—you and you and you and, yes, you, you've got to give them hope.

The hope speech was getting down to its final draft, though for Milk the idea had been a fundamental tenet of his personal philosophy since he had written Joe Campbell after the suicide attempt so many years ago, insisting life was always worth living because life always held hope.

Like most of the city's supervisorial hopefuls, Milk faced tactical problems because he would not know until after the August special elections whether he would be running citywide or in District 5. Moscone, Freitas, and Hongisto were also laying their political survival plans, which were introduced in a frank meeting with gay leaders. They would have to keep their distance from gays since their gay ties could cost them votes, their strategist told gays bluntly, but they still had to have gay votes to win, and they expected gays to rally around their liberal friends as they had before.

The duplicity angered Milk and he saw it as proof of his contention that in a pinch, liberals could be counted on to protect only themselves. "No longer should we allow any candidate, even our 'friends,' to evade the [gay] issue because it will hurt them with the voters," he publicly railed. "If none appear, then none should get our votes." Privately, however, Milk and the broad spectrum of other gay leaders had little room in which to maneuver. No acceptable alternatives stood on the horizon, especially if Moscone and Hongisto were thrown out of office. Moreover, the repeal of district elections would negate a cause for which every moderate and liberal interest group in the city had fought for years. David Goodstein broke ranks and supported repeal of district elections. Between the allies of all the city's major politicians, however, as well as the labor and neighborhood activists who had worked for district elections, the Democratic establishment built a mighty political effort for the August election.

"The last dying gasp of conservatives" was how one analyst sized up the returns on the night of the special election. The proposition to recall Moscone, Freitas, and Hongisto was beaten back by a 2–1 margin, with gay voters backing their allies by a massive 7–1 ratio. District elections won by a slimmer 58–42 percent margin, of which the 3–1 support from gay precincts was a key element. A jubilant Harvey Milk ran into his labor supporter Stan Smith and Smith's companion, Doris Silvistri, at a victory party. "We won, we won," he shouted. He brandished an empty petition and offered Smith and Silvistri his pen. "I want you to be the first ones to sign," he told them. In 1961, Jose had to scour the city for signers for his petition to run for supervisor; Harvey, of course, quickly qualified as a supervisorial candidate in District 5.

Though John Briggs began making regular pilgrimages to San Francisco to deliver pronouncements on this or that local vice and try to grab more media for his gubernatorial bid, his attempt to get an anti-gay teachers initiative on an early ballot fumbled on legal technicalities. The vote would be delayed until the 1978 elections. The torrid pace that had marked the weeks following Bryant's victory eased. Many gays were convinced that the gay cause—so close, they had thought, to being a juggernaut—had suffered a massive setback. Harvey Milk, for one, was gleeful at the turn of events, insisting gays should count their blessings. Gay groups had been holding press conferences for years and gained only a trickle of publicity, while it took an Anita Bryant to get the cause on the cover of *Newsweek.* "No matter which way the vote in Florida went, we won," he wrote in his column in the *Bay Area Reporter,* "The word homosexual has now appeared in every household in the country. More good and bad was probably written about it in the last few months than during the entire history of the world. Anita Bryant herself pushed the gay movement ahead and the subject can never be pushed back into darkness."

The conspiracy of silence was definitely broken. That, gay activists long complained, was what they had always fought; the silence that had haunted them since they were children and realized they were somehow different; the silence that said they were different in a way so evil as to be unspeakable.

A secret to kill and die for.

It didn't make sense, Al Asmussen's friends agreed. Acquaintances in his Young Republican club theorized that he may have been silenced so he would never reveal some secret he may have learned in an important investigation. One neighbor became so convinced San Francisco police were covering up a murder that she called the San Francisco FBI office to ask for a separate investigation. The suicide didn't make sense.

Asmussen's mother let the stories spread, even though Sheriff Hongisto had told her the details of Al's last night as delicately as he could. She would not open the screen door when a journalist came asking questions. "I don't know about *that* part of my son's life and I don't want to know," she shouted, angrily, as if the revelation of his homosexuality had added insult to the injury of her son's suicide. "My son is gone, dead and buried. No matter *what* he was, he was a fine and decent boy."

The district attorney's investigators had already been there, as had the police and public defender. Still, the chunky, late-fortyish contractor was surprised to see two reporters pull into his construction site. The man uncomfortably adjusted his beer gut over his belt as the reporters confronted him with what they already knew—that he had had a sexual relationship with John Cordova, the nineteen-year-old just convicted of stabbing Robert Hillsborough fifteen times in the face and chest.

"I got this call from this friend of mine who knew what I liked, said I should meet this kid," he explained. "He'd come over, drink a lot and say, 'I'm tired, let's go to sleep.' Then before long, he'd be on top of me or his legs would be in the air, but he never wanted to act like he knew what he was doin'."

The trysts occurred sporadically, he said. According to the contractor, Cordova would sometimes call and ask him to pick him up at an intersection four or five blocks from his home. The next morning, Cordova would always wake up as in a daze, insisting he had no idea what had happened the night before.

Then Cordova started degenerating. He'd show up at the man's front door, drunk, with his pants pulled down around his legs. Once he appeared naked, except for a coat, and the older man took him in, and in the morning, Cordova couldn't remember what had happened.

The judge at Cordova's trial denied a motion to introduce the information into the record, saying the subject matter was "too remote" from the case. Cordova was convicted of second-degree murder and sentenced to ten years in prison.

Two men dead in the late hours of June 21, 1977, one a victim in the year's most celebrated murder, the other an obscure suicide that rated only three paragraphs deep inside the early edition of the next day's *Examiner*. The real stories of John Cordova and Al Asmussen never made the newspapers, so the only thing the two deaths had in common was that, in the big black book where deaths are logged in the coroner's office, the autopsies for Al Asmussen and Robert Hillsborough are just one page apart.

eleven

Showdown on Castro Street

"We could castrate you, but we'll try shock treatment instead."

That was the studied opinion of the first psychiatrist, a man highly regarded in Oklahoma mental health circles. The second, younger doctor was more empathetic as he prepared the frightened and confused young man for his first rendezvous with the electrodes. "Your wife and your mother are the two people who really need this treatment," he assured him, "but you're the one who has been selected, so let's get on with it."

He would never forget the terror, sitting in the waiting room with the others, praying, hoping against hope that the next name they called would be someone else's. Please let someone else be next. The shot of Nembutal, slipping into a daze. The wooden machine is wheeled in. You're strapped on an ironing board with an axle, spinning through space, but you never really know what you're doing because you're unconscious. There's unspeakable pain but you're out so you can't scream or even open your eyes; you just feel your back arching and all you're left with is the profound sense that you've been hurt, hurt bad, because, as the doctor said, you were the one who had been selected.

By the time Rick Stokes ran for the

board of supervisors in 1977, this story of his electric shock treatment had been neatly packaged into a nationally televised documentary, sealed as part of the San Francisco gay community's heritage, along with comparable stories of bar raids, suicide attempts, dishonorable discharges, and, of course, Jose singing "God Save the Nelly Queens." There was already talk of heritage now, because it was obvious that a small part of history was being worked out in San Francisco and that a major turning point of that history would come in the November election, where District 5 voters were expected to elect the first openly gay big city official in American history. Rick Stokes and Harvey Milk were the two men most aware of that historic reality.

To most, the confrontation between these two leading gay candidates fell into easily definable components, as starkly contrasted as black and white. Rick Stokes was the gentleman politician, a moderate Democrat who had built a substantial reputation as a gay rights lawyer, working for the gay cause in some of the highest legal circles in the state, a reasonable, coolheaded, and respectable homosexual. Harvey Milk, by contrast, was still the *enragé*, given to shoot-from-the-hip hyperbole, the maverick forging a populist political niche, representing the scruffy studs on Castro Street, the shirtless ones. Respectable? Hardly. A reputable professional? Even to his detractors, Milk conceded that his business was little more than a front for his political activities. The contrasts could not be more distinct, but history has a way of playing tricks with scenarios that are so clearly etched; rarely has such a distinct dichotomy been, in fact, so clouded by subtle shades of ambiguity.

Born to an impoverished, west Texas family of cotton pickers, Rick Stokes spent his first years living in a dirt-floored shack. His parents pursued an upwardly mobile dream and moved to a ranch outside Shawnee, Oklahoma. It was on the ranch, about the time he turned six, that Ricky knew he was different. An only child, Rick spent most of his time playing with the kids on the ranch down the road, especially his best friend Joe. By the time the two were teenagers, they had started a passionate affair that lasted ten years, even after Joe got married. Rick was depressed and jealous when Joe took his vows and he confided to his parents the story of the love he and Joe had shared. So when Rick was seventeen, his parents knew all about his homosexuality; that was 1951, the year Harvey Milk joined the navy. While Harvey was leading a discreet but active gay life in the navy, Rick struggled to live up to the sexual norm, marrying and having a daughter. While Harvey contentedly lived his double life in New York City in the waning years of the 1950s, the family of Stokes's wife, appalled at the revelation of their son-in-law's homosexuality, sent Rick off to shock therapy and intensive psychiatric treatment.

The same year Harvey was passing out Barry Goldwater leaflets in Manhattan subways, Rick Stokes had found a political cause too— in Sacramento, where he had fled from his family and founded the area's first gay organization. While Harvey was arguing vociferously that America should bullishly *win* the Vietnam war, Rick was organizing gay protests and driving to San Francisco to participate in the fledgling Society for Individual Rights.

By 1977, of course, their roles had reversed and Harvey Milk was the candidate who talked most convincingly of the terrors perpetrated by a heterosexual society, even though Rick Stokes surely was the candidate who had more intimately experienced them; Harvey was the candidate who talked of the importance of coming out to parents and friends, even though Rick had done it years before the concept even dawned on Milk; Harvey was the outsider candidate who had once enjoyed a comfortable life of operas, gourmet cuisine, and fine apartments while Rick Stokes was the insider from a dirt-floored shack, the victim of some of the sternest blows meted out to those who are deemed society's pariahs. And all the compounded contradictions meant nothing in that election because politics reduces complexities to facile catch phrases and flossy symbols. So to most, the choice between Harvey Milk and Rick Stokes did not represent a conflict between two ambiguous men, but between two ways of life.

On Castro Street, that meant the rift between the teeming thousands of militant and angry street gays who had come during the 1970s and the older, more established professionals who had thrust deep roots into the city's political structure. The discordance bred deep animosities that began before the official campaign announcements were spoken and lingered long after election day. Both camps were convinced that the victory of the other would be a profound defeat for the entire gay movement. To Stokes supporters, Harvey Milk was a loudmouthed, unpredictable opportunist who had done little but run for office since he moved to San Francisco just five years before. To Milk supporters, Rick Stokes was just another part of the wealthy elite, salving his wounds by kissing ass to liberal friends. On a personal level, the conflict had been building since the first day Harvey Milk was rebuffed by Jim Foster in 1973 and the first time Harvey talked publicly of the Alice

B. Toklas club's "Uncle Toms." Heterosexuals, meanwhile, were amazed that gays, as embattled as they were by the summer of 1977, would spend so much time fighting each other.

"What is it you and Harvey had against each other anyway?" one local Democratic leader asked Jim Foster years later. Foster launched into an elaborate explanation about their different styles and political strategies. The wizened old politician listened carefully to Foster and then snapped that the whole explanation was bullshit. "I think the problem between you and Harvey was one of turf," he said. Foster had to concede the old-timer was probably right.

From the start, the District 5 race came off like the three-ring circus of the eleven district supervisorial contests. Seventeen candidates filed for the seat, more than in any other district in the city, and about half were gay. Straight challengers included such big names as former 49er football player Bob St. Claire and Terrance Hallinan, the son of the onetime Progressive Party presidential candidate who had championed radical causes in the Bay Area for a half century. The two great axes of liberal power in San Francisco divided between Milk's two most serious opponents, Stokes and Hallinan. Jim Foster made sure that the McCarthy clan would fall behind Rick when he had a casual conversation with Art Agnos. "Rick Stokes has a great political future," he mentioned to Art. "But I'm not sure what he should run for—supervisor or assembly." Assemblyman Agnos, of course, immediately chirped that he thought Rick would make a terrific supervisor and both he and Speaker McCarthy fell into his corner. Mayor Moscone, who also had little affection for Harvey Milk, did his part for Stokes by overlooking the no-candidate-no-commissioner rule and permitting Rick to keep his seat on the Board of Permit Appeals until the last possible day—long after Stokes had blanketed the district with his posters.

Many political gays thought Moscone's ulterior motive for tacitly supporting Stokes was to help the candidate who would most benefit from a divided gay vote: Terrance "Kayo" Hallinan. Moscone's ally, Representative Phil Burton, strongly backed Hallinan, who based his campaign on the hope that Milk and Stokes would split the gay vote to the extent that he could squeak to victory. The Burtons pulled out all stops for Hallinan. When Harvey led all hopefuls in balloting for the endorsement of the San Francisco Labor Council, for example, the congressmen's cronies pressured a major union into changing its votes from Milk to Hallinan. The council leadership, controlled by Burton allies, then refused to let a furious Stan Smith take the floor in support of Harvey. Once again, however, Milk deftly used the machinations to his advantage, and stories about the complex endorsement deals did less to promote Hallinan than to underscore Milk's perennial claim to the status of outsider and underdog.

Such PR left the other candidates shouting foul since Milk was, for once, anything but the underdog in the race. His basic strategy focused on running an incumbent's campaign, challenging his opponents to meet his record of involvement in neighborhood issues. Three campaigns had built a corps of experienced volunteers and by 1977, Harvey was able to assemble an impressive array of endorsements ranging from the Mexican-American Political Association to the gay Republican club and the usual assortment of unions. Members of the San Francisco Gay Democratic Club had infiltrated the Alice Toklas club to the point that they were able to deny Rick Stokes, a former Alice president, his own club's endorsement. All this had Milk's detractors muttering about the Milk Machine, to which Harvey snorted, "Well, at least a Milk Machine is healthy."

For all these advantages, Harvey ran hard, almost desperately in this, his fourth attempt for office in as many years. He raced through gruelling seventeen-hour days of bus stop handshaking, afternoon door-to-door canvassing and evening bingo games and candidates' nights. On one level, the immense funds pouring into the Stokes treasury and the political heavyweights behind Hallinan intimidated Milk; the panoply of minor candidates came as an unexpected challenge. Friends could also detect personal reasons for his uncharacteristic anxiety. His fabled stamina was beginning to fade; the years of nonstop campaigning had taken their toll. The massive publicity Milk had garnered as the primary gay spokesperson during the 1977 wave of militance had engendered an onslaught of macabre death threats. And just four weeks before Harvey made the formal announcement of his candidacy he turned forty-seven years old.

Broader historical forces were fueling the juggernaut of Milk's campaign. For proof, Harvey needed only to step outside his ex officio city hall and look down Castro Street. By the thousands, these men had flocked to the golden gates of the Castro, where even the store mannequins had washboard stomachs. The Castro had become the nation's chief liberated zone, as if the neighborhood's massive Castro theater marquee had asked, "Give me your weak, your huddled, your oppressed, and your horny looking for a little action."

Machismo was no longer fashionable, it was ubiquitous. Few hippies walked the streets any more; the hair was kept closely cropped à la Korean War era. Those who dared grow more than a few inches kept it tightly combed back circa Rick Nelson. The dress was decidedly butch, as if God had dropped these men naked and commanded them to wear only straight-legged levis, plaid Pendleton shirts, and leather coats over hooded sweatshirts. Everywhere, drugstore cowboys eyed laundromat loggers winking at barfly jocks. It was a 1957 beach party movie all over again, except the air bristled with the sexual tension of the seventies and there were few women. Most estimates put the gay population of San Francisco at around 125,000, but the guesswork left the estimators looking like medieval monks trying to figure how many gays could disco on the head of a peninsula. Milk privately estimated that at least 25,000 to 30,000 had settled into the Castro. His friend Tory Hartmann called them the Jeep People, since they were refugees who came not in tiny boats, but in their macho four-wheel-drive jeeps. The uniformity in dress and style had the Castro denizens jokingly branding each other Castroids.

The Castro Village Association had grown to include ninety merchants as the Castro business district sprawled from the two-block Castro Street strip itself to include virtually all the adjacent side streets. Milk estimated that businesses on the Castro strip alone grossed $30 million in 1976, up 30 percent from the year before. The local Hibernia Bank branch jumped from being the smallest branch in the Hibernia system to one of the largest, forcing the bank to add a new wing. The burgeoning business community consummated much of Harvey's early dream about gay economic clout. The mere rumor that beer magnate Joseph Coors had donated to Anita Bryant's campaign resurrected the old Coors boycott and every gay bar in the city dropped the popular beer; that alone ended Coors' long-held status as California's top-selling beer, and the company scrambled to take out ads in gay papers to deny Bryant connections. Florida orange juice also became a prime no-no and every gay bar prominently displayed signs explaining that any o.j. came strictly from California groves.

Television news crews and writers from publications around the world stalked the Castro to chart the story of the unprecedented powerhouse of gay political and economic clout. Most ended up at the doorstep of the unofficial mayor of Castro Street, who talked on about the neighborhood the way a proud father brags about a firstborn son, albeit Milk's enthusiasm for the street was often more lusty. With the growth of the Castro and the corollary development of economic and political strength, San Francisco replaced New York as the focus of the gay movement. Some called it Mecca, but to most gays it was nothing short of Oz, a place they had never hoped to see in their lifetimes. The area, however, maintained a small-town ambience. The neighborhood mailman was Harry Britt, the former Methodist minister, who could often be found chewing the fat with the neighborhood author, Frank Robinson, or the local pot dealer, Dennis Peron, in Castro Camera. The whole scenario brought back nostalgic memories for men like Allan Baird who knew of times when other villagers ambled casually along the friendly sidewalks.

Attacks came with the neighborhood's national prominence. The upsurge in violent assaults on gays forced the formation of local street patrols, which nonviolently corralled attackers until police responded, often tardily. The fact that a virile gay community was taking care of its own problems startled the city's establishment, which could barely deal with homosexuals of the Judy Garland vintage. The afternoon *Examiner* editorialized that the patrol was a "semi-vigilante" group and warned that "tolerant San Francisco has no quarrel with the gays as long as they don't get hysterical and create problems that call for a police crackdown." The comment indicated the extent to which city institutions were out of touch with the new realities being created by the gay influx to the city. At least 25,000 gays lived in the Castro, a quarter million showed up for the year's Gay Freedom Day Parade—and the *Examiner* still believed it could even suggest a police crackdown, as if they were still in the good old days.

The liberals in City Hall were also out of touch with the emerging political reality. By 1977, gays had obtained only three commission appointments out of the nearly four hundred the mayor could make, and two of these were the women's and human rights commissions, which had little real power. Gays were, at best, the unwanted stepchildren of city politics. Mayor Moscone refused to meet with leaders from groups like the San Francisco Gay Democratic Club, insisting that anyone with a problem to take up with city government had to go through Jim Foster. Since Foster and the entrenched gay leadership would have little to do with the unkempt gay militants of Castro Street, the new mass of gays, many of whom had arrived after the 1975 mayoral race and the repressive days of the Alioto regime, were, in effect, frozen out of City Hall. Politicos like Foster saw the process as simply part of the old political game of kings and barons. Harvey Milk, a baron, had challenged Moscone, the king; Moscone had no choice but to hang Milk in the public square and cut himself off from Milk's troops. That was how politics worked, reasoned the sophisticated political pro's. Among the less seasoned, however, an anger simmered just the same. This was not a matter of kings-and-barons politics, they thought, but of a movement—and, most significantly, a new gay consciousness—coming into its own in a neighborhood of its own, Castro Street.

Harvey's frequent bursts of enthusiasm had long ago stopped surprising Michael Wong, but even Wong was amazed when Harvey euphorically maintained he had finally found a campaign manager perfectly suited for his idiosyncracies.

"A manager?" Wong asked. "Who the hell can manage you?"

"This person, Anne Kronenberg!" Harvey exclaimed. "Wait till you meet her, Mike. She's really good at managing things for me."

"You're full of shit, Harvey," Mike snapped. "John Ryckman couldn't manage you and you want me to believe that someone is *managing* your campaign?"

Harvey was undeterred. "If I win, I intend to bring her to City Hall, but don't say anything, because I don't want people to start tripping over that."

"What's she like?"

"Sharp, young, and a good, good worker. You're gonna love her."

Wong was surprised when he finally did meet Anne. She seemed everything Harvey wasn't. Kronenberg was quiet by nature and spoke slowly and thoughtfully while Harvey yapped away in his characteristic breakneck pace; she was methodical, with a concern for details while the disorganized Milk carelessly forged ahead with little thought for specifics; she was relaxed and laid back while Harvey was his old hyperactive self. At twenty-three, Anne was half Harvey's age, but they proved a perfect match and her appearance completed the creation of the cadre of key aides who would work with Harvey for the rest of his career.

Anne knew from the first day she walked into a campaign headquarters as a junior high student in Everrett, Washington, that she liked politics. The headquarters always bristled with the excitement of people doing something that made a difference, even if it was just licking envelopes or sorting out precinct maps. Most of Anne's friends were Republicans, but at thirteen, Kronenberg figured out she was no traditionalist, so she joined the Young Democrats, often busing to nearby

Seattle to work on liberal campaigns there. She had always felt different, but her mom assured her it was normal to get jealous when her girl friends dated boys, so it didn't cross her mind until after she graduated from the University of Washington and moved to San Francisco that her difference had anything to do with sex. After a long bout with hepatitis, Anne was having a hard time establishing a career, so she was looking more for purpose than a job when she showed up at Castro Camera one day and said she'd like to volunteer. Since she was unemployed, she could work full time and, with his usual casualness, Harvey made Anne campaign manager.

Initially Kronenberg was not as taken with her candidate as he was with her. He was always running around and yelling; she was intimidated by his seemingly limitless energy. Harvey could not afford to pay her a salary, so she had to live off whatever extra $10 or $20 bill appeared in the Castro Camera register that day. The whole campaign had to be run on such a piecemeal basis. A $25 profit on developing a vacation's worth of slides meant that $25 worth of brochures could be printed up that day. It didn't bode well for long-term strategizing. On a more personal level, Anne worried that Harvey seemed hopelessly entangled in his complicated relationship with Scott Smith—using Scott as the scapegoat in his tantrums—while Harvey simultaneously maintained he was having a terrible time finding boyfriends. "You two act like you still are lovers," Anne told Harvey in her first weeks of campaigning. "No, we don't," Harvey said stubbornly.

Anne's lesbian friends, meanwhile, warned her that she should never get mixed up with a politician of the male gender. "He's a man," they counseled knowingly. "He's just going to use you and throw you out." Lesbian leaders had long ago spread the word that Harvey was anti-woman, partially for his close alliances with drag queens, and few ever backed Harvey. But the more Anne saw of Harvey, the more impressed she was. She was amazed that one man could have so much influence without ever having held public office; it never occurred to her that mere citizens could garner such power. And there was the endless stream of little old ladies and troubled young gay men who came to Harvey with their problems, big and small, and Harvey always had time for them. Anne soon found that Harvey was much more manageable than he would admit. The major problem was to learn how to put up with his constant ribbing—"We'll have to install a revolving door to handle all your girlfriends," he remarked at the sight of Kronenberg's frequent suitors—but that, she realized, came with the territory.

The sudden appearance of such a perfect campaign manager seemed suspicious to Harvey's old friend, Wayne Friday. Friday was convinced that she had been planted by the Stokes campaign to sabotage Harvey's effort. He even spent an hour grilling her before he would give his approval. The campaign, however, quickly evolved into a family affair. Kronenberg managed volunteers while Harry Britt worked for Harvey through the San Francisco Gay Democratic Club. Jim Rivaldo and Dick Pabich teamed up to design Harvey's campaign literature and took to consulting a number of political campaigns throughout the city. The Milk Machine was in full gear.

The guards at Peoples Temple eyed Anne suspiciously when she rode up to the locked gate on her Honda 550 with a boxload of Milk fliers strapped on the seat. The guard admitted her to the gate, but made her wait in a locked vestibule until he was authorized to admit her to a second locked vestibule, where she had to wait until she got still another authorization to walk inside the church, the guards standing stiffly at every door. She was then instructed to call before she came again, so she could get her name put on a special list that would enable her to enter. She left the Temple feeling queasy about the entire experience.

"They're weird, but they're good volunteers," Harvey told her. "You take help where it comes from, but don't trust them."

Bad press had plagued Peoples Temple that summer. An investigation by the *Chronicle's* City Hall reporter Marshall Kilduff had uncovered evidence that Jim Jones routinely faked his faith healings and that he kept Temple members sternly in line by regular beatings for the slightest infractions of the rules. The information startled Kilduff since Jones headed a powerful city commission, wielded considerable political influence, and had a top lieutenant serving in the district attorney's office, an appointment that effectively kept Temple dissidents from taking their complaints to the D.A. The *Chronicle* would not print Kilduff's revelations, so he had the story published in *New West* magazine. The city editor who squelched the People's Temple story, it turned out, had been well cultivated by the Reverend Jones. By fall, a besieged Reverend Jones headed for the Utopia he claimed he was building in the jungles of Guyana—named Jonestown, after himself. The city editor who stopped the *Chronicle* investigation of Jim Jones, meanwhile, would be gone by the time Peoples Temple made the news again.

Hallinan clearly stood as the most formidable challenger in District 5, but most of the talk at Milk's headquarters centered on Rick Stokes and his supporters, whom Harvey dubbed "Stokettes," as if the election were for control of the gay movement instead of District 5. When Harvey quelled the riots on Orange Tuesday, he pointedly kept asking, "Where was Rick Stokes? He's the highest gay official in the city, not me. And he wants to be a leader?" When real estate campaign contributions swelled Stokes's campaign chest to the largest of any nonincumbent in San Francisco, Milk talked of "blood-sucker real estate speculators" and piously maintained, "You can spend a fortune to buy 'name recognition' or you can earn it by helping people." All the money just proved he was once again the underdog, fighting the machine. The charge infuriated Rick, who knew well he was the underdog in the race. "Harvey was born to be a martyr," he fumed to one interviewer.

When not deriding Stokes, Harvey picked on his favorite nemesis, downtown business and tourist interests. "I don't know whether they're following some big plan of the Chamber of Commerce," Harvey speculated, but he made it clear that he thought the days were over when executives in skyscrapers could dictate the direction of the city. "Better watch out," one friend warned. "You keep talking like that and you're gonna get shot."

Harvey, however, had his own plans for the city. He wanted to reorient the tax structure to bring light industry back to the deserted factories and warehouses near downtown. The city could also use the structures for day-care centers where senior citizens, who frittered away their last years in lonely Tenderloin apartments, could tend the children of low-income mothers trying to work their way off welfare. The vision fit perfectly with the essentially capitalistic core of Harvey's own version of urban Jeffersonian democracy, focused on small businesses and industries working around decentralized neighborhoods which, like the Castro, could return the small-town flavor to big-city life. Harvey was fond of telling the story about the newspaper publisher who heard all these plans at Milk's endorsement interview and ended the meeting quizically saying, "You really are a dreamer, aren't you?" Harvey's favorite Broadway show had always been *Man of LaMancha,* so the question struck him as the highest compliment he received during the entire campaign.

The central element of Harvey's campaign appearances, however, were always the last paragraphs of his hope speech. By now, it had several permutations. Sometimes it was a boy in Des Moines, sometimes he was from Dayton, but always there was a young person out there who would hear of Milk's victory and know that even though he was gay and somehow different, he had a chance too. "It was funny," Frank Robinson later reflected. "Harvey had so much hope for the generic *you* and so much personal fatalism about his own life."

"Who's that drunk?"

Dick Pabich had little use for heavy drinkers and here he was, having the most successful fund raiser in Harvey's career, and there was this drunken Mexican, slobbering around, muttering epithets in a mixture of Spanish and English. "I'll show you the door," said Pabich, guiding the inebriated young man outside. A few minutes later, one of Milk's friends giggled, "He was Harvey's new boyfriend."

That was how Dick Pabich met Jack Lira; that was how most people met Jack Lira. Drunk. Harvey always had a penchant for young waifs with substance abuse problems, so Jack's appearance surprised few who had known Harvey in the days of Jack McKinley. Most of Harvey's San Francisco associates, however, had known only Scott Smith, who had for years served as the quintessential political wife, working on campaigns and managing the business while Harvey played politics. According to most accounts, Harvey had discovered Jack Lira one night on Castro Street, staring absently into the window of Castro Camera. His compact body made the twenty-five-year-old Latino irresistible to Milk and the pair made time for sexual trysts whenever they could be fit into Harvey's hectic campaign schedule. The older wealthy man with whom Lira lived at that time took a dim view of Jack's extracurricular activities. One day, Lira turned up tearfully at Castro Camera with a long letter explaining why he was being evicted from the comfortable Pacific Heights mansion. That night, Jack Lira moved into Harvey's slovenly apartment above the camera store.

Harvey quickly nicknamed Lira "Taco Bell"; Harvey's friends called him "the mistake." While campaign volunteers worked late into the night leafleting and stuffing envelopes, Lira spent afternoons watching soap operas and evenings drinking with a set of queeny buddies who also gained the disdain of Harvey's friends. He spent other hours sitting at the apartment window, staring silently out at Castro Street. Lira struck up a feud with Scott Smith, who was usually jealous of Harvey's new boyfriends anyway. Smith complained that Jack lashed out at his predecessor by mistreating the dog. When friends confronted

Harvey about his questionable choice of lovers, Milk would sketchily outline Lira's troubled past. The youngest child of a poor Mexican-American family, Jack had little education and no useful skills. The way Harvey told it, Jack's dad had declared he no longer had a son when he learned of Jack's homosexuality, so, like the many others, Jack trekked from Fresno to gay Mecca. Harvey insisted he was just trying to help out a troubled kid. Besides, he'd add with a wink, Jack was dynamite sex.

Former Toklas President Jo Daly and her lover Nancy Achilles had long planned some kind of marriage ceremony to solemnize their long relationship. Jo was taken aback, however, when she mentioned to her longtime friend Dianne Feinstein that she and Nancy were going to have a ceremony on a yacht cruising San Francisco Bay. Dianne was adamant; she wanted to go, but her husband was dying of cancer. They should have the ceremony in her backyard, Dianne suggested, so she could attend. Feinstein worked out the details and then poured over appropriate passages of Kahlil Gibran to read at the solemnization. The wedding was held on schedule in Feinstein's back garden and that, as much as the Orange Tuesday demonstrations, said a lot about where gays stood in San Francisco of 1977. Only several weeks before Feinstein faced the voters in one of the city's more conservative supervisorial districts, she held a lesbian wedding ceremony in her backyard. It barely caused a stir, and Dianne Feinstein was not generally considered to be among the more liberal politicians in city government.

An explosion shattered the night. Shards of glass sprayed across the sidewalks of Castro Street. Castro Camera's windows had been blown out by the M–80 mega-firecrackers; explosions shattered three more Castro Street stores within minutes. Supervisorial candidate Harvey Milk was on the front page of the next morning's *Chronicle* saying that, once again, Anita Bryant has goaded anti-gay violence. Years later friends hinted broadly that Harvey had more than a little foreknowledge that the explosions would happen. "You gotta realize the campaign was sort of going slow, and, well . . ." the confidante lets his voice taper off.

It's doubtful that Milk was responsible for the blasts, other friends say, if for no other reason than he could barely afford the cost it took to replace the window. The hints, however, indicate how badly friends knew Harvey wanted to win this election. Against such determination, Rick Stokes never had a chance. The early months did more to embitter than excite the soft-spoken attorney about the mechanics of electoral politics. Stokes was running because his years of drafting laws had intrigued him with the notion of sitting on a legislative board. He was never excited about campaigning. Harvey, meanwhile, was an inveterate campaigner who knew little of the nuts and bolts of legislation. The shy, affable Stokes found he had a hard time tooting his own horn as the campaign progressed. He enjoyed meeting people, but shied away from working crowds. Harvey, of course, proved as masterful as ever in 1977, jutting out his hand to every potential voter he saw and grabbing press at every turn. Rick just got more discouraged. Every day of campaigning you have to sell off bits and pieces of yourself, he thought. Before you know it, you're out the window with all the bits and pieces. At one point in the campaign, Stokes even toyed with the idea of dropping out. According to his early campaign manager, Ken Maley, David Goodstein and Art Agnos prodded him back into the race. "They're not interested in getting Rick elected," he observed. "They just want to put the final nail in the coffin of Harvey's political career." Stokes stayed in the race.

Harvey campaigned on maniacally, even as all the cards fell his way. He canvassed every precinct twice. His human billboards again lined Market Street. The big shocker came in the campaign's closing days when the *Chronicle* amazed everybody, especially Milk, and endorsed Harvey for supervisor. The endorsement editorial noted Milk's business experience as part of his qualifications, sending Harvey's friends into hysterics. For all the things Harvey had been charged with over the years, no one had ever accused him of being a good businessman.

On election day, Harvey dashed madly from precinct to precinct. His nightmare: that he would again lose by the razor-thin margin that had marked his assembly defeat. He relentlessly pushed on his well organized corps of get-out-the-vote workers to knock on every door. The fears, at last, proved unfounded.

Television kleig lights bathed Castro Camera's Victorian storefront with their surreal glow. The rowdy crowd overflowed into the streets and filled every available counter and tabletop in the store. The roar of motorcycles was heard as Anne Kronenberg pulled her Honda 550 to the front of the store with Sheriff Richard Hongisto behind her, while her latest lover pulled in on another motorcycle with a grinning Supervisor-elect Harvey Milk on the back, fresh from claiming his lopsided victory at City Hall.

The crowd cheered at the sight of the winner while television crews got ready to go live from the headquarters of the upset winner who had polled the highest tally of any nonincumbent supervisorial candidate in the city, making him the first openly gay elected official of any big city in the United States. Harvey had beaten both Terrance Hallinan and Rick Stokes by a better than two-to-one margin, garnering 30 percent of the vote against his sixteen challengers. Rick Stokes, Jim Foster, and Art Agnos came down the street to make their traditional concession handshakes, but Milk would not even let them inside the store. "It's too crowded," he said curtly.

"This is not my victory, it's yours and yours and yours," Harvey exhorted to the wildly cheering crowd. "If a gay can win, it means that there *is* hope that the system can work for all minorities if we fight. We've given them hope."

"Harvey for mayor," someone shouted and the crowd cheered more.

The next morning, Harvey and his cohorts were back on Market Street, smiling and waving, with their last human billboard, freshly crayoned signs that simply said, "Thank You." The drivers, fresh from seeing the morning *Chronicle* with the picture of the motorcycled Milk and Hongisto on the front page, waved back and honked their horns wildly. During red lights, Harvey jogged between cars to accept congratulations and shake hands. Trolley drivers rang their congratulations. Just like a Rice-a-Roni commercial.

When the traffic rush subsided, Harvey pulled Harry Britt over to the side. He was writing a note to Mayor Moscone, Harvey explained, just in case, well, anything happened. The letter would list the people Harvey wanted to replace him, and Harry should know that his name would be among them. Britt was surprised because he and Harvey had not been particularly close personal friends. They did seem to agree instinstinctively on political matters, but their relationship hadn't gone much beyond politics. Harry thought Harvey's disclosure was somewhat depressing and quickly dismissed the conversation, convinced that the rush of victory had kept Milk awake all night and left him emotionally drained. When Harvey told his friend Frank Robinson about the planned letter, Frank told him he was being downright morbid, attributing the political "will" to the black streak he had long ago noticed running on the underside of Milk's otherwise humorous demeanor.

It was well past midnight a week later when, after an exhausting day at the camera shop, Harvey slumped over a cassette recorder to tape the three messages he simply entitled "In case." Harvey listed who was and who was not acceptable as a successor. There was a chilling anatomical specificity to it all when Harvey's recorded voice was later heard saying, "If a bullet should enter my brain, let that bullet destroy every closet door."

Congratulations poured in from around the country in the days after the election. "Thanks to you that kid in Des Moines just bought a ticket for San Francisco," teased one friend. "Supe at last, supe at last, thank God Almighty, supe at last," wrote another. A sixty-eight-year-old lesbian who had been a San Francisco schoolteacher since 1932 wrote poignantly, "I thank God I have lived long enough to see my kind emerge from the shadows and join the human race." Her one regret was that she didn't live in District 5 to savor the victory as a constituent. Days later, Harvey added the finishing touches to his hope speech when he emerged with a vaguely apocryaphal tale of a sixteen-year-old boy from Altoona, Pennsylvania, who called to thank Harvey for giving him hope that he could make something of his life. No more talk of Dayton or Des Moines. For the rest of his career, Milk's hope speech talked of a sixteen-year-old boy from Altoona, Pennsylvania. There were other letters too, dozens of them, like the one addressed simply to "Milk the Faggot." It concluded with the cheery sign-off: "Maybe, just maybe, some of the more hostile in the district may firebomb your store or may even take some pot shots at you—we hope!!!"

The Irish Catholic cop-turned-politician and the gay Jewish neighborhood politico. The media like quick, easy juxtapositions that can be translated into the brief ninety seconds generally alloted to each television news story. The elections of Harvey Bernard Milk and Daniel James White to the board of supervisors were the natural peg to the election follow-ups. On one level, both typified the ultimate goal of district elections—to reflect the diverse citzenry of the city. Dan White reflected his working class, traditional native San Francisco district, just as Harvey Milk reflected his hip, heavily gay, non-native district. The contrast was too tantalizing for the television producers to pass up. In the weeks following the election, White and Milk made a number of joint appearances on local talk shows. Both warmly praised the other. White even publicly assured Harvey that his brochure's comments about "social deviates" referred to junkies, not gays. Milk began privately telling friends that he might be able to work with the conservative White.

Dennis Seely had been in the habit of arguing with Harvey ever since the two were neighbors on Castro Street, and Milk came to pound on Dennis' door complaining he couldn't hear his Mahler over the din of Seely's Jefferson Airplane records. The sight of Harvey buddying up with White on television was no more conducive to a smooth conversation between Dennis and Harvey than had been the sound of Grace Slick's piercing voice.

"Harvey, that guy's a pig," Dennis told him bluntly after he had seen a Dan-and-Harvey talk show. "I hate him."

"Dan White is just stupid," Harvey insisted. "He's working class, a Catholic, been brought up with all those prejudices. I'm gonna sit next to him every day and let him know we're not all those bad things he thinks we are."

"Look at him," Dennis said incredulously. "He's never gonna be different. He's a cop. All the analysts in the world aren't gonna reach that guy and your yakkin' ain't gonna make any difference either."

"As the years pass, the guy can be educated," Milk argued, adding huffily, "that's where *we* disagree. Everyone can be reached. Everyone can be educated and helped. *You* think some people are hopeless—not me."

PART III

Supervisor Harvey Milk

twelve

Media Star

"What do you think of my new theater?"
Supervisor Harvey Milk enjoyed posing that question to his friends as he would guide them up the grand marble staircase of San Francisco City Hall, and he pointed out the dramatic proportions the building seemed to lend to whatever history passed beneath its dome. "My stage," he would say, looking down at the expansive lobby from the balcony. From his first day in office, Harvey left little doubt that his term would be marked more by his unique brand of political theater than by the substantive tasks of the board. He managed to turn his ceremonial swearing-in into a major media event when he and Jack Lira led a procession of 150 supporters from Castro Camera down the fifteen blocks to the wide front steps of City Hall. "This is a walk of reconciliation with a nation of people," he lectured reporters. "This is a walk that will give to many people hope."

Mayor Moscone and a gaggle of other politicians greeted the cadre of outsiders who were about to take their seat of power at last. Milk insisted on an outdoor inauguration, saying all his supporters could not fit indoors. Besides, the pictures of Milk in front of the proud rotunda made much better television. As Harvey began to repeat the words of his oath, a gentle rain began falling. "Anita Bryant said gay people brought the drought to California," he joked, looking up at the sky. "Looks to me like it's finally started raining."

"This is not my swearing-in, this is your swearing-in," he told the crowd. "You can stand around and throw bricks at Silly Hall or you can take it over. Well, here we are."

Milk used his first board meeting that afternoon to strike an independent path. His first legislative proposal called for the enactment of a comprehensive ban on all forms of discrimination against gays in the city. During the board's first order of business—the election of its president—Milk tenaciously held out against the certain election of Supervisor Dianne Feinstein, maintaining the board should have its first minority president, the new Chinese-American supervisor Gordon Lau. After Feinstein won her 6–5 vote—the first of many 6–5 wins in the coming year—Milk refused to go along with Lau's courtesy motion to make Feinstein's election unanimous. The lack of tact horrified the newspapers. The *Examiner* ran an editorial saying Milk was off to a "disappointing start." But the anti-Feinstein swipe delighted both liberals, who viewed Feinstein as an ally of downtown business interests, and gays, who had grown uneasy with Feinstein's prudery. "I'm not concerned about the Emily Post attitude to life," Harvey snapped at critics. He privately noted that the *Examiner* editorial had served its most important purpose, spelling his name right. And no matter what the editorial page said, the afternoon paper's front page was dominated by one picture—Harvey with his arm around Jack, leading the march up Castro Street.

The formal inauguration in the elaborately carved oak-paneled board chambers was marred only when Harvey turned to introduce Jack Lira. Dan White had used his introduction time to pay tribute to his grandmother, an Irish immigrant; Harvey relished the juxtaposition of introducing his male lover, but Lira had slipped out of the room even before the meeting started, afraid of the cameras and bright lights being trained on him. "It's well known that I'm a gay person. I have a loved one but he was too nervous to stay here and he left," said Harvey. Milk had waited so many years for the day of his inauguration when he could stand as a homosexual to introduce the man he loved and the moment had fled him. Harvey instead used most of his introductory remarks to speak on his favorite theme. "A true function of politics is not just to pass laws, but to give hope," he said. "There have been too many disappointments lately. The real abyss that lies not too far ahead is that day when a disappointed people lose their hope forever. When that happens, everything we cherish will be lost."

"Hope is fine," Feinstein said tartly in her opening remarks, "but you can't live on hope. The name of the game is six votes."

Even the crustiest reporters, however, did not fail to note the symbolism Milk underscored in this, the first district-elected board in the city's modern history. Taking oaths were the city's first elected Chinese supervisor, the first black woman, the only Latino supervisor, the first gay city official in the nation, and, from another alternative life-styles category, even the first unwed mother supervisor, Harvey's friend and ally, Carol Ruth Silver. The inauguration also signaled what looked like the beginning of a new stability in city government after the turbulence caused first by Moscone's election, then the passage of district elections, later the whirlwind efforts to not only repeal district elections but recall the city's top officials, and finally the ouster of the citywide board in November. Feinstein called it "a new day in San Francisco politics"; the transition in power from downtown to the neighborhoods looked like a juggernaut now, a palace coup that could not be undone.

The best media event of inauguration day came not from Milk, but from his old nemesis David Goodstein, who sponsored a series of inaugural night parties at the city's three most popular gay discos. Publicly, Goodstein culled jargon from his est courses to insist he wanted to provide a supportive context for Milk and, publicly, Harvey said, "If Begin and Sadat can get together to talk, so can we." Privately, Goodstein quoted Machiavelli's *Prince*, not Werner Erhard, as the reason for the parties. "I want to coopt Harvey," he bluntly told an employee. For his part Harvey privately savored seeing Goodstein "kiss my ass," disdaining to do so much as even ride to the parties in the same car that Goodstein rode in.

Reporter Francis Moriarty later recalled the chilling irony at the end of that evening when Goodstein kissed Milk's hand as they parted company, saying "Goodnight, sweet Prince"—Horatio's famous farewell to the slain Hamlet. Goodstein later denied making the statement, but Moriarty insisted the moment stuck in his mind, since the quote came just after Hamlet, in his dying breath, endorsed Fortinbras in the coming struggle for power. Goodstein would not know for nearly a year that his parting line followed Milk's own secret taped nominations for his successor—nominations intended to squeeze out Goodstein's closest allies, Jim Foster and Rick Stokes.

The round of inaugural partying did not end until the next night when Milk threw a formal dinner to help pay off his campaign debt. The new supervisor used the occasion to wax eloquent again about his dreams for new cities and for hope:

> The American Dream starts with neighborhoods. If we wish to rebuild our cities, we must first rebuild our neighborhoods. To sit on the front steps—whether it's a veranda in a small town or a concrete stoop in a big city—is infinitely more important than to huddle on the living room lounger and watch a make-believe world in not-quite living color. . . .
>
> Yesterday, my esteemed colleague on the board said we cannot live on hope alone. I know that. . . . The important thing is not that we can live on hope alone, but that life is not worth living without it. If the story of Don Quixote means anything, it means that the spirit of life is just as important as its substance.

When Harvey met Jack Lira, he confided to his friend Tory Hartmann, "I've found the love of my life." Tory liked her gay friends because, as a Catholic, she thought they were God's lost people, but she could never get used to their easy romancing. "Just how many lovers for life are you going to have?" she asked Harvey; like most of Harvey's friends, she thought the politician could do much better than Lira. The night of the inaugural dinner she heard a whisper from the coat check. Jack was offended that he did not get to sit on the dais with Harvey and the important public officials, he told Tory, so he had thrown a tantrum and was hiding in the coatroom, refusing even to eat. Again, Tory had to wonder about Harvey's choice of boyfriends.

A huge American flag hung sternly from the balcony. The stirring fanfare of the "Theme from Rocky" blared. A handsome young man strode purposefully onto a balcony high above the crowd. It all gave Doris Silvistri the creeps. As a good friend of Building and Construction Trades secretary-treasurer Stan Smith, Silvistri got to attend more than her share of post-campaign fund raisers in the early months of the supervisors' terms. Nothing on the circuit bothered her more than the fund raiser for Dan White in the same spacious design center Harvey had used for his dinner. When White's turn to speak came, the balcony cleared, leaving only an oversized American flag draped in the rear, the "Rocky" fanfare and a disembodied voice introducing White. He walked stiffly across the balcony—like a robot, Doris thought.

"I'm not sure whether he thinks he's George Patton or Adolph Hitler, but he sure makes me nervous," Doris whispered to Stan.

Smith countered that everybody seemed to like the clean-cut young man.

"I don't care," Doris argued. "There's something wrong with that man. He's wound up too tight. Something's wrong." Talking personally to White did little to reassure her. "He responded like he was programmed," she said later. "He was like a spring ready to go off."

"I'm number one queen now. You can work with me or fight me. But if you fight me, be ready for me to do my best to make sure you don't get reelected."

Harvey Milk repeated this challenge to anyone who would listen. Mayor Moscone tried to start their first post-election conversation with small talk about how he could help Harvey erase his campaign debt when Harvey cut him off, pounded his fists on the mayor's desk, and laid out the ground rules for their relationship. Harvey wanted final say over any gay appointments. He also wanted the mayor to start producing substantive results for gays. Or else.

"You're never given power," he had railed for five years, "you have to take it." Milk knew his Machiavelli as well as any politico in town and he intended to use his clout as the first gay official to prove it. Moscone, for one, saw the new order shaping up in the gay community; he had bet on the wrong horse. At an open meeting with the gay community shortly after Milk's election, Moscone told gays to funnel complaints through Milk and that he would no longer pay heed to any "kingmakers" in the community, a direct slap at Jim Foster, who had long been called the gay kingmaker. Moreover, Moscone promised that he would appoint a gay member to the Police Commission, satisfying a demand gays had been making since the days of Jose's Black Cat. "Whatta difference a gay makes," touted one gay newspaper's headline at the breakthroughs. Milk returned the favor to Moscone. By the end of Harvey's first month in office, one political columnist observed that "Milk has become Moscone's strongest political ally on the board." Though the couple shared a similar liberal political philosophy, the newfound rapport between the two old foes surprised pundits both in and out of City Hall.

The new supervisor from District 5 was out to be more than the gay legislator and he used his first months on the board to build his populist image, inveighing against the interests he considered the bane of a healthy San Francisco—downtown corporations and real estate developers. He pushed for a commuter tax, so the 300,000-plus corporate employees who came downtown each day from suburbia would pay their share for the city services they used. When the Jarvis-Gann tax revolt started drying up local revenue sources, he joined Moscone in a push for higher business taxes, legislation that business-oriented Board President Feinstein managed to kill. The news that a parking garage for a new performing arts center near City Hall would replace housing units sent Harvey on a rampage. "It's a scandal of human nature to rip down sixty-seven housing units in this day so that the wealthy can have a place to park their cars," he lectured. "A place for an auto to rest is not as important as the need for a place for people to rest. There is a shifting of tides taking place toward the needs of people versus the needs of the auto." Real estate developers tried to persuade Milk to support a massive downtown development project with the argument that once built, it would provide thousands of jobs for minorities. "Jobs as what?" Harvey sneered. "Janitors, waitresses, and busboys. Big fucking deal. What kinds of opportunities are those?"

The centerpiece of Milk's legislative agenda remained his ordinance to discourage the real estate speculation that was running rampant throughout San Francisco, especially in the Castro. Harvey worried that the spiraling housing prices would force the poor and minorities out of the city. Milk went right to the belly of the beast and delivered the announcement of his anti-speculation tax to the San Francisco Board of Realtors. The group wasted no time in singling Milk out as their most formidable political foe. Still, conceded one Milk critic, "With Harvey, you never had to worry about a knife in the back. He gave you a frontal assault."

The Pentagon's announcement that it planned to close the city's Presidio military base had Board President Feinstein racing to shore up unanimous support for a resolution pleading for the complex's continued operation. Harvey stood as the lone dissenter, insisting the base's spacious grounds would be a dandy park and that the housing could better be used for his favorite special interest group, senior citizens. Besides, he confided to one friend, he'd seen too many lives wrecked by the military and its anti-gay pogroms; the less San Francisco had to do with the services, the better. The base ultimately remained open, but the freshman supervisor's anti-military posture only confirmed the editorial writers' view that Supervisor Milk was indeed a disappointment.

Though Milk and his closest board ally, Supervisor Carol Ruth Silver, ended up on the losing side of many a 9–2 vote, Harvey proved an effective ward healer once in office, practicing his own alderman brand of realpolitik to perfection. He saw to it that the once-weekly sweeping of Castro Street stepped up to a daily cleaning. He successfully thwarted the closing of the neighborhood's library branch, saying that cutting back on library services in a time of tight budgets was to cut "the bone, not the fat" in government. When the school district wanted to shut down the neighborhood grade school, Harvey fought to keep the school open and won; he still held true to his dream that the Castro could be the neighborhood where gays and straights could live together. Not one to get caught in abstruse political theory, Milk proudly counted fifty new neighborhood stop signs as one of his major accomplishments. He instructed his new City Hall aide, Anne Kronenberg, to give complaints about fixing potholes a top-priority status. "They might not remember how you voted on appropriations," he told her, "but every time they vote, they'll always remember that pothole in front of their house." Such matters represented the heart of politics to Harvey Milk. Even Harvey's most bitter opponents soon had to admit that Harvey was not the disaster they had predicted he would be.

As his early months in office wore on, Harvey gained greater confidence and poise. He reined his once galloping pace of speech to a reasonable canter. The formerly frenzied waving of arms gave way to a calmer, more confident gesture of one arm, index finger extended, which photographed better. He did his board homework meticulously. When a friend went to rouse him for a 2 A.M. emergency one morning, he found Harvey wide awake in his pajamas, reading the complicated city charter. Veteran Supervisor John Molinari thought Milk was acting driven at times in his effort to keep up on all the issues before the board, as if he had to prove that he was more than just a gay supervisor.

Harvey's good humor started outshining his natural abrasiveness, so that even while he was often in the minority of board votes, few colleagues disliked the politician with a penchant for puns and one-liners. Michael Wong found a thoroughly ecstatic Milk when he visited City Hall in March. Harvey recounted his excitement at a recent fund raising dinner.

"Mike, you should have been at the dinner," he enthused. "I told the audience, and a lot of Chamber of Commerce types were there, that the candidate I supported for President in 1976 was a populist named

Fred Harris. When the polls showed he was within striking distance of winning [his senate seat], the oil companies sent him a check for two thousand dollars. His manager said, 'Fred what should we do with the money?' Fred told him, 'Screw them and send it back.' The manager pleaded, 'But we need the money.' Fred said, 'Okay, deposit the money and then screw them.' And that's what I'm doing tonight."

"You're kidding?"

"Mike, they were stunned," Milk giggled. "No one knew what to say and finally they started to clap."

"Same old Harvey."

"And you know what else?" Harvey pulled out a jar of jelly beans which, because of his sweet tooth, was never far from his mouth. "I'm getting the board addicted to jelly beans. Every time they come in here, I feed them one, then another, then another. They're all hooked. And Dianne and Quentin [Kopp], let me tell you they're both assholes. They think they're so high and mighty. What I do is leave my door open when I'm on the phone and when I know that Dianne or Quentin is outside, I yell real loud, 'Shit, goddamn it, fuck' and all that street talk. It bugs the shit out of them."

The conversation shifted to Harvey's assessment of his colleagues, including the man who had emerged as the most conservative board member, Dan White. "White, I like Dan," Harvey insisted. "He's learning and he and I talk a lot. Give him some time."

Moments later, White was walking to his office across the hall and saw Wong in Harvey's room. He stepped in to greet Mike. Harvey took to clowning around.

"Dan, look at this toy," Harvey said, picking up a little statue of Mickey Mouse on a box. Harvey pushed a button and Mickey started running in place.

"Notice how Mickey is always the nice guy and Donald Duck is always the nasty aggressor?" Harvey asked. "Walt Disney was ahead of his time. Mickey Mouse represented black people and Donald Duck represented whites."

Wong was stunned that Harvey would say something like that to White. Dan just smiled; Wong figured he didn't understand what Milk was saying. The trio soon turned to talk of future politics. Wong asked Dan teasingly, "Are you going to challenge our great mayor in 1979?"

White smiled and gave the politician's answer. "No," adding pointedly, "not yet."

After Dan left, Harvey explained that he was trying to educate his fellow freshman. "He's basically a decent person, just uneducated," Harvey said. "He'll learn."

"I said he was safe."
"Out."
The shortstop threw his mitt into the dirt.
"C'mon, Dan," another player pleaded. He wanted White to let the matter slide.
"He was out," Dan White pouted from the infield.
And that's the way the whole game went. The game was the traditional summer standoff between the board and the mayor's office. Most of the legislators dropped any pretenses of august demeanor to lay back, drink beer, and shout at Mayor Moscone, who stopped briefly to shed his jacket, roll up his sleeves, and take a few whacks at the ball. But there was Dan White, making dramatic plays, running after every ball, arguing vehemently with the umpire, throwing down his mitt and stomping around the diamond when a call went against his team. John Molinari had to admit White was the perfect kind of guy to have on his team; a guy who hated to lose.

The same temperament marked his brief service as supervisor. Board President Feinstein, who had always stayed close to police and fire issues, took the novice under her wing and became his political mentor, but even with her steady hand behind him, he proved a poor protégé. He hated to lose at anything. When Supervisor Molinari made a routine request that a street be briefly closed for a Columbus Day bike race, White fought him in committee because the police said it might cause an inconvenience. When the closure passed committee anyway, White delivered an impassioned plea to the board, again citing police objections. That the board would turn a deaf ear to the police stunned and outraged him. His colleagues were shocked that he would fight so passionately over such a minor issue. After he lost the board vote, he didn't speak to Molinari for days.

White's biggest setback, and the one that permanently soured his relationship with Milk, came over a proposed psychiatric treatment center to be placed in an empty convent in his district. Even before White was sworn in, he was eagerly lobbying against the center, echoing neighbors' fears that the center would put "arsonists, rapists and other criminals" at their doorstep. Before learning much about the issue, Harvey indicated he would probably vote with Dan. When the final vote on the center neared, White had his 6–5 majority, but, as the gay legislator learned more about the center—and of the San Francisco children sent far away to a state hospital where they were removed from any daily contact with their families—he pondered switching his vote. "They've got to be next to somebody's house," Harvey finally decided, and tilted the majority for the center. After the vote, Supervisor Quentin Kopp reportedly saw Dan White mutter, "I see a leopard never changes his spots."

The loss infuriated White, who had made the center a major campaign issue in his district. He had lost, and he left little doubt as to whom was responsible for his failure. For months, White would not even speak to Harvey. The smiles with which he had once greeted Anne Kronenberg stopped abruptly. Harvey had to appoint his other aide, Dick Pabich, to serve as a liaison with White. Other supervisors noticed White stopped spending much time at City Hall; he moped and pouted during the weekly board meetings.

White's immediate anger fell on Harvey's pet project, the gay rights bill. At a committee meeting before Milk's vote on the psychiatric center, Dan voted for the bill, talking at length about his experiences as a paratrooper in Vietnam. "I found a lot of the things that I had read about—that had been attributed to certain people—blacks, Chinese, gays, whites—just didn't hold up under fire, literally under fire," he said. "I saw men I was in combat with perform as admirably as anyone else would perform from whatever background they were. I learned right there that people have many problems—we all have our problems and the sooner we leave discrimination in any form behind, the better off we'll all be." When the gay rights law came for a vote before the entire board—a week after Milk voted against White on the psychiatric center—White had significantly changed his views. "According to the city attorney's office, if a transvestite shows up at a public school with all the qualifications for teaching, they can't refuse to hire him for an opening, even if they object to having a man dressed as a woman in their school," White complained to one reporter.

White was not alone in his fears. Supervisor Feinstein, whose interest with the gay leather scene bordered on obsession, openly wondered if the bill would make landlords rent to S&M cultists. "One of the uncomfortable parts of San Francisco's liberalism has been the encouragement of sadism and masochism," she said. "The gay community is going to have to face it. There's a need to set some standards. The right of an individual to live his life-style in a way he or she chooses can become offensive."

Feinstein later regretted that she had felt obliged to publicly hold her nose while talking about gay rights, but in the end she overcame her trepidations about leathermen tenants and voted for the bill. By 1978, the political stakes were too high for any serious politician with ambitions for higher office to raise gay dander. Only Dan White voted against the measure. "A vast majority of people—I'll use the Roman Catholics for example—have very strong beliefs," he said. "Change is counterproductive when you force it on people. I fear that's where the problem is going to start."

White later told Dick Pabich why he had voted nay. "Harvey voted against me," he said, "so I voted against Harvey." White also told Pabich that he had interceded months before to persuade Board President Feinstein to appoint Harvey to the committee governing the city's bus system, a slot Milk wanted badly. He had helped Harvey; Harvey had betrayed him. That was the first time Pabich—and later Milk—ever learned of White's action on behalf of him.

Harvey would have preferred a unanimous vote for the bill, but the 10–1 margin was good enough, especially at a time when cities across the nation were taking up initiative repeals of local gay rights ordinances and as State Senator John Briggs geared up for his California anti-gay teachers initiative. On the day of the signing, Harvey presented Mayor Moscone with a powder blue felt-tipped pen to sign the bill, a camp gesture that assured the pair's photo on the cover of the afternoon paper. "I don't do this enough," said Moscone, "taking swift and unambiguous action on a substantial move for civil rights."

The fracas on the gay rights ordinance kicked off a public feud between White and Milk. White steadfastly opposed every street closing or permit that involved gays. When Dennis Peron's Castro Street pot supermarket got busted and both Milk and Supervisor Silver came to Peron's defense, White took to the board's floor to express his shock that Harvey would support a marijuana dealer.

Harvey, however, still maintained that White could be "educated," as Milk liked to put it. Harvey sometimes contrasted White with Supervisor Feinstein—the "Wicked Witch of the West," Harvey called her—whom Milk thought politicked from a sense of *noblesse oblige*. He thought Feinstein was intelligent enough to take a more progressive place in city politics, while White's conservatism stemmed from ignorance. For her part, Feinstein saw Milk as an unusual melange of characteristics. She was impressed by his tireless devotion to his job and the meticulous research he conducted on issues far beyond

the realm of gay concerns. Still, the grandstanding in Milk's showman-
ship at board meetings frustrated her. As board president, she had to
make sure the body got on with its business and Milk's theatrics did
not always make her task easy. Feinstein hoped Milk would mellow
with experience. Harvey, meanwhile, wrote her off and worked instead
to curry favor with White. He attended the young supervisor's baby
shower. He tried softening White with humor. During one exchange on
gays, Harvey told Dan, "Don't knock it unless you've tried it." Dan
White was not amused.

As White withdrew further from Harvey and his other colleagues,
he became closer to the sphere of interests Harvey bitterly opposed—
downtown corporations and real estate developers. White had started
as an angry blue-collar populist, but he quickly turned into the great
white hope of the downtown interests—a politician with a future. "The
guys at the Chamber of Commerce must have sat him down and started
talking about God, and Dan thought, 'Gee, these guys aren't so bad
after all,' " said one sympathetic leader of a union that had endorsed
White.

Feinstein helped connect White to Warren Simmons, a major real
estate developer who was opening a tourist development at Pier 39. The
Pier 39 project had all the trappings of old-fashioned political corrup-
tion and kept the city's muckrakers churning out reams of copy, since
a number of commissioners, supervisors, and other public officials who
were involved in securing approval for the project also ended up with
concessions for lucrative businesses there. Simmons gave White a concession for a fried potato stand to help augment the sparse $800
monthly salary supervisors earned. According to documents from the
Federal Bureau of Investigation, the FBI had started a probe into Dan
White's connections with Simmons to see if the concession was a payoff
for political favors. Before the probe turned up any substantive information, however, Dan White had been charged with far more serious
crimes and the FBI files noted that the investigation "should not be
discussed outside the bureau."

"How do you like Feinstein for mayor?"

Margo St. James had gained national fame as the organizer of
Coyote, an organization representing the interests of prostitutes. She
had also gained frequent phone calls from a police officer she nicknamed Joe the Pig. She had gone to San Francisco City College with
him twenty years before; now, he seemed to take pleasure in reaffirming

her worst fears about the city's police. A year before, in 1977, Joe had called to explain gleefully that the most right-wing police officers planned on murdering Police Chief Charles Gain. It would be easy, he said. Gain led an active social life, remained unarmed when he was off duty, and would not keep a bodyguard. St. James warned Gain who, hearing similar rumors on his own, started taking such precautions as never sitting with his back toward the door when in a restaurant. Now, Joe the Pig had called Margo to pass on the advice that he thought Dianne Feinstein might be mayor before the year was out.

"But Feinstein just said that she wasn't going to run in 1979, that George was bound to get reelected," Margo answered.

"What if George died?" the policeman asked.

"He's young and healthy," said Margo. "He's not going to die."

"Remember what they were gonna do to the chief last year?" Joe asked. "They couldn't get him, so they'll do the next best thing and get the guy who put him there."

St. James was incredulous.

"He'll be dead by Christmas," the police officer concluded.

Margo was surprised by the chipper attitude the officer took toward the topic of political assassination, but she was not taken aback by the hard feelings police rank and file held against Gain and his boss, George Moscone. The mayor was pressing hard for settlement of an old discrimination suit filed by the Officers For Justice (OFJ), a minority policeman's organization. The suit alleged that the nepotic department discriminated wildly against blacks in promotion and hiring; the SFPD was, according to one study, more racially segregated than the police force of Montgomery, Alabama. The OFJ wanted a multimillion-dollar settlement from the city and rigid enforcement of hiring and promotion quotas for minorities. Courts had long ago ordered that all hiring and promotion in the department be frozen, pending a settlement of the suit. Mayor Moscone had worked out a settlement that the Police Officers' Association detested. Both White and Feinstein spearheaded opposition on the board. Dan White fretted to a right-wing *Examiner* columnist, "Once they've taken over the law-enforcement mechanism of San Francisco, they've got the city cold." The settlement went down to a characteristic 6–5 defeat on the board. That was a precarious margin, as far as the POA was concerned. Even worse, both the mayor and the Civil Service Commission in 1978 announced that the new police recruitment drive would include a push to get openly gay cops on the police force. The POA monthly newsletter was filled with letters from members complaining about the development. No single police officer had made the decision to follow Chief Gain's advice and step forward as gay; now, gays would be forced on the department. One sergeant wrote that any gay officers should be given separate shower rooms, a solution which, he conceded, got sticky when the matter of showering locations for possible bisexual officers had to be sorted out. Even Gain's critics gave him credit for modernizing training and promotion procedures, but the rank-and-file discontent had seethed since Gain's first days in office and nearly every week brought new items in gossip columns that Gain was on the way out.

St. James forwarded a warning to Mayor Moscone's office. In August, she heard that Moscone had gotten a bodyguard.

"I can't believe it," sputtered an aide to another supervisor as he tossed the morning *Chronicle* across a table in the City Hall lunchroom. "Every time you pick up the paper, there's Harvey doing something new. How in the the hell does that guy do it?"

Like any good dramatist, Harvey Milk knew that the success of any show depended on good press. Milk's own flair for the theatrical as well as his well cultivated media connections quickly made Harvey the best covered supervisor in San Francisco. "Harvey and newspapers were made for each other; they were bound to have a love affair," said Harvey's friend, Frank Robinson, later. "For the papers, it was like having their own Flo LaGuardia in their backyard."

Even the routine rotation of the city's acting mayorship among supervisors became a front-page media event for Harvey once Mayor Moscone went on a Europeon vacation. As soon as the mayor's limousine chauffeured him to City Hall, Milk bounded into the Mayor's office and called a press conference, explaining to reporters that he was the first openly gay—albeit acting—mayor in the United States. This gave one more occasion for Harvey to talk piously about that sixteen-year-old from Altoona, Pennsylvania. Once the public pontification was completed, Milk spent the rest of the morning privately speculating to friends on the merits of the mayor's massive desk as a seduction site for any of a number of handsome young City Hall bureaucrats. For lunch, Harvey took Pabich and Kronenberg to Castro Street, keeping the mayor's limousine parked conspicuously in front of the restaurant. He later amused reporters when he opened a friend's new delicatessen with the quip, "I am the only mayor who is cutting the ribbon and then wearing it." The picture of Harvey behind the mayor's massive desk made page one in the afternoon *Examiner*.

Thinly veiled queer joking has always been considered good copy in San Francisco newspapers and Harvey was always quick to oblige. One gossip writer listed him as the "number one most ineligible bachelor of San Francisco" while columnist Herb Caen joked that Dianne and Harvey were fighting it out to see who got to be City Hall's official Avon Lady. When Jarvis-Gann budget cuts started squeezing the city coffers, Milk proposed legalized gambling in San Francisco. The plan had no chance of gaining approval, but it did make page one, permitting Harvey to retort to the plan's critics with, "Let he who is without sin cast the first dice."

The media coup of the year and the issue that best symbolized Harvey's theories on how government should work, centered on the mundane subject of dog feces. Survey after survey showed that sidewalk dog droppings were San Franciscans' biggest complaint about city life. Milk, therefore, sponsored a bill requiring dog owners to clean up after their pets, waxing philosophically that, "It's symbolic of all the problems of irresponsibility we face in big, depersonalized, alienating urban societies." Privately, Harvey lectured Anne and Dick, "Whoever can solve the dogshit problem can be elected mayor of San Francisco, even President of the United States." Years later, some would claim Harvey was a socialist or various other sorts of ideologues, but, in reality, Harvey's political philosophy was never more complicated than the issue of dogshit; government should solve people's basic problems.

The proposal, of course, got more fan mail than any other act Milk made as supervisor. For television cameras and newspaper photographers, Harvey gave demonstrations, using ersatz turds, of how his "pooper scooper" bags worked, concluding the news segments by stepping into some of the real stuff himself. Harvey walked away from the demonstrations with dirty shoes, but his picture went national on the A-wire. Only a few of his closest friends knew that he had spent an hour that morning walking up and down a park, finding a demonstration site that had the appropriate piles of dog droppings to sort-of-accidentally step in when the cameras arrived. Mayor Moscone publicly decried the fact that Milk's dog turd stories were making page one, while his stories about serious city problems were lucky to get to page eleven. Still, the story epitomized what Milk wanted to accomplish in office. "All over the country, they're reading about me and the story doesn't center on me being gay," he said. "It's just about a gay person who is doing his job." That, to Milk, was education.

Harvey's board colleagues were no more immune to the supervisor's pranks than the press. Milk frequently bandied with Chinese-American Supervisor Gordon Lau, partly because Harvey could never resist doling out ethnic slurs and partly because Milk figured that a gay-Chinese alliance could control the city one day, since both groups were migrating to San Francisco in such large numbers. When Harvey complained of being broke, Lau joked that he should do what every other gay in town was doing and become a realtor. "Then I could sell to all your Chinese cousins," Harvey deadpanned. When conservatives once dallied too long at the podium, Harvey turned to Lau to comment, "We'll fix them. We'll get all your guys to buy property from my guys and we'll be all set up." One day Milk plaintively asked Gordon, "When are you going to do my laundry?" Lau joked back, "When you redecorate my office."

Harvey also earnestly explained to his colleagues that the reason he kept jelly beans by his desk was because many years ago, homosexuals were derisively called jelly beans. "You can't imagine what I've got them believing," he'd snicker to gay friends. Supervisor Molinari, meanwhile, took to delighting both Harvey and his audience at one Republican event by talking about how he and Harvey had died and gone to heaven. They had only one command: If they had one lustful thought, their wings would fall off. As the story went, a shapely beauty soon walked by and Molinari's wings dropped to the cloud. When he bent down to pick them up, Harvey's wings fell. It was a variation of an old gay joke, but the fact that Molinari felt comfortable to tell him such jokes pleased Harvey immensely; it was another triumph. Milk came to judge his colleagues less by their politics than by their sense of humor. That ultimately is what bothered him about Dan White. He didn't seem to have a sense of humor.

"Here in Napa we kill cocksuckers who infiltrate city government." Wrote another, "What will the guys of Bayshore High School class of '47 think of Miss Harvey now?"

Even as Harvey clowned his way through press and politics, problems haunted his personal life. The hate mail increased with every new Milk clipping. Some of it was outright threatening. "Shoot fruit, not pool," read one card. Others revealed many a deeply disturbed psyche: "Nobody really gives a damn if you're homosexual. No one cares if you suck or like to be sucked or do sex in the ass. Even many who are not homos, if they have any sense, realize that under certain conditions, they also could enjoy being a homo. The right time, place, person, atmosphere, etc., etc. But to brag about it, many feel only a mentally disturbed person will." Harvey publicly joked about the mail and Anne sometimes posted a "letter of the week." But they took a toll. Anne noticed it one day when she fell into her old habit of musing about what it would be like forty or fifty years later when the whole group of idealistic young activists around Harvey became senior citizens. "I'll never live to be a senior citizen," Milk said casually. In other conversations, Harvey dropped remarks about how it would end; he always felt his would be a violent death.

Harvey's skimpy supervisorial salary of $9,600 a year kept both himself and his business in debt. The only reason he sustained an appropriate appearance in dress was because his friend, gay publisher Bob Ross, had an acquaintance who had died shortly after Harvey's election. By coincidence, the dead man was Milk's same gangly size, right down to the size 13 shoes. He also was a clotheshorse, so Harvey spent most of the year well dressed in a dead man's clothes.

Harvey's biggest problem was "Taco Bell," Jack Lira. At twenty-six, Jack had not finished high school and had learned few skills beyond how to drink massive amounts of alcohol and manage to drink still more. Even that, he did not do with élan. He maintained a complex love-hate relationship with Harvey's politics. On one hand, he enjoyed the chance to be Harvey's First Lady and sometimes pushed for invitations to dinners or events. But he was ill prepared for the social and political skills such a role demanded, so he would attend an event with Milk, become nervous, get drunk, create a loud, public argument, and then stomp out. Harvey offered to send Jack back to school; Jack didn't want to go back to school. Harvey found Lira many jobs, doing everything from Mexican restaurant work to bottling bootleg isobutyl nitrate in a downtown popper factory. It was weeks before Harvey learned that when Jack got up every morning and left the house, he wasn't going to work but to a Castro Street bar. Jack's jobs usually ended with his being fired for nonauthorized absences. The feud between Lira and Scott Smith intensified as the months wore on. Harvey might have been able to keep boys back in his Wall Street days, Smith reasoned, but not on his $9,600 supervisor's salary and the struggling camera store business that supported both Harvey and Scott. Seeing Harvey's subsidization of Jack draining the business, Scott found his own diversions on which to spend what he saw as his share of entertainment money. The business suffered further as tensions increased; Milk privately complained to one *Chronicle* reporter that Scott was blowing the profits; Scott figured the profits were going to Jack's favorite bars.

Agitated times were falling on San Francisco's gay community that year, as gay rights were beaten back in referenda in Wichita, St. Paul, and Eugene and as California homosexuals prepared for the Briggs Initiative. Lira became moody at the news and fell into severe depression after seeing the television movie "Holocaust," the story of the Nazi extermination of the Jews. Hints of Lira's troubled past sometimes emerged: the father who refused to call him "son," a mother who only fearfully spoke to him, afraid of incurring his father's potential wrath. A lonely childhood, turning to the lonelier world of alcoholism. Every personal and political friend Harvey had now prodded him to drop Jack. "I'm out to help people just like Jack, give them hope," Harvey explained to political associates. "I've got to help him." To his closer personal friend Tom Randol, Harvey gave a more candid explanation. "Jack is truly good sex," he said. "When I come home to him, I don't have to talk politics. I don't have to talk intelligently. I don't have to think. I can just relax. Besides," he added pragmatically, "Where is a forty-eight-year-old man like me going to get such a hot-looking young guy?"

Gossip flowed in some knowledgeable gay circles that Harvey indulged himself in more exotic sexual practices in these later years. Surprisingly, though, Harvey's sex life never came under any public scrutiny and rarely emerged as any kind of an issue. That was not the case for many of the city's political figures. The city's worst kept political secret, for example, was that a major liberal city office holder had a fondness for black prostitutes. Though publicly portrayed as an ethnic family man, the politician's proclivities and the mishaps that they got him into were so legendary that two newspaper reporters tailed the leader one night when they saw the official leave North Beach Restaurant in the company of a new woman friend. The pair walked to the woman's Volkswagen in the front of SS. Peter and Paul Church —the city's major Italian Catholic institution—where the politician got a quick blow job. Newspaper stories later that year would only obliquely talk of how the Reverend Jim Jones bragged of providing black followers to a "major public official." The whole story, however, made the rounds at reporters' bars. As one *Chronicle* staffer put it, "We got the general impression that he liked black prostitutes to sit on his lap, play with his nipples and call him daddy."

That particular politician's nemesis, meanwhile, was a dour conservative who was known around San Francisco as the town grump. The way reporters told the story, this conservative had been a fairly sociable guy until his wife ran off with his law partner. Losing both his business partnership and his wife in one blow would do in anyone's good humor, pundits observed. Meanwhile, at least one board member was surprised when, in the course of talking to Board President Feinstein, Dianne opened her purse and a gun was nestled inside. Feinstein later publicly discussed carrying the rod as a means of protection against potential assassins. Given all this, it wasn't surprising that Harvey's sometimes kinky love life never got much attention; against the ensemble of the lusty liberal, the cuckolded conservative, and the pistol-packing socialite, Harvey's quirks were hardly conspicuous.

You get to know a guy, really get to know a guy on the campaign trail, Art Agnos thought. You might never be friends but you watch them so much, you can practically predict just what they're gonna do. After bitterly slugging it out with Milk in the assembly race two years before, Agnos didn't need a crystal ball to see Harvey's political plans. He was mending fences with all the gay leaders who had opposed him so long—Foster, Stokes, and Goodstein—while building his bridges back into the political establishment with people like Moscone and even Agnos himself. The overtures to Chinese voters were smart moves, as was the fact Milk had not let himself sit as simply the gay supervisor, Agnos thought. Milk candidly admitted to his former opponent that he wanted to make a stab at the board presidency once he got reelected in November 1979. The next step, to Agnos, was obvious. "He's going to run for mayor," Agnos counseled friends. "You know what? I think he can win."

The wiser political observers pooh-poohed the notion that Milk, a homosexual, would consider, much less run for mayor. That flew too much in the face of reality. A homosexual for mayor? But Agnos knew all too well that Harvey had no compunctions against flying in the face of reality. "That guy will one day be the mayor of San Francisco," Agnos said.

Harvey was less guarded about his future agenda when talking to Michael Wong. On the day of his acting mayorship, Milk ran into Wong and promptly offered his old friend a ride in the mayor's limo.

Young Harvey Milk on a pony. (courtesy of the Estate of Harvey Milk)

Harvey and Robert Milk at Coney Island on September 1, 1942. (courtesy of the Estate of Harvey Milk)

Harvey Milk with his mother Minerva and father
William at his college graduation on June 17, 1951.
(courtesy of the Estate of Harvey Milk)

Harvey Milk in his navy dress whites, circa 1955. (courtesy of Estate of
Harvey Milk)

Harvey Milk with Joe Campbell
September, 1956. (courtesy of
the Estate of Harvey Milk)

Harvey Milk with Joe Campbell
on July 13, 1958 at Riis Park
Beach where they met two years
earlier. (courtesy of Estate of
Harvey Milk)

Harvey Milk on the Plymouth Savoy in which
he and Joe Campbell moved to Texas in 1957.
(courtesy of the Estate of Harvey Milk)

Harvey Milk and Scott Smith, 1971. (courtesy
of the Estate of Harvey Milk)

Harvey Milk with Jack Galen McKinley and
their dog, Trick. (courtesy of the Estate of
Harvey Milk)

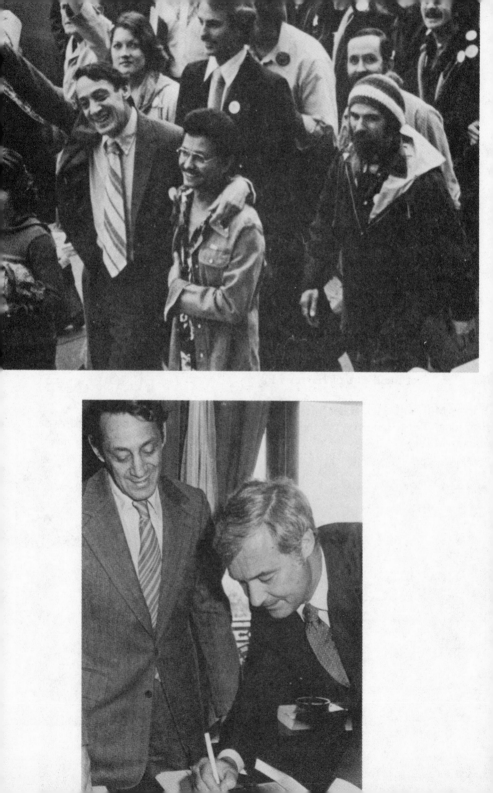

Harvey Milk with Jack Lira under his arm walks to City Hall on the day of his inauguration. Dick Pabich in suit and tie is walking directly behind Milk. (photo by Daniel Nicoletta)

Mayor George Moscone signs the San Francisco Gay Civil Rights bill with Harvey Milk looking on. (photo by Efren Ramirez)

Harvey Milk's swearing-in on the steps of City Hall. Supervisor Gordon Lau is directly above Milk with Anne Kronenberg to Lau's left and George Moscone applauding to Lau's right. (photo by Efren Ramirez)

A human billboard from the 1975 supervisorial campaign. At far right is Jim Rivaldo. Dennis Seeley is fifth from right. Carl Carlson, Scott Smith and Harry Britt are ninth, tenth and eleventh from right, respectively (photo by Leland Toy)

Harvey Milk in his clown outfit on May 21, 1978. (photo by Daniel Nicoletta)

Harvey Milk greets a constituent at the 1978 Gay Freedom Day Parade. (photo by Robert Purzan)

photo by Jerry Pritikin

Harvey Milk speaking at Union Square rally on the night of Anita Bryant's victory in Miami.

Michael could tell Harvey was enjoying his chance to play Andrew Jackson in the White House, but deferred the ride and mentioned that all the day's publicity might lead to speculation that Harvey wanted to be mayor.

"Who said it's speculation?" Harvey asked.

Wong told him he was crazy: a gay supervisor yes, a gay mayor, no. "Not even San Francisco is ready for that," he insisted.

"I'm not so sure, my little fortune cookie," Harvey said. "Besides, it doesn't hurt to let people think I'm interested in the job."

Harvey proudly showed Allan Baird the pen-and-pencil set Allan had given him during the first supervisorial campaign in 1973, when Baird made his first trip to City Hall. The Teamster friends who had once worried that Baird might be queer for hanging out with Harvey were now complimenting Allan on his foresight, and occasionally trying to nudge a favor from the supervisorial friend.

"Are you going to be the next mayor of San Francisco?" Allan bluntly asked Harvey.

"Allan, you can be the next mayor of San Francisco, anybody can be," Harvey said. "All you have to do is work hard and you can get it."

Harvey figured he had already pretty much proved that point with his election as supervisor.

With the specter of a statewide fight on the Briggs Initiative looming ahead, Harvey took to building a statewide political machine geared to his nuts-and-bolts approach to politics. He met the Los Angeles end of the planned machine before his election when he ran into Don Amador, a gay studies professor at a local college. With characteristic tact, Milk told him the best way to educate people about gays was through politics, not colleges.

"How many students do you have?" Harvey demanded.

"Thirty," said Amador.

"How long do you have them for?"

"Sixteen weeks."

Harvey made his instant calculations. Only thirty people every sixteen weeks. "No," he said tersely. "That's too slow."

The two struck up a friendship. Once in office, Harvey lobbied Los Angeles Mayor Tom Bradley to appoint Amador as his official liaison to the gay community. Amador got the job and Milk started persuading

the teacher that he should run for office if he really wanted to educate
people about gays. On a spare afternoon, Harvey jotted out his ten rules
of how to win an election:

1. Interviews with all major papers. [All was underlined three times.]
2. Knock on all doors.
3. Ride buses.
4. Visit non-gay bars during the daytime and any singles bars at nite.
5. Coffee shops and restaurants. Stop off early in morning and late at
night.
6. Shake hands.
7. Shake hands.
8. As few meetings as possible—just meet the people.
9. Door to door of registered Demo's is very best thing you can do
outside of media coverage.
10. Don't stop.

Harvey's new friendship with Amador gave him rare chances to
escape the tensions of home and office to stay in what became his own
room in Don's comfortable home. One day, Amador and his lover
returned to find the house covered with orange juice promotional signs.
"Orange Juice Just Isn't for Breakfast Anymore" posters hung from the
chandeliers while o.j. cardboard table tents covered all counters and
promotional bumper stickers graced the windows. Harvey had a new
boyfriend, an employee of Anita Bryant's boss, the Florida Citrus
Commission. Bob Tuttle had seen Harvey standing alone after speaking
at a Los Angeles gay rally. It seemed funny to see somebody that
important standing all by himself, Tuttle thought, like a lost little boy.
"I just want to tell you that I appreciate what you're doing because if
this ever turns against us, you'll be the first one they go after," Tuttle
impulsively told him. Milk beamed back, "Yeah, I know."

Tuttle was twenty-eight, but looked all of twenty-one, an appearance that put him in Harvey's favored age bracket, so the pair started
a long-distance romance. During a four-day stay at Tuttle's Venice
Beach apartment, Harvey confided he was then having his longest
vacation in six years.

During another visit to Amador's, the phone rang. A young voice
said he had read about Don in a *People* magazine story about Amador's
gay courses. He was seventeen years old, in Richmond, Minnesota, he

explained—and about to kill himself because his parents were going to institutionalize him for being gay. Harvey took the call, confident he could do some crash counseling; the young man was, after all, the lonely teenage constituent for whom Harvey had tailored all his candidacies. "Run away from home," Harvey urged. "Get on the bus, go to the next biggest city—New York, San Francisco, Los Angeles, even Minneapolis, it doesn't matter. Just leave."

The young man started crying. He was confined to a wheelchair and couldn't get on any bus he said. That moment marked one of the only times Amador would ever see tears come to Harvey's eyes. Everything was so much more goddamn complex than he could say in his hope speech.

thirteen

Willkommen Castro

"On this spot, four days ago, a young citizen was murdered because he was a homosexual."

Ribbons in the colors of the Catalonian province, yellow and orange, laid silently on the street next to the cardboard flowers by the hand-scrawled epitaph. It had been years since Cleve Jones fulfilled his adolescent dream and come to San Francisco for his first San Francisco Gay Freedom Day Parade. Like most of his friends, he too had been swept up in the tide of militance after the Anita Bryant controversy. Weeks after Orange Tuesday, he had left his Castro Street apartment to take a hitchihiking tour of Europe. In Barcelona, he had heard there would be a rally, here, where the blood of a gay man had spilled just four days before. The fledgling Spanish gay activists were cautious as they first approached the spot. This was the first gay demonstration since the death of Francisco Franco, they explained to Cleve; that meant the first gay demonstration in Spanish history. Ever.

Slowly, the momentum grew as Jones and a cadre of the braver gays marched down Los Ramblos from the waterfront to the Catalonian provincial capitol. From nowhere, La Guardia Civil appeared,

211

firing rubber bullets into the crowd. Jones turned to see bullets tear off the scalp of the woman marching at his side. Blood, broken glass, and tear gas filled the streets. Rather than surrender, the gay protestors launched into an elaborate game of cat and mouse with the police through the winding alleys and lanes of Barcelona. They took the chairs and tables from sidewalk cafés and built barricades, taunting the police to fire on. Cleve threw his first rock. The street fighting in Barcelona excited his long latent anger even more than the frenzied chanting of the San Francisco demonstrations after Orange Tuesday. When the days' fighting waned, he wrote a long letter enthusiastically recounting the day to a friend; the letter was widely reprinted in gay papers across the country. When Jones returned to Castro Street that fall to work in Harvey Milk's supervisorial campaign, he still talked ecstatically of that day in Barcelona. He had suddenly realized that the gay movement meant more than an annual parade and that it would soon be bigger than anyone imagined; too much anger simmered beneath the surface, all over the world.

Jones couldn't have come to a time and place that could better nourish that conviction. A sense of gay manifest destiny gripped San Francisco by 1978, as if it were ordained that homosexuals should people the city from sea to shining bay. Harvey's bold public role as Castro Street's neighborhood supervisor—and the national publicity he garnered as the city's gay spokesperson—certainly fueled that attitude. But the import of the San Francisco gay phenomenon had implications far beyond the pillared walls of City Hall, and the gays of San Francisco saw themselves as the avant-garde of a burgeoning national movement.

Dade County marked the beginning, not the end, of organized opposition to the gay civil rights cause; the issue moved to the forefront of the nation's social agenda. Fundamentalists filed petitions in rapid-fire succession in St. Paul, Wichita, Seattle, and Eugene to repeal local gay-rights ordinances. Even more significantly, State Senator John Briggs was targeting his initiative for the November general election ballot, when one in ten American voters went to the polls to vote for, among other offices, California governor.

Gays seemed on the defensive around the country. The Oklahoma legislature enacted their own version of Briggs's proposal to ban gays from teaching in public schools. From Oklahoma City soon afterward came the news that one hundred teenage boys had formed their own Klu Klux Klan chapter and had picked gay bars as their primary targets, slashing tires and beating patrons with baseball bats. In nearby

Arkansas, the legislature took up a bill that not only banned gays from teaching, but denied credentials to gays in the fields of pediatrics, psychiatry, child psychology and youth counseling. Moreover, the bill empowered the state to strip existing licenses from anybody discovered to be gay and penalized gays caught lying about their sexuality by five years in prison. Adolf Hitler had started his final solution for Jews by just such methodical, restrictive legislation, and the analogy was not lost on the startled gays of San Francisco. The pink triangle, which Hitler forced gays to wear in his death camps, soon became the most prominent symbol of the San Francisco gay rights movement.

The courts provided few hopes for judicial remedies. The U.S. Supreme Court refused to even hear the case of a Tacoma teacher with a flawless record who was fired from his job not for any misdeed, but solely because his principal learned of his homosexuality. In a more extreme case, the Supreme Court refused to review the conviction of a North Carolina man guilty solely of having sex with another man, a proverbial consenting adult. The Jacksonville police admitted they had recruited the man to entice their prey, a local massage parlor owner, and that the eventual seduction was "deliberate and planned." The man was sentenced to nine months in prison for committing a crime that according to Dr. Kinsey's statistics, one in 10 Americans routinely indulge—and the Supreme Court would not even listen to arguments that the man's privacy and equal protection rights might have been violated.

Given the courts' timidity on homosexual issues, gays didn't feel any more reassured when Anita Bryant gave a long magazine interview in which she said gays should be locked up for at least twenty years if convicted of commiting just one homosexual act. "Any time you water down the law, it just makes it easier for immorality to be tolerated," she explained. "Why make it easier for them? I think it only helps condone it and this makes it easier for kids who wouldn't be so concerned. If it were a felony, [it] might make them think twice, especially the younger ones." Of course, Bryant held out hope for salvation. "They'll have plenty of time to think in prison," she said.

Though a few dozen congressmen bravely introduced federal gay rights legislation, hopes of any congressional action withered; few major national politicians wanted to take the risk of being tied to gays. In an effort to recruit a big-name speaker for his San Francisco Gay Democratic Club and to get a major public figure to stand with gays against their increasingly virulent opposition, Harvey Milk sent letters to President Carter, Senator Edward Kennedy, Governor Jerry Brown, and Georgia State Senator Julian Bond, imploring them to make some kind of pro-gay statement, hopefully at an S.F. Gay dinner. Each letter ended with a plea roughly like the one Harvey sent to Carter:

> Sooner or later, the massive gay population will indeed win their rights, as other groups have already done. Sooner or later, the strife and anger and hatred and violence against gay people will be put aside. What we seek now is to leap over the many years and great turmoil that will take place by having the person who represents these people speak out now.

A Carter aide sent back a two-sentence reply a week later explaining the President had prior commitments, but that he "appreciates your thoughtfulness and sends his best wishes." Julian Bond wrote to say he had forwarded the request to his booking agent.

Fear and anger dominated many street-corner conversations among the young women and men who had moved to Castro Street. Though representing the entire spectrum of American life, most of the migrants—like most Americans—came from typical middle-class, mid-American backgrounds, so they were not prepared to have their backs shoved up against the wall for any reason. They may have grown up being called queers and getting beat up in locker rooms, but the attacks were so pervasive in the broad psychological and physical scope that the enemy barely seemed tangible. Now the threats could be defined as flesh and blood religious activists mounting concrete political efforts for specific election days. It was all so . . . so real. Cleve Jones started spreading word among his many street friends in the neighborhood as the day of the first post-Miami referendum vote neared in St. Paul. "Now is the time for us to get our army together," he said.

A preternatural smile spreads slowly, tremulously across Pat's lips while she speaks, as if the forty-six-year-old southern California housewife can almost see the Sunday School picture of Jesus Christ drifting into sight. "And the Bible says that just before Jesus comes to take all Christians to heaven, there will be times when men will have unnatural affections toward other men," she says calmly, her smile never losing its benevolence. "Then, God says He will visit great wrath upon the earth."

A few hours earlier, Pat had sat in the front pew of the Central Baptist Church of Pomona and filled out the three-by-five index cards on which newly saved Pomonans recorded their vital statistics before wading toward the promise of ever-lasting life in Central Baptist's plastic-walled baptismal font. Last Tuesday, Pat had had her first day of work in a different kind of heavenly project, though she saw it as no less essential to her salvation than her daily prayer studies. That's when Pat had folded fliers for the California Defend Our Children Committee, the political arm of State Senator John Briggs's efforts to ban gay teachers from public schools. Like Cleve, Pat saw herself as part of an army, one of the "foot soldiers of God" that Anita Bryant talked so glowingly about. Pat had never taken part in politics before, but this was clearly different. "This isn't politics," she insisted, "it's the Lord's work."

Gay leaders had made a vast mistake in 1977 by underestimating the intense dedication of the legions of born-again Christians because of the ease with which their spokespeople could be dismissed. John Briggs, for example, scarcely made a secret of the fact that he viewed his anti-gay teachers' drive as little more than a publicity stunt for his gubernatorial bid. Anita Bryant's later confessions about her own love life also made it unlikely that she would be God's number one draft choice to throw the first stone. Behind these foppish leaders, however, were an ardent corps of true believers who were only beginning to flex their political muscle in 1978—and the issue that initially motivated them was fighting against homosexual rights.

Religious revivals have swept America at fairly regular intervals since the nineteenth century, and throughout the mid-seventies a substantial revival of evangelical fundamentalism had swept the country's heartland. Thousands of generally sincere born-again Christians echoed Pat's fears about the Final Days in the early months of 1978 and went on to stir up the most frenzied fundamentalist politicking since Prohibition. In St. Paul, fifty couples from the Temple Baptist Church spent weekends going door to door with the provocative question: "Would you want your children taught by an overt homosexual?" Without much problem, the couples quickly collected enough signatures to put that city's four-year-old gay rights law up for a repeal vote in late April. In Wichita, like-minded parishioners of Glenville Bible Baptist Church had circulated petitions to put that city's new gay rights law up for a referendum vote two weeks after the St. Paul election. A similar movement of fundamentalists in the mellowed-out college town of Eugene,

Oregon, followed suit and petitioned to have that city's gay rights law on a special election ballot just two weeks after Wichita's. A Seattle coalition of fundamentalists, Mormons, and members of the John Birch Society successfully put another repeal measure on the Queen City's general election ballot in November.

The quick series of repeal referenda that swept west from Miami startled gay activists, who grew convinced that they were the victims of a massive New Right conspiracy. Though this initial politicization of fundamentalists over the homosexual issue certainly went on to aid the subsequent New Right emergence, gays in 1978 were the victims of nothing more vile than a conspiracy of belief. "Look right here," explained a housewife volunteer at the Wichita anti-gay headquarters when a San Francisco reporter asked for her ideaological impetus. She whipped out a pocket-sized Bible and started poring over the dozen fairly specific scriptural condemnations of homosexuality. "Look what happened to Sodom and to even the world of Noah's day when they turned away from what God said," she goaded. The fact that the nation's gay Mecca sat smack on the nation's most unstable earthquake fault only buttressed her case, she thought. Debating such campaigners produced negligible results. As one California fundamentalist shouted at a lesbian activist during a heated exchange at a Briggs organizing meeting, "You can argue with me, lady, but you can't argue with God."

Few groups were as evenly suited to battle each other as gays and fundamentalists. Both gays and evangelicals shared a profound experience that shaped their politicking; they had both been born again. For evangelical Christians, it was a theological experience, finding God in a sinful world. For gays, it was a social experience called "coming out," expressing one's gay sexuality and identity in a generally hostile heterosexual world. For both sides, the born-again experience usually meant breaking with the past, establishing a new social network and building a new life, one that was happier than the life left behind. Both sides also put great faith in the necessity for testifying to the born-again experience. Fundamentalists did this in their routine rounds of testimony for the Lord; gays did this by acknowledging their homosexuality to friends and relatives, a move that practically represented an article of faith for those in the gay movement. Both camps also saw themselves in an ultimate struggle. For gays, that meant the eradication of prejudice; for fundamentalists, it was the scripturally demanded battle against sinners and their sins. Most significantly, the costs for losing the struggle were incredibly high. During the fundamentalists' anti-gay groundswell of

1978, gay activists talked ominously of how failure could lead to a Hitleresque extermination of gays. Born-again Christians needed to go no further than *Revelations* to see that gays were the harbingers of the Final Days, times when Christians must fight sin or go to hell. Both sides, however, stood on polar opposites of society, with fundamentalists calling for a return to the most traditional American morality while gays stood for some of the least traditional social values. The troops of both sides were also incredibly motivated—gays were fighting to keep themselves out of modern-day Dachaus while, for fundamentalists, fighting gay rights became the surest way to keep their polyester leisure suits from melting in hell.

The rhetoric flared. Homosexuality, said Wichita's anti-gay spokesman, the Reverend Ron Adrian, "is a sin so rotten, so low that even dogs and cats do not practice it." The brochure from the St. Paul Citizens Alert for Morality outlined the frightening world facing fundamentalists in the Twin Cities:

> They've opened gay rap parlors, saunas, and night clubs supported by extensive advertising obviously aimed at the "uncommited" as well as their own kind. They've imported gay films for public showings. Again, obviously welcoming the "uncommitted." They've infiltrated state and city government offices and other activities, including the clergy, with homosexuals or sympathizers.

A Seattle anti-gay spokesperson chose more nostalgic phrases when she called on "Christian patriots" across America to help their anti-gay effort, saying, "This would be a step forward in preservation of Aryan culture and western civilization."

The widespread attacks hit a movement that suffered from factionalism and had little national direction. Only a handful of gay groups could claim a national constituency, and they often lacked funds to carry on a meaningful effort. The leader of one national gay organization, for example, had to supplement a meager salary by illicitly running counterfeit transit tokens for organized crime. This moonlighting was even known to members of the group's board of directors, one of whom shrugged, "I guess it shows we should pay more money." The lack of a major national group forced each city to sink or swim on its own, while the leaders who claimed to speak for gays nationally—generally based in New York—took to calling the referenda local 'brushfires' that could not be tended by the national organizations.

Harvey Milk railed on about fundamentalists being the new Nazis, but privately Harvey, for one, was thrilled at the turn the gay rights fracas had taken. News about one or another initiative made the papers daily, reaching into the homes of every American family, including those of closeted teenagers who would grow up hearing of homosexuality as a civil rights issue, not just a matter of sin, crime or perversity. Liberals may have passed the laws, but in so vociferously seeking their repeal, the born-again Christians had aided the gay cause much more profoundly by making gay rights a daily conversation topic.

At twenty-three, Cleve Jones did not have the disposition to ponder these complex interrelationships between the media, politics, and long-term social change. He was just pissed. As the April date of the St. Paul vote neared, he talked more heatedly as he cruised the corners of Castro Street. They had to do *something.* At 3 A.M., just days before the balloting in Minnesota, Cleve and a handful of friends made their move. Armed with staplers and cheaply reproduced fliers, they blanketed all available walls and phone poles in the neighborhood with the announcement—come to Castro Street at 10 P.M. on the night of the St. Paul election. In evening sessions at Jones's Castro Street apartment, the covert activists trained monitors to serve as a buffer between the expected crowds and police. There would be no notification of authorities, no police permits, nothing polite—just a raw, spontaneous expression of anger.

Even the most pessimistic gay activists were stunned at the proportions of defeat in St. Paul, which was even worse than in Dade County. Hundreds of young men in fleece-lined bomber jackets milled around the corner of Castro and Market as the news of defeat swept the neighborhood. Jones took a bullhorn and held up a police whistle, which so many gay men carried to ward off attackers. "You have whistles," he shouted. "You use them when you have been attacked. Tonight, we have been attacked."

With whistles shrieking, the crowd surged past Castro Street's gay bars, attracting hundreds more. The size and intensity of the throng startled even Jones, not to mention the police, who gave up trying to restrict the crowd to a sidewalk. By the time the raucous demonstration passed City Hall, at least two thousand were shouting and blowing their whistles in unison. They cut the traditional five-mile swath through the city, the path they had followed on Orange Tuesday, and a lively rally at Union Square lasted past midnight. Afterward, Jones and his angry young friends decided they must further organize so that they could call a spontaneous demonstration with only a few hours' notice. They also had to stake out Castro Street as the locale for gays to go to during times of crisis. "Castro Street has to be made into *our* territory. Strictly," said Jones.

One week later, State Senator John Briggs appeared on the wide granite steps of City Hall to file the petitions that would assure that his initiative, now dubbed by gays the Briggs Initiative, would appear on the November ballot. Briggs's gubernatorial campaign had fizzled by then. The initiative represented his last chance to get statewide recognition for whatever ambitions for higher office he might have held. The chants of gay demonstrators assured lead-story coverage: "John Briggs, you can't hide, we charge you with genocide."

As usual, the state senator from Fullerton had his dollop of hyperbole. He was launching the drive in San Francisco again because, he explained, the city was "the moral garbage dump of homosexuality in this country."

Not about to be outdone, Supervisor Harvey Milk told reporters, "Nobody likes garbage cause it smells. Yet eight million tourists visited San Francisco last year. I wonder how many visited Fullerton."

Within a week, Wichita voters rejected their city's gay rights ordinance by a whopping five-to-one margin. The posters had been put up secretly, only days before that march too; monitors were ready to keep the crowd in line so police would have no reason to attack. Over one thousand assembled at Castro and Market, angrily surging about like a herd of impatient cattle waiting to stampede. A true child of the Television Age, Cleve Jones had already arranged a march route that would assure the best pictures for the television cameras ready to get the tantalizing live shot of the demonstration for the late-night news. Cleve took his bullhorn to address the crowd, but before a dozen sentences came from his mouth, the throng spontaneously turned and pushed toward City Hall, leaving Cleve scrambling to catch up and take his ostensible post as leader. On the sides, walking inconspicuously in his cordoroy jacket, blue jeans, and sneakers, was Harvey Milk. The militance he had been urging gays to gain since 1973 had become a fait accompli. The shouts were no longer courteous slogans like "Gay Rights Now," but chants like, "Civil Rights or Civil War."

As the crowd turned off Market Street on the final blocks toward the City Hall rotunda, a wave of anger swept over the throng, an invisible yet palpable tide that rose cathartically like a small waft of gasoline vapor rising toward a spark, and then ebbing, falling back slowly, only seconds before the moment of ignition. "It only came *this* far from being a riot," Harvey confided to a reporter later that night. The reporter noted that Harvey didn't seem particularly upset by the prospect.

At the rally after the march, Jones took his bullhorn to note that the day marked the fortieth anniversary of the year Adolf Hitler issued his first anti-homosexual decrees banning gays from many jobs and making homosexual thoughts a punishable offense. "Forty years ago tonight, the gay citizens of Germany found out they no longer had civil rights," Cleve exhorted. "Tomorrow morning, the gay citizens of Wichita will also awaken to find that they too have lost their civil rights."

> *"Take the clown suit off Harvey and all you end up with is another clown,"* Harvey's friend Carl Carlson said later.

Barnum and Bailey's circus had come to town, and, as a publicity stunt, offered to make up a number of public figures as clowns. Harvey, City Hall's most ardent circus lover, stepped to the front of the line; Harvey could finally be a clown—a real one—for a change. A *California Living* magazine writer, Ira Kamin, was on hand to record Harvey's transformation. His description has eerie implications, given both the bizarre sequence of events that followed the story's publication and the later historic significance of the date, May 21, just one day before Harvey's forty-eighth birthday.

> "How do you feel," asked the make-up artist.
> "I'm getting into sadness," said Milk. . . .
> You don't realize someone's sad, really, till you see them in clown make-up. The eyes will always give you away. And Harvey Milk in white face had these terribly sad eyes. . . . Harvey Milk jutted out his lower lip, and drooped his shoulders. It was as if, getting into sadness, he was picking up the horror, the real horror of the world and there was absolutely nothing anyone could do about the real horror of the world, but jut out your lower lip and drop your shoulders and apply white cream to your face and feel it.

Once outside, Kamin wrote, "something snapped" and Harvey gleefully started running up to cable cars, shaking tourists' hands. "Hey, I'm a supervisor," he explained, in full clown regalia. "I pass laws. I run this city. I'm an elected official." The fact that the bozo claimed his name was Harvey Milk didn't do much to convince the skeptical visitors.

The circus' major problem was that once in a clown outfit, Harvey didn't want to give it up. After terrorizing tourists and charming children with his antics, Harvey went on to make his appointed rounds of political events that day—in his clown drag.

The day after the clowning, while supervisors deliberated their serious municipal measures, Board President Feinstein was startled to see a man in a huge gorrilla costume come traipsing into the board chambers, lean over the railing separating supervisors from the gallery, hand Milk a red rose, and plant a big kiss on the legislator's lips. It was Harvey's last birthday.

Caught up in the tide of events that seemed so unrelenting in those early days of 1978, voters in Eugene repealed their gay rights ordinance the day after Harvey's birthday. Once again, thousands took to the streets of San Francisco to chant, blow whistles, and then rally. After the successive losses in Dade County, St. Paul, and Wichita, a gay cartoonist depicted the new vote with one scoreboard: Lions—4, Gays —0. Few had any doubts that the Christian lions would chalk up another win when the Briggs Initiative—just qualified as Proposition 6 for the November ballot—came up for a vote. David Goodstein wrote that any fight was hopeless but that gays should slip into the background and let experienced campaign managers handle the effort. Less moderate gays condemned this as elitist Uncle Tomism, but they were not much more optimistic. "We're going to be creamed and it's important that we not deceive people into thinking we can win," warned Chris Perry, former President of the S.F. Gay club.

Gay politicos responded to the Prop 6 threat by doing what they usually did when faced with a tough fight—splintering into factions. Moderates aligned with the Goodstein-Foster axis formed the statewide Concerned Voters of California (CVC), which would serve as the top-level professional side of the statewide campaign. The group hired Don Bradley, a veteran campaign warhorse whose experience included managing the statewide campaigns of John Kennedy, Lyndon Johnson, former Governor Pat Brown, and many local politicians, most notably George Moscone. Bradley was well connected with political machines, which would ensure endorsements from virtually every major public figure and union in the state. Radicals, meanwhile, jelled into a state-wide network of groups highlighted by San Francisco's Bay Area Committee Against the Briggs Initiative (BACABI). These groups stuck to the tactics they knew best, organizing demonstrations and rallies. BACABI moved quickly to shore up support among all gays activists to the left of Goodstein.

Neither group satisified Harvey. At a meeting of local gay leaders with CVC strategists, Representative Phil Burton proudly held up a brochure that talked in nebulous terms of human rights and the U.S. Constitution. "This is masturbation—shit and masturbation," Harvey shouted, convinced the brochure was merely a tepid response to what he considered a dangerous threat. All he'd get from CVC, he decided, was liberal bullshit. Milk also doubted that the rowdy demonstrations and leftist rhetoric of groups like BACABI would do much to convince California voters either. Harvey and his corps of close followers formed their own group, San Franciscans Against Prop 6. Since winning the election seemed out of the question, the group had only one primary goal: to make sure Prop 6 was defeated in San Francisco. A statewide loss might be tolerable, but losing in San Francisco would have national significance and prove a devastating blow to the image of gay power Harvey had promoted for so many years. Harry Britt was now president of the San Francisco Gay Democratic Club; he and activists like Cleve Jones, Dick Pabich, and Jim Rivaldo put together the framework of S.F. Against, deciding to avoid the high-budget media strategy of CVC and to leave picketing to the hard-core radicals. Instead, they would use the political tactics Harvey had lectured on through his four campaigns—registering voters, walking precincts, and gaining support through old-fashioned door-to-door canvasing. Harvey spurned suggestions that big names be brought in to direct and staff the group. "Always take people from the streets," he urged. So the two directors, Bill Kraus, a UC-Berkeley graduate student fresh from the anti-Jarvis–Gann campaign, and Gwenn Craig, a black lesbian from Atlanta, were activists with little organizational experience.

The formation of Harvey's own anti-6 group outraged both radicals and moderates. The CVC forces had long distrusted Milk's type of volunteer-intensive campaigns, fearing that all those unkempt Castro Street gays wandering the neighborhoods might scare voters away from the gay side. Radicals, meanwhile, saw the new organization as a naked power play by Harvey, another step toward building the political machine he had started to put together with San Francisco Gay Democratic Club. To a large extent, the radicals were right. Harvey had every intention of building a machine trained in his pragmatic theories of realpolitik; it was no accident that the people he assembled in his City Hall office and anti-Briggs campaign—people like Kraus, Craig, Anne Kronenberg, Pabich, Rivaldo, Cleve Jones, and Harry Britt—would indeed prove to be the people who, in a few months, would be leading the gay community, their hands on more power than Harvey could have imagined.

With State Senator Briggs appearing regularly on nightly news broadcasts with anti-gay tirades that made Anita Bryant sound like Gertrude Stein, gays did not have much time to bicker. The three major groups learned to take up a policy of peaceful coexistence and coordinated their various efforts. It had been nearly a year since Briggs first announced his campaign, so the hysteria with which gays first viewed the Briggs Initiative had given way to calmer determination as the hard work of the campaign neared.

"You get the first bullet the minute you stand at the microphone." The neatly typed postcard bore only that simple message, underscoring all the fears Harvey had about his appearance in the 1978 Gay Freedom Day Parade. A number of threats had promised Milk death on that day. Milk talked freely of the potential of assassination; maybe it would happen while he was riding in the open car, maybe on the stage, but he refused police protection. The Briggs Initiative had cast the eyes of the nation on California and especially on the San Francisco gay community. Harvey had to be there.

The 1977 parade had been marked by strident militance in reaction to both the unexpected Bryant victory and the Robert Hillsborough murder; the 1978 parade, on a warm, sunny Sunday at the end of June, turned into a confident show of strength. A musician had organized a ninety-piece marching band to lead the parade. Near the head of the crowd stretched a long banner touting Jimmy Carter's classic quote: "Human Rights Are Absolute." Contingents from over one hundred gay groups—everything from gay doctors, teachers, and plumbers to the roaring Dykes on Bikes—filled the streets. Pink triangles dominated many of their posters. The *Los Angeles Times* estimated the crowd at 375,000—the largest assemblage of people that would meet in one place in San Francisco during the entire 1970s. Only the helicopters hovering overhead with their network cameramen could see the broad expanses of people eking their way slowly toward the beautiful Civic Center plaza. Parade organizers had asked marchers to carry a sign saying where they were from, so the television cameras could record that San

Francisco's homosexuals were indeed refugees from all over the United States. With a flowered lei thrown casually over his white T-shirt, Harvey Milk, sitting in the back of a convertible, carried his hand-lettered sign, "I'm from Woodmere, N.Y." He waved to the crowd that swelled around his car, cheering wildly as he passed. "This is such a great crowd," Harvey enthused. "They'd even elect me mayor."

Wayne Friday carefully held Milk's legs in case the car had to make a sudden lurch forward. As she drove slowly toward the City Hall rally site, Anne Kronenberg kept retracing the routes to the nearest hospital in case it happened. Less than a year ago, Anne had walked into Castro Camera to volunteer for some campaign work because she didn't have anything better to do; now, she was driving one of the nation's most famous gay leaders, bracing herself for the sound of gunfire. So much had happened so fast. And it had only begun.

Harvey and Frank Robinson had prepared one of the dramatic pieces of oration Harvey loved so much for that day. Maybe the assassination threats had made him think of Martin Luther King, because he quoted King freely during the speech, even calling for a march on Washington for the next July 4. Few politicians in American history got the chance to directly address a crowd the size of the one stretched out before him and Harvey wanted to make the best of it.

My name is Harvey Milk—and I want to recruit you. I want to recruit you for the fight to preserve democracy from the John Briggs and Anita Bryants who are trying to constitutionalize bigotry.

We are not going to allow that to happen. We are not going to sit back in silence as 300,000 of our gay sisters and brothers did in Nazi Germany. We are not going to allow our rights to be taken away and then march with bowed heads into the gas chambers.

On this anniversary of Stonewall, I ask my gay sisters and brothers to make the commitment to fight. For themselves, for their freedom, for their country. . . . Gay people, we will not win our rights by staying quietly in our closets. . . . We are coming out. We are coming out to fight the lies, the myths, the distortions. We are coming out to tell the truths about gays, for I am tired of the conspiracy of silence, so I'm going to talk about it. And I want you to talk about it. You must come out. Come out to your parents, your relatives. I know that it is hard and that it will hurt them, but think of how they will hurt you in the voting booths. . . .

Jimmy Carter, you talk about human rights. You want to be the world's leader for human rights. There are 15 to 20 million gay people in this nation. When are you going to talk about *their* rights?

If you do not speak out, if you remain silent . . . then I call upon lesbians and gay men from all over the nation, your nation, to gather in Washington one year from now . . . on that very same spot where over a decade ago, Dr. Martin Luther King spoke to a nation of his dreams, dreams that are fast fading, dreams that to many in this nation have become nightmares rather than dreams. I call upon all minorities and especially the millions of lesbians and gay men to wake up from their dreams, to gather in Washington and tell Jimmy Carter and their nation: "Wake up. Wake up, America. No more racism. No more sexism. No more ageism. No more hatred. No more . . . And to the bigots. To the John Briggs, to the Anita Bryants . . . and all their ilk: Let me remind you what America is.

Listen carefully:

On the statue of Liberty, it says, "Give me your tired, your poor, your huddled masses yearning to be free . . ."

In the Declaration of Independence, it is written: "All men are created equal and they are endowed with certain inalienable rights . . ."

And in our national anthem, it says: "Oh, say does that star-spangled banner yet wave o'er the land of the free."

For Mr. Briggs and Ms. Bryant . . . and all the bigots out there: That's what America is. No matter how hard you try, you cannot erase those words from the Declaration of Independence. No matter how hard you try, you cannot chip those words off the base of the Statue of Liberty. And no matter how hard you try, you cannot sing the "Star Spangled Banner" without those words.

That's what America is.

Love it or leave it.

The sight of the hundreds of thousands gathered in front of the stately City Hall, overflowing from the large Civic Center plaza, flashed on television sets across the nation that night. The press had a field day with human interest side stories to the event. One white-haired, seventy-four-year-old woman, for example, told reporters about her two gay sons who were both teachers. "My older son committed suicide when his local school board found out he was gay and made moves to fire him," she said. "My other son is afraid to be here today because of that S.O.B. Briggs and what he wants to do to teachers. I lost one son to the likes of Mr. Briggs and I don't intend to lose another one."

Also granting interviews that day was Supervisor Dan White, who stood grimly on the sidelines of the parade as the thousands marched by. White was the only supervisor who had voted against closing Market Street for the annual parade. "This is our only opportunity to approve or disapprove of what goes on in our streets," he said. "The vast majority of people in this city don't want public displays of sexuality."

Anita Bryant asked Christians to pray for San Francisco on that Sunday.

Harvey was ecstatic about the response to his speech. As usual, he never mentioned the assassination fears once the imminent threat had passed. Instead, he spoke enthusiastically about the crowd and carefully handed out copies of his speech to every reporter he could buttonhole. Already, he could imagine the tens of thousands walking by the White House next year, assembling under the shadow of the Washington Monument. Such good theater.

Bienvenidos Castro. Willkommen Castro. Bienvenue Castro, in seven languages, the large canvas banner festooned over the intersection of Eighteenth and Castro spoke to the new role the Castro neighborhood now fulfilled in the homosexual collective conscious. The corner had been dubbed the crossroads of the gay world, and by the summer of 1978, the neighborhood had become an international gay tourist mecca. Thousands more were moving to the neighborhood, prompting gay politicos to speculate not *if* gays would become a numerical majority of San Francisco adults, but when. A new gay chauvinism ran rampant, complete with a lexicon of pejoratives. Heterosexuals became known as breeders—"Today's breeders, tomorrow's cows," went one slogan—and the game of spotting heterosexuals on Castro Street replaced the old heterophile game of picking out queers.

The neighborhood represented less a trend than a bona-fide sociological phenomenon. An entire Castro life-style evolved, fixed squarely on machismo. A gym membership became a prerequisite to the neighborhood's social life. Solid pectorals and washboard stomachs were highly valued for their aesthetic benefits during the ritualistic tearing off of sheer tank tops during the sweaty nights on the disco dance floor. The milieu was more macho than anything in heterosexual life and early settlers were disquieted by a profound shift in the neighborhood. No longer was the area a social experiment in the throes of creation; the life-style had solidified. Gays no longer came to the Castro to create a new life-style, they came to fit into the existing Castro Street mold. The summer of '78 seemed the Castro gays' equivalent of the Haight-Ashbury hippies' summer of love eleven years earlier; like its predecessor, the hot sunny days marked the end of an epoch as well as the beginning.

The continuing influx of gays from across the country strained housing stock and once distinct neighborhoods adjacent to the Castro soon became "Castroized," as Harvey called it. The renovating gay immigrants bought up tract after tract of century-old Victorians, often at extragavant prices. Housing prices skyrocketed further because of the high demand—and the real estate speculators, who were taking advantage of the boom to quickly buy and sell the homes. The rate of real estate transactions jumped 700 percent between 1968 and 1978, according to one federal study of the Duboce Triangle neighborhood a few blocks off Castro. The gay immigrants bought heavily into neighboring black and Latino areas, whose low-income minorities could not compete economically. Black leaders were especially vocal in asserting that gays were shoving minorities out of the city. By the end of 1978, gay neighborhoods dominated roughly 20 percent of the city's residential expanses.

No single strip in San Francisco felt the pinch of the inflated real estate values like the two-block core of the Castro district. Leases rose dramatically, killing marginal businesses to make way for establishments oriented toward the high-profit services needed by tourists and the increasingly affluent residents. A few hundred feet from the Willkommen Castro banner was another sign that spoke as meaningfully of the changing Castro. In the window of Castro Camera: "We need a new home."

The trouble started when Harvey learned his landlord, a Castro Street gay realtor, had kicked an elderly woman out of a nearby apartment where she had lived for decades to make way for a title insurance company. Harvey repeatedly used the eviction as an example of why the city needed an anti-speculation tax. Harvey's landlord was understandably miffed at being paraded about as the city's number one "bloodsucker," as Harvey was fond of calling realtors. He even mentioned Harvey's indiscretion in a letter informing the supervisor that his store's rent was increasing from $350 to $1200 a month. Rent on Milk's apartment above the store was also boosted.

With characteristic delicacy, Harvey posted the old and new rent figures on his store window, alongside the name of the offending realtor. Harvey didn't need the extra hundreds of square feet any more, since most of his obligations as the mayor of Castro Street had shifted months before to the real City Hall, so he found a small cubbyhole on Market Street right off Castro and moved the still skimpy inventory. Harvey's friends looked at the move as something of an end to an era on Castro Street, and sneered when the space was soon taken up by a bourgeois boutique that sold such utilitarian items as $350 crystal vases.

Virtually all of Milk's aides and friends saw the move from his Castro Street apartment as an opportunity to unload Jack Lira. As the months of Harvey's supervisorial term wore on, it became obvious to them that Jack was Harvey's major liability. His drunken tantrums often embarrassed Milk publicly and certainly provided no role model for the nation's first gay city official. His depression from watching *Holocaust* on TV never lifted. Moreover, Jack was always hassling Harvey's City Hall aides, insisting that they record his lengthy messages word for word while they were in the midst of heated political activity. Jack, however, usually refused to take any messages for Harvey and simply hung up the phone on many political callers, including a state senator and a number of other supervisors.

Anne Kronenberg pushed Harvey to move into his new apartment without Jack. But Harvey had prepared a dozen reasons to keep him. Jack was improving; he might take a job next week; he might go back to school; he seemed to be getting better the last few days; and, of course, the old standby, "He needs me." Sometimes Harvey pointed to Lira's occasional voter registration work as proof Jack was straightening out; he registered 123 voters in one week alone, Milk boasted. But the only money-making project Anne ever saw him get behind was a scheme to write all the major cash prize quiz shows in Los Angeles, suggesting they bring on this hilarious San Francisco politician as a contestant. Anne figured that Jack liked the project because it was a way to make money without him having to get a job. In the end, Jack made the move with Harvey.

It would be another year before Anne understood Harvey's ill-fated attraction to Jack and other men with dependent and often troubled personalities. She was studying alcoholism and ran across research about a pandemic, though little-known, problem known as co-alcoholism. Alcoholics, by definition, usually need someone to take care of them, since they are ill-suited to take care of themselves; their caretaker is the co-alcoholic, a person who, like Harvey, is often a nondrinkier. The co-alcoholics are the people who drive the drunk home from the bar, pay the rent and offer hope to otherwise dismal lives. By doing this, the co-alcoholic fulfills an addiction as dangerous as alcohol—the need to be needed. Harvey had all the classic symptoms of the co-alcoholic, Kronenberg thought later. But then it was too late.

fourteen

Deadline Pressure

"This is not a civil rights question. This is not a human rights question. It is simply a question of morality."

The senator perspired lightly under the glare of the television lights and the derisive sighs of the overwhelmingly hostile audience. Briggs cited the apocryphal statistics he brought up in every debate: a third of San Francisco's teachers were gays, as were 20 percent of Los Angeles.' "Most of them are in the closet," he concluded, "and frankly, that's where I think they should remain."

"If Senator Briggs thinks he's better than Christ, that he can decide what's moral," the supervisor snapped back, "then maybe we should have elected him Pope."

Harvey was reading the line off one of the dozens of five-by-nine inch pieces of paper on which he had methodically typed each pat answer to all the equally pat charges which arose in his debates with the Fullerton senator. The debate in a high school auditorium in suburban Walnut Creek—televised live to the Bay Area— looked like as heated an exchange as could be found in American politics. But by late September, each combatant had honed his argument into prepackaged, easily digestible quotes for media consumption. Fast food politics. The John and Harvey show.

Since the governor's race was nothing more than a dull cakewalk to victory for Jerry Brown, Proposition 6 became the most talked about contest in California's 1978 general elections. Reporters from around the world trekked to America's most populous state to cover the first time an entire state had voted on gay rights. Each side had a champion, one of two forty-eight-year-old public officials, both Korean war veterans and both scrappers who had struck maverick political careers. Prop 6 had yanked both men from regional notoriety and into a national spotlight as they slugged it out over this new and ambiguous social issue of homosexuality. Both were given to buzzwords, bugaboos and apocalyptic visions. For John Briggs, the battle was his one last chance to build a statewide following to expand on his backwater Orange County roots. For Harvey Milk, the fight was the latest act of a political drama that started with his hippie board candidacy five years earlier; finally he had the platform to say everything that had needed to be said, and heard, for so many years, since that traumatic day in Central Park when he took off his shirt.

"Homosexuality is the hottest issue in this country since Reconstruction," said John Briggs. On that, at least, nobody at the debate disagreed. A handful of suburban Briggs supporters watched aghast as buses deposited hundreds of San Francisco gays at the auditorium doors. Sitting with his San Francisco friends was Harvey Milk's new boyfriend, Doug Franks. Everybody liked Doug much more than Jack Lira and they nodded knowingly as they purveyed Doug's short, muscular body. Just Harvey's type. The television technicians focused their instant eyes and adjusted their blaring lights—and the debate continued. Briggs quoted the statistics about one-quarter of gay men having over five hundred sexual contacts. "I wish," Harvey jabbed back.

Briggs insisted he was only out to defend the family. "There are no organizations to defend children. There are all kinds of organizations to abuse your children. Pornographers want your children. Dope addicts want your children. Homosexuals want your children." And the issue *is,* he maintained, again and again, children. "They don't have any children of their own. If they don't recruit children or very young people, they'd all die away. They have no means of replenishing. That's why they want to be teachers and be equal status and have those people serve as role models and encourage people to join them."

"Children," Harvey shot back, "do need protection—protection from the incest and child beatings pandemic in the heterosexual family." Milk glanced down to point number four in his notes. The heading:

Teaching Homosexuality. "How do you teach homosexuality—like French?" As far as role models, "If it were true that children mimicked their teachers," Harvey joked, "you'd sure have a helluva lot more nuns running around."

In the end, both posed their visions of two imminent dark futures. "We cannot exist without the family, without the church and without the nation," Briggs concluded. "And if the initiative is defeated, I think it portends for a period of moral decay in this country that is going to lead to the carrying out or the bearing out of the prediction of General MacArthur, who stated that no civilization has ever been recorded having survived when it falls into a period of general economic decline and moral decay.... As of late with this free love, this zero population and gay liberation, we are in effect weakening the moral fiber, not only of the family and the child and the parents, but the country. And this is a greater danger than communism."

A greater danger than communism, Harvey thought to himself. Did he first hear that on the public television debate, read it in the Los Angeles *Times* interview, or see it at one of Briggs' City Hall appearances? All the charges had become so interchangeable, and Harvey's eyes darted down at his notes for his now-familiar windup. "John Briggs knows that every one of his statements has been repudiated by facts," Harvey began. "Yet he never stops making wild inflammatory remarks that, to anyone who knows the facts, sounds as if it were the KKK talking about blacks or Hitler about Jews. There is absolutely no difference between those types of morality." Harvey picked up the pace for the ending, so rote he needed no notes, just the right dramatic intonations. "In your own drive for personal power, how many careers are you willing to see destroyed? How many lives will you destroy in your lust for power? And when will you stop?"

The crowd cheered Milk on. The lights blinked off and Harvey collected his neatly typed notes for the next debate. That's the way all the debates went, Harvey had explained to Doug on the way to the auditorium. But Doug saw Milk was exhilarated at the unique chance for televised rebuffs to the old stereotypes of child molesters and recruiters that had haunted gays since his own childhood in Woodmere more than forty years ago. After the debate, Doug easily slipped into the background as scores of fans came to congratulate Harvey. Doug enjoyed watching the idolatry younger gays heaped on the supervisor. Harvey, meanwhile, liked finally having a boyfriend who could fulfill the role of political wife. Jack had never done that, he told Doug. Jack couldn't handle it when they'd go somewhere together and Harvey would get all the attention, leaving Lira in the background. Other than that brief assessment, however, Doug knew little of Jack, except that anger crept into Harvey's voice every time the name came up.

Harvey had little time to dwell on the past. An election had to be won, and Harvey threw himself into his role as the chief campaigner for the gay side with a desparate pace that worried his friends. When not poring over his speech notes or flying all over California for debates and fund raisers, Milk had his heavy workload as San Francisco supervisor and his less official responsibilities as Castro Street ward healer to tend to. But there was a pathos to all the activity and it was rapidly taking a toll on the supervisor. For the first time, Harvey actually looked his age. The air of immortality that had always made him look years younger had faded into wrinkles and furrows. Harvey would come home from one of his seventeen-hour days, plop himself on the couch, strike up a conversation with a friend, and then, in mid-sentence, drop off to sleep in dead exhaustion.

"Harvey, you're killing yourself," pleaded Don Amador in Los Angeles. "You've got to slow down." Amador later remembered, "He was acting like there wasn't enough time to do everything that had to be done. He never complained that there was too much work—it was always that there wasn't enough time."

At City Hall, Anne Kronenberg grew more concerned as she saw the grueling campaign wearing out her boss. But he insisted that he had to keep going. No invitations could be turned down; it was all too important. A few friends guessed what caused those frantic weeks of activity that fall, tracing Harvey's full-throttle campaigning back to that tragic Monday evening in late August.

A dynamite day at City Hall, Harvey thought as he started walking home. His dogshit ordinance had finally passed its third and final reading. Everybody at work had ribbed him about the clown story, which had appeared in the previous day's newspaper magazine supplement. Had he really been running up to cable cars telling people he was an elected official? they asked.

The only small blot on the day was Jack Lira. He'd called during the board meeting, insisting that Anne had to pull Harvey out of the board chambers so he could talk to him. In the background, Harvey could hear that Jack had turned his radio to a live broadcast of the board meeting. Jack had known he was pulling Harvey out of the

meeting, but he did it anyway, Harvey thought. Harvey had already
confided to friends that Jack had to go. The moods, the drinking, it was
all too much. Jack had even run away to Los Angeles briefly a week
before, staying with Don Amador, making drunken scenes and public
embarrassments for his host throughout his stay. Harvey always felt a
fatherly impulse to protect his friends. The fact that Jack had held
Amador up for potential ridicule rankled Harvey more than the humiliating scenes with which Lira had long harassed Harvey. Jack had to
go.

Harvey kept a cheerful spring in his pace as he walked the eleven
blocks from City Hall to his new flat on Henry Street. He should have
been home at 6:15, but he'd stayed an extra forty-five minutes to stick
his head into a committee meeting. No obligation to be there, but he
enjoyed making his presence known. Harvey fumbled for his keys as he
arrived at his flat; the first thing he saw as he opened the door mystified
him.

A trail of voter registration forms. It led from the front door down
the hall into the living room. Harvey quizzically followed the trail from
living to dining room. Now, wadded-up anti-Briggs fliers also littered
the floor and dropped sporadically on the voter forms were empty cans
of Coors beer. The path grew messier as it wound from the dining room
into the kitchen, through the bathroom, back into the hallway, through
Jack's room and finally onto the enclosed back porch. A huge black
velvet curtain was draped from the beam. Jack had pinned a note to
it: "You've always loved the circus, Harvey. What do you think of my
last act?"

Harvey pulled back the curtain and saw Jack's body, cold and
discolored, hanging from the beam. Milk ran into the kitchen and
grabbed a knife. As he cut the rope, he looked at the beam and saw that
Jack had nailed to it a paperback novelization of the television series
Holocaust. Distrusting police, Harvey ran to a firehouse a few doors
down the street and then called two of his most trusted friends, Anne
Kronenberg and Scott Smith. Anne motorcycled over in time to see the
firemen attempt and fail at resuscitation. The coroner later estimated
that Jack had been dead forty-five minutes before Milk got home, at
about 6:15. Jack had timed it so his legs would still be kicking when
he thought Harvey would walk in the door.

The body was gone by the time Scott arrived. The trio got to work
cleaning up the house before the police came. Jack had left notes all
over the apartment. A long suicide message scrawled in both Spanish

and English rambled about the anti-gay tide he saw sweeping the country. Other notes, which were never made public, ranted vindictively against Milk. "You're a lousy lover, Harvey." Jack had carefully hidden the taunting reminders throughout the house. Over the next few days, Scott found many notes tucked into odd drawers, out-of-the-way nooks, in the seams of Harvey's underwear and between the pages of books and magazines that Jack knew Harvey would pick up some day. A six-pack of empty Coors beer cans sat in the refrigerator. Months later, Anne got a sinking feeling in her stomach when she remembered a note taped prominently on a kitchen wall: "Beware Of The Ides of November."

Both the police and press treated the death gingerly. Though the suicide made page one the next day, it quickly faded. An avalanche of sympathy notes poured into Harvey's office. About half came from other lesbians and gay men who had lost a lover to suicide, often after they'd been arrested on a trumped-up charge, fired from a job or dishonorably discharged from the military. A sixty-four-year-old wrote of how his lover of fourteen years had committed suicide in 1953. With another man, the lover's suicide was six years ago, another three and one was "just last month." A grandmother wrote of how her grandson, a promising sixth grade teacher, had years ago been seen going into a suburban gay bar by a colleague, and how the school principal drove the young man to the pharmacist to get the dosage of pills that would save the teacher from an embarrassing hearing in front of the school board. Exactly fifty letters came from a small jungle outpost in South America, all sending regrets and extending an invitation. "I had the opportunity in San Francisco when we were there to get to know you and thought very highly of your commitment to social actions and to the betterment of your community," wrote Sharon Amos, who had organized the Peoples Temple leafleting for Harvey's Assembly campaign before moving with Jim Jones to Guyana. "I hope you will be able to visit us here sometime in Jonestown. Believe it or not, it is a tremendously sophisticated community, though it is in a jungle."

Even then, the packet of letters was chilling. It was as if it had never crossed the writers' minds that the appearances of exactly fifty letters—many of them identical word for word, and none of them wavering from the condolence-invitation formula—written on identical pieces of paper with similar pencils would look like anything but a spontaneous outpouring of sympathy.

"Everything I've ever done was to give hope to people like Jack,"

Harvey repeated over and over to his friends after the initial shock wore off. "And here I failed." Milk had suffered many political defeats, almost humorously, because he could always find some germ of victory in them—a little old lady converted from anti-gay prejudice, a new union supporter, or, if nothing else, higher name recognition. But the defeat had been final with Jack. There could be no hope for a victory the next time. Harvey had failed.

The guilt dissipated within hours of Milk's arrival in Fresno for Lira's funeral. He met and took an instant disliking to Jack's father who, Jack claimed, had so consistently rejected him. Harvey learned of Jack's previous suicide attempts; nobody in the family had bothered to inform him about them before. Jack's sister later wrote Harvey, "I hadn't told you about how bad the family was because I didn't think you'd ever have to be exposed to them. Now you see. Don't feel guilty about Jack. You were better to him than anyone else."

Harvey returned from the funeral relieved. "The guy never had a chance," he told Anne. Within a week, Harvey had met a young bartender, Billy Wiegardt, who had just moved to the Castro from Long Beach, Washington. Harvey registered him to vote and then proceeded with the mushy love notes and bouquets of red roses. Billy moved into Harvey's apartment a week later.

"You've got to remember, Bill, you're in the direct line of fire," Harvey warned as the young man unpacked.

"What do you mean?" This was, after all, pretty heavy stuff for a twenty-two-year-old who had just left Long Beach, Washington.

"If I get killed, you can be killed too," Harvey said matter-of-factly. "Somebody could walk through the door and blow both our brains out."

Harvey had grown to dislike mixing politics with romance, so most of the courtship employed the sentimental tactics he'd used successfully since nabbing Joe Campbell in 1956. Unaware of the details of Jack's suicide, which Harvey rarely discussed, Billy was delighted to come home one day and find paper footprints leading down the hallway, into the dining room, through the kitchen, down the hall and into Billy's new room. At the end, a vase of flowers. Billy noticed that the flowers Harvey frequently left never looked like they came from a florist shop. In fact, they looked like they might have just been plucked from somebody's front yard. Billy had the good sense never to ask Harvey about their origins.

The passion soon fled their affair. Like a sailor on his first leave, Billy was having his first taste of gay life, and in San Francisco no less. Neither the time nor the environment encouraged him to settle into the type of marriage in which Harvey had been involved for well over twenty years. Instead of being lovers, they became roommates who sometimes slept together. Harvey started complaining to friends that he wasn't getting enough sex. "Get it while you can," he counseled Harry Britt. "Nobody likes an old queen." The comment was based more on self-pity than fact; Harvey had few problems rustling himself up new boyfriends.

Within weeks of meeting Wiegardt, Harvey was courting twenty-four-year-old Doug Franks, a graduate student at San Francisco State University. Harvey registered him to vote and talked woefully of the loneliness of the campaign trail. Once he had earned Franks' sympathies, Harvey brightened up and asked him for a date. The event was a Nationalist Chinese dinner Milk was attending as a favor to John Molinari, Chinatown's district supervisor. Doug expected to be picked up for the date in a swanky big car, the kind he figured all supervisors drove. Instead, Harvey picked a rendezvous point on the city's bus system. On the way up the stairs to the dinner, Franks started seeing a panoply of political notables, as well as scores of sedate Chinese couples.

"Harvey, this is like I'm going as your date."

Harvey pulled Doug aside and gave him careful instructions.

"Now remember, if anyone says one thing to you that is snotty or condescending, you have my permission to say this." Harvey changed his voice tone into a sprightly conversational cadence. "You say, 'No, no, no. You've got it all wrong. Harvey doesn't fuck me. I fuck Harvey.'"

The statement's accuracy did not convince Doug it was appropriate. "Harvey!" he answered incredulously. "I can't say that."

"No, say it," said Harvey grinning.

Milk could barely restrain his laughter while speakers droned on about how the Taiwanese would inevitably reclaim the mainland. Doug found himself sitting with the city's public health director on one side and a representative from Governor Brown's office on the other. Harvey nudged Doug as the lazy susan loaded with Chinese delicacies was brought to the table.

"Go for it, Doug," Harvey prodded. "Don't worry about anybody else. It's *their* dinner," Harvey said, pointing to the would-be conquer-

be honest with everybody about where you're at. They in turn can do the same thing and it can open up a bigger sphere."

A sphere of love, always growing. That ultimately was what his politics were all about, Harvey decided. Lovers were not meant to be chattel, locked into only one finite relationship. Harvey never had any use for organized religion, but he was convinced that his notion of love was what Jesus was probably talking about years ago, not the hate that John Briggs and the fundamentalist Christians kept bringing out. Such lectures on the nature of love and the corny romantic courtship poems and flower bouquets came only in brief moments, the few which Harvey could spare from his hectic schedule. Every other waking minute was the campaign. Harvey had always enjoyed feverish activity, but now, friends worried, he acted like a driven man. He rose at 6 A.M. every day and rarely got to bed before midnight. Billy frequently came home from his bartending job at 3 A.M. to find the supervisor passed out on the couch. But there were sleepless nights too. Billy would awaken in the early morning hours before dawn started filtering into the sky and he'd see Harvey awake, staring at the ceiling. "The whole world is watching this," Harvey said once. Billy would doze off again, because he'd already heard so much about the Briggs Initiative, but Harvey would still be staring up blankly. The whole world was watching.

"You can act right now to help protect your family from vicious killers and defend your children from homosexual teachers."

With a picture of a bludgeoned teenage youth lying in a pool of his own blood, the brochure read like a grisly clearance sale, advertised with a political motif. Though it was Proposition 6 that gained the nickname the Briggs Initiative, the ambitious Fullerton senator had sponsored two ballot initiatives for the election—Prop 6 and Proposition 7, enacting a tougher death penalty statute. Briggs earnestly insisted that the two issues were inexorably tied together. The fund raising letter for both Propositions 6 and 7 drew the parallels, over the picture of a victim of the odious trashbag murderer. "The ruthless killer who shot this poor young man in the face can be SET FREE TO KILL AGAIN because California does not have an effective death penalty law." A few paragraphs later, Briggs explained that homosexual teachers represented an equally horrendous threat, what with the proliferation of gay teacher-recruiters in the classrooms. The brochure lacked subtlety, but the skillful use of direct mail techniques initially brought hundreds of thousands of dollars into the coffers of Briggs's campaign.

Moreover, the gruesome brochure for the two initiatives was not particularly wild rhetoric compared to other fliers Briggs circulated for Prop 6. The major leaflet of his campaign featured fifteen different newspaper clippings with headlines like: "Teacher Accused of Sex Acts with Boy Students," "Senate Shown Movie of Child Porn," "Police Find Sexually Abused Children," "Former Scoutmaster Convicted of Homosexual Acts with Boys," "Why a 13-year-old Is Selling His Body," "Ex-Teachers Indicted for Lewd Acts with Boys," "R.I. Sex Club Lured Juveniles with Gifts." One full-color newspaper advertising supplement featured pictures from the San Francisco Gay Freedom Day Parade on its cover with the words "Moral Decay" emblazoned across them. "Politicians Do Nothing—Decent Citizens Must Act. You Can Help! Start by Signing Up to Save Our Children from Homosexual Teachers." Pictures of Briggs with Anita Bryant adorned the inside pages.

In September, Briggs further startled gay activists when he said he was about to publish a book entitled *Everything You've Always Wanted to Know About Homosexuality But Were Afraid to Ask*. The planned 150-page opus would include pictures of victims of the trash bag murders and the Houston sex-torture ring, he said. San Francisco would dominate the booklet with lengthy discussions of the seedier sides of gay life, including fist-loving sadomasochistic cults and sexual activity in parks, beaches, bathhouses, back rooms, and private male clubs.

Briggs' speeches were similarly peppered. "If you let one homosexual teacher stay, soon there'll be two, then four, then 8, then 25—and before long, the entire school will be taught by homosexuals," the senator said in a speech in Healdsburg, a tiny Sonoma County hamlet that gained national attention during the Prop 6 campaign when a local second grade teacher publicly acknowledged his homosexuality. In the course of that one forty-five-minute speech Briggs managed to equate homosexuals with adulterers, burglars, communists, murderers, rapists, Richard Nixon, child pornographers, and effeminate courtiers who had undermined the Greek and Roman civilizations.

The rhetoric was less startling than the fact that Briggs's law just might have passed if it were not for the brief definition of one three-word phrase in its language: *Public Homosexual Conduct*. The phrase may sound like a description of a round of fellatio on Main Street, but the initiative sweepingly defined "public homosexual conduct" as "advocating, imposing, encouraging or promoting of private or public homosexual activity directed at, or likely to come to the attention of, school children and/or other [school] employees." Walking in a gay pride parade "encourages" homosexual activity, so any teacher, gay or straight, could have been fired for walking in a gay march. Having a drink in a gay bar, assigning books written by a gay author, attending a meeting where gay rights was discussed, all constituted activity that might advocate or promote homosexuality, and all were therefore punishable by termination, be the teacher gay or straight. The reason that Briggs picked Healdsburg as a showcase city was because the second grade teacher had said he was gay in a statement opposing the Briggs initiative. Opposing the Briggs Initiative might be grounds for termination.

In front of a crowded Healdsburg audience, Briggs defended the clause to teachers who worried that their stance against Prop 6 would later cost them their jobs, since a defeat for the initiative would encourage the gay movement. One teacher rose to ask if her defense of the embattled gay teacher might endanger her job in a school district twenty miles away.

"You don't have to worry," Briggs assured her. "The law is not retroactive."

Another Healdsburg teacher, an admitted heterosexual, wanted to know if she could lose her job if she continued to support the gay teacher *after* the election.

"It would depend on the limits of your support," said Briggs.

Where did Proposition 6 end and the First Amendment begin? "That," Briggs said, "is up to the courts to decide." He did note, however, that the Supreme Court had recently turned down the appeal of the Tacoma schoolteacher fired solely for his homosexuality, so he had no doubts about the constitutionality of his law.

The sheer breadth of the law, as well as Briggs's own heavy-handed hyperbole, made it easy for gays to dismiss the Orange County legislator as a contemporary incarnation of Hitler. This characterization genuinely mystified Briggs, who, on his home turf in southern California, was the epitome of the backslapping, gladhanding down-home politician. Privately, he was somewhat bemused by many of his fundamentalist followers—"They really know how to whoop it up," he said once—and he often told the Anita Bryant jokes he heard from his gay adversaries. He made it clear that he thought Bryant's propensity to burst into verses of "Battle Hymn of the Republic" put her somewhere out in "left field." Asked if it were any more fair to compare all gay teachers to the Houston or trash bag murderers than it would be to compare all heterosexuals to Richard Speck or the Boston Strangler, Briggs would nod thoughtfully, "I believe the Good Lord is watching us, but this is a political battle—and in politics, anything is fair."

The Briggs Initiative may have had the trappings of a moral crusade, and the fundamentalist followers believed that, but for the senator, it was just politics. John Briggs in the eyes of John Briggs was just a politician riding abreast a popular cause. Ronald Reagan had his nonsense about the Panama Canal treaty. Howard Jarvis had his property taxes to complain about. Briggs had his homosexual teachers campaign. Though his gubernatorial attempt failed against much bigger names, he did little to allay speculation that he was gearing up ambitions to seek a U.S. Senate seat in 1980 or 1982. That gays were calling him Adolf Hitler only proved their essential emotional instability, he thought. The private Briggs counted gays lucky that this public crusade was not led by a zealot but a pragmatic politician.

"Aren't you guys glad *I'm* leading this and not one of those people from way out in left field?" he asked one gay reporter with whom he had struck a rapport.

The reporter wasn't sure what Briggs meant.

"I mean, I don't want to put you people in prison or anything. It could be a lot worse." Briggs leaned across his desk and asked sincerely, "Aren't you guys glad this isn't being led by some crazy?"

If gays constantly harped about Hitler and concentration camps, Briggs had his death threats too. The FBI had caught four members of the Weather Underground crawling toward Briggs's office with a pipe bomb. Some observers even credited an unusual clause of Briggs's death penalty initiative to the death threats Briggs himself had received. The clause invoked an automatic death penalty for anyone convicted of murdering a public official in an effort to prevent that official from carrying out his public duties. Many people later noted the irony that Harvey Milk and George Moscone vigorously opposed Proposition 7 while Dan White supported the tough new capital punishment law.

"I see the Christ moving always to outcasts to stand with them. My own priesthood, my own humanity, ask me to do the same. I stand there this day. I have always stood for them.

"Friends of mine have asked me, 'Bill, we understand this. But when are you going to stop standing for them and stand honestly as one of us? Can we not see ultimate honesty in the church?' And so this day, my beloved people, I believe I am called by God Himself not only to stand up for them, but this time, now more honestly, to stand as one of them. I, of course, am speaking about gay people. I am gay."

A soft rustle swept through the chapel of San Francisco's Episcopal Church of Saint Mary the Virgin. Some had suspected that the Reverend William Barcus would make such a pronouncement when they saw Supervisor Harvey Milk quietly slip into a rear pew that morning. With only two weeks until election day, many California pulpits turned their attention to Prop 6. That Sunday, fundamentalist preachers around the state recited the Levitican incantations against gays, but the parishioners of St. Mary's heard a different message; the excesses of the Briggs campaign had gays throughout California running scared and many were fighting back.

"Those of us who have heard the debates and read statements on the subject believe the bigotry and poison spread by John Briggs need speaking to, not only by those studying the phenomenon of homosexuality, but by those of us who can give you a clear example of who we are," the Reverend Barcus told the congregation. "We who will live with what a 'yes' vote on Proposition 6 will mean. Jobs are at stake, yes, but far more importantly, lives are at stake. Countless numbers of lives and professional careers already have been destroyed, and even taken in desparation. I mean suicide. The witch-hunt has already started. Teachers in this state have already been irresponsibly charged with being homosexual, and some are very happily married people. The burden falls hideously upon them now just to prove their innocence. Their innocence of what, in the name of God? The witch-hunt cannot be allowed to continue. You can help by being willing to morally put yourself on the line, not after the fact, not after November 7th, but now."

The first statewide poll on Prop 6, released in September, showed the measure leading by a whopping 61 to 31 percent margin. Pollsters said they had rarely seen an issue with so much public opinion already galvanized with so few undecided voters. The prognosis rattled the comfortable gays who had easily assimilated their homosexuality into the California life-style. Thousands of homosexuals who had shunned politics for years stepped forward to fight the law in many ways. Frustrated that anti-Briggs campaigners were focusing their work in the heavily populated San Francisco Bay and Los Angeles regions, Frank Vel, an advertising copywriter, quit his job and walked through California's lightly populated agricultural heartland from the Mexican border to the Oregon state line. An efficient corps of advance people lined up interviews with scores of small-town newspapers along the sweltering 1,203-mile route. News that the Beverly Hills Chamber of Commerce was about to endorse Prop 6 brought hundreds of angry calls from well-heeled gay shoppers, threatening to have a massive credit card burning on Beverly Hills' chic Rodeo Drive. The chamber ended up taking a "no position" on the measure. One San Francisco gay man came out of the closet to tell gossip columnists how he had dated John Briggs's daughter in high school. "Can you *really* spot one by looking at him?" reporters asked Briggs. A graphics artist created "Homosexual Identification Cards," which were widely distributed in gay neighborhoods. The cards had boxes to designate assembly areas—Camp Bryant or Camp Briggs—where each homosexual was supposed to report in the event of a special executive order. Even punk rockers got into the act by sponsoring a "Save The Homos" fundraiser, advertised with posters featuring an appropriately tasteless drawing of a speared and bleeding whale.

Bigger guns came in to fight the Briggs Initiative as well. Republicans had long been embarrassed by Briggs's antics in the state senate, so G.O.P. legislators lined up against Prop 6 in the hope that defeat might finally shut the senator up. Former Governor Ronald Reagan—who had promised to veto any decriminalization of gay sex during his eight-year term as governor—went on record against Prop 6, observing, "Whatever else it is, homosexuality is not a contagious disease like measles." Briggs brushed off the rebuff, saying Reagan was part of "the whole Hollywood crowd." Gay insiders, however, credited Reagan's help to the fact that he had no small number of gays among his top staff. Former President Ford came out against the measure, saying it represented an unconservative expansion of state power. The Catholic and Episcopal Bishops of San Francisco took firm stands against the measure. Boards of education throughout the state also voted opposition to the initiative, fretting over the considerable sums—an estimated $12,000 per teacher—it would take to hold the hearings that would determine whether teachers were guilty as charged. Many heterosexual teachers, meanwhile, promised to clog the school boards with hundreds of confessions that they had violated the "public homosexual conduct" clause. The California Teachers Association, California Federation of Teachers, American Federations of Teachers and the National Education Association, as well as the state AFL-CIO, which sent out 2.3 million slate cards, also took a firm No-on-6 posture. From show business came a panoply of stars who helped raise considerable sums to fight the measure. They ranged from the expected entertainers-cum-politicos like Shirley MacLaine, Ed Asner, and Joan Baez to such normally apolitical figures as Cher, Carol Burnett, Helen Reddy, Donna Summer, Sandy Duncan, Shelly Winters, James Garner, Dennis Weaver, and Natalie Wood. Paul Newman and Joanne Woodward sent out a fund raising appeal on their personal letterhead. Ironically enough, it was stars with huge gay followings like Barbra Streisand and Liza Minnelli who would not take a stand on the issue, following the old Hollywood dictum that taking positions on controversial issues can hurt audience appeal and, therefore, cut profits.

Liberal politicians were often more reticent to take a stand against the measure than the conservatives. Governor Jerry Brown waited until the last minute to state his opposition to the proposal. President Carter said nothing, even after Milk telegrammed repeated pleas for a statement—any statement. "How many lives must be destroyed before you speak out?" he asked. What angered Harvey most was that the San Francisco Chamber of Commerce pointedly turned a deaf ear to gay pleas for a "no" stance on Prop 6, saying it had "studied" the issue and would release no position. More proof that the Chamber thought homosexuals were bad for business, Milk complained.

The lack of gut liberal outrage at the Briggs campaign provided more fodder for Harvey's contention that the future of the gay movement lay not with nurturing liberal friends through high-level politicking, but in forging strong power for gays at the grass roots. "It's not enough to have friends represent us, no matter how good friends they might be," he told a statewide caucus of gay Democrats. "If we remain invisible, we will be in limbo, people with no brothers, no sisters, no parents, no positions of respectability. The anger and frustration some of us feel because we are misunderstood—friends cannot feel that anger and frustration. They can sense it in us, but they cannot feel it. . . . It's time we have many legislators who are gay, proud of that and do not remain in the closet."

Such pleas were always followed by Harvey's insistence that all gays should come out of the closet to show the world that gays indeed were everywhere and not an exotic tribe beamed to San Francisco from Mars. Harvey's call to come out became as adamant as his protestations that everyone should register to vote. Coming out represented the assertion of personal power, of the personal belief that one person *can* make a difference and play a role in changing the world. To surrender the opportunity to make a dent in history was to Milk like surrendering the point of one's very existence. "All human beings have power," Harvey had said in his 1973 campaign. "You are just one person, but you have power. That makes power so significant." Harvey's basic campaign theme hadn't changed in the five years since then.

Polls, meanwhile, confirmed the political value of gays being up front with friends and relatives. Voters who knew gays personally were twice as likely to support gay rights than those who said they had never known a homosexual. On a fundamental level, however, Harvey was more concerned with what coming out meant to gays themselves than to heterosexuals.

Miraculously enough, gay factionalism submerged during the campaign, partly because of the steadying hand of the no-nonsense veteran Don Bradley at CVC, and the radicals and moderates coordinated their efforts with a unity previously unknown in the gay movement. In an attempt to head off competition for scarce funds, Milk started the United Fund Against the Briggs Initiative to dole out money to various groups around the state—and, some politicos sniped, to give Harvey's new protégé, Cleve Jones, a job as its director. The grass-roots politicking at the San Franciscans Against Prop 6 headquarters was also creating a cadre of activists well trained in Harvey's own brand of meet-the-people campaigning. Once these new volunteers learned the political ropes, Harry Britt took them aside to sign them up as members of Harvey's San Francisco Gay Democratic Club. By the closing week of the campaign, the club had surpassed the older Toklas club in its ability to get large numbers of volunteers out to the precincts on short notice.

Milk proudly brought Congressman Phil Burton and Mayor Moscone down to his headquarters to show off his humming operation. Once considered a wild-eyed radical himself, Burton smiled at the sight of all these militant gays being drawn from street protests into the nuts-and-bolts politics of the system. Both George and Harvey started making regular Saturday morning visits to the headquarters to give volunteers pep talks as they set out to ring doorbells and canvass precincts. Harvey eagerly accepted invitations from around California, refusing to accept honorariums for his talks. "I'm going to speak out about what I believe in," he told Anne. "I can't take money for that."

Still, many gays around California did nothing—some out of apathy, others out of terror. Every day at City Hall, Anne and Dick Pabich took fearful calls from around the state and the nation. "What happens if it passes?" fearful teachers called to ask. "What do we do—where else is there to go?" Psychiatrists with large gay clienteles reported growing caseloads not only of teachers, but of pediatricians, counselors, and child psychologists who feared that Prop 6 was merely the first step.

"Harvey, I think there's gonna be riots if this thing passes," Cleve Jones warned one day.

"There goddamn better be," Harvey snapped back.

"When are we going to fight back?" Harvey asked Chris Perry. "I can't say it because I'm a public official, but for God's sake, fight back."

What Harvey did say publicly—certainly was not tepid. "At what point do we say 'Enough?' " he wrote in his column for the gay *Bay Area Reporter*. "At what point do we stand up—as a total group—and say we will not allow it to happen any more? Enough is enough! Should we wait until the Bryant camps are built?"

Gay rights lawyers had suits challenging the law's constitutionality ready to be presented in court the morning after the election. But that was not the response most gays on Castro Street were discussing. Riots. Most activists did not speak of them publicly, but with so many convinced that defeat was inevitable, the potential was never far from the minds of gay activists in the Milk camp. Already many militant gays were circulating a "Statement of Conscience," swearing to take part in nonviolent civil disobedience if Prop 6 passed. Many were signing up, even though some objected to the inclusion of the term "nonviolent." The news that the Atlantic-Richfield oil company had contributed to Briggs's gubernatorial campaign had insiders warning, "If Prop 6 passes, I wouldn't be around the Castro Street Arco Station on election night."

Harvey relished the opportunity to caution reporters about possible rioting, always prefacing the warning with, "I'm not for violence, but . . ." One CBS reporter looked at Milk incredulously when the supervisor brought up the possibility of a violent reaction to the passage of Prop 6. "You mean homosexuals can be violent?" he asked. That comment, if nothing else, made Harvey actually look forward to rioting. That would show them gays weren't a bunch of pantywaists to be pushed about like sissies in a locker room.

"The Lord said, 'Go find me ten righteous men.' "

The Reverend Ray Batema seemed pleased with the analogy, as he sat back in his paneled office behind his Central Pomona Baptist

Church, his head silhouetted on a Mexican-made American eagle tapestry, the kind you buy in the parking lots of deserted Exxon stations in San Bernadino County. The Reverend Batema was co-chairman of the Citizens for Decency and Morality—the other co-chairman was John Briggs himself—and he saw no problem with using that Biblical quote from the story of Sodom as the basis of his campaign tactics. "That's going to be our strategy. We'll ask each of our people to go find ten righteous men to support morality. And they'll find ten righteous men and *they'll* find ten more."

"That's just why we're going to win this campaign," commented CVC director Don Bradley upon hearing of the plan. "The other side is a bunch of religious fanatics who won't be able to put together a campaign."

Even while gay activists were signing their Statement of Conscience slips, the Yes-on-6 campaigners like the Reverend Batema were sowing their own destruction. Briggs could rally few political figures to his side, so he was surrounded exclusively by fundamentalist preachers who figured that God, not campaign managers, would give them victory. Even as conservative opposition to the measure dried up the Yes campaign's funding, the preachers were convinced that Batema's Ten Righteous Men plan would win the election. By late fall, the campaign was broke. In the closing weeks before election day, only three well-known political organizations had endorsed the measure—the state Nazi party, the Ku Klux Klan, and the Los Angeles County Deputy Sheriffs Association. An October poll showed support slipping drastically. In one month, the 61–31 margin for Prop 6 fell to a razor-thin 45–43 lead.

A big boost for gays came in the final weeks of the campaign when President Carter came to California to campaign for Governor Brown's reelection. Carter had finished his speech and was walking away from the podium when a television microphone picked up Brown telling Carter, "Proposition 6. You'll get your loudest applause. Ford and Reagan have both come out against it. So I think it's perfectly safe." Carter walked back to the mike and added, "I also ask everybody to vote no on Proposition 6." The crowd cheered wildly, though it was never clear whether Carter actually knew anything more about Proposition 6 than that, by late October, opposing it was a "perfectly safe" stand.

An emboldened Harvey Milk issued a sweeping challenge to debate John Briggs at any place or any time. "He can pick the town and the audience and I'll ask our supporters not to attend," Milk said. "His issues are so phony, I think even an audience stacked in his favor would see through them."

A week before the election Briggs responded, inviting Harvey to debate in his Orange County home turf for an evening sponsored by the "Pro-Family Coalition." The debate's location appealed to Harvey. If John Briggs could mount the steps of San Francisco City Hall, Milk could damn well go to Orange County. He was not about to be up-staged. Friends, however, warned of an assassination attempt. The local police offered bodyguards, but Harvey refused. "Listen, *you* know it's going to happen and *I* know it's going to happen some time," he said. "There's no use worrying about it—it'll happen when it happens."

At the Orange County Airport, Harvey and Dick Pabich ran into John Briggs, his wife, and his State Police bodyguard. Briggs offered to drive the pair to the debate, but Harvey wanted to wait for a ride from his boyfriend, Bob Tuttle. The quintet decided to have a cup of coffee at the airport lounge and for a half-hour Briggs and Milk bantered back and forth about the campaign like two old World War II buddies reminiscing about their days in the trenches. Dick Pabich never forgot the friendly exchange. They were two seasoned politicians who had spent years breaking all the political rules, relying on sheer showman-ship for their successes, and delighting in the give-and-take of politics. When Briggs left, Harvey giggled to Dick, "This really is a big joke to him."

At the debate, the pair viciously ripped into each other.

Bob Tuttle was startled at the vehemence of the many Briggs supporters who came to jeer Milk. "That," he said later, "was when I realized that Harvey was right—he was going to get shot some day."

By the campaign's closing days, pollsters called the race too close to call, though gays had clearly seized the momentum. It wasn't so much that homosexuals were winning, but that John Briggs was losing. Another spokesperson could have pulled it off, but the public didn't like the senator. In a last-ditch effort to grab the media spotlight, Briggs called the San Francisco Police Department on the afternoon of Octo-ber 31 to say that in four hours he intended to show up at Polk Street. Halloween, of course, had been the city's high homosexual holiday since the times of Jose's Black Cat. In recent years, crowds around the gay Polk Street neighborhood had grown so massive that police rou-tinely closed off the street and let the drag queens have their annual field day. Some 80,000 revelers were partying on Polk Street when Senator Briggs arrived. A battery of media had also come to try to grab the expected shots of Briggs confronting drag queens. "I'm going because this is a children's night and I'm interested in children," he solemnly told reporters who asked why he was dropping in on that particular street on that particular night.

The police car carrying Briggs, however, took him not to the Polk Street action but to a special delegation that had been arranged to greet the senator a few blocks away. Mayor Moscone, Police Chief Gain, Supervisors Milk and Silver all stepped forward to shake Briggs's hand when the shocked legislator saw them. The mayor suggested it was not in the best interests of law and order for the senator to wander to Polk Street. The police chief, flanked by about twenty-five officers, agreed. The senator testily gave in and started his drive back to Sacramento.

Just fifteen years ago that night, the police and city authorities had forced The Black Cat to close. The confrontation between Briggs and city authorities on Halloween 1978 was but another indication of how fully the tables had turned since that Halloween in 1963.

Election night. Harvey Milk was hopping mad.

The pollsters had been wrong. The vote wasn't even close. Around the state, voters were smashing Briggs's ambitions by gigantic proportions. In San Francisco, the proposition was losing by a 75–25 percent margin; only one supervisorial district produced a majority for Prop 6 —District 8, Dan White's district. It looked like the measure would lose by over a million votes statewide and Harvey was pissed. All fall he had been looking forward to, at best, a narrow loss—and then some riots. People fought best with their backs to the wall, he thought, and he wanted his people to keep fighting. "You've heard of sore losers," he complained to Cleve Jones. "Well, I'm a sore winner."

But the show had to go on. An empty hall off Castro Street had gone through a one-day refurbishing for the dozens of television cameras from all the networks that had assembled for the victory party that night. Mounted on the stage's television-blue backdrop was a huge cutout of the Statue of Liberty, holding not a Bible but a large No-on-6 poster. The poster concealed a jockstrap that the artist had jokingly painted on Liberty. At 11 P.M., when Harvey figured the television newscasts would cut to the headquarters for live coverage, Milk gave the signal. From downstairs came the sound of a brass band, which marched into the hall blaring "San Francisco," the perfect background music for the announcement of the results which showed a 2–1 victory for gays statewide. Harvey mounted the stage. "This is only the first step," he told the roaring crowd. "The next step, the more important one, is for all those gays who did not come out, for whatever reasons, to do so now. To come out to all your family, to come out to all your relatives, to come out to all your friends—the coming out of a nation will smash the myths once and for all."

Mayor Moscone got a massive ovation when he made a surprise appearance at the rally. The election, he said, proved that "this country is really worth fighting for and the people over the years who have made so many sacrifices for this statute, for that principle did not fight in vain . . . that this country is a great country and anyone who in the future attempts to make political advances on the backs of those who it appears are at the bottom of the spectrum will be repudiated. . . . This is your night. No-on-6 will be emblazoned upon the principles of San Francisco, liberty and freedom for all, forever."

From Seattle came the news that gays had thwarted the attempt to repeal that city's gay rights law, the first time gays had won a municipal gay rights referendum. After so many defeats, gays were finally winning. Police had to close off a block of Castro Street after the party, since celebrating gays had taken it over, dancing in the streets until 4 A.M.

Late that night, Harvey called his friend Don Amador, who had been celebrating the victory at a party with an eighteen-year-old from Richmond, Minnesota, whom Harvey might remember. The disabled young man who, a year before, was ready to kill himself because his parents were going to institutionalize him had followed Harvey's advice, taken his crutches, and boarded a bus for Los Angeles. He had registered to vote and that day cast his first ballot—against Prop 6. Harvey rarely showed emotion, but his voice cracked when he heard the news. The eighteen-year-old could hardly wait to meet his hero.

Three days later, Harvey and Doug Franks were sitting in Castro Camera, closing up the shop for the day. Harvey took a phone call and within moments was jumping up and down shouting, "That's terrific. I can't believe it. That's too terrific to believe."

Once off the phone, Harvey started dancing around the store, unable to contain his excitement. "Dan White's resigned," he told Doug. "It's just too good to believe. Now I've got my sixth vote—the sixth vote. Now I'll really be able to get things moving on the board."

As Dianne Feinstein had said on inauguration day, "The name of the game is six votes." Harvey and the other liberals had lost so many battles by the 6–5 conservative majority that year that the resignation of Dan White—caused, White said, by the financial hardship of the supervisors' puny salaries—seemed a godsend, the final move that would give liberals complete control over City Hall. Harvey spent most of the weekend calling his political cronies with the good news. "We've got our sixth vote."

fifteen

Curtain Call

"You're the asshole that passed that dog-shit ordinance, aren't you?"

The twenty people standing in line at the Haight-Ashbury ice cream parlor were in for a show. Doug Franks shrank back while Harvey adopted the most defiant New York demeanor he could muster.

"Yeah, I'm that person."

"What's wrong with you? What do you have against dogs? Are you a dog hater?"

"What do you have against blind people?" Harvey shot back. "Do you know what it's like to be blind and step in dogshit?"

Everybody in line clapped. Milk could hardly hold back his smile as he railed on.

"If you feel so strongly about it, why don't you make it an issue and run against me?"

The dog lover skulked back into the line while a beaming Milk congratulated himself on the performance. How he loved applause. And it wasn't even from gays or about anything gay. Everything was falling into place the way he had always wanted it to.

The weeks following the unexpected victory against the Briggs Initiative gave Harvey a much-needed respite from the grueling schedule that had dominated his life since Jack Lira's suicide. Never had Milk's star seemed brighter. His role as chief gay spokesperson during the Prop 6 campaign thrust him to the forefront of the gay movement. The numerous televised debates had built him into a significant statewide presence as well, giving him added credentials as the chief gay wheeler-dealer with state and national politicians. In San Francisco, meanwhile, Harvey had long ago ceased being known as "the gay supervisor" and risen to be the most articulate champion of progressive causes. His particular interests in the concerns of the disabled, senior citizens, and Chinese-Americans had given him a constituency well beyond the boundaries of District 5.

Harvey also was looking forward to his reelection campaign the next fall when, for the first time in his political career, he would be a shoe-in. He was far less concerned with the problems of winning District 5 than with winning the race by such a huge margin that he could lay claim to the board presidency. He had enlisted the popular Assemblyman Willie Brown to be his honorary campaign chair and lined up most of his major 1977 supervisorial opponents—Rick Stokes, Bob St. Claire, and Terrance Hallinan—to serve as Brown's co-chairs.

After 10 months as supervisor, the routine board tasks bored Milk, so he had taken up a host of other projects. He looked forward gleefully to the march on Washington. With Harry Britt he planned his debut in national Democratic Party politics as a delegate to the upcoming midterm convention, where he would make a dramatic appeal for gay rights.

Harvey's affair with Doug Franks blossomed. Doug could hardly have found a more ardent suitor. The usual romantic trimmings of any Milk affair, love notes and freshly cut flowers, flowed in abundance. When the pair attended a musical revue doing a takeoff on a *Casablanca* love scene, Harvey leaned over to croon softly in Doug's ear "As Time Goes By" in harmony with the singers. For years, Harvey's life had been a web of loose ends; now they were coming together as he had always wanted them to. One night while making love, Harvey and Doug both spontaneously broke into tears. They never talked about why.

Relieved and cheerful, as if a load was finally lifted, Dan White acted like a new man after he resigned from the board, thought White's colleague, John Molinari. The pressures that had forced White's impromptu resignation had, by now, become front-page news: the supervisors' $9,600 annual salary wasn't enough for White to support his wife and four-month-old son. His fried potato stand at the new Pier 39 complex needed his attention or it would fold. White's resolution to quit politics made Molinari feel downright guilty. Molinari had spent the last seven years at boring meetings, decimated his family life, ruined any chance of getting ahead in his insurance firm, and even moved his family to a new part of town so he could qualify for a district seat. And what for? For $9,600 a year salary? Dan White is a man with his priorities straight, Molinari thought to himself as he watched the young man pack up. He hadn't seen White in such a good mood in months.

That's why Molinari and the rest of the city's political establishment was surprised when, ten days after the sudden resignation, White emerged from a meeting with leaders of the Police Officers' Association and the Board of Realtors to say that he wanted his seat back. Mayor Moscone quickly handed White his letter of resignation and told reporters, "As far as I am concerned, Dan White is the supervisor from District 8. . . . A man has a right to change his mind."

That same afternoon, Congressman Leo Ryan from the San Francisco suburb of San Mateo arrived in Georgetown, Guyana, with a troupe of reporters and relatives of Peoples Temple members. Ryan had come to investigate the complaint of a constituent who worried that his grandson was being held in the Peoples Temple colony of Jonestown against his will. Ryan exuded a gruff Irish optimism that his mission would be a success, but he was privately worried about reports that Jones was degenerating into madness at the jungle compound.

The news that George Moscone was going to actually reappoint the former police officer shocked Harvey, who quickly set up an appointment with the mayor. Milk reminded George that White had been the swing vote in many of the 6–5 defeats that the mayor's proposals had suffered in the board. Beyond that, White was the only city politician who had stepped forth as an active anti-gay spokesperson. You *are* up for reelection next year, Harvey goaded, and reappointing the city's major anti-gay politico is no way to lock up the gay vote. Seeing the wisdom of Milk's assessment, Moscone soon backed down from his earlier promise to reappoint White, and, sure enough, the city attorney issued an opinion citing a city charter passage that could be interpreted as blocking White's reentry to the board. Moscone told White that in order to be reappointed, he would have to demonstrate support in his home district. That, Moscone knew, would be no easy task. Many of

White's original supporters had grown disenchanted with the novice politician, since White seemed much more interested in currying favor with police, business, and real estate interests than with his blue-collar constituents. When White held an angry press conference to pressure Moscone into reappointing him, he was flanked not by neighborhood activists, but by officials of the Board of Realtors and the Police Officers' Association. Both groups had good reason to push for White's reappointment, and, according to most accounts, both were instrumental in pressuring White to seek his old job back. Realtors were understandably shaken at Harvey Milk's announced intention of passing a strict rent control ordinance to put the lid on skyrocketing rents. The loss of Dan White's conservative swing vote might make that proposal a reality. The Police Officers' Association, meanwhile, had been battling Mayor Moscone's settlement of a racial discrimination suit against the SFPD. The settlement, which had thus far escaped board approval by a 6–5 vote, would have forced promotion and hiring of more minorities in the department. Moscone was pushing hard for the settlement in an effort that further infuriated many of the more right-wing officers. A police beat reporter was not particularly shocked to see written on a police station bathroom wall, "Who's going to get the mayor?"

The fight over White's reappointment was little more than a political sideshow. Most of the politicking was done behind closed doors. Supervisor Dianne Feinstein was the only board member to publicly back Dan White. Milk would make no on-the-record comments, using the opportunity instead to rally support for his proposal to raise supervisors' salaries. The low salaries, he said, were part of a city government designed for the interests of those who wanted "only the wealthy class to run the city."

Harvey quickly got some personal insight into the problems of low salaries when he started reviewing Castro Camera's books shortly after the Prop 6 election. During his fervent campaigning, Harvey had simply stopped working on the store's accounting. A survey of the store's debits and credits led him to one inescapable conclusion: Castro Camera had to close. The business had been thousands of dollars in debt before—after both the 1975 and 1976 campaigns—and managed to pull through, largely because Harvey *had* to have the business as a base of political operations. Ever since moving off Castro Street, however, both Harvey and Scott had been losing interest in the business. Its status as an informal community center had slipped away when Harvey went to

City Hall. Without politics, Castro Camera was just a camera store and neither Harvey nor Scott had ever been interested in running just a camera store. Scott immediately agreed that Castro Camera was no longer worth the effort it took to keep it going. Harvey started looking around for a new job for Scott. A sign went up on the door announcing the business's December 1 closing date.

Other financial pressures were building up in those last weeks, problems Harvey did not confide to anyone, like the notice of garnishment from his bank. "The balance of your account has been held, pending a release or demand for payment," he was told. By late November, his major credit card account had also been declared in default and closed. Two banks were pressuring him for payments on past-due business loans. Harvey was scrambling for a way to solve his financial problems.

Congressman Leo Ryan has been shot.

Details were sketchy on that startling Saturday night. Day after day, the story came out in bits and pieces. First the murder of Ryan, *Examiner* photographer Greg Robinson, an NBC crew, and the shootings of several others at the Guyana air strip. Then, the first stories of how hundreds had committed suicide. Sharon Amos, the woman who had served as liaison between the temple and Milk's assembly campaign, was found with her three children, their throats slit with a butcher knife. The Reverend Jones had long ago code-named his suicide drill plans "white night." The San Francisco *Chronicle,* which had spurned its reporter's attempts to investigate Jim Jones during his rise to influence, started running the grisly banner headlines: "400 Stood in Line to Die."

Congressman Ryan's aides would later raise eerie questions of the State Department and the CIA's role in the Jonestown tragedy, but early media attention in San Francisco turned to the many politicians who had worked with Jim Jones, particularly Mayor Moscone and District Attorney Freitas. The press doggedly researched the Temple, a research project that, had it been launched two years earlier, might have saved over nine hundred lives.

This was only one of the mayor's problems. An ongoing FBI investigation of an alleged $10,000 political pay-off from Howard Hughes' Summa Corporation was beginning to draw media attention. Another FBI probe of both Milk and Moscone was looking into the pair's attempts to get federal money for a gay community center. Conors of Beijing. "If we run out of food, they'll just have to put out more."

On the way home, Doug mentioned he'd never been to City Hall. "You've never been to City Hall?" Harvey asked in amazement. He wanted to give Doug a private tour right then, but he'd left his keys at home, so he instead launched into a long lecture about the intricate friezes adorning the inside of the stately rotunda. He told of how sometimes, in the beautifully carved board chambers, he simply sat back and stared up at the crystal chandeliers and the carefully crafted scrolls carved into every corner. And of course, there was the grand marble staircase that flowed elegantly into the spacious colonnaded lobby. Like the steps of a grandiose Roman palace in a Cecil B. DeMille movie. "Never take an elevator when you're in City Hall," Harvey explained. "Always take that stairway. You can make such an entrance with it." Harvey paused, pondering the building on which so many of his aspirations had been centered. "You can make such an entrance— take it slowly."

When the pair finally trollied to Harvey's door, Doug was initially intimidated by the old blow-ups Harvey still had out of Jack McKinley's derriere. Doug wondered if he would measure up. The next morning, Harvey assured him he did and, as usual, Harvey jumped headfirst into a passionate love again. The relationship bloomed rapidly. Both were rebounding from collapsed affairs. Doug had broken up with a man he had lived with since he divorced his wife four years ago; he had only moved to San Francisco in August. Harvey talked little of Jack or how the relationship had ended. Given the anger that Harvey seemed to harbor against his former lover, Doug wasn't surprised that Jack never called or that Harvey never ran into him, even though Harvey stumbled into no small number of former flings at the numerous gay fund raisers the pair attended. Doug didn't worry about it; Jack Lira didn't sound like anybody Doug wanted to meet anyway. Harvey confided one night that at twenty-four, Doug was the oldest man Harvey had ever started an affair with; Doug thought he was kidding.

Explaining the waning affair with Billy and the ongoing romance with Bob Tuttle in Los Angeles required a full exposition on Harvey's theories of neo-homosexual romance. "As homosexuals, we can't depend on the heterosexual model," Harvey explained to Doug one night. "We grow up with the heterosexual model, but we don't have to follow it. We should be developing our own life-style. There's no reason why you can't love more than one person at a time. You don't have to love them all the same. You love some less, love some more—and always vinced it was prompted by one of his gay adversaries who was jealously trying to get funding for his own community center, Milk didn't take the investigation seriously. With the specter of scandal hanging over the mayor from both the Summa investigation and his Peoples Temple connection, however, it was a politically vulnerable George Moscone who emerged from the Guyana tragedy—and Harvey Milk knew it as the day of the final decision on the Dan White appointment neared.

"That man is dangerous."

Harvey and Doug were walking up the grand marble stairway beneath the City Hall rotunda when Harvey nudged Doug and pointed to the handsome young man walking stiffly toward them. Doug thought the man looked more handsome than dangerous.

"Who's that?" Doug asked.

"That's Dan White," Harvey said. "He's a real closet case." Every trace of Milk's usual good humor dropped from his voice. "There's nothing more dangerous than a closet case, someone fighting that inside of himself. He's that much more hostile to anyone who is open."

Doug mentioned that he thought Dan White was cute.

"Dan White is a closet case," charged Milk, "and he's dangerous."

Only in those final weeks did Harvey—who had previously talked of how White was "educatable"—use the word "dangerous" to describe White. Some associates later speculated that the pair might have had a run-in that drastically hardened Milk's feelings against White, because the term now popped into Harvey's conversations frequently when he talked about Dan. Harvey was not engaging in his normal political hyperbole. In an interview with gay activist-journalist Jack Davis, Harvey said that White was able to consider going back to the board because real estate developers had advanced him long-term, low-interest loans. The forces Milk most distrusted were behind White: Police Officers' Association, realtors, developers, and downtown business interests. There was talk that White had only reluctantly allowed himself to go after his seat, that he had been pushed. Pushed hard. These interests had lost too many fights in recent years, with Moscone's election, district elections, and the new, more liberal board, and they didn't want to keep on losing.

At a dinner with neighborhood activists that week, Milk button-holed *Chronicle* reporter Dale Champion, a president of a District 5 neighborhood group, to warn, "You news guys should be looking into Dan White. He has a history of mental instability." Milk explained to the rest of the activists that he chiefly opposed White because of the former policeman's anti-gay posture. Champion later thought of the ironic picture that was used on the front of the invitations for the dinner, a reproduction of da Vinci's classic "The Last Supper."

Mayor Moscone set the next Monday, November 27, as the day he would announce whether he would reappoint Dan White or put someone else on the board. In a conversation Harvey boastingly repeated to his friends, Milk bullishly gave the mayor an ultimatum. "You reappoint Dan White to the board and you won't get elected dogcatcher," Harvey told him. With Peoples Temple bearing down on him, Moscone knew that the gay constituency was an important one he could nail down in advance. Newspaper stories, meanwhile, started carrying comments from "an unnamed supervisor" vociferously opposing White's reappointment. That this supervisor was Harvey Milk soon became one of the city's worst-kept political secrets.

Charles Morris, the publisher of a local gay paper, had the comments in mind when he ran into Dan White at a political fund raiser. White was in a jovial, affable mood when they struck up a conversation. As for talk of opposition to his appointment, White said, "Those are just political pressures."

"There are some in the gay community who think that you might be anti-gay," Morris said, putting the comment as gently as he could. White froze up at the suggestion: "He got so cold," Morris recalled later, "that hell couldn't have melted him. It sent chills down my spine."

"Let me tell you right now," White said. "I've got a real surprise for the gay community—a real surprise."

With that, White turned and stalked away.

Dan White did not like to lose. He was convinced he could win this one. "When the smoke clears Monday," he told one television interviewer, "I'll be a supervisor again."

The holiday season was approaching, Harvey's favorite time of year, but even as the Thanksgiving weekend neared, an unusual calm settled into Milk's life, and he suddenly became preoccupied with wrapping up any outstanding business. He arranged to borrow several thousand dollars from his friend Carl Carlson so he could consolidate his debts. He turned in his leased car. He had been able to afford this luxury because it was a business expense. Now that there was no business, it had to go. He began making comments that didn't make much sense at the time. Over lunch a friend suggested that they start strategizing about the run for mayor Harvey wanted to make in 1983. "I'm not going to be around then," Harvey said. "Let's talk about today."

Though Harvey wouldn't talk of his own future, he gave an eloquent interview to activist Jack Davis about his vision of the future of San Francisco. Gays and Chinese would control the city within five to ten years, he said. He pointed to the many neighborhoods where gays were moving in and talked of the "beautiful flow" of communication between gays and heterosexuals in these newly integrated areas. He saved his most enthusiastic words for the neighborhood he had helped pioneer. "I could never have imagined five years ago that it would become like today," he said. "I came out at fourteen. Even though I lived at home for several more years, it was never 'home' again, for in that home, I was closeted. In fact, I never had a home again and especially no hometown. Then came Castro Street. Castro Street became my hometown. For the first time in my life, there was a place to live, to shop, to play, to be where I felt at home. To many, Castro Street became their hometown. Even if for only a short time. It has become a symbol to many gay people—a symbol of being. You can go home again."

Like the other buildings of the Beaux Artes Civic Center plaza, the San Francisco War Memorial Opera House stood in neo-Classical splendor, its colonnaded front the perfect entrance for Harvey's night at the opera that weekend. The night was a grand event for opera buffs —Magda Olivera, at 71, was making her debut in *Tosca,* Puccini's violent tale of love, jealousy, and political intrigue, in which all the main characters either get murdered, executed, or commit suicide by the end. Harvey was the guest of local opera impressario Kurt Herbert Adler in Box A. At Harvey's left sat Bidú Sayão—the grand diva who had sung at the first opera Milk had ever attended back at the old Met some thirty-five years before. The crowd went wild when Sayão was introduced. When the heavily gay throng saw her companion, shouts of "Bravo, Harvey" went up as well. When Harvey got home, he jotted off a quick note to his friend Tom O'Horgan in New York:

Tom—
Sitting in a box next to and talking with Bidú Sayão and listening to
Magda Olivera in her San Francisco debut at age 71.

The crowd went so wild that Mick Jagger would have been jealous
—I can't remember any reaction like that—and Sayāo—was like a
youngster hearing her first live opera—
Ah—life is worth living.

                                                              Love, Harvey.

The night Harvey sent that letter, George R. Moscone celebrated his forty-ninth birthday.

The next morning, the papers reported that the original estimate of the Jonestown death toll was a gross underestimation. Instead of 400 dead, there were at least 780 bodies, maybe more. Authorities said they had undercounted because they had not seen that many more bodies laid under the top layer of dead who were rotting in the jungle sun. The same paper reported that Dan White had lost his attempt to get a temporary restraining order to block Moscone from appointing a new supervisor on Monday. White insisted he would be in the board chambers to take his seat whether Moscone appointed him or not. When *Chronicle* reporter Martland Zane told White that the mayor planned to counter White's legal attempts to get the seat back, the former police officer fumed, "Well, now, the gloves are off."

"I'm worried about Dan White," George Moscone reportedly confided to his wife. "He's taking this hard. He's acting sort of flakey."

The next day, the newspapers reported that 910 bodies had been found in Jonestown.

"The mayor makes the appointment tomorrow," Harvey told his roommate, Billy Wiegardt. Billy knew that Harvey and George had spent long hours wrangling over the Dan White issue, but Harvey didn't seem to know what was happening, so, as he cut Harvey's hair, Billy refrained from asking more questions. The pair slipped into small talk. Billy had never cut anyone's hair before, but Harvey had decided he *had* to have his hair cut tonight. Harvey was pleased that Billy had just written his mother in Long Beach, Washington, to tell her he was gay. Harvey always viewed such moves as personal victories. When Billy was done, Milk glanced briefly at his hair and then returned to shuffling his paperwork. Billy had to tend bar that night, so he kissed Harvey good-bye and left him in the house, alone.

It isn't like Harvey, to talk so long, Don Amador thought. But there was Harvey, on the phone for thirty-five minutes, talking on about how he was turning in the car and closing the store. Small talk, Don thought; Harvey, however, never called for small talk. Don asked Harvey whether he should run for city council or school board. The city council race was inviting, but that was three years away and he could start running for school board right now. "Your job is to run for city council," Harvey directed. "Don, you have time and age on your side. I don't want you to be like me." Amador never figured out what that comment meant. He finally found an excuse to cut the conversation off, but he couldn't help later mentioning to his lover how odd it was that Harvey just kept on talking. Not like him at all.

"The strangest thing happened," Bob Tuttle's roommate told him later that night. Harvey had called earlier. No, he wasn't calling to say he was coming down or anything. He just called to talk. When Bob wasn't home, Harvey just started talking to his roommate, on and on as if he didn't want to get off. Bob thought of all the phone conversations he had had with Harvey. Milk never seemed to like talking much on the phone. Always brief, to the point, and good-bye. Both Bob and his roommate agreed, it was weird.

Harvey Milk, it seems, was lonely that night.

Mary Ann White returned from her trip to Nebraska at about 7 P.M. that Sunday night. She expected Dan to ask her if she had had a good time or a nice flight back, but he said nothing when she walked back in the house.

"Oh, it was nice," she said enthusiastically.

But Dan White just walked through the house, plopped himself on the bed, and started watching television. The response didn't particularly surprise Mary Ann. The pair had stopped having sex weeks before; White spent the nights in a sleeping bag on the living room couch. Dan hadn't talked much in the past few weeks either. As usual, Mary Ann blamed herself, wondering what she had done wrong. When she mentioned that she was tired and wanted to go to sleep, White glanced up briefly and told her, "Well, I'm going for a walk."

"I'm Barbara Taylor from KCBS. I'd like to speak to Dan White."

Mary Ann had heard the phone ring, though she couldn't make out what Dan was saying in the other room.

"I have received information from a source within the mayor's office that you are not getting that job," Taylor told White. "I am interested in doing an interview to find out your reaction to that."

"I don't know anything about it," White said.

White sounded surprised, Taylor thought. That, in turn, surprised her since she assumed White would already have heard the news. But Taylor needed a sound-bite for her story.

Taylor rephrased her question, and got no usable answer so she thought of a different phrasing and asked again. Dan White hung up the phone.

"Who was that?" Mary Ann asked.

"Oh, it was just some newsperson."

Billy got home from work at about 3:30 that night. He slipped into bed next to Harvey who, as always, was snoring loudly. At about 6:30, Billy groggily heard the coffee grinder in the kitchen and the usual clatter that accompanied the creation of Harvey's ritual morning cup of coffee. Harvey always tried to keep the noise down, but he was too much the klutz to be very quiet. Billy went back to sleep, only vaguely hearing the noise of the closing door as Harvey left for City Hall.

sixteen

No Cross, No Crown

The glimmer of dawn was obscured by a dark curtain of clouds hanging over San Francisco.

Dan White had stayed up all night, eating cupcakes, drinking Cokes, and finally watching the sun work its way over the horizon. White was still moping around the house when Mary Ann woke to go to work at the fried potato stand. She dressed the baby and left for the baby-sitter's at 7:30 A.M.

White's aide, Denise Apcar, called at 9 A.M. to tell Dan that a group of his supporters planned to present Mayor Moscone with petitions and letters of support from District 8 voters. Since Mary Ann had the car, Dan asked if Denise would come and take him to City Hall. White hung up the phone, showered, shaved, and slipped into his natty three-piece tan suit. He walked downstairs to his basement den and picked up his .38 Smith & Wesson, the Chief's Special model so favored by police officers. He checked the chamber; it was loaded. Stepping into a small closet off the den, he reached to the top shelf and pulled down a box of Remington hollow-headed bullets. He methodically pulled each bullet from the styrofoam case where they were individually packed. He counted out ten, two chambers' full, slipped the gun into his well-worn holster, snapped the holster to his belt, and then carefully tucked the gun under his vest.

Cyr Copertini, George Moscone's appointments secretary, was surprised to see the mayor's black Lincoln limousine parked by the Polk Street entrance of City Hall when she arrived to work at 8:40 A.M. The mayor rarely arrived before her, but then she remembered today was to be a special day at City Hall. Cyr found her boss ebuliant that morning. He'd gotten a good response to his private soundings about appointing a liberal neighborhood activist to Dan White's supervisorial seat. He'd finally have his working majority on the board. Moscone had originally planned a 10 A.M. press conference to announce the appointment, but he asked Cyr to delay the gathering until 11:30. George decided to take care of some phone work before then.

A cadre of Dan White's supporters were waiting in the mayor's office when Cyr arrived. They wanted to present a stack of petitions to the mayor. Cyr offered to take the papers to him. No, they insisted, they wanted to see Moscone. Copertini returned to her office. George told her he did not want to see the delegation. Copertini was not surprised. Moscone was by nature a jovial man who avoided potentially nasty confrontations at all costs. He still had not told Dan White that he would not be reappointed. Copertini went back to White's supporters, told them the mayor was busy, and promised to give them a receipt swearing that Moscone would have the petitions on his desk within minutes of when they handed them over to her. They relented and gave Cyr the petitions, shortly after 9 A.M.

At about the same time, George Moscone dialed Dianne Feinstein's Pacific Heights home. No, he was not going to reappoint White, he explained, even though the former supervisor insisted he would physically take his seat at that day's board meetings, whether he got it back or not. George returned to writing out by hand his comments for the press conference. Later that morning, his close ally, Assemblyman Willie Brown, dropped in briefly and the two made arrangements to do some Christmas shopping that weekend.

A worried Dianne Feinstein was sitting in her small City Hall office a half hour after talking to Moscone. As president of the board, the decorum-minded Feinstein felt it was her responsibility to prevent the kind of donnybrook that might arise when two men, both claiming to be supervisor from District 8, tried to get in the same chair at that afternoon's board meeting. She called a hurried meeting with a deputy city attorney and the board clerk to see if there were any legal tactics that could circumvent the problem. Finally, she decided she would try to dissuade White from forcing his way into the chambers. She told her aides to try to find White, and tell him she'd like to have a chat before the meeting.

Dick Pabich and Jim Rivaldo had rarely seen Harvey in as good a mood as when he bounded into the office at 9 A.M. He was always bouncy on Monday mornings, since each board meeting gave him the chance to put on another show, but that morning, Harvey seemed particularly cheerful. Funding for a gay community center would be voted on that day, and Harvey figured he finally had his sixth vote. He chatted briefly with Jim and Dick, then strolled over to the mayor's office where Moscone told him the news he wanted to hear—Dan White would not get his seat back. Buoyant, Harvey walked down the grand marble staircase and started to make his way toward a cafeteria where he could have his morning roll.

Doug Franks had been thinking about Harvey all morning. Just couldn't get him off his mind, even as he left the senior citizens center where he worked and headed for the library. He was suprised when he ran into Harvey striding down the street.

"I've never seen you so radiant," Doug told him.

"I am," Harvey said. "I'm happy. I just came from George's office. He's not going to reappoint Dan White."

Milk wasn't sure whom the mayor would appoint, but he knew he had the gay center vote and he was confident he had a sixth vote for many other decisions to come. The couple walked together to the cafeteria for breakfast. Harvey spent most of the next fifteen minutes talking excitedly about the march on Washington. No senators or congressmen could speak, he decided, unless they came out. They walked back to Civic Center, where Doug turned to go to the library and Harvey to City Hall. They agreed to get together that night for dinner after the board meeting.

Denise Apcar told Dan White she had seen Harvey leave the mayor's office when she picked White up, about 10:15. Dan told her he wanted to see both George and Harvey once he got to City Hall. Denise noted he was rubbing his hands together and blowing on his fingertips as he talked. "I'm a man. I can take it," he told her. "I just want to talk with them, have them tell me to my face why they won't reappoint me."

Denise dropped White off at City Hall and left to gas up her car. William Melia, a city engineer with a lab overlooking the supervisors' parking lot, first noticed a nervous young man pacing by his window at about 10:25. The man walked back and forth, anxiously glancing into the window where Melia was working. The phone rang and Melia stepped briefly into another room to take the call. As soon as he left the room, he heard the lab window open and the sound of someone jumping to the floor and running out of the lab and into the hall.

"Hey, wait a second," Melia shouted. He knew such an entrance was a sure way to avoid passing through the metal detectors at the public entrances of City Hall.

"I had to get in," White explained. "My aide was supposed to come down and let me in the side door, but she never showed up."

"And you are—"

"—I'm Dan White, the city supervisor. Say, I've got to go." With that, White spun on his heel and left the office.

Mildred Tango, a clerk-typist in the mayor's office, saw White hesitating near the main door of the mayor's office as if he didn't want to use that entrance. Inside sat the mayor's police bodyguard; White knew that, since he had once worked the relief shift as the mayor's police bodyguard during the Alioto administration. White saw Tango unlocking a side door to the mayor's office on her rounds to collect the morning mail. She recognized White and let him follow her into the hallway that led to the mayor's suite. White presented himself at Cyr Copertini's desk at about 10:30 A.M.

"Hello, Cyr. May I see the mayor?"

"He has someone with him, but let me go check."

Moscone grimaced at the news. He was clearly uncomfortable with the idea of a confrontation on what promised to be such a splendid morning.

"Give me a minute to think," the mayor said. "Oh, all right. Tell him I'll see him, but he'll have to wait a minute."

Cyr asked if George wanted someone to sit in on the meeting. Press secretary Mel Wax often served such duty to make sure disgruntled politicos did not later lay claim to specious mayoral promises.

"No. No," George said, "I'll see him alone."

"Why don't you let me bring Mel in," Copertini persisted.

"No, no. I will see him alone."

Copertini told White the mayor would be a few minutes. Dan seemed nervous.

"Would you like to see a newspaper while you're waiting?" Copertini asked.

He didn't.

"That's all right. There's nothing in it anyway, unless you want to read about Caroline Kennedy having turned twenty-one."

"Twenty-one? Is that right?" White shook his head. "Yeah. That's all so long ago. It's even more amazing when you think that John-John is now eighteen."

Moscone buzzed for White.

"Good girl, Cyr," Dan White said.

An aide told Dianne Feinstein that he had just seen Dan go into the mayor's office. She sent her administrative assistant, Peter Nardoza, to find White. As an extra precaution, Feinstein opened her office door so she could see him if he slipped into the long hallway on which the supervisors' offices were clustered.

Around the same time Dan White walked into George Moscone's office, Harvey Milk was stepping up the marble staircase to his aides' offices. Dick Pabich was working on correspondence. Jim Rivaldo was talking to a gay lawyer, who, Harvey knew, had a fondness for leather during his late-night carousing.

"Well, where are your leathers?" Milk asked.

"Don't worry," Jim joked. "He's got leather underwear on."

Milk excused himself to go to the bank. He was expecting Carl Carlson with the cashier's check. Jim and Harvey agreed to get together again at 11:30 so they could go to the swearing-in of the new supervisor.

Harvey walked to his office, but Carlson hadn't arrived yet. Harvey was on the phone when he came in, about 10:50; Carl sat down to do some typing until Harvey was finished.

Dan White and Moscone hadn't been in the mayor's large ceremonial office more than five minutes before Cyr heard White's voice raised, shouting at Moscone. George hated scenes and decided to try to mollify the former supervisor by inviting him to a small den off his office where he kept a wet bar. He lit a cigarette, poured two drinks, and turned to see White brandishing a revolver. White pulled the trigger and fired a bullet into Moscone's arm, near the shoulder, and immediately shot a second slug into the mayor's right pectoral. Moscone sank to the floor as the second bullet tore into his lung. Dan White knelt next to the prostrate body, poised the gun six inches from the right side of Moscone's head, and fired a bullet that ripped through Moscone's earlobe and into his brain. He pulled the trigger again and another bullet sped from the revolver, through Moscone's ear canal and into the brain.

White methodically emptied the four spent cartridges and the one live bullet from his Smith & Wesson and crammed them into the right pocket of his tan blazer. He had special bullets for his next task; the hollow-headed dum-dum bullets that explode on impact, ripping a hole into the victim two to three times the size of the slug itself. White slipped the five bullets into the revolver's chamber, stepped out a side door, and dashed toward the other side of City Hall where the supervisors' officers were.

The four dull thuds sounded like a car backfiring, Cyr thought, so she looked out her office window, but saw nothing. Rudy Nothenberg, Moscone's top deputy, had an 11 A.M. appointment with the mayor. He was ready to cancel it when he noted that George's meeting with White was taking longer than expected. He was relieved when he saw White hurriedly leave the office; he'd get his chance to talk to the mayor after all.

Dick Pabich saw White dashing toward the supervisorial offices. What a jerk, Pabich thought, running around here like he's still somebody important.

Peter Nardoza saw him rushing into the hallway outside Dianne Feinstein's office.

"Dianne would like to talk to you," Nardoza said.

"Well, that will have to wait a couple of moments," White answered sharply.

Feinstein heard the exchange, then saw White flash by her office door.

"Dan," she called.

"I have something to do first," White said.

Harvey and Carl were getting ready to go to the bank when White stuck his head into Milk's office.

"Say, Harv, can I see you?"

"Sure."

White took Harvey to his old office across the hall. He noticed that his name plate had already been removed from the door. Once Milk stepped inside, White planted himself between him and the door. He drew his revolver and fired. A sharp streak of pain sped through Harvey.

"Oh no," Milk shouted. "N—" He reflexively raised his hand to try to protect himself.

White knew that bullets went through arms, and he fired again, cutting short Harvey's cry. The slug tore into Harvey's right wrist, ripped into his chest and out again, finally lodging near his left elbow. Another dum-dum bullet pounded Milk in the chest. He was falling now, toward the window. As he crumpled to his knees, Dan White took careful aim from across the office. The first three bullets alone would not have killed Harvey. White took careful aim at the staggering figure and fired a fourth bullet which sliced into the back of his head and out the other side, spraying blood against the wall. The shots sounded so loud they startled White; louder than the shots in Moscone's office. Harvey had fallen to the floor. White gripped the revolver's handle and pulled the trigger once more. The bullet left only a dime-sized wound on the outside of Harvey's skull, but shards from its hollow tip exploded when they struck Harvey's skull, tearing and ripping into his brain. Harvey Milk died at approximately 10:55 A.M. on the dark gray morning of November 27, 1978, a year and a half short of his fiftieth birthday.

Dianne Feinstein had heard the first shot and known exactly what it was—Dan White had committed suicide. Then she heard more shots and felt an unspeakable horror. She had to get up from her desk. She had to force her brain and body to function together, to move her out of her chair, out of her office. But she felt she was going too slow, too slow, she had to go faster. She saw White walk by her door. She couldn't move fast enough as she smelled the odor of gunpowder that wafted down the hall.

Carl Carlson thought at first maybe the sounds were firecrackers, but he had heard Harvey shout and knew it was not firecrackers. Carlson stepped out of Harvey's office in time to see White walk out of his office, pull the door shut behind him, glance coldly at Carlson, then walk calmly down the hall. Feinstein joined Carl at the door to White's office.

Feinstein shoved the door open and saw Harvey's body sprawled out, his face toward the window, lying in a spreading pool of blood. Feinstein's mind shifted into automatic. All her emergency medical training told her to take the injured man's pulse. She knelt to take Harvey's arm; she put her finger to Harvey's wrist and it quickly oozed into the wound left by the second bullet. Blood and tissue engulfed her finger.

White ran into Denise Apcar's office. "Give me the keys," he shouted to her. "Give me the keys."

Apcar nervously handed White her car keys and he dashed out the door.

Only two or three minutes had passed since Dan White had left the mayor's office. Rudy Nothenberg was waiting for George to buzz him for their 11 A.M. appointment. It didn't make sense—Rudy had seen Dan White leave. What was taking George so long? Tentatively he stuck his head in Moscone's main office, then walked into the adjoining den and saw George's feet. He figured Moscone had fainted until he got closer and saw the blood flowing from his head onto the carpet. Moscone still held a lit cigarette in his right hand; it was burning a hole into the back of his tie.

"Get in here," he shouted to Cyr. "Call an ambulance. Get the police."

Dianne Feinstein bounded into Harvey's office with Carl. She grabbed a phone, frantically calling the police chief. The chief's lines, however, were all busy with calls from the mayor's office, but Feinstein didn't know that and kept dialing desperately. What's the matter she thought. Why can't I get through?

A few blocks away, Dan White was at a fast-food joint calling Mary Ann. Something happened, he said. He needed to meet her right away at St. Mary's Cathedral.

Carl Carlson was on Harvey's other phone, buzzing Dick Pabich. Dick had just come into his office telling Jim Rivaldo how weird White had looked. He answered Carl's call.

"Harvey's been shot. Call an ambulance."

"Oh, sure," Pabich answered sarcastically.

"No time for messing around. I'm serious."

"What?"

Pabich jumped from his desk and raced toward Harvey's office. Rivaldo followed him into the corridor and saw a cadre of armed police racing toward the mayor's office. He followed them, thinking that was the best way to find the source of the ruckus, when Pabich ran back and shouted at the officers, "No, no. It's not the mayor's office. It's down here." Several officers split off and followed Pabich to the supervisors' offices. Chief Gain arrived shortly after and sought out Feinstein, telling her the mayor had been killed too.

"Oh, no," Feinstein gasped.

Aides now circled Dan White's office door. Dick Pabich remembered seeing White rush by and arrived at the obvious conclusion. "Dan White did it," he said. A conservative board clerk who had never had much use for either Milk or his gay entourage scolded Dick: "How can you say such a thing?"

Mary Ann White left the cab and hurried across the wide brick terrazo that stretches in front of the modernistic St. Mary's Cathedral. She quickly spotted her husband in the chapel.

"I shot the mayor and Harvey," he told her.

They talked for a few minutes. Mary Ann said she'd stand by him through any ordeal. They started walking the few blocks to Northern Station, the police station where White had once worked as a member of the San Francisco Police Department. As they walked, Mary Ann kept her hand around Dan White's waist, holding firmly onto the revolver in the belt holster, fearing he might suddenly grab the gun and shoot himself.

Hundreds of reporters were rushing to City Hall. Stories were muddled. Was the mayor shot? Was he dead? No, it was Harvey Milk. Milk and one of his aides? Were they dead? And, of course, the question that immediately came to all the reporters' minds: Were the shootings the work of a Peoples Temple hit squad? Jim Jones's code word for the suicide rituals—"white night"—was also supposed to trigger cadres of Peoples Temple assassins, according to reports from Jonestown. Had they started doing their bloody work?

At 11:20 A.M., a shaken Dianne Feinstein stepped from the supervisors' offices to make the announcement. Her face looked haggard; Police Chief Gain had to support her as she spoke.

"As president of the board of supervisors, it is my duty to inform you that both Mayor Moscone and Supervisor Harvey Milk have been shot and killed."

The reporters recoiled with a collective gasp that nearly drowned out Feinstein's next words.

"Supervisor Dan White is the suspect."

Across City Hall, outside the mayor's office, press secretary Mel Wax made the same announcement to another knot of reporters. Wax added that under the provisions of the city charter, Board of Supervisors President Feinstein was now acting mayor.

Doug Franks easily found the book he sought in the library, checked it out, and walked the five blocks back to the senior center where he worked. When he arrived, he saw that somebody had taken a portable television to the living room where the seniors now huddled, murmuring in shock. He heard the announcer's raspy voice: "Again, Supervisor Milk and Mayor Moscone have been killed."

Doug stumbled; he felt he was going to faint; he had just hugged Harvey, checked out a book, walked five blocks and now Harvey was dead. That's all the time it took—and someone you love is dead.

At 11:25 A.M., Dan and Mary Ann White arrived at Northern Station.

"It's there," White said, pointing to his right hip.

The officer took the revolver from White's belt and the four spent .38 special casings and one bullet from his blazer pocket. White wanted to turn himself in at Northern Station because his friend, Paul Chignell, the vice-president of the Police Officers' Association, worked there. White asked Chignell to make sure the press stayed away from his wife. White seemed calm and detached, not particularly distraught, Chignell noted. White asked, "Is he dead, Paul?"

Police and officials from the coroner's office busily snapped pictures of the two undisturbed bodies for nearly an hour. Cleve Jones and Scott Smith arrived at City Hall shortly after the shootings. At first, wary supervisors' aides would not admit Smith to Harvey's office; nobody recognized him. Jones finally pulled Scott into the secured area, where grim-faced police mixed with sobbing board clerks and the small group of Harvey's stunned aides.

"It's over. We've lost it," Jim Rivaldo kept muttering to no one in particular. He felt drawn to the door of Dan White's office where Harvey still lay. The police officer at the door warned him away from the grisly sight, but Rivaldo felt he needed to connect with the physical reality of Harvey's death. He stood outside the door as policemen were turning the corpse over to put it in the black rubber body bag. Jones stepped up and peered over Rivaldo's shoulder as the officers struggled with Milk's lanky frame. Harvey was blue now, his discolored head rolling limply, his suit and thick dark hair stained with clots of blood. Jim stared at the bloodstained wall and tried to retrace the path of Harvey's stumble to calculate what Milk had seen last. Harvey had fallen facing the window, so that before Dan White had pumped the last bullets into his staggering victim, Harvey could have looked out the window and seen the grand facade of the San Francisco War Memorial Opera House across the street.

The police finally succeeded in getting Harvey's body into the bag, which was then put on a gurney, covered with a crisp, creased hospital sheet and pushed down the hallway past his old office. At noon, the doors of the supervisors' offices opened and police wheeled the gurney into a nearby elevator—the elevator Harvey had always forsaken in favor of the grand staircase—then out a side entrance of City Hall into a waiting coroner's ambulance.

At about the same time Milk's body was being slipped on a rack beneath the stretcher bearing George Moscone, Dan White was sitting down with homicide inspectors Ed Erdelatz and Frank Falzon. Falzon had attended St. Elizabeth's Grammar School with White and later coached him on the police softball team; Dan had been his star player. Falzon read White his Miranda rights and then taped his twenty-four-minute confession. The interrogation of White—or, some said, the lack of it—would later prove to be one of the most controversial aspects of the murder case.

By noon, a small silent crowd was gathering outside City Hall, standing below the dome, staring dumbly at the police, reporters, and city officials who scurried up the wide stairs. The golden-bordered city flag above the portico was pulled to half-mast as the crowd grew. Some dropped flowers on the steps. Before long, a mound grew and an angry young man put a hand-lettered sign amid the blossoms: "Happy, Anita?"

The EXTRA editions were hitting the newsstands on Castro Street with their bold headlines: "Mayor, Milk Slain; Dan White Seized." Knots of Castro residents clustered on the corners, reading the newspapers in disbelief. Many of the bars and businesses quickly closed their doors and hung black bunting at their entrances. Black-bordered pictures of Harvey appeared in shop windows, store clerks slipped on black armbands. People started coming to Castro Street, to gather where they had so many times before in past crises.

Frank Robinson had spent the morning working on his new submarine disaster novel when he took his afternoon break and heard the news from a restaurant waitress. He went home, tuned into a news radio station, and started taking the dozens of calls from Harvey's other friends. He remembered the early days he and Harvey had spent bullshitting about politics on the old maroon couch in the funky Victorian storefront on Castro Street. A sense of isolation gripped Robinson as he realized this all was over now. He had no anger or hatred for Dan White. For Frank, White did not even exist as a person; White was just a tool, he thought. It was the whole society that hated gays; the game had always been stacked. You could be the best man in the world, he thought, and still the society would crucify you.

A few blocks away, Harvey's political friends from the San Francisco Gay Democratic Club were conferring at Harry Britt's house. They decided to respond to the assassinations just as they had responded to the crises of past years—a march from Castro Street to City Hall. The permits, details, and announcements fell into place as the afternoon wore on. They asked mourners to bring candles.

President Carter's statement that afternoon expressed "a sense of outrage and sadness at the senseless killing" of the two men. He praised Supervisor Milk as "a hard-working and dedicated supervisor, a leader of San Francisco's gay community, who kept his promise to represent all constituents."

The board met briefly for its regularly scheduled Monday meeting at 2 P.M. "This is an unparalleled time for San Francisco, and we need to keep together," said Acting Mayor Feinstein. "I think we all have to share the same sense of outrage, the same sense of shame, the same sense of sorrow and the same sense of anger." Feinstein urged the public to "go into a state of very deep and meaningful mourning and to express its sorrow with a dignity and an inner examination. . . ."

Medora Payne was on her lunch break at Lowell High School when a friend told her that Harvey and the mayor had been killed by Dan White. She had to be kidding, Medora thought, but her chemistry teacher confirmed the news. Medora could tell by the look in her teacher's eyes that it was true. She broke into tears, apologized to her friend for not believing her, and asked if she would stay with her while she wept for the funny man she had met so many years before when she took her parents' film to get developed at Castro Camera. She spent the next few hours walking around the high school's cinder track, crying and remembering the nights she had spent licking envelopes and handing out brochures for Harvey Milk.

Tom O'Horgan heard the news in New York City only hours before he went to the mailbox to find the letter Harvey had posted after he went to the opera, the letter ending with the exclamation—"Life is worth living." A few hours later, Jack McKinley, hysterical from grief, joined him. O'Horgan loaned him the money to make the trip to San Francisco.

Mrs. Gina Moscone and the mayor's mother were attending a cousin's funeral seventy miles north of San Francisco when the assassinations occurred. The mayor's four children had converged on their home from their various schools by 1 P.M., when they finally arrived home. Gina took a few steps from her car and collapsed into a friend's arms. She had heard of the news of her husband's killing on the car radio.

"This is Harvey Milk, speaking on Friday, November 18, 1977. This is to be played only in the event of my death by assassination. I've given it considerable thought to this, not just since the election. I've been thinking about this for some time prior to the election and certainly over the years. I fully realize that a person who stands for what I stand for, an activist, a gay activist, becomes the target or potential target for a person who is insecure, terrified, afraid, or very disturbed with themselves. Knowing that I could be assassinated at any moment or any time, I feel it's important that some people should understand my thoughts, so the following are my thoughts, my wishes, my desires, whatever, and I'd like to pass them on and played for the appropriate people."

Most of the people in the room had known Harvey had made this tape. Now, only three hours after the shootings, they were following Harvey's wish that it be played. Harvey knew enough about the machinations of City Hall politics to understand that the outer trappings of sorrow would not keep politicos from immediately maneuvering to grab his seat. He had made the tape to ensure that his post would not fall into the hands of the gay moderates, whom he had so long opposed. Pabich, Rivaldo, Jones, Carlson, and Scott Smith, along with a handful of others, had originally walked into Harvey's office to play the tape, but Scott had seen Harvey's honorary clown certificate and the memorabilia cluttering Harvey's walls and could not bear to stay in the room, so they now huddled in Supervisor Carol Ruth Silver's cubicle, listening to Harvey's political will.

"I stood for more than just a candidate. I think there was a strong differential between somebody like Rick Stokes and myself. I have never considered myself a candidate. I have always considered myself part of a movement, part of a candidacy. I've considered the movement the candidate. I think there's a distinction between those who use the movement and those who are part of the movement. I think I was always part of the movement. I wish that I had time to explain everything I did. Almost everything was done with an eye on the gay movement."

Harvey launched into vociferous attacks on the four people who he said should not succeed him: Jim Foster, Rick Stokes, Jo Daly, and Frank Fitch, all past presidents of the Alice Toklas Democratic Club Harvey had battled so long. He then listed the four people who he said should be considered as replacements, strongly praising Frank Robinson and Bob Ross, his first choices, suggesting Harry Britt as a third choice, and offhandedly mentioning Anne Kronenberg as well. Scott sat through the tapes silently, still numbed by the killing. Cleve broke into sobs as Harvey's voice talked on. Jim Rivaldo, meanwhile, began to marvel at the perfection of the destiny Harvey had created for himself. There Harvey was, carefully instructing his friends on what to do next, weighing the political situation and prodding his allies to keep up the fight. Rivaldo felt torn between the tragedy of the day and this sense of marvel that Harvey was living out an extraordinary final act. He had known that his death would be another step in a historical process, and was even now counseling his associates in how to use it. Rivaldo began to think less of Harvey, a man who had been killed, than Harvey the actor, still performing exquisite political theater.

Even as they listened to the tape, reporters were clamoring for a statement from Harvey's friends. In the next paragraphs, they found it.

"The other aspect of the tapes is the business of what would happen should there be an assassination. I cannot prevent some people from feeling angry and frustrated and mad, but I hope they will take that frustration and that madness and instead of demonstrating or anything of that type, I would hope they would take the power and I would hope that five, ten, one hundred, a thousand would rise. I would like to see every gay doctor come out, every gay lawyer, every gay architect come out, stand up and let that world know. That would do more to end prejudice overnight than anybody would imagine. I urge them to do that, urge them to come out. Only that way will we start to achieve our rights."

Harvey closed his tape with the lecture most in the room had heard many times before; maybe that's why it wasn't included in the press release that Harvey's lawyer, John Wahl, read to reporters soon afterward. The last words that most of them would ever hear Harvey Milk speak concerned the one commodity he believed he had brought to gays —hope: "I ask for the movement to continue, for the movement to grow because last week I got the phone call from Altoona, Pennsylvania, and my election gave somebody else, one more person, hope. And after all, that's what this is all about. It's not about personal gain, not about ego, not about power—it's about giving those young people out there in the Altoona, Pennsylvanias hope. You gotta give them hope."

At Harry Britt's house, the leaders of the San Francisco Gay Democratic Club were beginning to arrive at the same consensus developing in Harvey's office about who should follow Milk as supervisor. Frank Robinson, Harvey's first choice, had neither the experience nor the desire to be a supervisor. The second choice, Bob Ross, had never been close to Harvey's younger political coterie. They worried his instincts were more conservative than their own liberalism, so they decided to try to engineer the selection away from him. Few of Harvey's intimates took Harry Britt seriously as a potential successor. His political experience was largely limited to Milk's campaigns and their own fledging Democratic club. His long sideburns and west Texas drawl convinced most that he was an unrefined yahoo, ill-suited for the role as the city's chief gay spokesperson. That left Anne Kronenberg. As Harvey's aide and former campaign manager, Anne knew many of the political connections who would be necessary to persuade the next mayor. Though the group making the decision was almost exclusively male, most liked the idea of advancing a lesbian for the job, since lesbian-feminists frequently carped that the gay movement seemed dominated by men. Slowly, with many phone calls between Britt's house and City Hall, the consensus began to build for Kronenberg who was then on a plane, flying home from a visit with her parents.

Joe Campbell saw a bold headline mentioning something about a mayor, but since stories about mayors usually meant talk about politics, Joe didn't bother to give the paper an extra glance. He wasn't interested in politics. Later that same Monday afternoon, he was driving toward his isolated Marin County home when he picked up a hunky young hitchhiker.

"Too bad about the mayor and that other guy," the rider casually said.

"What about?"

"You haven't heard? They got shot. The mayor and some other guy. He was a supervisor."

"Milk?"

"Yeah, that's it. Harvey Milk."

"Are you sure he's dead?"

"Yeah. Shot in the head."

Campbell careened his station wagon to the shoulder of the gravel road and collapsed into tears.

"That's my lover," he sobbed.

The hitchhiker held Campbell for five minutes as Joe wept for the man he had lived with for six years in what seemed like another lifetime. As the late afternoon sun began to set over the Pacific, Campbell began his frantic drive into San Francisco.

Though most of his friends at City Hall spent much of the day saying how shocked they were that Dan White would kill the mayor and supervisor, Undersheriff Jim Denman had no trouble believing that Dan White was capable of the crime. Denman had spent years working with the police subculture and his brief meetings with Dan White had indicated the former supervisor fit the police mold well—rigid, conservative, and anti-gay. But White was also a prisoner who needed protection. With the image of Jack Ruby shooting Lee Harvey Oswald haunting him, Denman personally supervised Dan White's first day in jail. Denman was not particularly surprised that police treated White with deference, though he was taken aback when one policeman gave White a pat on the behind, as if the killer had just scored the winning touchdown for the high school football team. What did amaze Denman was the cool calm with which White handled himself. He was controlled, businesslike, and exceedingly polite. If he was in shock, Denman thought, it was at best a very mild shock. The only time White showed any sign of emotion was when he called his mother. "Hi, mom, how you doing?" he said. "I guess you heard." A few minutes into the conversation, White's voice turned soft and caring, like it might crack —and then White caught himself and his voice turned hard again.

When the cell door slammed behind him, White betrayed no hint of emotion. He simply laid back on his cot, folded his arms behind his head and stared at the ceiling. For three days Denman watched White for any sign that he understood what he had done. Never did a tear, a questioning glance, or any sign of remorse crossed the former policeman's face.

From radio reports, Joe Campbell learned of a memorial service for Harvey at a makeshift gay community center near City Hall. He sat near the back of the hall, still in shock, and overheard someone whisper that Harvey's lover was in the front row. Campbell glanced to Doug Franks but couldn't think of anything to say. As the service began, Campbell realized that the speakers were talking about a man he didn't know, certainly not about the Harvey Milk he had met at Riis Park Beach in 1956. Joe never understood what Harvey had meant with all his politics business, but he had no doubt that it wasn't anything worth getting shot about. He was still dazed when he left the service. Since Joe knew little of Castro Street or the marches, he didn't know that as he left the memorial service, thousands were converging on Castro Street. Instead, Joe drifted to a friend's apartment, where he spent the night.

The crowd started gathering at 7:30 P.M. on the corner of Castro and Market Streets, the place that would one day be called Harvey Milk Plaza. Hundreds, then 5000 and soon 10,000 came with their candles. From a nearby balcony came the mournful wail of a conch shell as the crowd silently grew. The businesses had all closed now, their commercial displays replaced with tributes to Harvey Milk and George Moscone. Cleve Jones and his street radical friends had been training monitors all afternoon at Jones's apartment a block up Castro. The police were worried about violence, but the throng, which had been so rambunctious during protests over gay rights referenda, needed little quelling as it stood dumbly, waiting for direction. A bank of television lights flicked on across Market Street and the crowd started moving toward it. The monitors, however, were not yet in place. As titular leader of street marches, Jones scrambled to a promontory where he could soothe the crowd. From a bullhorn, he shouted words from a folk song by lesbian singer Meg Christian:

> Can we be like drops of water
> Falling on the stone
> Splashing, breaking, dispersing in air
> Weaker than the stone by far
> But be aware that as time goes by
> The rock will wear away.

The crowd stopped and stared mutely at Jones while the monitors raced into position.

Three men, carrying the American, California, and San Francisco flags, took their places at the beginning of the procession, flanked by a lone drummer, slowly thrumping a muffled beat while in the night, the sound of a distant trumpet murmured the old Bob Dylan song "Blowin' in the Wind." Slowly, the march pushed down the boulevard, stretching for five and then ten blocks while thousands more were still arriving on Castro Street. The tens of thousands of candles glimmered in the night, their flickers merging with the lights on the hills around Castro Street so that from a distance it appeared that a thousand stars had fallen onto the avenue and were moving slowly toward City Hall, flowing from the hills of San Francisco and the dark night above.

Medora Payne walked with her parents and John Ryckman, Harvey's campaign manager from 1976, and gazed at the crowd around her. Young and old, men and women, gays and straights, walked slowly to the drum's dirge. Medora thought how much Harvey had wanted gays and heterosexuals to come together and experience themselves beyond the superficial delineations of sexuality and now she saw Harvey's dream finally dawning on these tens of thousands and Harvey wasn't there to see it and this too made Medora want to cry. Harry Britt marched with Harvey's many other friends—Pabich, Rivaldo, Robinson, Tom Randol, and Michael Wong—and while he was moved by the immensity of the demonstration around him, he was worried. Harvey had always been there before; now he was gone; was this the end or the beginning? Suddenly, Harry felt like the little boy in Altoona. All he had was hope. Behind him he heard a woman talking in muffled tones about who should succeed Harvey. "There's a mailman we want to get

Dianne to appoint," she said. This came as disquieting news to Britt, the mailman.

The massive crowd stretched the entire distance from City Hall to Castro Street, some 40,000 strong utterly silent. A reporter standing on the sidewalk heard a cough from the center of the throng a half-block away. A carload of punks sped by and shouted "Goddamn queers"— and nobody bothered to shout anything back as the procession moved toward the grand rotunda. The Civic Center plaza was awash with the still-flickering tapers, stretching out around the wide granite stairs of City Hall while the strong and resonant voice of Joan Baez sang "Swing Low, Sweet Chariot." The march ostensibly memorialized both George and Harvey, but few speakers quarreled that the crowd had amassed chiefly to remember the gangly ward politician who had once called himself the mayor of Castro Street.

"He was a leader who represented your voices," Dianne Feinstein told the crowd. "Those of us on the board will remember him for his commitment, for his sense of humor, and for his ability to develop a sense of destiny. I ask you to take up that legacy and I give you my assurance that as long as I have any say in city government, we will remain a city that strives for human understanding and rights."

Milk had taught gays, Harry Britt said, that "no matter what the world has taught us about ourselves, we can be beautiful and we can get our thing together. . . . He was to us what Dr. King was to his people. Harvey was a prophet. Like Dr. King, he lived by a vision. As I look out over this crowd, I think the city has bought this vision. Something very special is going to happen in this city and it will have Harvey Milk's name on it. . . . How many times have we made that walk down Market Street and known that when we got there to City Hall, Harvey Milk would be there? Harvey will be in the middle of us, always, always, always."

The crowd was still somber when the speeches ended. Many took their candles and set them on the statue of Abraham Lincoln near City Hall's front portico. Most trudged silently back to the Castro where, on the corner of Eighteenth and Castro Street, spray-painted graffiti posed the larger social question so troubling to gays, so inexplicable to straights: "Who Killed Harvey Milk?"

In the Sunset District, a labor organizer who had met Milk in the district elections campaign spent much of the early evening pacing his living room in the district where he had lived nearly all his life. Sure he had once worried about the fruits and kooks, but by late 1978, he knew Harvey Milk was a friend of the union man, a voice for the regular guy like him. And as for George Moscone, he had held a neighborhood coffee for George right in his own living room back in the watershed 1975 campaign. Something had to be terribly wrong in the world when two men like that could just get offed in a matter of a few minutes, he thought. Something terribly wrong. He paced further. Finally, after darkness fell, he hopped in his car and went to City Hall where he listened to Joan Baez, Dianne Feinstein, and Harry Britt. But he was still agitated as the mourners turned back to Castro Street; he knew where he had to go. On a hill overlooking the Castro, his daughter had moved in with another woman. Just a few weeks before, she had told her stolid father that she was gay. His wife had been more shaken than the machinist himself. After all, he had known Harvey for years. Still, he had not gone to her apartment without an express invitation before, but on this, of all nights, he felt that's where he needed to go. She answered the door, her face still red from the day's tears, and within moments the father and daughter had fallen into each others' arms, sobbing. "Knowing Harvey Milk," he said later, "was a blessing."

With meticulous precision, the coroner worked on the bodies of George Moscone and Harvey Milk, collecting the necessary forensic data. Once washed down, it was amazing to see how small the bullet holes that riddled Harvey's body actually were. Harvey would have survived the body wounds, the coroner concluded, but, as he shaved the back of Harvey's head to reveal the wounds into which Dan White had pumped his coup de grace shots, he could see that the final bullet had brought instantaneous death. Once the autopsy was completed, the coroner fulfilled Harvey's last request and removed his dead eyes to be transplanted into the living.

By Tuesday, the immediate jolt had passed and the newspapers had started speculating about the political ramifications of the shooting of the city's two most dynamic liberal politicians. Few politicos wanted to be quoted by name, but their assessments were nearly unanimous. As one neighborhood activist put it, "This sets back the liberal cause fifteen, maybe twenty years."

Jim Rivaldo and Scott Smith were punchy with exhaustion when they rummaged through Harvey's closet that afternoon to pick out

Harvey's final attire. Talk was already spreading that Harvey would lie in state at City Hall, so Jim first suggested that only one outfit would suit Harvey for such august surroundings—his blue jeans, plaid shirt, and sneakers. After deciding that might be too much for the sober morticians to appreciate, they ferreted through Harvey's more respectable outfits. Rivaldo was amazed to see that most of Harvey's clothes, from his suits to his underwear, were tattered and threadbare. They had a hard time finding socks that didn't have holes in them.

By Tuesday afternoon, most of Harvey's inner circle agreed that Anne should succeed Harvey. Anne wasn't enthusiastic at first, but she agreed to make the push. She and Doug Franks bused to Macy's and bought what they called a Dianne Junior outfit, complete with a wool skirt, a purse, and a frilly bowed blouse. In twenty minutes, Kronenberg —who had not one dress to her name—looked like a serious young businesswoman.

John Wahl was standing in a phone booth when he recognized a troupe of men he had seen at the Hall of Justice. He couldn't remember whether they were policemen or sheriff's deputies. They apparently recognized him from his appearance on the local television stations when he had read the publicly released portion of Harvey's will; when they walked by him, they started chanting, "Dan White is all right. Dan White is all right."

Jack McKinley was in the second day of a drunken binge on Tuesday. "I want to fuck Dan White to death," he kept telling friends in New York.

The very suggestion enraged Harvey's friends. During the preparations for the planned lying in state, the mayor's staff decided that George Moscone alone would lie beneath the City Hall rotunda. Harvey's casket would be left in the front lobby for mourners to file by on their way to see the main attraction. Harvey's aides argued bitterly against the plan, sensing that even in death, the political establishment was trying to shove Harvey's casket to the back of the bus. The mayor's staff finally relented.

That night, the San Francisco Gay Democratic Club voted unanimously to change its name to the Harvey Milk Gay Democratic Club.

The thick layer of clouds that had so relentlessly shrouded the city since the assassinations still hung over City Hall on Wednesday morning when the hearses arrived to deliver the bodies of George Moscone and Harvey Milk to their final appearance in City Hall. Hundreds crowded around the side entrance just a few feet away from the window Dan White had crawled through forty-eight hours before to see the two coffins carried into the building.

An hour later, the memorial service began and Acting Mayor Feinstein spoke from a black-bunted stage erected on City Hall's front stairs. "The murders of Mayor George Moscone and Supervisor Harvey Milk shake and pain us all. In the wake of the tragedies in Guyana, this additional senseless monstrosity seems simply unreal. Yet our anguish and grief permeate everything we do. We silently rail at the manifest injustice of these untimely deaths. We cry out to reverse the irrevocable. In our sorrow, this lovely jewel of a city seems a dark and saddened place."

Doug Franks sat with Anne Kronenberg during the service. At the end, an elderly woman came to pat Anne on the shoulder and assure her, "Don't worry. At least now he's with Jack." It was the first time that Doug realized that Jack Lira was dead. He vaguely remembered reading something about a roommate of Harvey's committing suicide before they had met, but Milk himself had never alluded to the incident, much less indicated that the suicide represented the demise of Harvey's relationship with Jack.

Once the service was over, lines formed on the steps of City Hall to view the closed caskets that lay under the great rotunda. Flowers crowded each step of the grand staircase. Mourners followed a long crimson carpet to where the two coffins lay. Over ten thousand filed by the coffins that afternoon. A militant lesbian in jeans and leather jacket strained against the velvet cord to drop a single rose on the casket of the Italian family man who was the thirty-seventh mayor of San Francisco. An old Irish crone genuflected by the coffin of Harvey Milk, a gay Jew. One woman left a pair of black gloves on George's casket, a dapper man left a silk black top hat on Harvey's. For hours, the stream of people walked by silently, touching the coffins to gain some physical connection to the tragedy.

Scott Smith looked down at the scene from the second floor promenade. He kept staring at Harvey's plain wooden coffin, trying to convince himself that Harvey's body was really inside it, that it was all over. Really. For good. Trying to imagine what Harvey's body looked like under the layers of red roses and white chrysanthemums. An old friend of Harvey's from Dallas stood next to Scott and remembered that he had stood with Harvey at that very spot earlier that year when Harvey had waved his hand across the marble lobby where his coffin now laid and asked, "What do you think of my new theater?" At the mention of such a moment, which Scott recognized as quintessentially Harvey, Smith broke into tears and collapsed in the friend's arms.

Later that afternoon, a special memorial service was held for Harvey at Temple Emmanue-El, the city's most prestigious synagogue. The service marked the first time an openly gay rabbi was permitted to officiate at that temple.

That night, a portly man and his wife stepped off a jet at San Francisco International Airport. Reporters immediately noted how much Robert Milk resembled his brother, except that he looked many years older, carried many more pounds and had a much bigger nose. Robert told reporters he had always thought his brother was a minor office holder, and only realized his broader significance when he turned on his television Tuesday morning to see the vast crowd carrying candles in the darkness for his younger brother. Heterosexuals had so long viewed gays as people without pasts or families that Robert Milk was immediately accorded a dignitary's status as reporters probed to find something more in the background of the politician who had entertained them for so many years. Robert told of how he and Harvey had once doubledated and how Harvey had kept his homosexuality a secret for many years, probably to protect his parents, he figured. He spoke convincingly of the meaning of Harvey's career. "Harvey was a pioneer of the twentieth century," Robert said. "His struggle and his deeds will prove to history that there's no such thing as a gay way, that there is only one way. . . . The citizens of San Francisco can make Harvey live forever by continuing to do things his way, in the deeds and in the accomplishments of their daily efforts to make their great city live." As for any concerns Robert might have had about his brother's homosexuality, the elder Milk simply said, "I didn't feel it was important."

Some of Harvey's closer friends grimaced at the sight of Harvey's estranged brother belatedly embracing the slain supervisor's cause. But they politely let Robert speak his piece and never made public the provision of Harvey's will, which explicitly excluded Robert from receiving any benefit from his estate.

The clouds lifted briefly on Thursday morning when several hundred San Francisco firemen, policemen, and sheriff's deputies stood in rigid formation on the broad brick terrazo of St. Mary's Cathedral where George Moscone's casket was slowly carried for his Mass of Christian Burial. Over six thousand crowded outside to watch this final procession. Inside, a host of mayors, state legislators, and lesser officials took their seats with the governor and presidential representative, and the archbishop conducted the final service for the mayor. George Moscone was buried later that afternoon.

Many of the thousands who converged on the San Francisco War Memorial Opera House late that Thursday joked that Harvey's last memorial should be at an opera house, since few knew Harvey well enough to imagine that the fast-talking, maverick populist could have had anything to do with something so refined as opera. The service's program simply bore the handful of speakers' names and a handwritten motto Harvey had recently copied from a book and pinned to his office wall: "All the forces in the world are not so powerful as an idea whose time has come.—Victor Hugo."

His face and body bloated by years of drinking, Jack McKinley had lost much of the good looks that had attracted Harvey to him back in 1963, but his flamboyance remained intact as he appeared at the service in a silk puffy-sleeved shirt unbuttoned to the navel, his chest covered by garlands of gold chains. Joe Campbell spent his first minutes of the service looking for familiar faces. He glanced up the center aisle and saw Billy Sipple heading for the section roped off for Milk's friends. Something embarrassed Joe about seeing Billy, and he turned his head away, ignoring the man he had once loved so passionately. Only Audrey Milk recognized Joe. Knowing of the Milk family disagreements, Joe leaned over to Robert Milk. "Harvey left a lot of fractures in his life," he said haltingly. "He was rash and left a lot of things behind. We're just some of the fractures."

Over five thousand crowded into the seats and aisles of the opera house. Another thousand listened over a special loudspeaker set up in the lobby. Robert Milk sat in the front row, flanked by Governor Jerry Brown, the lieutenant governor, and the California Chief Justice on one side, with the acting mayor and the White House representative on the other.

"These past few days have been the saddest days of my life and the saddest in the history of the city," said Dick Pabich, starting the service. "This is not a night for tears and sadness—Harvey would not have liked that. Harvey reached out and touched us all and made us all his friends. Maybe here tonight, though we are tired and discouraged, we can gain strength from each other. . . . We never got to tell Harvey how much we loved him. We must never forget his smile, his courage and his sense of justice. That is why he spent so much of his time with us and why he gave us everything he had."

Harvey's aides and friends decided that Milk would have preferred a political rally to a wake, so much of the evening was spent rousing the gay spirits—much to the discomfort of many of the esteemed dignitaries who had come expecting eulogies. "Tradition would expect me to tell you Harvey's gone to heaven," quipped the Reverend Bill Barcus, who had so dramatically come out during the Briggs campaign. "Harvey," he said, "was much more interested in going to Washington."

A gay doctor spoke of a conversation he had had with Milk a few months before. "What can we do for gay people in the area?" the doctor had asked Milk. "Write more prescriptions for quaaludes," Harvey had answered. While the crowd roared and cheered, Dianne Feinstein leaned over to her fiancé to ask, "What's a quaalude?"

"Harvey told me that if I ever had to speak at something like this that I should either, one, show up in full leather, or second, that I would show up in a dress," began Anne Kronenberg. "I think he would have been more shocked to see me in a dress."

Kronenberg read from a poem Harvey had written during the height of the Briggs battle a month earlier:

> I can be killed with ease
> I can be cut right down
> But I cannot fall back into my closet
> I have grown
> I am not by myself
> I am too many
> I am all of us

"Harvey understood the necessity of us all working together," Kronenberg said. "Harvey would prefer often to build new bridges stone by stone. He knew that it was not something that was done overnight. But he knew our time would come," she concluded, raising her fist. "And our time is now."

The crowd rose to its feet, stamping, applauding, and yelling its approval for Kronenberg's strident message. Harvey's cronies were amused to see the black lieutenant governor nudging a shocked Governor Brown who remained seated, as in a daze, while all the dignitaries around him rose, however reluctantly, to join the standing ovation. The sight of the politically powerful rising to cheer some of the most militant homosexual rhetoric that could be doled out left many of Harvey's old cohorts laughing.

When the service ended, a speaker implored the women and men to take the blossoms from the thousands of floral arrangements that crowded the opera house stage, saying, "Nothing should be allowed to die here." On the buses and streetcars of San Francisco that afternoon, the lesbians and gay men passed the flowers out to strangers. Already, people had started talking of a Harvey Milk legend.

Dianne Feinstein left the opera house for an appearance on San Francisco's public television's nightly news show. While technicians miked her blouse, she privately complained that she felt the service's strident tone was entirely inappropriate; it bothered her sense of decorum. Once on the air, the reporters' questions turned to politics, a subject that had been politely avoided until the final services for George and Harvey. Feinstein acknowledged she would be among the candidates for mayor when the board met the following Monday to select Moscone's successor. With speculation about Milk's successor already running rampant, a reporter asked if Feinstein felt obliged to appoint a gay to Milk's seat and whether she would follow Milk's tape-recorded wishes about who should—and should not—succeed him. Feinstein clearly was not expecting the question, especially since knowledge of Harvey's "no" list had not yet surfaced in news accounts. Yes, she would appoint a gay supervisor, she said, and she would try to follow Harvey's wishes.

Depression still hung heavily over the city at the week's end. Crisis centers reported that suicide threats had doubled in the days after the assassinations. Business in restaurants and bars tapered off dramatically; few seemed interested in going out to party. Department stores noted that Christmas buying had fallen to a fraction of the previous year's sales. Many of Harvey's friends thought the lack of holiday cheer probably would have disturbed Harvey more than any other aspect of the post-assassination gloom. Harvey had always loved Christmases.

Coming at the heels of Jonestown, the assassinations raised the usual talk of San Francisco as "Kook Capital" in both the national and local media. "Will we ever learn that there is no such thing as 'just a harmless kook?' " asked Herb Caen in a *Chronicle* column quoted widely around the country. "This is every misfit's favorite city," complained *Examiner* editor Reg Murphy, a Southerner who had never had much use for San Francisco's idiosyncracies to start with. *Time* magazine ran the definitive kook capital story by somehow tying together Patty Hearst, the SLA, Zebra killings, hippies, and Golden Gate Bridge jumpers to prove that San Francisco was indeed a magnet for wackos. The thesis raised no small irony, since much of San Francisco's kook image in the late 1970s was borne of its reputation as a place where tolerant political leaders like George Moscone encouraged a massive gay immigration of people like Harvey Milk. The stories, of course, never mentioned that Dan White, the killer who had caused the city's major tragedy, was spawned not in a hippie commune but from such all-American institutions as the Catholic Church, the U.S. Army, and the police and fire departments. In the curiously twisted logic of the media, the victims became the victimizers, while the criminal represented the morality from which an errant San Francisco had tragically wandered in its path toward kookiness. Local anger at the kook capital stories grew so severe that Herb Caen retracted his "harmless kook" comment. After all, he noted, nobody had ever called Dan White a kook.

Scott Smith drove with Jack McKinley and Tom Randol to the mortuary Friday afternoon to pick up Harvey's ashes. The undertaker offhandedly greeted Scott and made Smith follow him through the lab where morticians embalmed bodies. The room seemed grisly to Smith. Had he been a bereaved widow, the undertaker would have respectfully turned over the remains with appropriate sympathy, Scott thought. But he had long ago come to expect that as far as most heterosexuals were concerned, gays were people with no family or loved ones, so ordinary concerns of courtesy were not necessary. The mortician unceremoniously handed Smith a brown plastic box with the label, "Cremated Remains of Harvey B. Milk."

Repercussions came in all hues, not just those of regret and compassion. Harvey's Los Angeles boyfriend, Bob Tuttle, asked for the week off from his job with the Florida Citrus Commission, explaining that Harvey was a close friend. When he returned to work, his supervisor called him into a special conference. "I've got something I want you to do for me," he said. "We think it would be in both of our interests if you submit your resignation." Tuttle complied, though he would always wonder what Harvey would have told him to do.

The day after the candlelight march, Steve Hollonzine, a nineteen-year-old graduate student who had carried the California flag in the solemn procession, received an unexpected phone call from his parents. They had flown from their home in Toronto to San Francisco immediately after seeing a telecast of the march on Canadian television. Both parents were Auschwitz survivors who had lost their entire families in Nazi death camps. Hollonzine's father was an orthodox rabbi who had proudly watched his son graduate from high school at sixteen and then go off to the University of San Francisco to start work on a master's degree in philosophy as preparation for his own rabbinical career. The elder Hollonzine was not pleased to see that his son had appeared on television carrying a flag in a march mourning a dead homosexual.

"Are you a sodomite?" he demanded when he got to his son's apartment. Steve allowed that he was. "Either you get on the next plane home with us or we no longer have a son," the rabbi ordered. The parents left without their only surviving child. Two years later, Steve's friends would call from Toronto to see why he had not attended his own mother's funeral; that's how Steve learned his mom had died. Gays have long been disowned by irate parents, but the story of Steve Hollonzine's estrangement carried an extra twist since both his parents knew that he was suffering from a malignant brain tumor that was slowly spreading cancer throughout his body. They had left their nineteen-year-old son to face his early death alone.

Press speculation settled on three leading candidates to succeed Harvey Milk: Rick Stokes, Jo Daly, and Frank Fitch, all past presidents of the Alice Toklas club. Milk's cohorts wanted to ensure that their favorite, Anne Kronenberg, proved the most viable candidate, even though she did not live in District 5. A Milk aide called the city attorney's office to check the legal technicalities. The office said it had prepared an opinion on the subject just a few weeks before, when George Moscone was pondering who to appoint to Dan White's seat. No, the office stated decisively, an appointee did not need to be a district resident. Milk's allies decided to make an all-out push for Anne and quickly leaked to the press the news that Harvey's list of unacceptable successors included just the names newsmen were discussing. Kronenberg, meanwhile, was touted as Harvey's favorite choice. Kronenberg's supporters decided to move Anne into the district, so on Friday night,

Billy Wiegardt heard the door of his flat open and came into the living room to see a half dozen of Harvey's friends moving Anne's furniture into Harvey's old apartment.

The release of Harvey's enemies list to the media incensed Harvey's lawyer, John Wahl, who felt that the four activists were being unfairly tried in the press without the chance to hear the still-secret tape themselves. He arranged a meeting for the four Milk opponents to hear the message. Jim Foster turned red with rage when he heard Harvey insist that "the Jim Fosters never understood the movement." This was only further proof that Harvey was a megalomaniac, Foster said. Harvey's exhortation that gay lawyers, doctors, and architects should come out raised cackles from the veteran activists who had only days before read Robert Milk's newspaper statements that Harvey had never come out earlier because he didn't want to hurt his parents. "Come out, come out, but please don't tell my mother," mocked one of the four unacceptables. Rick Stokes angrily told reporters that the tapes should have been destroyed and that the refusal of Milk's friends to publicly release the full contents of the tapes represented "Nixonian Watergate" tactics to obscure Harvey's vindictive character. "We had a hero," Stokes said. "We all could have used a hero. This is not in the best interests of Harvey at all."

Scott Smith was ecstatic to see Harvey alive again, sitting in a Paris café sipping wine. "Things were getting too heavy," Harvey grinned. "I had to get out." Scott could barely contain his joy and then he woke up and realized that he had been dreaming and that Harvey was still dead, and he started to cry.

Like all the shrouded mornings of that week, Saturday promised to be another overcast day, but brilliant sunshine broke through the clouds late in the morning while two dozen of Harvey's closest friends gathered at a San Francisco pier where an antique 102-foot schooner, the *Lady Frie,* was berthed. The captain remarked that San Francisco Bay sat remarkably calm that day; only four or five days a year saw that kind of glassy peace on the normally turbulant Bay. Harvey's old lovers, friends, and political cronies arrived: Tom O'Horgan and Jack McKinley from New York, lovers like Joe Campbell, Billy Wiegardt, Doug Franks, and Scott, and friends like Tory Hartmann, Danny Nicoletta, Tom Randol, Bob Ross, Jim Rivaldo, and Dick Pabich. Dick passed around cigar-sized joints while Jack freely shared whiskey from his hip flask. After a dreary week of death and eulogies, they were ready for a party. A curious shrine greeted the revelers when they went below into the ship's cabin. Neatly arranged on the top of a color television set was a dictionary-sized box wrapped in Doonesbury comics and topped by a single long-stemmed crimson rose. Spelled out in rhinestones on the cartoons were the initials R.I.P. Arranged neatly around the package was a box of bubble bath and an array of grape Kool-Aid packs, the drink with which, according to early news reports, the Reverend Jim Jones had mixed cyanide during the Guyana suicide rituals. Jack explained that he had decided to wrap the box in comics since Harvey would never want to be seen publicly in plastic.

The ship glided gently across the Bay, under the Golden Gate Bridge, and into the open sea. Once out to sea, Tom Randol tore the funny papers off the plastic box while Jack ripped open the Kool-Aid packs and the bubble bath. Under the clear California skies, the ashes, Kool-Aid, and bubble bath fell gently from the schooner and Harvey was gone, a bubbly patch of lavender on the cold, glittering Pacific Ocean.

That night, the "Saturday Night Live" comedy show ran a news flash about the assassinations on its Weekend Update segment. To mourn the deaths of George Moscone and Harvey Milk, 350,000 Chinese homosexuals had marched in San Francisco, the newscaster deadpanned. The mourners wearing red collars were dominant while the marchers with keys on their belts were passive.

San Francisco officialdom erupted with moral outrage at the spoof and demanded an apology from the NBC network. Most of Harvey's friends, however, agreed that the comic take-off on the candlelight march probably would have been the tribute that amused Harvey most.

By Sunday, the political chips were rapidly falling in favor of Dianne Feinstein's election as mayor. Even her most bitter detractors had to admit that Feinstein handled her role as acting mayor during the tragic week with incredible poise and grace. Both the Saturday and Sunday *Examiner* editions editorialized for her. Politicking remained frenzied. Supervisor Molinari was the first to openly commit himself for Feinstein, reportedly after he got Feinstein's promise that she would back his election as board president. Supervisor Silver also endorsed Feinstein on two key conditions—that she would get the powerful chairmanship of the Finance Committee and, as a concession for Silver's gay following, that Feinstein would promise not to fire Police Chief Charles Gain for the duration of what would have been George Moscone's term.

Exactly one week after the assassinations, the board voted 6–2 to elect forty-five-year-old Dianne Feinstein the thirty-eighth mayor of San Francisco, the first woman to hold that office. In the same meeting, the board appropriated $375,000 to finance a gay community center to be named after Harvey Milk. The long-planned Yerba Buena Convention Center was renamed after George Moscone. "Though we are crippled with our grief and our sadness, we must and we will resume the important tasks of governing this city," said Feinstein after assuming the office she had said she would never seek again. "Despite our grief, I know these two leaders would have insisted that we get on with the business of putting this city back together again—that we see how our spiritual health depends on tomorrow's visions not yesterday's sorrows."

That afternoon, the newly elected legislature was sworn in at the state capital in Sacramento. The California Senate session was largely spent eulogizing George Moscone, its former majority leader. Hardened conservatives broke down and cried as they recounted the good-natured jostling with the jovial mayor. The body unanimously passed a resolution honoring their onetime colleague. When a San Francisco state senator offered a similar resolution for Harvey Milk, State Senator John Briggs led a cadre of nine conservative senators who would have nothing to do with honoring a homosexual. "I don't think anybody is sadder over the death of Harvey Milk than I am," said Briggs. "But this wasn't a resolution memorializing him. I think it memorialized what he did and stood for—and that's the issue." The resolution ultimately passed with thirty ayes and nine abstentions. The state assembly adjourned its session in honor of Representative Leo Ryan, Moscone, and Milk. Because of the conservative objections voiced by Briggs, however, the senate adjourned only in the memory of Ryan and Moscone as well as "the others slain in a senseless way."

Shortly after the board meeting, Anne Kronenberg held a press conference on the steps of City Hall, flanked by a panoply of District 5 leaders. Members of the Harvey Milk Gay Democratic Club handed out fliers bearing the   picture of Harvey joking with Anne, headlined: "Continue the work Harvey Milk started—Make sure we get the supervisor that Harvey Milk wanted: Anne Kronenberg." Dick Pabich and Jim Rivaldo proved key strategists in the campaign to get Mayor Feinstein to appoint Anne. They soon found that their most powerful ally remained Harvey Milk. After a week of tributes that endlessly repeated the phrase George-and-Harvey, Milk had attained a higher status than he would ever have received had he been killed alone, largely because the simultaneous deaths of both the mayor and supervisor had equalized the two officials in the eyes of the mainstream political establishment, symbolically elevating Milk to the rank of the slain mayor. Leaders in the Chinese, black, Latino, environmental, labor, neighborhood, and Democratic Party groups now rallied behind Milk's powerful memory. Since virtually all Harvey's old aides said supporting Milk meant supporting Kronenberg, an argument based on the tapes they kept secret, Anne achieved an immense base of broad support.

Anne's fans seemed everywhere—except in the mayor's office. Feinstein worried that the twenty-four-year-old Kronenberg was too young to hold the job. On the afternoon of Dianne Feinstein's first day of office, the city attorney's office told Rivaldo that it had reversed its residency ruling of a few days before, insisting that new research indicated that any appointee had to live in the district for at least thirty days. Fine, Kronenberg's supporters responded, she had moved into the district; in a matter of a few weeks, she would be a resident. Feinstein remained unenthusiastic. Stories began to spread that the mayor was particularly upset about the comment Kronenberg had made at the opera house about showing up in a dress or in leathers. The idea that homosexuals donned leather in the dark of night had long disturbed the mayor's sensibilities. "Would Anne dress in leather when she attended board meetings?" Feinstein reportedly asked gay politicos. Harvey's aides dug in their heels for a long fight.

Running, panting, the footsteps chasing him down, tapping loudly on the marble hallways of City Hall. Cleve Jones would have this dream many times in the months following the City Hall assassinations, but it first came in the week after the killings. He was being chased around a dark, empty City Hall. He didn't know who was chasing him, but he knew he was in danger and he had to escape. Up the grand staircase and through the colonnaded halls Jones ran until finally he reached the door to the complex of supervisors' offices. Cleve had a key to this door. Once inside, he slammed the door resolutely behind him. He started running down the hallway, knowing he was safe now, but looking for a place to hide. Then he heard the sound of another key slipping into the lock and the door opening, the door that Dan White had used on his way to see Harvey that last time. Cleve started running hard again, running down the narrow hallway that seemed miles long in his dream, the hallway that Dan White's office was on, where Harvey had died. Running and panting and then in front of him, floating in the air, Cleve saw the pale blue dead face of Harvey Milk, rolling above him, as it had when Cleve had seen the police turning over the corpse on that dark Monday morning. The pale blue face was rolling and then Cleve woke up.

Cleve was still sobbing as he shook the sleep from his head. He grabbed a paperweight near his bed and threw it at a framed painting across the room, sending the portrait crashing to the floor. He stumbled over to his crowded desk, swept his hand across the surface, kicking and flailing at the papers that filled the air. He knocked over his bookshelf, threw the heavy volumes against the wall and hurled his bedside water glass against his door. He began to cry and pick up the room, so his roommate would not see what he had done; crying, trying to pull order out of the chaos while the grief started turning to rage.

PART IV
The Legend Begins

seventeen

Justice and Thieves

A man may see how this world goes with no eyes. Look with thine ears: see how yond justice rails upon yond simple thief. Hark in thine ear: change places, and handy-dandy, which is justice, which is the thief?

—King Lear, *IV, vi.*

". . . It's about giving those young people out there in the Altoona, Pennsylvanias hope. You gotta give them hope."

John Wahl reached over and turned his Panasonic cassette recorder off. Dianne Feinstein hadn't expected Milk's tape-recorded voice to leave such an impact on her, but the sound of a man talking about himself in the past tense shook her. She thought it was like Harvey was talking from the dead. Carl Carlson was surprised to see Feinstein lose the patina of control she seemed to maintain in every situation. Feinstein confided none of her personal anxieties to the two men who had come to play Harvey's tape and instead delved straight to the issue at hand. "Who do *you* think I should appoint?" she asked.

Both Carlson and Wahl insisted their duty as Harvey's friends was solely to relay what Harvey wanted. The responses left Feinstein facing the most bizarre polit-

299

ical twist she had confronted in a decade of city government—a dead man was essentially dictating one of her most important decisions from the grave.

Anne had virtually eliminated herself from serious consideration in her first meeting with the mayor. Supervisor Silver had carefully coached Kronenberg that Feinstein's primary consideration in making the appointment was loyalty. Do what you want once you get on the board, Anne's supporters urged, but at least tell her now you'll be loyal. Once Feinstein raised the loyalty question, Kronenberg would only say, "I promise to give you every bit of consideration Harvey did." Anne later defended the statement by saying Feinstein never would have believed a blanket pledge of loyalty; politicians familiar with Feinstein, however, saw Kronenberg's answer as a kamikazi flight for honesty. Harvey Milk, after all, rarely gave Feinstein's views anything resembling serious consideration; Anne's promise, therefore, did scarcely anything to assuage the fears of a politician who would be seeking reelection in a matter of months.

Feinstein easily filled Dan White's vacant seat, appointing the man Moscone had selected because, she said, the bullets from Dan White's gun should not alter planned city policy. For the seat left vacant by her elevation to the mayor's office, Feinstein had appointed a blue ribbon panel of district leaders who sifted through applications and found a replacement closely aligned with the new mayor's moderate policies. Feinstein refused to appoint such a committee for Harvey's district. Virtually every district leader had already endorsed Anne by then anyway. Feinstein still had few options, since she had publicly said she would follow Milk's wishes and appoint a gay successor. Author Frank Robinson had pulled himself out of consideration; Harry Britt had endorsed Kronenberg; Bob Ross was nixed because he had recently been elected the emperor of San Francisco, the male counterpart to the city's drag queen empress. Feinstein didn't like drag queens any more than leather. Feinstein stalled on making the decision for weeks.

Pabich and Rivaldo first hoped that the mayor was postponing the appointment to let Anne creep in under the thirty-day residency requirement. When word leaked that the mayor opposed Anne, they decided to try to intimidate Feinstein. "Kronenberg For Supervisor" posters appeared throughout District 5, pointedly employing the same colors and typeface of Harvey's campaign posters. Over two thousand district residents signed petitions endorsing her. But Feinstein would not be bullied and as other hopefuls began submitting their names for the seat, the contest to succeed Harvey Milk became the city's major political circus. Former Air Force Sergeant Lenny Matlovich announced his availability for the seat, even though he had lived in San Francisco only six months. One heterosexual woman aspirant said she "would don leathers or chains or do whatever is necessary to meet the qualifications" Feinstein had set for the gay seat.

Local reporters' favorite candidate was a man who had done nothing in gay politics, since he had only come out on the day of the Moscone-Milk killings. Scott Beach, a local radio personality, had long hung out on the fringes of San Francisco's haute crowd, frequenting singles bars and journalists' watering holes. Once Milk's seat became open, however, Beach announced he had been gay all along and that Milk's murder had inspired him to come out of the closet. To advance his candidacy, he wrote a song based on the Milk poem Anne had read at the opera house—"Our Time Is Now"—and played it for every approving reporter who showed up at his house. After singing the jingle, Beach would piously insist he was the man to carry on Milk's legacy. When one gay reporter pointed out that Beach had tape-recorded commercials for Terrance Hallinan's campaign against Harvey in 1977, Beach confided, "Well I did that for Terry as a favor, but when I went into the voting booth, I pulled the lever for Harvey Milk."

Newspaper columnists proclaimed Beach the best candidate for supervisor. He may not have taken part in any gay political activity, but the newspaper people had never considered such activity to be serious in the first place. Beach had never bothered them with uncomfortable prattle about homosexuals' rights. Besides, Beach made great copy. He even played his song on network television, garnering more air time than any of the serious gay candidates. Gay politicos complained that once again the media were trivializing a serious issue, but these activists never understood that few reporters thought the gay movement was anything but trivial.

All the while, Feinstein pondered and delayed the decision, impressing Harvey's aides by her sincerity in really wanting to replace Milk with a politician in tune with Harvey's populist views, and yet frustrating them by her apparent conclusion that none of the candidates acceptable to Milk were qualified to sit on the board. The indecision left gays feeling leaderless and angry. "If it took the Roman Catholic cardinals less than two days to choose a pope," the Bay Area Reporter wrote after a month of waiting, "surely the mayor could have come up with a qualified supervisor in like time."

"Free Dan White."

Reporter Mike Weiss instantly recognized the slogan as the battle cry policemen had taken up after the assassinations. Still, he was taken aback when he unexpectedly saw the quote that surrounded this slogan on the t-shirt beneath the unbuttoned uniform of a police officer in the Hall of Justice. Encircled around "Free Dan White" was the John Donne quote: "No man is an island entire to himself."

Within a week of the killings, Dan White had become a cause célèbre for police officers who never had much use for either Harvey Milk or his liberal ally, George Moscone, the man who had appointed Chief Gain. Gays were enraged at the news that police and firemen had raised a reported $100,000 for White's defense fund. Graffiti soon appeared throughout the city with such slogans as "Kill Fags: Dan White for Mayor" and "Dan White Showed You Can Fight City Hall." An Irish Catholic friend of the White family joked with Weiss: "Why did Harvey Milk die a faggot's death? Because he got blown away."

Feinstein had spent much of Mayor Moscone's term lambasting Chief Gain, so rumors spread swiftly that Feinstein would soon can the controversial chief and replace him with a man from the ranks. Sensing a shift in the wind, some policemen removed the "lavender glove" which, they complained, Gain had insisted they don when dealing with gays. When a hotel manager objected to police beating several transvestite tenants, a police sergeant explained, "Well, they're only fruits." When the manager turned out to be a radical gay activist who filed charges against the sergeant, the police officer returned to casually ask, "How is your health? How is your life expectancy?"

Cleve Jones got a call from two friends one morning who told of how a gang of Latino thugs had chased them through the Castro the previous night, right to the door of their Mission District apartment. When the police came, they did nothing, even though the attackers still sauntered defiantly around the gays' apartment building. Once the cops left, the punks literally broke through the door, leaving the victims to fend them off with kitchen knives. Jones hadn't spent his political stewardship under Harvey Milk for nothing: He quickly issued a press release, called television stations, and instructed his friends on how to reenact the crime for the TV news cameras.

On Castro Street, police started making random identification searches. For the first time in years, uniformed officers started appearing in gay bars during peak hours to undertake such important business as checking pinball licenses. Gain no longer had control of his officers, activists feared, and the police were reverting to the harassment of years past. The stories coming from all corners of the city's gay community later had politicos terming the months after the assassinations "the winter of our discontent."

Nobody works on New Year's Eve.

Harry Britt glanced at his clock; it was 11:30 P.M. on New Year's Eve. He couldn't believe Mayor Feinstein was working at that time on that day, but there she was on the phone, asking Harry if he could drop by her Pacific Heights home to discuss Harvey's replacement. By now, some five weeks after the killings, Harvey's aides were convinced that they had lost the seat to the moderates. Though they still ostensibly backed Anne, they were desperately floating trial balloons for other candidates. Harry could tell that he had impressed both Feinstein and her fiancé Richard Blum, who seemed to have a major role in the mayor's decision making. He was at Feinstein's door at what seemed a most ungodly hour the next morning. Over coffee, the mayor wondered aloud if she should appoint a caretaker replacement. A federal employee who was unknown to gay political activists had caught her favor and she was eager to appoint him. Britt counseled that it would be politically foolish to lose control of the seat by appointing someone who would never turn into a gay leader and help promote Feinstein's own election in November. Who was Britt's second choice, after Kronenberg? Feinstein asked. Harry refused to forward any other names. The mayor pressed further. "If I can't appoint Anne, who should I appoint?"

Harry suggested another name from Harvey's list—his.

As soon as news surfaced that Feinstein was seriously considering Britt for supervisor, gay moderates spread rumors that he was a communist, a member of the Socialist Workers Party. Pabich, Rivaldo, and Britt corralled all the Democratic leaders they could to make one point: Harry was a Democrat. They also struggled to fabricate a respectable image for Harry. Though he was now more apt to be found at meetings of the local Gay Atheist League than at MYF gatherings, Britt's backers highlighted Harry's background as a Methodist preacher. Though his politics indeed lay at the socialist end of the spectrum, he now was presented as a stolid Democrat. Harry was no homosexual militant, but a Texas-bred, soft-spoken minister who would bring mature leadership to the gay community. They would promise Feinstein his loyalty and support—anything to keep the seat. The strategy often stepped over the line between politicking and deception—and it worked. On Thursday, January 8—almost one year after Harvey Milk and Jack Lira had led the inaugural march from Castro Street to City Hall—Feinstein and Britt held a joint press conference to announce that Harry Britt, Jr., would be the new supervisor from District 5.

Anne went into seclusion. Her lesbian friends had long told her that in the end, the gay men would screw her over and now, she was convinced they had been right. Her original backers, who had defected to Britt, felt Anne missed the point. The necessity was not to get Anne or any specific individual in Harvey's seat, but simply to get someone committed to Harvey's progressive and militant gay politics. Anne had been plucked from obscurity and essentially created and marketed, the way a company markets a new laundry soap, they felt. She shouldn't take the defeat personally. With this analysis, the aides closest to Harvey had taken their first steps away from Milk's ward politics. They had learned that once you have power, you don't have to bother spending years to stake out a score of stands on a score of issues; candidates can be created and marketed and imbued with the power that connections and political savvy can bring. Harvey had brought them this power. Now it was theirs to use.

Harry Britt was just over forty years old. He spent the Saturday between the press conference and his formal swearing-in wandering around the familiar haunts of Castro Street, watching the hot young guys guzzle beer and shoot pool. He viewed this scene with a certain nostalgia now. He knew it was his last weekend to be an anonymous Castro clone. He had come to the Castro because of the murder of his first hero, Martin Luther King, and now he was leaving it because of the killing of his second, Harvey Milk. That afternoon he went downtown to buy something he hadn't needed in years—a suit.

Harry's inaugural speech at the board was emblematic of his first months in office. "Decisions about gay people must be made by gay people," he said. "Decisions that affect women must be made by women. The decisions that affect human beings must be made by women because they are free from the macho mentality." Even Harry's close friends glanced at each other nervously when Britt fumbled over the last sentence. What the hell was that supposed to mean?

Modern lawyering requires careful use of the press, Dan White's lawyer, Doug Schmidt, later told a barrister's convention. The press speculation surrounding Dan White's preliminary hearing—just one week after Harry Britt was sworn in—certainly represented a masterful stroke of media manipulation, perhaps, some observers later guessed, the move that won Schmidt the trial. The list of prospective witnesses Schmidt presented at the hearing read like a Who's Who of city government. A judge, congressmen, current and former supervisors, and even State Senator John Briggs were among the forty politicians Schmidt indicated he might call during his client's trial. The list mystified most of the people named on it. A number of former supervisors complained that they had never served on the board with White; some had never even met him. One miffed judge filed a motion to squash any subpoena of herself, pointing out she had met White only once and could offer no information about either the crime or criminal.

For his part, Schmidt would only say he was basing his defense on a "broad spectrum of social, political, and ethical issues," arguing against the judge's motion by vaguely insisting he would present a unique defense, unlike anything seen in courtrooms before. The "broad spectrum" quote caught the reporters' fancy and after a number of well-timed leaks, the story of Dan White's possible defense emerged. White's case obviously would not question whether the former policeman had actually fired the bullets that killed George and Harvey. That point was obvious. White might instead plea that he had killed the pair in a heat of passion bred because, one newspaper report speculated, a "profound change had occurred in the political climate at City Hall and that this had offended White's sense of values." The "broad spectrum of social, political, and ethical issues," therefore, could include everything from excesses at Gay Freedom Day Parades to the seamier sides of some of the major city politicians' sex lives to such issues as the tremendous clout Peoples Temple wielded in city government. Confronted with this snake pit of San Francisco politics, the theory went, Dan White's traditional all-American values were so offended that in a moment of moral outrage, he killed the two politicians.

Lawyers debated whether such a broad argument with all its particulars would even be admissable in court. But many also noted that a major figure in any snake pit scenario would be the man prosecuting White, District Attorney Joe Freitas. A top lieutenant of the Reverend Jim Jones had literally lived in the D.A.'s offices when he was an assistant D.A. for Freitas, and the ambitious district attorney owed his election in no small part to aid from the temple. Some attorneys reportedly advised Freitas to hand the case over to a special prosecutor or to the state attorney general's office. He had known both Milk and Moscone and could rightly say that his office would be biased in its prosecution. But Freitas pressed ahead with his plans for prosecution, despite the snake pit speculation. He charged White with two counts of first-degree murder, invoking for the first time the clause in John Briggs's new capital punishment law that called for the gas chamber for any person who assassinated a public official in an attempt to prevent him from fulfilling his official duties.

"Look, it's easier to grab fruits," the policeman explained to the bystander who asked why five police officers had yanked two men about to walk into a gay bar, dragged them to the street, and started pummeling them with their nightsticks. When another gay man protested the beatings, an officer tartly informed him, "Shut up, faggot, or I'll knock you out." The two beaten men were arrested for "blocking an entrance."

"Let's get the dykes," shouted the ten men as they ran toward the doorway of Peg's Place, a lesbian bar, in another incident.

"Call the police," shouted the bouncer to the bartender.

"We *are* the police," one of the drunken men shouted. "We can go anywhere we damn well please."

A melee broke out between the men and the women patrons who rushed to the bar employees' defense, beating the intruders with pool cues.

The police lieutenant who came soon afterward shook his head when told of the behavior of the men, two of whom were off-duty cops. He knew one of the attackers, the lieutenant said, and he was "a good guy." He had a hard time believing the policeman would do such a thing. The lieutenant then checked the bar's various licenses and inquired if the bartender wasn't really drunk.

The Peg's Place brawl hit the front pages with gay complaints that the fracas was only part of a concerted increase in police intimidation of gays. Feinstein said nothing for two weeks and then released a statement calling for stern prosecution of the policemen involved. The response satisfied no one. The POA criticized her for taking the gays' side while gay leaders were miffed at the two weeks it took to get a response.

Homosexual rancor grew further when, at a meeting with gay leaders, Feinstein refused to promise to appoint a gay police commissioner. George Moscone had pledged such an appointment before his term was out and Feinstein's reneging on that promise seemed further proof that the climate for gays had turned considerably colder under Feinstein. A *Ladies Homes Journal* interview with the mayor set off more controversy when she worried about how gays' flouting of community standards might "set up a backlash" in the city. "The right of an individual to live as he or she chooses can become offensive," Feinstein said. "The gay community is going to have to face this. It's fine for us to live here respecting each other's lifestyles, but it doesn't mean imposing them on others." As far as gays were concerned, Dan White and his police friends were the parties guilty of imposing their lifestyles on others—and the mayor's continued fretting about gay sexuality tendered further proof of her own prudery, many gays thought. Around the Castro, posters soon appeared depicting Feinstein in sadomasochistic leather drag, cracking a cat-o'-nine-tails, under the caption, "The Ayatollah Feinstein."

Supervisor Britt could do little to counter the growing disatisfaction. He never rallied from the initial burst of criticism over his strange inaugural remarks. He was intimidated by the charges of sexism lesbians leveled against him after the Kronenberg affair. He had none of Harvey's skill at dealing with reporters, insulting them and even hanging up on them if he didn't like the direction he thought the interview was taking. In public appearances, Britt was a frumpy dresser. His contact lenses made him blink uncontrollably when put under television lights. People frequently called him Harvey instead of Harry, a habit which infuriated Britt and delighted his critics who insisted that the novice politician suffered in comparison to the late Milk.

"The change began with the assassinations of Moscone and Milk. The pair were put out of the way to destroy what they stood for and to dismantle what they had achieved," editorialized the *Bay Area Reporter,* echoing the fears that many gays were voicing at the increased gay problems. "The evidence is coming in day after day: Violence against gays is on the rise. Police harassment (both covert and overt) is on the rise. . . . At this writing, the Dan White plan seems to be succeeding, for once again, gays are targets and victims."

Such an assessment left Police Chief Gain in a curious position. During his three years as chief, relations between police and gays had evolved into the most cordial between any police agency and gay community in the United States. The majority of his police officers were far more sophisticated in dealing with gays than police in other major cities. Police Officers Association president Bob Barry, for example, was outspoken in his opposition to the Briggs Initiative. In another time, the outbursts of police harrassment might not have been seen as a barometer of a changing social climate in the city. Coming just months after a former policeman killed the city's first gay official, however, they seemed part of a concerted effort by the police to pull San Francisco back. Gain, who was more sympathetic to gays than any other police chief in the nation, was powerless to change this growing perception that he reigned over the most anti-gay institution in the city.

"Have you ever supported controversial causes, like homosexual rights, for instance?"

Doug Schmidt asked this question of potential jurors since the judge had forbade him to ask directly if people were gay. Homosexual activists complained that few judges in America would allow black jurors to be systematically excluded from a jury weighing the murder of the nation's most prominent black public official. But the first days of the jury selection for the Dan White trial saw precisely the analogous drama unfold. One heterosexual woman was disqualified from the panel when she said she had gay friends and had once walked with them in a Gay Freedom Day Parade. One man was disqualified from sitting on the case when he answered the question about controversial causes by saying, "I sign anything that comes along Eighteenth and Castro." When a juror appeared in a plaid shirt, blue jeans, and a thick, dark mustache, Schmidt asked with whom he lived. A roommate, he explained. "What does he or she do?" Schmidt asked. *"He* works at Holiday Inn," the young man said, putting special emphasis on the sentence's subject. Schmidt asked the judge to pass the juror "for cause," meaning it was prima facie that the man would not be a fair juror; the judge agreed. For the duration of the trial, gay papers pointedly referred to the panel on the case as the "all-heterosexual jury."

Like almost every aspect of the Dan White trial, the jury selection process defied predictions. Legal observers had expected the selection to draw on for a week, maybe longer, so the court impaneled 250 prospective jurors instead of the usual one hundred. Prosecutor Tom Norman, the fifty-seven-year-old warhorse of over one hundred homicide prosecutions, asked the usual questions about whether jurors could vote for the death penalty. Doug Schmidt, however, took a much more unusual tact, asking about church attendance habits and choosing San Franciscans from white working-class and, most significantly, Catholic backgrounds. Such jurors are usually the very people most prone to

support a law-and-order prosecution, but Doug Schmidt clearly had a
novel strategy.

Reporters began to suspect that prosecution of Dan White would
be less than aggressive when potential juror Richard Aparicio took the
stand. Aparicio said he had worked briefly as a San Francisco policeman years back and had spent much of his life since then as a private
security guard. He shopped at the same meat market where Dan
White's uncle sold raffle tickets for his nephew's defense fund. When
Schmidt asked Aparicio why he thought White killed Milk and Moscone, Aparicio said, "I have certain opinions. . . . I'd say it was social
and political pressures." Minutes after Aparicio made the statement—
nearly a blueprint of the precise arguments Schmidt was expected to use
in White's defense—Tom Norman told the judge he was happy with the
jury and that he was ready to proceed with the trial.

The decision stunned both legal and journalistic observers, coming
after only three days of jury selection and after Norman had used only
six of his twenty-six preemptory challenges. The jury contained no
blacks, no Asians, and no gays. Most of the jurors were white working-
class ethnic Catholics, like Dan White. Four of the jury's seven women
were old enough to be Dan White's mother. Half the jurors lived near
Dan White's old supervisorial district; none, of course, lived in or near
Milk's. Dan White would truly be judged by a jury of his peers.

As reporters rushed to file stories of the surprise denouement to
what was expected to be a lengthy jury selection process, a woman in
a brown leather jacket with a fur collar smiled from the back of the
courtroom. On a chain around her neck dangled a swastika and a
medallion with a Hebrew inscription which, she said, translated to
"Hitler was right." Sister Barbara explained that her friends in the local
Nazi party had held a prayer meeting for Dan White right after a recent
memorial service for "our beloved Führer." Said Barbara, "I came to
the trial because I care about Dan White. You see, we call him 'Gentle
Dan.' All over the city you see signs that say 'Free Dan White.' He did
what he had to do."

"The city's gays pose what is probably the most serious challenge
she has faced since becoming mayor," wrote the *Examiner*'s political
columnist in a story released on the last weekend that the new Dan
White jurors spent at home before being sequestered for the trial.
Evidence of the growing gay discontent with Feinstein came from
throughout the city. "Dump Dianne" buttons sold briskly at meetings
of gay businessmen. The Harvey Milk Gay Democratic Club had

unanimously voted to send a letter to Feinstein expressing the "club's disappointment" over her first months in office. Harry Britt talked openly of how a gay candidate for mayor might surface if problems with police continued.

"White's attorneys have said they will dig deeply into the political atmosphere at City Hall, hunting out the sources of pressures on the former supervisor, spotlighting the behind-the-scenes maneuvering for power in San Francisco," reported a front-page *Examiner* story the day before the trial opened.

Dan White walked stiffly into the courtroom on Tuesday, May 1, the first day of his trial for the shootings of George Moscone and Harvey Milk. White, his lawyers, the prosecution team, the judge, and jury sat in front of a bullet-proof plastic wall that separated the court proceedings from the packed gallery. As she would every day of the trial, Mary Anne White sat anxiously in the front row. Her husband never gave any sign of recognition to his pretty young wife as he walked to the defense table. He stared blankly at the floor, and as the days of the trial wore on, reporters would strain to find new words to describe White, since the early descriptions—that he acted like a robot, a zombie, or an automaton—became redundant. Doug Schmidt used his opening argument to present a paean to the man he said Dan White had once been:

> He was a native of San Francisco. He went to school here, went through high school here. He was a noted athlete in high school. He was an army veteran who served in Vietnam and was honorably discharged from the army. He became a policeman thereafter and after a brief hiatus developed, again returned to the police force in San Francisco and later transfered to the fire department. He was married in December of 1976, fathered a child in July 1978. Dan White was a good policeman and Dan White was a good fireman. In fact, he was decorated for having saved a woman and her child in a very dangerous fire, but the complete picture of Dan White perhaps was not known until some time after those tragedies on November 27 occurred.

The next sentence became the key to Dan White's defense:

> Good people, fine people, with fine backgrounds, simply don't kill people in cold blood. It just doesn't happen and obviously some part of him has not been presented thus far.

That previously unknown part, Schmidt said, was a history of manic-depression, a "vile biochemical change" in the body that made a decent man like Dan White fly off the handle.

> Dan White was an idealistic young man, a working-class young man. He was deeply endowed with and believed strongly in the traditional American values, family and home. I think that he could be classified as almost rigidly moral, but above all that, he was an honest man, and he was fair, perhaps too fair for politics in San Francisco. . . . Dan White came from a vastly different life-style than Harvey Milk. Harvey Milk was a homosexual leader and politician, and Dan White, though they were from vastly different life-styles, sought to befriend Harvey Milk after being a member of the board of supervisors and tried to be tolerant and protective of the issues that his constituency felt were important, and those issues were the traditional values of family and home. . . . Dan White was supremely frustrated with crime and the politics of the city and saw the city deteriorating as a place for the average and decent people to live. . . .

The pressures built on Dan White, Schmidt said; White was "the voice for the family" on the board.

Tom Norman's task was to prove the three elements that mark the legal definition of first-degree murder—premeditation, deliberation, and malice. In a dull monotone, Norman recounted the events leading up to the assassination: How Dan White had brought his gun and extra ammunition to City Hall, crawled through a window, snuck in a side door of Moscone's office, killed him, reloaded, summoned Milk and then killed Harvey, coolly aiming his revolver at the stem of Milk's brain. This, Norman said, was cut-and-dried first-degree murder. The litany of facts implied the elements of premeditation and deliberation, but one key element was absent—malice. Norman gave the jury no motive for why White had killed the two politicians. Schmidt clearly was making White's background the centerpiece of his case; Norman, meanwhile, said nothing of the background rancor between Milk and White.

Norman presented his first witness that afternoon, Coroner Boyd Stephens. Stephens talked of the technicalities of the deaths and made repeated references to the "high-velocity blood splatters" on the wall where Harvey was shot. Stephens felt that the splatters showed White had fired his first shot at the back of Milk's head while Harvey was still falling. Such precise aim certainly indicated that White was not deranged, so Stephens kept trying to pull his testimony back to the splatters; Tom Norman, however, did not seem interested. The next witnesses reviewed the familiar ten minutes it took White to kill Milk and Moscone. Carl Carlson was one of the last witnesses for Norman's side. When Carl looked across the dozen faces of the jury, he thought, It's all over. We've been screwed. He had no doubt what verdict the twelve conservative-looking faces would return. After his testimony, Carl ran into Dan White in a hallway behind the courtroom. He stared into the eyes that had been so zombielike during the session; now they were cold, steely, and calculating, Carlson thought.

The prosecution took only three days to present its case. The last witness called for the people was Frank Falzon, who played the tape-recorded confession White had made an hour after the shootings. The first halting question Falzon put to White became one of the many controversial aspects of the tape. "Would you, normally in a situation like this, ah . . . we ask questions," said Falzon. "I'm aware of your history as a police officer and also as a San Francisco fireman. I would prefer, I'll let you do it in a narrative form as to what happened this morning if you can lead up to the events of the shooting and then backtrack as to why these events took place."

White started talking of the financial and political pressures of the past weeks and the sense of betrayal he felt at losing the appointment. The second question similarly struck an odd chord to some observers, as the police prodded White to tell *more* of his problems: "Can you relate these pressures you've been under, Dan, at this time?" White said he had no plan when he went to City Hall and faltered when he tried to explain why he had worn his Smith & Wesson. "This is the gun I had when I was a policeman. It's in my room and ah . . . I don't know, I just put it on. I, I don't know why I put it on, it's just . . ." The police officer interrupted White just as the former supervisor was struggling with the sticky issue of whether he premeditated the killings to interject a question some felt was irrelevant. "Where is the gun now, Dan?" he asked.

The subject shifted to how White had gone to Moscone's office, pleading that he had overwhelming support in the district. Moscone conceded he knew this, White said, but added he would not reappoint White because "it's a political decision and that's it." Moscone took him into the back den and poured him a drink, White said, and he started hearing strange noises: "It was like a roaring in my ears and, and then, em . . . it just came to me, you know, he. . . ." Once again, the interrogator interrupted White, just as he was about to describe the shooting.

Within a few minutes, White's voice was rising to a whine as he talked of shooting George and running over to see Milk. "I wanted to talk to him, and, and, and just try to explain to him, you know, I, I didn't agree with him on a lot of things, but I was always honest, you know, and here they were devious and then he started kind of smirking cause he knew, he knew that I wasn't going to be reappointed. And ah . . . it just didn't make any impression on him. I started to say you know how hard I worked for it and what it meant to me and my family and then my reputation as a hard worker, a good honest person and he just kind of smirked at me as if to say, too bad and then and then I just got all flushed and, and hot and I shot him."

Four jurors cried as they heard the tortured confession. Even some reporters shed tears, while Mary Ann White broke out into sobs. The tape turned into the most sympathetic device for White in the trial so far—challenged only by the testimony Falzon next gave under cross-examination. Falzon talked of how he had met White years ago in Catholic grammar school and the years he had coached White on the police softball league back when Dan was named most valuable player for the California all-star team in the state's law enforcement league. Just a year before, Frank had given Dan a list of his own friends from whom White could gain support for his supervisorial bid. During all the years he had known White, Falzon said, he had only seen the man lose his temper once. Was the Dan White Falzon saw on November 27 the same man he had known for years? "Destroyed," said Falzon. "This was not the Dan White I had known at all." Dan White, he said, used to be "a man among men."

After his testimony Falzon returned to the chair in which the investigating police officer sits for every murder case—the seat at the side of the prosecuting attorney. Falzon had become the most convincing character witness for Dan White; for the rest of the trial, he sat at the hand of the man who was supposed to convince the jury that Dan White was a cold-blooded murderer. Reporters later scolded Norman for not trying to impeach Falzon's glowing testimony about White, for not ripping him with questions about whether their long friendship had compromised his objectivity. He would not consider doing such a thing, Norman reportedly told one reporter. Falzon's family was sitting in the audience that day. How could he be expected to tear apart a police officer right in front of his family? After Falzon's testimony, Norman rested his case. The political feuding between White and Milk was never brought up. Politics never entered Norman's case. Norman had so far managed to present his entire side without even using the word "assassination."

"This is a bunch of shit."

Warren Hinckle reread the line from the *Examiner* story that opened the trial: "White had led an exemplary life and no one seems inclined to challenge that statement." Hinckle slammed the newspaper on the counter of his favorite Irish bar and ordered another screwdriver. The forty-year-old reporter had followed the daily press reports of the trial and got more nauseated with each newspaper edition. As a fourth generation Irish San Franciscan, the scion of families of Irish cops and dance hall girls, Hinckle felt he too knew Dan White's background and his frame of mind on the day of the assassinations. He had grown up among the Irish working class who bred White and still spent no small portion of his days in the city's Irish watering holes, even after he had forged his career as San Francisco's foremost sob sister muckraking journalist. Hinckle had served variously as editor of *Ramparts, Scanlan's Monthly,* and *City* magazine. They all eventually went broke, but not before he had liberally peppered their pages with political exposés and his own genre of sentimental and often heavy-handed prose. Now a *Chronicle* columnist, Hinckle focused his attentions on the San Francisco scene and had spent much of the last year intrigued by growing working-class complaints about the gay invasion. From the start, he had considered Dan White to be little more than a contemporary model of Dennis Kearney, the nineteenth-century San Francisco mayor who built his political fortunes on the promise to drive the Chinese from the city. Everybody else may have thought White was the cat's ass, Hinckle thought, but he knew all along that White was a fascist lunatic. He hadn't been able to avoid dropping a few "I-told-you-so's" after the shootings, but any smugness turned to rage when he saw the trial unfolding. As far as Hinckle was concerned, the assassinations were little more than Dan White's Final Solution for the Homosexual Problem in San Francisco. Kill the queer and the queer-lover and turn the city to the right—perhaps permanently. He kept waiting for Norman to introduce this obvious angle to the case—and kept waiting. He was appalled when the prosecution closed its case after Falzon's testimony.

Norman had never given the jury any evidence pertaining to the

key element of any first-degree murder charge, malice. Where was the
motive? The key to the trial was homophobia, Hinckle decided, and as
he ruminated about the case over successive screwdrivers, he decided
that in order to really try this case, San Francisco needed to be put on
trial. Every little bit of bias against gays would need to be aired, since
anti-gay prejudice, he had no doubt, is what drove White to kill George
and Harvey. He was certain that it was precisely men from fine Irish
Catholic backgrounds who would relish murdering a gay leader and a
gay ally. After ranting and raving through Irish bars all over the city,
Hinckle decided to do his own research on Dan White's much vaunted
background.

The trail led quickly to former Undersheriff Jim Denman. The
soft-spoken Denman had always liked Hinckle, but he was well aware
of Warren's notorious reputation for sousing interviewees and then
extracting just about any quote he wanted. Denman wasn't reassured
when Warren told him they should meet at the Dovre Club, a den of
IRA supporters where Hinckle frequently passed his afternoons. Denman decided he wouldn't have a drink. Hinckle, of course, immediately
offered Denman a drink on the house; Denman decided he would have
just one. "A rum and coke, with lots of coke," he said. Hinckle brought
a drink with lots of rum and hardly any coke. A half-dozen rum and
cokes later, Denman unfolded the story about Dan White's first night
in jail, the friendly pats on the ass from the other cops, the reports of
policemen joking and smiling about the killings, and, most significantly,
White's apparent lack of any shame or remorse over the killings. After
six months, Denman added, he had never heard a single report of White
showing any regret or any emotion over the killings, beyond his daily
transformation into an automaton for his court appearances.

Hinckle pressed further. Denman thought he was trying to get him
to say that there had been a police conspiracy in the killings. Jim had
worked with police for years and certainly didn't rule out that possibility, but he had seen no evidence of such a conspiracy and decided it was
unlikely. Instead, Denman tried to explain that it could have been a
covert, even unconscious conspiracy, revolving around subtle nuances
of the police subculture. Nobody ever had to sit down and order White
to kill Milk and Moscone, but White knew that he would be a hero to
some if he killed the pair. As a former policeman, he would know
exactly what to say—and not say—in his confession. One point still
troubled Denman, however. He again told Warren about White's first
night in jail and the lack of any characteristics that indicated any lapse

of sanity. Schmidt was now basing his case on a "diminished capacity" argument, so Jim figured that he would be called as a prime witness for the prosecution. He had already told D.A. Freitas that White sure didn't act insane just an hour after the killing; he didn't even seem sorry. But Freitas had never called Denman; it didn't make any sense.

Hinckle suddenly became enthusiastic and cheerfully ordered another round of drinks. He had his story. The exposé that could pressure Freitas to push a *real* prosecution, he thought. Hinckle stumbled home later and started typing his opus on his Smith-Corona portable: "The Witness the Prosecution Isn't Calling."

Warren was enraged when his *Chronicle* editors refused to run the story. They didn't want to bias the jury, they said. Hinckle pointed out that the sequestered panel had their daily newspapers censored for just such reasons. The editors, however, remained unimpressed. The issue of fair trial versus free press had been haunting editors with greater frequency in recent years. *Chronicle* editors did not want to be accused of poisoning Dan White's right to an unbiased hearing. The only news that would be covered in the trial was the story of what happened within the four walls of the courtroom. That's how both newspapers were covering the story. Hinckle argued that the story about the trial concerned what was *not* happening in the four walls, but to no avail. When *The New York Times Magazine* called Warren to do a major piece on the trial, Hinckle shifted his allegiances to the Manhattan-based publication. Hinckle got to work on more research about Dan White's background. Each interview made him angrier, especially as the defense unfolded its case.

While Dan White sat impassively staring at the courtroom floor like a pod person from *Invasion of the Body Snatchers,* Doug Schmidt presented an array of psychiatrists who all agreed that Dan White could not have even been capable of premeditation, deliberation, or malice in the killings of Milk and Moscone. One psychiatrist insisted that the reason White took his revolver and extra rounds of ammunition to City Hall that morning was because the gun represented a "security blanket" at a time when White felt threatened. The killings, he said, represented an "uncontrolled breakthrough of primitive uncontrolled rage." Another psychiatrist told the court that the reason White crawled through a basement window instead of going through the front door—and the metal detector—was because White "didn't want to embarrass the police officer" at the door by forcing him to deal with a gun-toting politician. "It seems to me he takes special considerations not to hurt their [other people's] feelings," the psychiatrist insisted, causing some reporters to ask how a man so concerned with hurting a policeman's feelings one minute could moments later blow away a mayor and supervisor. One expert testified that the reason White shot Moscone was because he was too moral a man to punch the mayor in the nose; shooting was a much more impersonal and therefore a moral, means of violence, he said. Another psychiatrist talked about how Dan White's habitual consumption of junk food—particularly Twinkies, potato chips, and Coca Cola—led to the killings, since the extreme variations in blood sugar levels excaberated existing manic-depression. This soon became known as the Twinkie defense. Another expert noted that White's paternal grandmother had once suffered from mental illness. White was a hard-working, sincere supervisor, he added, caught amid devious politicians who had not a fraction of his honor. Faced with such a repudiation of his own naive faith in the democratic process, the psychiatrist said, the "American dream had become a nightmare." A string of character witnesses from White's family and the police and fire departments, meanwhile, testified that Danny had always been an exemplary boy, a man who had shown not a hint of the capability to kill people.

At every turn, Schmidt also brought up the issue of homosexuality, never overtly attacking Milk, but never allowing the jury to forget that Milk was the leader of the city's homosexual vanguard. Often, the references were just dropped offhandedly in cross-examination, like during Schmidt's question to Carl Carlson: "Harvey Milk was considered to be a leader in the gay or homosexual community. Is that fair?" Schmidt had no follow-up to the question, nor any apparent reason to ask. Coming the day after Schmidt had called Dan White "the voice for the family," however, the contrast was clear. When Dick Pabich testified about seeing White run from the mayor's office to the supervisors' complex, Schmidt asked if Harvey was pushing Moscone to apoint a homosexual to White's seat. No gay replacement, of course, was ever considered for the vacancy, and by then the newspapers had reported that Milk was advancing a heterosexual woman, but the specter was raised for the jury nevertheless. The most unusual introduction of homosexuality came when Supervisor Carol Ruth Silver testified. "You are part of the gay community also, aren't you?" Schmidt asked Silver.

"Myself?" she asked.

"Yes," said Schmidt.

"You mean, am I gay?" Silver persisted; the publicity she had gained as the first unwed mother to serve on the board should have put such questions to rest.

"Yes," Schmidt pushed.

"No, I'm not."

Gay leaders thought the exchange represented the basest form of queer-baiting.

The trial's key moment came and went so fast that most reporters missed it altogether. Dr. Martin Blinder was giving the familiar defense testimony about how an honorable Dan White had faced a devious city government. "He would put in hours wrestling with an issue, working to discern its merits," Blinder explained, "and then when he found out the merits of an issue and voted accordingly, he found his colleagues didn't give a damn about his merits but how useful their votes would be. Supervisor Molinari voted against a ball field tax exemption because he didn't get the right tickets—"

"—Doctor," Schmidt interrupted. "We decided not to mention any names with regard to specific supervisors and that sort of thing."

The psychiatrist later told a reporter that he had never heard of any such decision about what was and was not to be discussed, though he assumed Schmidt was referring to instructions Schmidt's partner was supposed to give him. By the time Blinder testified, it was obvious that Schmidt was not mounting the type of snake pit political defense he had first hinted he might undertake. The only politicians whose names were brought up were the two dead men. There was no talk of the "broad spectrum of social, political, and ethical issues." The lack of politics was surprising not only for the defense, but for the prosecution, since it was in politics that the roots of possible malice could be found. Speculation grew among reporters and lawyers that the prosecution and defense might have made some agreement that neither side would refer to politics, but both Schmidt and Norman denied that any gentleman's understanding existed.

Warren Hinckle sat at his Smith-Corona, trying out sentences for his Dan White story:

"Background" and "hardworking" are buzzwords used repeatedly by the defense when describing White; they are code: read "white and straight." The defense argument is that such a nice kid from such a good family wouldn't shoot anyone unless something snapped inside,

and, subliminally, unless the victims somehow deserved it. White is
being portrayed as innocent as a Jamesian heiress; it is suggested,
successfully, that the naif's exposure to the dirty world of politics had
allowed his becoming unglued. Moscone and Milk, the liberal and the
gay, are allowed to be seen somehow as the bad guys. The semantics
of how to characterize the prosecution are at best imprecise. There
have been arguments over whether the case is being "blown" or
"thrown." A word frequently invoked is "fix", although in S.F. it is
subject to as many interpretations as the King James Bible.'

Hinckle liked his semicoloned sentences, heavily laden with literary
allusions, showing, if nothing else, that he wasn't just any hard-drinking
Irish writer, but a *good* hard-drinking Irish writer. For this story,
however, Hinckle would let the facts stand out more than the style. The
research he had undertaken in just two weeks of surveying Dan White's
district gave him more ammo than he could ever lob at the ex-cop in
an encyclopedia, even as White came off as a "babe in the woods" at
his trial.

Over a styrofoam cup of coffee in her sweets shop in District 8,
Goldie Judge told Hinckle why she had quit as Dan White's campaign
manager midway in the 1977 race. She had resented the cops who were
always hanging out at the headquarters. White was the spoiled child,
throwing tantrums and pouting when he did not get his own way. Once
White became a supervisor, the manager joined a chorus of former
supporters who thought White had forsaken District 8 in favor of police
and real estate interests; like many others, she had urged Moscone not
to reappoint White.

White, however, had spent much of his taped confession and the
subsequent psychiatric interviews talking about how his constituents
had backed him, how 1,100 letters of support were delivered to the
mayor the very morning of the shooting. Judge and many others argued
this. Hinckle soon heard that Dan White was seen at the supervisors'
Xerox machine in City Hall photocopying many of those letters himself. Hinckle sharpened his pen: "The big lie," he called White's claims
of constituent support.

More disturbing stories quickly emerged. One former opponent
revealed that White had packed the meetings of other candidates with
youth gangs who would disrupt speeches and chant for White. When
four Nazis showed up at a district meeting with swastikas and "Unite
and Fight with Dan White" buttons, one of White's opponents begged

the ex-policeman to kick them out. Gentle Dan refused. White routinely bullied and intimidated political adversaries, Hinckle learned. The pattern was not new for Dan White. A subsequent probation report revealed that just as he had once beat up blacks who were integrating his high school in the early 1960s.

What rankled Hinckle the most was the defense claim that White actually liked George and Harvey. Prosecutor Norman never once objected to that point. The most cursory investigation revealed that White had barely spoken to Harvey for months and that Harvey had taken to calling White "dangerous" in his final weeks. None of this was coming out at the trial. Instead, Norman had simply given the chronology of the murders without a hint as to the motive. Hinckle's major question was trying to decide whether D.A. Freitas was responsible for the poor prosecution or simply irresponsible. The absence of any talk of politics made Hinckle suspicious. Discussion of politics in the prosecution might have led the defense to talk of some messy matters of city politics, a point of no small concern to a vulnerable district attorney seeking reelection only six months down the road.

Nobody else had bothered to do the legwork to find out if Dan White's angelic image stood the test of truth. Hinckle saw that his own research would not be printed in a San Francisco newspaper, much less used in a trial that revolved around Dan White's character and background. All this made him want to go out and have a drink, which is what he decided to do. Under the flag of the Irish Republic, hanging from the wall of Paddy Nolan's Dovre Club, Hinckle started putting his forebodings about the case to the best use he could, taking hefty bets that Dan White would get off the hook and be found guilty only of voluntary manslaughter.

The defense called its last witness, Mary Ann White, on Friday, May 11, and then rested its case.

On Saturday, hundreds of shirtless young men tanned their pectorals, smoked joints and circulated around the corner of Eighteenth and Castro, enjoying the first warm day of the summer. A hippyish-looking man was casually tacking up posters on a telephone pole outside the Elephant Walk when a local rent-a-cop stalked up to him. Putting posters on telephone poles violated a city ordinance, the officer announced, as he handcuffed the man and called for a paddy wagon. A dozen men soon surrounded the officer and his handcuffed charge, taunting the guard. A bartender happened by and blew his police whistle, alerting the rest of the street. Within minutes, the pair was engulfed in an angry mob of gay men. The officer nervously radioed for help. By the time a half dozen police cars arrived moments later, nearly three thousand swarmed over the intersection, throwing their cigarettes and pennies at the police, shouting, "Dump Dianne." From a nearby corner, a gleeful Cleve Jones started chanting, "Dan White was a cop. Dan White was a cop."

When the paddy wagon arrived to take the arrested man away, police could barely struggle through the crowd engulfing the van. Some of the more daring Castro denizens darted around the vehicle letting the air out of its tires. The police reinforcements pulled back into a tight formation, unsure of how to handle the strange new phenomenon of violent homosexuals. The shrieks of police whistles echoed through the neighborhood while thousands chanted "Dan White was a cop." The police were able to briefly clear the way for the paddy wagon, which hobbled up Castro on its airless tires. After several more uncomfortable minutes, the police again pulled back and slowly started driving away, accurately seeing that without their presence, the throng would have nobody to shout at. The uneasy mob moved to the corner of Castro and Market Streets, where they sat down and blocked traffic for a half-hour before dispersing into a routine Saturday afternoon of cruising and drinking.

Cleve Jones, for one, was ecstatic. Once again, he saw the potential of what Harvey Milk had so frequently discussed during the Prop 6 fight—a gay riot.

On Monday, Tom Norman started delivering the final summation of his case. He again recounted the facts of the shootings. "It seems to me that someone so dazed at the time and suffering from mental illness wouldn't necessarily be able to do these things," said Norman of the various ruses White had used to enter Moscone's office undetected. "Actions speak louder than words."

Norman, however, was not one to spare detail. He droned on for four hours. At least two jurors went to sleep while he plodded through his summation. Reporters spent much of the time throwing each other winks and knowing glances, doodling on their note pads, and perfecting their afternoon leads. The sight of sleeping jurors at what should have been the city's trial of the century infuriated other journalists. After the closing arguments, a local television reporter told Norman about the ongoing arguments in the press box about whether the trial was being blown or thrown.

Schmidt had walked amiably through the court room for most of the case, but for his closing arguments, he brought in a high lectern from which he addressed the jury. Few could escape noticing how much Schmidt acted like a parish priest at his pulpit; one reporter watched his second hand for a quarter hour and figured that Schmidt invoked the name of God about once a minute. His speech was brief and dramatic, a stark contrast to Norman's long and dull oration.

"Lord God," he said of Dan White's pressures, "nobody could say that the things that were happening to him wouldn't make a reasonable man mad. Surely he acted rashly and impulsively out of some passion." Calling for a voluntary manslaughter verdict, Schmidt continued, "A good man, a man with a fine background, does not cold-bloodedly go down and kill two people. That just doesn't happen. I beg you. I would do anything to convince you of what I am saying.... The pot had boiled over.... He will be punished.... His child and his family will have to live with this.... God will punish him.... Please. Please. Just justice. That's all."

At the same time Doug Schmidt was delivering his impassioned final argument, Cleve Jones and a handful of gay leaders were meeting with a police captain to discuss plans for handling gay response to a possible manslaughter verdict for Dan White. The captain assured Jones that homosexuals were far too responsible to do anything so troublesome as riot.

"You're not listening to me," said Jones, pounding the captain's desk. "There's going to be trouble, and we're not leaving here until we have some contingency plans."

"Okay, Cleve," said the captain, thoroughly amused by Jones' outburst. "What do you think is going to happen?"

"If he gets off with anything less than first-degree murder, within an hour there will be five thousand people on Castro Street out for vengeance."

"Okay Cleve," the captain calmly advised. "If the crowd gathers, you get your bullhorn. You'll get a police escort and you can march them down to City Hall like you always have and you can have a rally."

Jones returned to the Castro to find fliers on phone poles throughout the neighborhood:

Dan White Gets Special Treatment!
Why?
Because: He's an Ex-Cop?
He's a "Family Man?"
He's White?
Has Financial Problems!?
He Eats Junk Food!?

We Denounce Trial And Verdict.
Protest! 8 P.M. Night of Verdict, Steps of City Hall.

The group claiming to sponsor the posters was "Lesbians and Gay Men's Coalition Against the Death Penalty," a group of radical lesbians and gay men few had heard of. Jones called the police to tell of the posters. "This is out of my hands now," he said; he could tell the police didn't take his warnings very seriously.

The case went to the jury the next day. Reporters started their long vigil for the verdict, anxiously swapping theories and scenarios for possible decisions. Given the weak prosecution, most thought White might get a manslaughter verdict for Moscone's killing, but since White had to reload in order to kill Milk, a verdict of at least second-degree murder seemed inevitable on at least one count. One reporter offhandedly asked Defense Attorney Doug Schmidt if he felt society would feel justice was served if the jury returned the two manslaughter verdicts Schmidt wanted. "Society doesn't have anything to do with it," Schmidt said. "Only those twelve people in the jury box."

eighteen

The Final Act

Looking tired and spent, the seven women and five men of the Dan White jury filed into the warm, windowless courtroom in the Hall of Justice. Only juror Richard Aparicio, the retired policeman, seemed pleased with his work; he beamed at Dan White as he walked into the room and when White sat motionless, Aparicio rapped his knuckles loudly on the defense table in front of the defendant. The jurors had deliberated thirty-six difficult hours over their decision, producing some speculation that the trial might have created a hung jury, but at 5:28 P.M. on Monday, May 21, the dozen San Franciscans were ready to announce their verdicts.

"Mr. Foreman," Judge Walter Calcagno asked, "Has the jury reached verdicts in this case?"

"Yes, it has, Your Honor."

"Will you read the verdicts, please."

The foreman slowly told the judge that the jury had found Dan White guilty of violating section 192.1 of the penal code in the slaying of George Moscone. Voluntary manslaughter. The judge polled each juror to see if this represented the unanimous verdict. Dan White's family and the hundred reporters waited anxiously for the Milk verdict, since the second shooting represented the likelier case of murder.

His voice quavering, the foreman told the judge that the jury had found
White guilty of again violating section 192.1 of the penal code—voluntary manslaughter. The stunned reporters sat motionless, some calculating the sentence for two counts of voluntary manslaughter. Seven
years, eight months. With time off for good behavior, White would
probably be out of jail in less than five years. Dan White raised his hand
to his eyes and cried. Mary Ann White and several of the jurors also
broke into tears. Richard Aparicio walked from the jury box to the
defense table and gave Doug Schmidt a firm and hearty handshake.
Prosecutor Tom Norman sat in stony silence, flushed.

A radio station had called Cleve Jones' Castro Street apartment
moments before the verdict was announced, so it could get an instant
live response from the twenty-three-year-old activist. The reporter had
left the receiver sitting next to her own radio connection. Jones could
barely believe the words she broadcast: "Oh, my God! I can't believe
it—he got off on both. Manslaughter for Milk. Manslaughter for Moscone."

From the next room, Cleve's roommate started shouting that the
verdicts had just flashed on the television news.

"What does this mean?" the shaken reporter asked Jones.

"This means that in America, it's all right to kill faggots," Jones
said. He hung up the phone and raced to the bathroom, where he
started throwing up. He remembered the days he had thrown up in gym
class bathrooms after getting beat up by high school bullies, he remembered the blood on the wall of the flophouse hotel where he had spent
his first night in San Francisco, he remembered the blood on the wall
in Dan White's office where Harvey's pale blue face had lolled on his
dead shoulders, and he threw up some more. By the time Jones emerged
from the bathroom, a small crowd had already gathered in his living
room, Jones's militant young friends coming to the Castro apartment
where they had assembled to plot marches and demonstrations in years
past. Reporters were demanding Jones for instant interviews down on
Castro Street, where most TV stations werer setting up their microwave
discs to go live.

By a strange twist in timing, the next day, May 22, would have
been Harvey Milk's forty-ninth birthday. Jones and the Harvey Milk
Club had long ago planned a street celebration for that night. Once on
Castro Street with reporters, Jones was besieged with questions about
the planned party.

"Will the reaction to the verdict come here tomorrow night?" a journalist asked Jones.

"No," Cleve said. "The reaction will be swift and it will be tonight."

Already, a crowd of several hundred had gathered around the corner of Castro and Market, dazed and angry. Jones raced back to his apartment and searched for the battered white bullhorn Harvey had used in so many street demonstration. He grabbed Milk's old bullhorn and headed back to Castro Street.

Dianne Feinstein held an impromptu press conference when she heard the verdict. She had found Harvey's body, she noted, and had no doubt what the verdict should have been. "As I look at the law," the mayor said, "it was two murders."

Supervisor Carol Ruth Silver put her assessment of the verdicts more succinctly. "Dan White has gotten away with murder. It's as simple as that."

Supervisor Harry Britt locked himself in his office for forty minutes after hearing the outcome and emerged after 6 P.M. to deliver his own enraged reaction. "Harvey Milk knew he would be assassinated. He knew that the lowest nature in human beings would rise up and get him. But he never imagined that this city would approve of that act. It's beyond immoral. It's obscene. This is an insane jury. This man's homophobia had something to do with this verdict—and it *was* murder."

A gallows humor pervaded the city's newsrooms as journalists started shaping their verdict reaction stories. "Sara Jane Moore got life for *missing* Gerald Ford," a reporter commented. "Doug Schmidt's such a good lawyer he could get sodomy charges reduced to a citation for following too closely," joked another. Gay journalist Randy Alfred wondered aloud why the jury had not just gone ahead and convicted Milk of "unlawful interference with a bullet fired from the gun of a former police officer."

Journalist Francis Moriarty was standing next to a police radio when he heard the SFPD dispatcher cheerfully broadcast the verdicts and then burst into a chorus of "Danny Boy." In the background, another officer started whistling the Notre Dame fight song.

Cleve Jones clasped his bullhorn firmly as he stared at the milling throng gathering on Castro Street. "Today, Dan White was essentially patted on the back," he told the crowd of five hundred that had gathered below him, reading their EXTRA editions. "He was convicted of manslaughter—what you get for hit and run. We all know this violence has touched all of us. It was not manslaughter. I was there that day at City Hall. I saw what the violence did. It was not manslaughter, it was murder."

With the chant of "Out of the bars and into the streets," Jones started leading the mob down Castro where scores more emerged from each bar. The crowd circled the Castro, past Most Holy Redeemer Church, with its chants:

> Out of the bars and into the streets
> Dan White was a cop
> Out of the bars and into the streets
> Dan White was a cop

The crowd surged up Castro again, a thousand strong. There, a wispy, blond-haired young man held a handscrawled sign: "Avenge Harvey Milk." He was Chris Perry, the first president of what was now the Harvey Milk Club, an old Milk political croney who remembered Harvey telling him seven months before that gays needed to fight back. Perry thought about this and all the times in the past months that he and his friends had been kicked around by thugs and police on the sidewalks of the Castro; today it made sense that, even after his years of registering voters and nudging gays into nuts-and-bolts Democratic Party politics, he should be standing on this corner, a block from Harvey's old ward headquarters, holding his sign: Avenge Harvey Milk. One year ago that very afternoon, Harvey Milk had been dressed in a clown suit, jumping aboard passing cable cars to tell tourists, "I'm an elected official. I run this city." A year later, Harvey was only a memory, his ashes spread in the cold waters of the Pacific, but an angry mob took up the chant as it passed Chris Perry's sign and started down Market Street toward City Hall, and hundreds more joined in from every side street, echoing the mantra of a thousand voices:

> Avenge Harvey Milk
> Avenge Harvey Milk
> Avenge Harvey Milk

As the crowd passed out of the Castro, Cleve sought out the policemen he had been promised a few days before in his stormy meeting with a police captain. "I hope you have my escort."

"Yes, Mr. Jones," said the officer, with newfound respect.

New chants rose and fell as the throng, now 1,500 strong, moved down Market Street:

> Dan White, Dan White
> Hit man for the New Right
> Dan White, Dan White,
> Hit man for the New Right.

And the chant that had become increasingly popular during the mounting tensions of the past months:

> Dump Dianne
> Dump Dianne
> Dump Dianne

Police whistles shrieked at the fading day. The crowd had followed this path so many times before, but today their anger was not directed toward a nebulous electorate in the Midwest and they bore no candles. Slogans rose, evaporated, and were forgotten amid each successive wave of angry mottos that deafened commuters trying to wend their way up Market Street.

> All-straight jury
> No surprise
> Dan White lives
> And Harvey Milk dies.

Fresh crimson paint now dripped from the wall of the hamburger joint across the street from City Hall, a few feet from the phone where Dan White had called his wife after the killings: "HE GOT AWAY WITH MURDER." The crowd had swelled to over five thousand by the time it reached City Hall. The handful of police officers inside were confused. None of the experienced police brass, who had spent so many years of their careers watching courteous homosexuals walking docilely into paddy wagons during the decades of bar raids, could have imagined a gay crowd literally screaming for blood.

> Kill Dan White
> Kill Dan White
> Kill Dan White

The anti-death penalty coalition that had organized the march had a sound system waiting on the wide granite stairs of City Hall, but as the crowd surged toward the building's glass doors, the handful of officers decided they had to make a stand. They charged up the steps, knocking over the public address system's generator and mortally mangling the loud speakers' wiring. The officers quickly retreated back into City Hall as the thousands pressed in upon them. As dusk fell, the first rock crashed through one of the doors and the crowd roared its approval.

The throng had grown far beyond the first five thousand who had marched from the Castro. While the first hundred at the front tried to storm the City Hall doors, thousands more stood by confused, trying to figure out what was going on as the sounds of shattering glass echoed through the darkening sky. A dozen young men tore the gilded grill ornamental work from the front doors and then used the spears to batter through the thick glass at the entrance. Stones hurled from all directions began smashing every first floor window in the building. The outbreak of violence surprised many of the more sedate gays who were expecting another rally. Scuffling broke out between the protesters. As one man hurled a rock, he was confronted with a pair of well-dressed professionals arguing for peace; the professionals were then threatened by a half dozen angry youths who were engulfed by still more gays arguing nonviolence.

The first storming of the doors brought together an odd ensemble of Harvey's friends, lovers, and cronies, as they dived to the front of the crowd to try to contain the imminent riot. About two dozen joined hands and lined themselves between the mob and the doors. Terror and purpose overwhelmed Harvey's 1976 campaign manager John Ryckman as he tried to hold back the marauding crowd; Ryckman came from the old school and was truly opposed to any violence. Jim Rivaldo and Dick Pabich thought a violent response was not entirely inappropriate, but tried to hold back the rioters for fear that a riot might harm Harry Britt's reelection chances. Scott Smith had no doubt that Harvey would have loved the theater unfolding that night, but Smith also remembered how much his former lover had adored City Hall and would have considered any violence against the building to be desecration of good culture. For a dozen reasons, the thin line of monitors held firm, pushing the demonstrators back off the City Hall steps, even while rocks whizzed by their heads and glass sprayed at their feet.

Gay leaders tried to quell the violence. "Harvey. Remember Harvey Milk. He'd be ashamed of us," shouted Harry Britt. But the crowd knew him only as the man put in office by Dianne Feinstein; they didn't know who he was then, they didn't know who he was now. They booed and jeered him. In frustration, Britt screamed, "Stop this. You're acting like a bunch of heterosexuals." And the jeers rose again.

A well-known lesbian university professor yelled into a feeble bullhorn, "Harvey Milk lives." From the mob someone shouted back, "Harvey Milk's not alive. He's dead, you fool."

From the north side of the Civic Center Plaza, a wedge of police appeared. They started their march through the crowd, braving the fusillade of rocks and bottles that flew at them. Relieved at the support, the monitors decided to sit down on the cleared steps to show that they were part of the peaceful gays. The officers quickly reached the stairs, but rather than reinforcing the monitors, they summarily started beating them with their night sticks. The odor of tear gas began to fill the night air as the monitors scrambled for cover, away from the marauding nightsticks. While the police pummeled on, a young man kicked his Frye boot through the window of a lone police car parked in front of City Hall, lit a pack of matches, threw it in the front seat, and watched the upholstery burst into flames. Another man kicked in a newspaper stand and used the street editions to kindle a fire beneath a tree near the City Hall front doors. The flames leaped into the darkness and from the inferno that was once a police cruiser came a loud wail, the shrieking of a melting siren, punctuated dramatically by the dull thud of the gas tank's explosion. The crowd cheered the sight of the burning police car. From police radios, reporters listened to the codes shifting from warnings of 911's, broken windows, to 404's, possibility of riots, and then to 528's, fire.

The police secured the portico and stood stoically as the mob pelted them with rocks and chunks of asphalt pryed from the street. When other officers attempted further forays into the crowd, the rioters tore up parking meters to ram them back, holding lids from garbage cans as shields. They tore apart massive concrete trash receptacles and hurled the chunks at police, newspeople, any visible symbol of institutional authority.

Police Chief Gain watched the riot unfold from inside City Hall and issued one stern order. Police were not to attack the rioters but simply hold their ground. Even some of the police force's sternest critics were amazed at the restraint officers showed in those early hours.

Supervisor Carol Ruth Silver decided to wade into the crowd as a last-ditch effort to end the rampage. As she stepped away from City Hall, however, a chunk of concrete hit her in the face and she had to be carried back through the glassless doors.

Mayor Dianne Feinstein arrived at City Hall at 8:30 P.M. While she huddled with aides and supervisors, more rocks crashed through her second-floor office, allowing tear gas to waft in from the night. The group retreated to the supervisors' offices, where Feinstein was greeted by the sight of Silver stretched on a couch, her face streaming with blood. Downstairs, standing in neat rows between the pillars of City Hall's marble-floored lobby, scores of police waited in full riot gear. Each new wave of shouting and each successive onslaught of missiles stiffened them further. Many beat their clubs rythmically against the columns. Their tempers throbbed as they heard that other police outside were being ordered to only stand their ground as the rioters taunted and stoned them.

The police cars that had escorted the marchers from the Castro had lined up on the north side of the Civic Center Plaza, deserted hours ago during the early moments of rioting. Cleve Jones was stunned as he watched a dozen gay men with helmets and clubs start darting from car to car, coordinating their actions with intricate hand signals. The youths would first kick in a car window, light a book of matches, throw it onto the car's upholstery and then methodically fan the flames until the blaze was well underway. Within minutes, a block-long line of police cars had burst into flames, their gas tanks exploding and their melting sirens screeching into the cool May night. Several of the braver rioters leaped into the broken basement windows of City Hall and set fire to printouts in the city's computer center. Police rushed from the lobby to squelch the flames.

Nearly three hours after the first rock had shattered the City Hall doors, a wide wedge of officers appeared, the flames of the burning police cars casting ominous shadows on their helmets. They marched sternly into the pandemonium, beating their batons on the pavement before them like a Roman legion out to make their final conquest. Minutes after wading into the crowd, small groups of police broke away from the wedge to take on knots of rioters. With the formation destroyed, Civic Center plaza became a mélange of skirmishes between gays and police. Police were surprised and enraged at the depth of resistance they encountered. Gays beat back police with branches torn from trees, chrome ripped from city buses, and slabs of asphalt torn from the street. As a young man torched a last police car, he shouted to a reporter, "Make sure you put in the paper that I ate too many Twinkies."

The fighting edged further into the night, and slowly, as the police forced the rioters from Civic Center, the battles dispersed to the side streets around City Hall as random cadres of police confronted the odd groups of hoods and hustlers who took advantage of the City Hall melee to begin looting stores. Civic Center soon turned from a grim portrait of chaos to an empty wasteland of broken glass and smoldering police cruisers.

Mayor Feinstein held a midnight press conference, praising the police restraint and promising to get on with the business of putting the city back together. The riots represented the most violent episode in city history since the racial rioting of 1966, but, Feinstein noted, not one person was killed that night and none of the reported injuries was critical. "The city," she said, "is secure."

As reporters left the press conference, however, policemen standing guard around City Hall seemed anything but in control. "The faggots had their day," a cop shouted to no one in particular. "We'll get ours."

Cleve Jones escaped being hunted down by the roving bands of police by hitching a ride on the back of a punk rock songstress's motorcycle. Once home, Jones climbed the fire escape of his apartment building to see if trouble had spread to the Castro. Below him were the silhouettes of dozens of helmeted officers gearing up for new action.

At about the same time, Warren Hinckle arrived in the Castro with a friend who had served many years on the police department. The night seemed remarkably quiet for Castro Street, though many of the neighborhood bars were crowded with nonviolent gays who had fled the rioting for the peace of the Castro. Moments later, however, Hinckle was aghast to see police cars cruising slowly down Castro, crammed with officers in full riot gear. Some smiled with grim satisfaction as crowds gathered on the corners, hurling epithets and an occasional beer bottle.

Hinckle and his friend, the police veteran rushed to the captain, who impassively watched the gathering storm. "You guys are gonna start a police riot here," he accused. "We lost the battle at City Hall," the captain retorted angrily. "We're not going to lose here."

After several bottles crashed on the cruisers' hoods, the police spilled out, went into battle formation, and started their march into the

Castro. Sensing trouble, many crowded into the Elephant Walk bar, where Harvey Milk and Allan Baird had once talked of how gays and straights could live together. The police gazed through the bar's plate glass windows at the sight of a homosexual haven that so brazenly exhibited its goings-on through picture windows. With neither orders nor method, two dozen officers suddenly charged into the Elephant Walk, flailing their clubs at everyone in sight and shouting, "Banzai." Hinckle watched the attack with amazement. Most of the officers had hidden their badges so they could not be identified.

The surprised bartenders ducked behind the bar, stretching themselves out on the floor, so the policemen simply jumped on top of the bar and coldly aimed their batons for the prostrate employees' skulls, shouting, "Sick cocksuckers." The bar's ornate engraved glass work shattered to the floor, further scarring the women and men the police were beating and kicking. After fifteen minutes of carnage, the police returned to the streets, where dozens more officers were haphazardly beating any gay they could spot.

By now, Cleve Jones and his roommate were making brief forays onto Castro Street to drag the wounded back to their apartment. On one trip outside, Jones looked across the street and spotted two gay men on a rooftop holding rifles. Blood stained his carpet, and when he heard a new wave of police sweep past the apartment for another attack, he ordered everyone to lie on the floor. Cleve had come to San Francisco to be free and march in a gay pride parade; tonight he felt like Anne Frank dodging the Gestapo.

Harry Britt left the City Hall press conference and was heading toward his Castro home when the sight of dozens of police cars drew him to the marauding police on Castro Street. He ran up to a police sergeant who was watching the mayhem. "I'm Supervisor Harry Britt and you work for me," he shouted.

"Buddy," the cop answered. "I work for the city, not for you."

From the corners, gays mocked Britt. "Okay, Harry," they shouted, "if you got clout, use it."

The police were regrouping again on the corner of Market and Castro when Britt caught sight of Police Chief Gain. "The police don't belong on this street," he railed. "Get them to leave." By now, Gain had heard the reports of the Elephant Walk rampage, an excursion he had not ordered. A mob now was marching toward the new police line, shouting, "Go home. Go home. Go home." They were ready for another fight. Gain ordered his men out of the Castro. The officers were itching for more action, but they reluctantly withdrew.

Later that night, a friend of Mike Weiss, a free-lance reporter, ran into a cheerful group of police officers who were whooping it up at a downtown bar. "We're celebrating," one cop explained. "We were at City Hall the day it [the killings] happened and we were smiling then. And we were there again tonight and we're still smiling."

The glass cleared from the streets, the windows of City Hall now neatly boarded up, the city's gay leadership assembled in a board of supervisors committee room the next morning, just hours after the police had made their final sweep of Civic Center. By now, the statistics were being endlessly repeated by the media: At least sixty-one police officers were hospitalized and an estimated one hundred gays. A dozen police cars had been burned. Police estimated total damage to be near $1 million, a figure that later proved to be exagerated threefold. Only nineteen rioters had been arrested. Different journalists had variously tagged the riots as the "Twinkie Riots" or the "Night of Rage," but the name beginning to stick was the "White Night Riots," a bizarre echo of the "white night" code word Jim Jones had dubbed his suicide rituals. Mayor Feinstein had hastily called a meeting with gay leaders for that morning. Gays had now come together for an earlier conference, because Supervisor Britt and the more militant gays from the Harvey Milk Club wanted to make one point clear to the more stolid gay moderates: *No one* was to apologize for the riot. Harvey's party would go on as planned.

Mayor Feinstein clearly would have preferred gays to cancel that night's street celebration, but the Harvey Milk Club's leaders pointed out that over ten thousand posters had gone into circulation weeks before, all featuring a picture of Harvey Milk in his clown outfit, and it would be impossible to stem the tide of gays going to the Castro that night. "We have a choice between escalation or resolution of this," Cleve Jones told Feinstein. The solution, Milk Club leaders advised, was not to keep gays out of the Castro, but to keep police away; the party must go on. Feinstein assented and Jones feverishly started training monitors and coordinating contingency plans with police. At another meeting, that night's planned speakers decided that they could variously address whatever issue they wished in their talks, but on one condition—no one should apologize.

"Harvey Milk's people do not have anything to apologize for," Harry Britt told a gaggle of reporters after the Feinstein meeting. "Now the society is going to have to deal with us not as nice little fairies who have hairdressing salons, but as people capable of violence. We're not going to put up with Dan Whites anymore." The reporters were shocked that a public official would condone violence. Britt was shocked they would expect anything else. The journalists asked if such a riot would not set back the gay movement. "No one has ever accepted us," Britt snapped. "What sets a movement back is not violence. What sets us back is Uncle Toms."

Newspeople scurried to try to find a gay leader who would apologize. They had a tough time. "Political and cultural leaders haven't apologized for creating a jury where Dan White is a hero and for creating a jury where Dan White can be found a moral man incapable of cold-blooded murder," snorted Bill Kraus, the new president of the Harvey Milk Club. "They have a lot more to apologize for than we do."

Graffiti around Castro Street took an even more strident tone. Slogans filled all available walls:

Gay Riots Now

Feinstein Will Die

Death Dan White

Islamic Justice—An Eye for an Eye

Dan White & Co. You will not escape, for violent fairies will visit you even in your dreams.

On a wall a few doors down from the old Castro Camera site was a tribute to the man who was becoming legend: Happy Birthday Harvey —At Least We Love You. Across the street from the devastated Elephant Walk, a spray-painter had scrawled a variation on the dramatic sentence from Harvey's taped political will: Let the Bullets that Rip Through My Brain Smash Through Every Closet Door in the Country.

The only person remotely aligned with Harvey to denounce the riots was his estranged brother Robert, who pleaded that gays should "respect and honor his feelings and my feelings by not demonstrating."

Down the Long Island Railroad tracks from Robert Milk's Rockville Centre home, Harvey's old basketball teammate from Bayshore High, Dick Brown, read the news of the riot that day with considerably

less antipathy. When blacks have a riot, they burn their own neighborhoods, Brown thought. At least when gays riot, they have the sense to
get out of their own neighborhood.

Officials from the Police Officers Association spent much of that
day in press conferences angrily denouncing the restraint which Chief
Gain had ordered during the early hours of the City Hall fracas. Gain
defended himself by saying he had avoided a bloodbath; POA leaders
said that sixty-one injured officers was, by their standards, a bloodbath.
Cops also flayed at Gain for ordering the withdrawal from the Castro.
One police officer even filed charges of "inciting a riot" against Harry
Britt because of the supervisor's insistance that police did not belong
on Castro Street.

The newspaper editorials and columnists, of course, condemned
the gay rioting, but the news coverage of the night worked to balance
the public's perceptions of the events. Spot news, after all, demands
simplification of even the heaviest news events, so on the day after the
riots, only two stories emerged: the story of the gay brutality against
police at City Hall and the story of police brutality against gays on
Castro Street. The police attack on the Elephant Walk was something
of a lucky break, not only because it balanced the homosexual excesses
at City Hall, but because media people were crawling all over the Castro
before police arrived, permitting every police abuse to be fastidiously
documented in both print and film. The fact that police had beaten
reporters at both City Hall and Castro Street did little to engender
journalistic sympathy for the SFPD.

Still, gay activists fretted about the political fallout from the rioting. The elections for mayor, D.A., sheriff, and six of the eleven supervisors were to be held less than six months away. They could provide a
likely platform for any politician who decided to fan the flames of
conservative voter discontent. As in the militant days after the Anita
Bryant vote and again during the Briggs Initiative, the specter of an
anti-gay backlash haunted the politicos who had worked so long to
achieve gay political power.

By the afternoon newspaper editions, stories of the tense hours of
jury deliberations began to emerge. Only one juror had voted for a
charge of first-degree murder, and that was only on the first of many
ballots. The jury had then spent hours trying to decide whether White
might be guilty of second-degree murder, but arrived at the dual manslaughter verdicts, because, as one seventy-five-year-old woman juror

put it, "It just all came together as if God were watching over us, as if God brought us together." She had hoped that the decision would be best for San Francisco. "We didn't want to give the city a worse name," she said. "We wanted things to just quiet down and be over with."

Another juror said that Dan White certainly was a "moral man" and was particularly impressed by the psychiatric testimony that said White had shot Moscone because he was too moral to punch him in the nose. "Many of us were praying for guidance," said a Catholic juror who maintained that the verdict "must be God's will or it would not have turned out this way." Virtually all the jurors made the same point —for all the evidence the prosecution presented about the facts of the killing, they never had a sense that the prosecution had done anything to show that Dan White harbored any malice or motive to kill Milk and Moscone. They were amazed that prosecuter Norman thought he had had such an open-and-shut case of first-degree murder.

A radio blared in Cleve Jones's apartment as he coordinated the training of some three hundred monitors for that night's birthday party. The disc jockey was playing "Ain't No Stoppin' Us Now" and dedicating it to the memory of Harvey Milk. Down the street, volunteers were hoisting a huge blowup portrait of Harvey to hang from the theater sign, which spelled out CASTRO in three stories of neon. On the marquee, the theater had written: Harvey Milk Lives. Police blocked off the street so workers could erect the huge entertainment stage, as they had so many times before at the Castro Street fairs Harvey had once masterminded. Other volunteers printed up hundreds of T-shirts for the monitors with the slogan: "PLEASE—No Violence." Late in the afternoon, Cleve and Scott Smith made their final plans with police, helping them set up a secret command post over Cliff's Hardware. Other police officials were scouting hidden assembly points for the hundreds of uniformed police who would wait on the periphery of the Castro for any sign of trouble. Gays were making their own secret preparations too. First aid stations were covertly established in a number of neighborhood locations. Legal observers were donning green armbands so they could witness any arrests police tried to make. Though both sides had called a truce, neither trusted the other. Police felt humiliated by the gay show of strength at City Hall; gays still fumed over the unprovoked Elephant Walk bash-in. As dusk fell and thousands began descending on the

Castro, Jones was enthusiastic: "We'll disco right in the police's faces." Many of the celebrants were wearing helmets, however, and the neighborhood police captain called Jones over a special radio he had given him to say, "Don't worry, Cleve. I'm right here in front of your apartment. We'll see what happens."

By the time the party started, twenty thousand had gathered in the Castro to hear Jones' opening words:

> Thank you for being here. Last night the lesbians and gay men of San Francisco showed the rest of the city and the rest of the world that gay people are angry and on the move. And tonight we are here to show the world what we are creating out of that anger and that movement. A strong community of women and men working together to change our world.
>
> It seems highly appropriate to celebrate Harvey's birthday in this manner, a party on the street he loved. Castro Street was Harvey's home. Where he lived, worked, and organized.
>
> How many have moved here, to this new home from somewhere else?
>
> How many are not native San Franciscans?
>
> We have come here from all the old hometowns of America to reclaim our past and secure our future and replace lives of loneliness and despair with a place of joy and dignity and love.

The crowd cheered and Jones began introducing the acts. The Castro's own star, Sylvester, got the crowd dancing to his latest disco hits and before long, the street was filled with the bobbing heads of people dancing, slurping beers, and generally congratulating themselves on the unique homosexual ability to stage a stormy riot one night and then disco peacefully in the streets the next. The most disgruntled folks on hand were the plainclothes vice cops who could do nothing while the celebrants happily passed marijuana cigarettes among each other. When the late-night chill crept into the partying throng, the event's organizers assembled on stage to sing one last tribute to the man who would have been forty-nine years old that day. The words echoed by the storefronts Harvey had once organized into his business group, through the alleys where Harvey had walked precincts, and down the streets where he had cruised, demonstrated, and registered voters. Twenty thousand voices singing for a dead man who had spent most his life as an unsettled drifter with strange forebodings until six years before, when he had found a home on this obscure street in San Francisco. "Happy birthday, dear Harvey," they sang. "Happy birthday to you."

In New York City that night, several hundred gay pickets gathered in Sheridan Square, across the street from the location of the old Stonewall bar, where gays had first rioted a decade before. They knew nothing of the cheerful birthday party a continent away and were still outraged by the verdict. Some signs bore just one phrase: "We all live in San Francisco."

Epilogue

Attempts to investigate and prosecute those involved with either the gay rioting or the police brutality largely fizzled. The anti-gay backlash some activists feared also failed to materialize. With the 1979 municipal elections only months after the White Night Riots, most concern about the city's gay community focused solely on its political clout.

By the November elections, gays wielded unprecedented power. The surprisingly strong showing of a virtually unknown gay mayoral candidate—David Scott, Rick Stokes's successor on the Board of Permit Appeals—forced Mayor Feinstein into a runoff against conservative Supervisor Quentin Kopp. Feinstein promptly apologized for her "community standards" remarks, promised a gay police commissioner, lunched nearly every day in the Castro, and ultimately gained lopsided percentages in gay precincts to win her own term as mayor.

Other incumbents had an even tougher year. Voters sent District Attorney Joe Freitas into political exile, handing him a three-to-one margin of defeat and electing novice politician Arlo Smith, the mild-mannered attorney general's staffer who had once stuffed envelopes in Castro Camera for Harvey Milk. All incumbent supervisors in contested races that year also lost their bids for reelection except one—Harry Britt.

Those 1979 supervisorial elections, however, were the last to be held under the district elections system that politicians like George Moscone and Harvey Milk had worked so hard to enact. In a special election in the summer of 1980, voters narrowly repealed district elections and reinstated citywide, at-large elections of supervisors. An attempt to repeal this repeal failed three months later. Though the new citywide board had roughly the same liberal-conservative balance of the district body, liberals saw the city rapidly shift away from the neighborhood-oriented course charted during the height of the Milk-Moscone era. In the same election, voters also rejected a proposal to raise supervisor's salaries.

340

Once mayor in her own right, Feinstein nudged the city back toward the pro-business polices of the pre-Moscone years. Feinstein no longer peopled planning boards with troublesome environmentalists who worried about the Manhattanization of San Francisco. Developers and business interests once again had a friendly ear in City Hall. As for Feinstein's pet city agency, the police, one of the mayor's first moves after her election was to announce the appointment of a new police chief, Cornelius Murphy, a stolid Irish Catholic from the ranks. Murphy decreed that police cars were no longer to be painted powder blue, they were again to be macho black-and-whites; and this made the men of the San Francisco Police Department happy with their leadership once again. Murphy, however, swore to keep Gain's progressive policies toward gays. One of his first appearances as chief-designate came at a fundraiser for a gay police recruitment drive. By 1980, one in seven new police recruits were either lesbians or gay men. Feinstein appointed her old friend Jo Daly, a former Alice president, to the Police Commission, fulfilling a gay demand that dated back to Jose's first campaign for supervisor. Chief Charles Gain did not leave without his own burst of glory. In one of his last appearances at a major gay function, he told a roaring crowd that he fully expected to see the day when San Francisco had both a gay mayor and police chief. Saying this, Gain retired and moved to a small town near Fresno, where he bought and managed a mobile home park.

By the opening of the 1980s, San Francisco had spent a half decade in turmoil unmatched by any other American city of that period: Moscone's 1975 election coup, the 1976 enactment of district elections, the attempts to repeal district elections and recall the city's major officials in 1977, the first district-elected board, the gay unrest of Orange Tuesday and the midnight marches, Peoples Temple, the assassinations, the riots, and the ultimate reinstatement of citywide elections. All this had wearied both conservative and liberal activists, and few responsible politicos were eager to push any new initiatives as the decade opened. Wounds from the long battles may not have completely healed in subsequent years, but neither did they fester. The city remained bound together by the curious sentiment that San Franciscans of all stripes share—that San Francisco is somehow a special city. Still, when reformers sometimes talked late into the night and wearied of the gossip about contemporary politicians, their conversations often drifted into memories of the Milk-Moscone years which, in reflection, seemed a bright, magic epoch which was not likely to happen again soon.

The loss of so many liberal advances made during the brief Moscone-Milk era kept some of the more suspicious bandying conspiracy theories about the assassinations. Many of Harvey's closest friends remained convinced that George and Harvey had been the victims of a byzantine conspiracy, plotted by those who had millions of dollars to gain by taking city government out of the hands of neighborhood-oriented liberals and returning power to the more steady moderation of a Dianne Feinstein. Signs at gay demonstrations sometimes carried such mottos as, "I'd like to see Joe Freitas' Swiss bank account." *Examiner* reporter Russ Cone, a veteran of a quarter century on the City Hall beat, took a more prosaic approach and wrote a long story tying the killings to conservative policemen's fears about Moscone's proposed settlement for the police discrimination suit. Killing Moscone effectively ended chances for the mayor's pro-minority settlement, Cone wrote, while "taking out the ever-present irritant, Milk, was insurance that six votes for the Moscone settlement would not exist" on the board. The *Examiner* declined to run the account, so it was published in a Los Angeles-based magazine. Nor was any major publication interested in Warren Hinckle's hypothesizing about the role of political chicanery and homophobia in Dan White's prosecution. Hinckle had to make a living and he soon found other subjects to fuel his ongoing fires of moral outrage. Since the San Francisco media assiduously avoided analyses of the troublesome implications of the killings and trial, the entire Dan White affair soon slipped into an uneasy niche in the public memory. Occasionally, however, spray-painted across a barren wall in the Castro, appeared the question: "Who killed Harvey Milk?"

The disparate currents of history and personal aspirations drove the enemies and lovers, friends and cronies of Harvey Milk toward their own destinies:

Dan White was sentenced to the maximum imprisonment for his dual convictions of voluntary manslaughter—seven years, eight months. Upon entering state prison, White was examined by psychiatrists who decided against prescribing therapy since, they said, Dan White had "no apparent signs" of mental disorder. White's expected parole date: January 1984. He reportedly plans to move to Ireland after his release.

State Senator John Briggs returned to Sacramento and, though any plans for statewide office were shattered in the Prop 6 landslide, he easily won reelection in 1980. A year later, however, he stunned the capitol by announcing that he was going to resign and become a lobbyist. "Have you heard of job burnout? I've done it," he told reporters. "You aren't going to have me to kick around anymore." The *San Jose Mercury* best summed up the reaction of both conservatives and liberals to the impromptu resignation with a two-word editorial that simply said, "Good riddance."

David Goodstein largely withdrew from gay politics after Milk's death and devoted most of his energy to organizing his own idiosyncratic marriage of the gay and human potential movements. Patterned after Werner Erhard's est, Goodstein's Advocate Experience gave him the opportunity to be guru to thousands, even after his failure at becoming a political leader. Jim Foster, meanwhile, aligned himself with Harry Britt to become an important fund raiser in Britt's future campaigns. The role he had fashioned in national politics at the 1972 Democratic Convention helped bolster his party status to the point that he was northern California chairman for Teddy Kennedy's 1980 presidential campaign. Rick Stokes returned to his law practice, shunning most involvement in local gay politics.

Robert Milk turned up in San Francisco on the first anniversary of his brother's assassination. He gave reporters copies of a poem he had written bemoaning his brother's death. Later, however, he took to asking writers to pay him for interviews he granted about his early memories of his slain brother.

Joe Campbell determined to have a career as he entered his midforties, and joined a surveyor's crew in Marin County. After Harvey's death, Jack McKinley became a born-again gay liberationist, drunkenly ranting about gay politics as he moved from cheap hotel to cheap hotel. One friend says he wrote his family to announce his homosexuality; an older brother sent him a religious tract explaining the finer details of damnation awaiting sodomites. On February 14, 1980—St. Valentine's Day—McKinley was drunk, playing a tape of one of Harvey's political speeches, and threatening to jump off a ledge of Tom O'Horgan's loft apartment on Broadway. Several minutes later, somebody noticed McKinley was no longer on the ledge. His broken and bloody body was found on the street, eight stories below. He was thirty-three years old, the same age that Harvey had been when the pair first fell in love in 1963. A portion of his ashes were scattered into the Hudson River off Manhattan; by his request, the rest were cast off the Golden Gate

Bridge, a few miles from where Harvey's ashes had been scattered more than a year earlier.

Scott Smith fell into a grave depression after the killing of the man who had guided his personal and professional life since he was twenty-two. Since most media attention focused on the political heirs of Harvey Milk—who had long considered Scott to be little more than the camera store's clerk—Smith became increasingly embittered in the months after the assassination, complaining that he had never gotten due credit for propping up the business that gave Milk his political base. As executor of Harvey's estate, Scott was saddled with Milk's debts but none of the recognition. Friends hoped Smith's anxieties would lessen as time distanced him from Harvey's brutal end. But they didn't. Finally, the city's public health director, a longtime admirer of Harvey's, helped Scott find some counseling, and Smith began reconstructing his life, two years after the assassination.

Milk's last series of boyfriends fared better than his lovers. Billy Wiegardt became manager of a gay bar on Polk Street. Bob Tuttle moved to San Francisco and fell in love with a business executive from Sausalito. Doug Franks spent much of the year after the killings heeding Harvey's advice about opening a greater "sphere of love" with pluralistic nonmonogamous relationships. Within a few months, Doug was simultaneously dating three men and two women. As Harvey insisted, Doug was honest about his multifaceted romancing with each participant. As Milk hadn't predicted, however, this candor engendered disaster. The men turned out to be stuck more on the heterosexual models than the heterosexuals themselves, and soon split with Doug to seek a monogamous male mate. The women hung on longer but became disgruntled when the ménage narrowed to a threesome and both women left him. Franks went back to school to finish his graduate degree.

Frank Robinson toyed with writing a book about Milk but gave up on the idea and continued writing science fiction in his Castro area home. San Francisco never seemed the same to Tom Randol after Milk's killing, so he moved to New York City and built stage props for Tom O'Horgan's various theatrical ventures. Medora Payne left San Francisco to complete high school in England. Carl Carlson gained unwanted notoriety as the only person who had seen Dan White summon Harvey to his death. The resulting publicity over his ties to the gay leader cost Carlson his job as an airline pilot, and he launched plans to found the first gay charter airline. Dennis Peron continued to deal marijuana and continued to get arrested for it. Finally, in 1980, he ran for supervisor on a marijuana legalization platform and garnered an impressive tally of votes, though not enough to win. The 1976 Assembly race forever soured Michael Wong on the promise of running for office, so he stuck to working for issues instead of people in his continued political activity, championing a range of causes, from neighborhood issues to anti-nuclear energy work. The ballot described his occupation as "agricultural products distributor." John Ryckman met the unlikeliest fate of all Harvey's friends. After his lover died, he took to spending his spare time with an old friend who had recently lost her husband; they were married several months later and Ryckman frequently joked to friends that he wished Harvey could have come to the wedding to give him away to his bride.

Harvey's cohort from the Coors boycott, lifelong Castro denizen Allan Baird, lost a round of internecine Teamster politicking and returned to drive a truck for the *San Francisco Chronicle*. Within a few years of Harvey's death, he began to give up on the dream he and Milk had once discussed, about making Castro Street a model neighborhood gays and straights could peacefully share. Not many heterosexuals stuck around. By 1980, there weren't enough Catholic kids in the parish to justify Most Holy Redeemer's School, so it graduated its last class and closed down. The blustering expansion of the Castro business district had transformed the gay Oz into a homophile Fisherman's Wharf with bars and boutiques catering to gay tourists. The Castro became more tourist trap than small town. The Castro Clone became a caricature against which younger gays started revolting, just as the early Castro immigrants had revolted against the effete homosexuals of the 1960s. But few minds reared in rebellion anymore, about anything. The thousands who still came to the Castro from all over the world had their eyes set upon the smorgasbord of beautiful men, not on the panoply of injustices about which activists had once complained. Few on Castro Street talked of a new age, a better order, or a changed world. The dream of the Castro became a victim of its own success.

So it also went with Harvey's political legacy. The Harvey Milk Gay Democratic Club quickly grew into the largest Democratic organization in California and one of the most potent and sought-after groups in San Francisco. The club's leadership soon learned the art of power-brokering and compromise. They learned how to be responsible gay leaders, how to play ball with political bosses and machines. It became a matter of some debate whether a candidate who abrasively refused to play the game with powerful machines—a man like Harvey Milk— would be endorsed by the Harvey Milk Gay Democratic Club.

Virtually every aspect of the San Francisco gay community laid claim to some part of Harvey's legacy. Gay Jews used Harvey to eke out greater acceptance from the city's Jewish establishment, while the Gay Atheist League published a number of essays discussing Milk's atheism. Harry Britt was a socialist, so he frequently raised Harvey's memory to defend his socialist positions. Gay Democrats used Milk's status as a martyr to weasel concessions from the local Democratic party, while gay Republicans spent no small effort noting that the Democratic establishment had opposed Milk through most of his political career. Some of Harvey's closer allies found great convenience in the fact that dead leaders can be counted on to say the most quotable things at the most timely occasions. Brochures were frequently dressed up with stirring Harvey Milk quotes written long after the supervisor's demise.

Harvey's political cronies prospered, to be sure. Though Anne Kronenberg pulled back from gay politics, she was appointed to a good-paying job in the Feinstein administration. Harry Britt's gay militance and unbending leftist politics easily made him the city's most controversial politician, but he carved a solid constituency among the city's reformists and emerged as one of the top vote-getters in the citywide election of supervisors in November 1980. Cleve Jones quickly took Harvey's place as the most media-wise—and impish—gay politico, and earned a job as an aide to the California assembly speaker, the first openly gay legislative aide in the country. The appointment, by Assemblyman Agnos, spawned speculation that Jones might one day be the first machine-anointed candidate for the assembly seat Harvey had futilely sought. Jim Rivaldo and Dick Pabich teamed to form one of the more successful political consulting firms in the city, shoring up ties with some of the very establishment politicians who had so spurned Milk in his lifetime.

Harvey's successors proved adept at learning the skills of marketing candidates. By the 1980 election, for example, they helped engineer the citywide election of Harry Britt's roommate-turned-aide to the community college board, implementing a strategy much like Rick Stokes's campaign for the same post eight years earlier. The campaign relied on heavyweight political endorsements; the candidate's brochures did not mention his homosexuality or discuss complicated issues of hope or teenagers in Altoona, Pennsylvania. As Harvey had once said of Rick Stokes's campaign style, "You can either buy name recognition or you can earn it"; within two years of Harvey's death, his political disciples had learned the art of buying it.

For their part, Harvey's protégés argued that while Milk played the politics of the outsider, they were faced with the even tougher task of playing the politics of power. If some carped that Harvey's inner circle did not remain faithful to their mentor's populism, few argued that the successes Milk forged remained. Harvey's political heirs shored up gay power in dozens of subtle ways not apparent on the street level. Every political endorsing organization in San Francisco knew that at least one acknowledged gay candidate should appear on any slate, right down to the conservative Chamber of Commerce which in 1980 endorsed a gay Republican for supervisor. The sight of mustachioed young men in tight straight-legged jeans became increasingly common in City Hall too, as the civil service bureaucracy started assimilating gays into its ranks, as it had drawn in so many other minority groups before. If the spirit seemed absent from the San Francisco gay politics of the 1980s, it was because the spirit that grew in the Castro Street gay community had dimmed as well. The wave of history that crested so dramatically in the late 1970s could not sustain itself indefinitely; like all waves, it fell back.

Some did occasionally remember that a glimmer of idealism had once lit up the street. Perhaps that nearly forgotten hope for a changed world helped to fuel a certain seething, undefined anger which still lurked like an inarticulate memory in the hearts of Castro Street gays, years after the drama of Harvey Milk had passed into history. In the end, however, San Francisco had a Harvey Milk Library, a Harvey Milk Arts Center, a Harvey Milk Democratic Club and a Harvey Milk Plaza on the corner where Milk had announced his first candidacy for the Board of Supervisors in 1973; but on Castro Street, businessmen were largely concerned with business, politicians were largely concerned with candidates, and homosexuals were largely concerned with sex. The old slogans were already sounding hollow the night at City Hall when police cars were exploding into fireballs and a lesbian leader shouted "Harvey Milk lives," and somebody yelled back, "Harvey Milk's not alive. He's dead, you fool."

If Harvey Milk lived on Castro Street, it was mainly in the memories of the lives he touched. Even if he did not move society the great length toward final understanding and acceptance of homosexuality, he did demonstrate one significant point: He had spent the last years of his life clinging tenaciously to the naive notion that one person could change the world. Because he so dumbly believed he could change the world, Harvey Milk did.

To a fledgling national movement still starved for legends, Harvey Milk's legacy was less ambiguous. In October 1979, over one hundred thousand marched on Washington as Harvey had wanted, and thousands of them carried placards and portraits invoking the slain leader's memory. Harvey Milk had clearly become the first martyr of the young gay movement. These people, of course, knew little about the particulars of Milk's life, only what they had heard about the Harvey Milk of legend, a story that could be summarized in a few sentences: Milk was a gay leader who talked about hope, struggled for his political successes against all odds, and won. Since he was strong and found victory, he had to be killed, because, most gays knew, society does not want homosexuals to be strong and succeed. That Harvey Milk's killer should be an all-American boy and ex-cop added poetic embellishment to this tale, for the thousands who had come to revere Harvey Milk as a martyr knew all too well that hating homosexuals is a solid part of the all-American ethos. Since the killer was heterosexual and the victim was homosexual, it only made sense to gays that the killer found succor in the criminal justice system; heterosexuals had long been free to violate homosexuals with impunity. The revenge of the White Night Riots provided a measure of success for the legend's ending as well—for the politically committed, revenge is better than resignation.

The entire story of the life and death of Harvey Milk rang so true to the experiences of gays throughout the country because it already seemed a part of the homosexual collective unconscious, even before it happened; that it happened to one man in San Francisco was a mere formality. It had been happening for a long time. This is why a politician who had lost three out of four of his elections and served only forty-six weeks in public office ultimately became a legend. His story already existed in the lives and minds of millions of gays; had it not been Harvey Milk in San Francisco, the legend would have settled on someone else, in another city, at another time. Harvey's sense of staging merely ensured that his legend would also prove good theater. So for years after Harvey's death, when dull moments fell over a gay demonstration and the old slogans felt thin, someone could shout, "Harvey Milk lives," and it would not be hollow rhetoric; Harvey Milk did live, as a metaphor for the homosexual experience in America.

Appendix
I. A Populist Looks at the City

On September 10, 1973, in the midst of his first political campaign, Harvey Milk laid out his basic populist platform at the endorsement session of the San Francisco local of the Longshoremen and Warehousemen's Union. The basic themes of this speech remained the core of Milk's four campaigns and his year in office. (The speech manuscript was provided by the Estate of Harvey Milk.)

A city, any city, can take one of several approaches to the future; whichever approach it takes not only affects the citizens of today but also greatly affects the children of tomorrow—the citizens of tomorrow.

San Francisco, like any other major city, has that choice, and before we get too far down any route we must be sure that it is the route we really want to travel. The present leadership seems to have taken the money route: bigness and wealth. They would like to be remembered as making San Francisco a major money center: a big bankbook. The trouble with this approach is that there is no way whatsoever that this city can ever gain anywhere near the wealth that the New Yorks, the Chicagos have. No matter how much we try we will always be somewhere down on the list. If someone ever wants to add up the bank accounts of our cities, New York is always going to come out on top.

Or our city could take the route of becoming the seat of learning. But, there is no way we will be able to surpass the Bostons . . . there are just too many great universities throughout the land. We can never become *the* seat of learning.

Then there is the route that, for some reason or other, no major city has ever tried. That is the route that has little room for political pay-offs, deals . . . that is the route that leaves little in the way of power politics . . . that is the route of making a city an exciting place for *all* to live: not just an exciting place for a few to live! A place for the individual and individual rights. There is no political gain in this nonmonied route and, thus you do not find people with high political ambitions leading this way. There are no statistics to quote . . . no miles of highways built to brag about, no statistics of giant buildings built under your administration. What you have instead is a city that breathes, one that is alive, where the people are more important than highways.

How does this route stand with our present leadership? They are more impressed with statistics than with life. I want a city that is not trying to become a great bankbook.

San Francisco can start right now to become number one. We can set examples so that others will follow. We can start overnight. We don't have to wait for budgets to be passed, surveys to be made, political wheelings and dealings . . . for it takes no money . . . it takes no compromising to give the people their rights . . . it takes no money to respect the individual. It takes no political deal to give people freedom. It takes no survey to remove repression.

We can start immediately by rereading the Constitution of the United States. We can start immediately by no longer trying to legislate morality. The Constitution calls for the separation of the church and the state . . . and, yet we find that our legislators end up spending millions of dollars and years of their lives legislating morality. . . . That money, that time, that energy should be spent in making the city a place for all people. When our Supervisors are more concerned about tearing down a freeway than dental care for the elderly or child-care centers, when our Supervisors are more concerned about the Muni drivers' benefits and not the least bit concerned about improving service for the riders, when our Supervisors are more concerned about building a multi-million dollar tourist-and-convention center instead of putting that money into an "Operation Bootstrap" to teach the unemployed of San Francisco skills so that there will not be the need to rely on the tourist for jobs, when our Supervisors realize that the best way to attract visitors is not through convention centers but through giving the people of San Francisco real job opportunity so that we can beat poverty, when such a consciousness takes place, when such a human sense of priorities gains hold, we will indeed be number one.

We can start immediately by giving the people of San Francisco and not the people who live in Marin first priorities. . . . We can start immediately by giving the people who live here and not the tourists first priorities. When we hire someone from outside the city to work for the city that person takes our tax money and spends it in Marin. . . . He can not be loyal towards the city for he does not live here. The rent he pays, the food he buys, the products for his home . . . all that is purchased with San Francisco tax money from business outside the city. He does not understand the problems of the city. . . . How could he? . . . He does not live here at nighttime. To make the city a better place . . . to lower the city's unemployment rate, all city employees must be residents of the city. The policeman who works in the city during the day is not involved in the city's nighttime problems. Right now San Francisco has seen an increase in the police force, an increase in the police budget, an increase in stolen cars, an increase in burglary and a decrease in our population! Why? Two reasons: 1. Many police do not live in the city. . . . I never want to hear what I heard last week . . . a police officer in the downtown sector made this comment to me: "I wouldn't live in this city if you paid me!" . . . We do pay him! The second reason is that half of the police budget and effort is wasted on trying to enforce victimless crime laws. . . . *That is like trying to bring back Prohibition! All prohibition did was to create the greatest crime waves and syndicates this country has ever had . . . and it created a lot of murder.* AND ALL IN THE NAME OF MORALITY!! Can't we learn? It was the moralists of the 20s that created Crime Inc., and now these same moralistic types are once again, in their blindness, trying to force their morality on others, creating organized crime . . . can they not learn? Do they ever read history? Because of the failure of their family, of their church, they are attempting to make the police force into ministers, while crimes against victims increases. . . . This false morality is against the Constitution. If they do not like the Constitution, let them amend it. Let them scrap the Declaration of Independence and in the meantime let them go back to God with their morality and become ministers . . . true ministers. *Instead of spending time trying to get the death penalty passed let them reread the Ten Commandments.* Let them teach the Commandment: Thou Shall Not Kill. I know of no Commandment that says Thous Shall Not Smoke Marijuana. I know of no Commandment that says: Thou Shall Not Read Dirty Books. I know of no Commandment that says: Thou Shall Not Walk Around Naked. Why are they such moralists when it comes to man-made Commandments and such anti-moralists when it comes to God's Commandments?

Let me have my tax money go for my protection and not for my prosecution. Let my tax money go for the protection of me. Protect my home, protect my streets, protect my car, protect my life, protect my property. Let my minister worry about my playing bar dice. Let my minister and not some policeman worry about my moral life. Worry about gun control and not marijuana control. . . . worry about dental care for the elderly and not about hookers . . . worry about child-care centers and not about what books I might want to read . . . worry about becoming a human being and not about how you can prevent others from enjoying their lives because of your own inabilities to adjust to life.

II. A City of Neighborhoods

Though California Lieutenant Governor Mervyn Dymally was the keynote speaker at the fundraising dinner the day after Harvey Milk's inauguration, the new supervisor stole the show with this speech outlining his vision of San Francisco's future. (The speech manuscript was provided by the Estate of Harvey Milk.)

In 1977, a large seaport city on the East Coast voted to take away the rights of some people. Later that year, another large seaport city, this time on the West Coast, voted into office one of those same people. That same West Coast city once had a frightening nightmare of the future—and the next morning promptly voted against Richard Nixon. Soon a nation followed the lead. That same city voted to decriminalize marijuana and now sees states like Mississippi follow its lead.

That city, our city—San Francisco—has now broken the last major dam of prejudice in this country and in doing so has done what no other city has done before.

How does one thank a city? I hope, with all my heart, that I can do the job that I have been charged to do and do it so well that the questions raised by my election will be buried once and forever—and that other cities will once again follow San Francisco's lead.

I understand very well that my election was not alone a question of my gayness, but a question of what I represent. In a very real sense, Harvey Milk represented the spirit of the neighborhoods of San Francisco. For the past few years, my fight to make the voice of the neighborhoods of this city be heard was not unlike the fight to make the voice of the cities themselves be heard.

Let's make no mistake about this: The American Dream starts with the neighborhoods. If we wish to rebuild our cities, we must first rebuild our neighborhoods. And to do that, we must understand that the quality of life is more important than the standard of living. To sit on the front steps—whether it's a veranda in a small town or a concrete stoop in a big city—and talk to our neighborhoods is infinitely more important than to huddle on the living-room lounger and watch a make-believe world in not-quite living color.

Progress is not America's only business—and certainly not its most important. Isn't it strange that as technology advances, the quality of life so frequently declines? Oh, washing the dishes is easier. Dinner itself is easier—just heat and serve, though it might be more nourishing if we ate the ads and threw the food away. And we no longer fear spots on our glassware when guests come over. But then, of course, the guests don't come, because our friends are too afraid to come to our house and it's not safe to go to theirs.

And I hardly need to tell you that in that 19- or 24-inch view of the world, cleanliness has long since eclipsed godliness. Soon we'll all smell, look, and actually be laboratory clean, as sterile on the inside as on the out. The perfect consumer, surrounded by the latest appliances. The perfect audience, with a ringside seat to almost any event in the world, without smell, without taste, without feel—alone and unhappy in the vast wasteland of our living rooms. I think that what we actually need, of course, is a little more dirt on the seat of our pants as we sit on the front stoop and talk to our neighbors once again, enjoying the type of summer day where the smell of garlic travels slightly faster than the speed of sound.

There's something missing in the sanitized life we lead. Something that our leaders in Washington can never supply by simple edict, something that the commercials on television never advertise because nobody's yet found a way to bottle it or box it or can it. What's missing is the touch, the warmth, the meaning of life. A four-color spread in *Time* is no substitute for it. Neither is a 30-second commercial or a reassuring Washington press conference.

I spent many years on both Wall Street and Montgomery Street and I fully understand the debt and responsibility that major corporations owe their shareholders. I also fully understand the urban battlefields of New York and Cleveland and Detroit. I see the faces of the unemployed—and the unemployable—of this city. I've seen the faces in Chinatown, Hunters Point, the Mission, and the Tenderloin . . . and I don't like what I see.

Oddly, I'm also reminded of the most successful slogan a business ever coined: The customer is always right.

What's been forgotten is that those people of the Tenderloin and Hunters Point, those people in the streets, are the customers, certainly potential ones, and they must be treated as such. Government cannot ignore them and neither can business ignore them. What sense is there in making products if the would-be customer can't afford them? It's not alone a question of price, it's a question of ability to pay. For a man with no money, 99¢ reduced from $1.29 is still a fortune.

American business must realize that while the shareholders always come first, the care and feeding of their customer is a close second. They have a debt and a responsibility to that customer and the city in which he or she lives, the cities in which the business itself lives or in which it grew up. To throw away a senior citizen after they've nursed you through childhood is wrong. To treat a city as disposable once your business has prospered is equally wrong and even more short-sighted.

Unfortunately for those who would like to flee them, the problems of the cities don't stop at the city limits. There are no moats around our cities that keep the problems in. What happens in New York or San Francisco will eventually happen in San Jose. It's just a matter of time. And like the flu, it usually gets worse the further it travels. Our cities must not be abandoned. They're worth fighting for, not just by those who live in them, but by industry, commerce, unions, everyone. Not alone because they represent the past, but because they also represent the future. Your children will live there and hopefully, so will your grandchildren. For all practical purposes, the eastern corridor from Boston to Newark will be one vast strip city. So will the area from Milwaukee to Gary, Indiana. In California, it will be that fertile crescent of asphalt and neon that stretches from Santa Barbara to San Diego. Will urban blight travel the arteries of the freeways? Of course it will—unless we stop it.

So the challenge of the 80s will be to awaken the consciousness of industry and commerce to the part they must play in saving the cities which nourished them. Every company realizes it must constantly invest in its own physical plant to remain healthy and grow. Well, the cities are a part of that plant and the people who live in them are part of the cities. They're all connected; What affects one affects the others.

In short, the cheapest place to manufacture a product may not be the cheapest at all if it results in throwing your customers out of work. There's no sense in making television sets in Japan if the customers in the United States haven't the money to buy them. Industry must actively seek to employ those without work, to train those who have no skills. "Labor intensive" is not a dirty word, not every job is done better by machine. It has become the job of industry not only to create the product, but also to create the customer.

Costly? I don't think so. It's far less expensive than the problem of fully loaded docks and no customers. And there are additional returns: lower rates of crime, smaller welfare loads. And having your friends and neighbors sitting on that well-polished front stoop.

Industry and business has made our country the greatest military and economic power in the world. Now I think it's time to look at our future with a realistic eye. I don't think the American Dream necessarily includes two cars in every garage and a disposal in every kitchen. What it does need is an educational system with incentives. To spend twelve years at school—almost a fifth of your life—without a job at the other end is meaningless. Every ghetto child has the right to ask: Education for what?

It's time for our system to mature, to face the problems it's created, to take responsibility for the problems it's ignored. Criminals aren't born, they're made—made by a socioeconomic system that has turned crime into a production line phenomenon. "In 1977, there were so many burglaries per second, so many murders per hour. . . ."

It also sounds simplistic to constantly say that jobs are part of the answer. But there are things to consider. As huge as they are, corporations frequently have more flexibility than the people who work for them. A company headquarters can leave town, a factory can literally pull up stakes and move someplace else. But the workers they leave behind frequently can't. The scar that's left isn't just the empty office building or the now-vacant lot; it's the worker who can no longer provide for his family, the teenager who suddenly awakens from the American Dream to find that all the jobs have gone south for the duration.

It was an expensive move the company made. You see the empty buildings but you don't see the hopelessness, the loss of pride, the anger. You've done a lot more than just lose a customer. And when I say losing a customer, I don't mean just your customer. There are other businesses and when they move or shift, the people they leave behind are also your customers, just like yours are theirs.

I think, perhaps, many companies feel that helping the city is a form of charity. I think it more accurate to consider it a part of the cost of doing business, that it should be entered on the books as amortizing the future. I would like to see business and industry consider it as such, because I think there's more creativity, more competence perhaps, in business than there is in government. I think that business could turn the south of Market Area not only into an industrial park but a neighborhood as well. To coin a pun, too many of our cities have a complex, in fact, too many complexes. We don't need another concrete jungle that dies the moment you turn off the lights in the evening. What we need is a neighborhood where people can walk to work, raise their kids, enjoy life.

That simple.

And now, I suspect, some of the business people in this room are figuring—perhaps rightly—that they've heard all this before. Why is it always business that's supposed to save the city? Why us? Why isn't somebody else doing something? How about you, for a change, Harvey? What the hell are the rest of the people in this room doing? And you've got a point. But I merely suggest that business must help, that we must open up a dialogue that involves all of us. A businessperson's decisions aren't his alone, for the simple reason that they affect far more people than just himself. And we have to consider those other people. Those are the ghosts that sit on your board of directors and they must be respected.

And now I think it's time that everybody faced reality. Real reality. So for the next few minutes, it's going to be slightly down and dirty.

A small item in the newspaper the other day indicated what the future might be like. Mayor Koch of New York turned his back on the elegance of Gracie Mansion and opted for the comforts of his three-room apartment—and I'll refrain from any comparison to our good Governor. Mr. Koch chose his three-room apartment because he likes it. Nothing more complicated than that. He likes it.

And believe it or not, that's the wave of the future. The cities will be saved. The cities will be governed. But they won't be run from three thousand miles away in Washington, they won't be run from the statehouse, and most of all, they won't be run by the carpetbaggers who have fled to the suburbs. You can't run a city by people who don't live there, any more than you can have an effective police force made up of people who don't live there. In either case, what you've got is an occupying army.

The cities will be saved. The cities will be run. They'll be saved and they'll be run by the people who live in them, by the people who *like* to live in them. You can see it in parts of Manhattan, you can see it along Armitage Street and on the far North Side of Chicago, and you can certainly see it in San Francisco.

Who's done the most for housing in our city? The federal government? The state? Who's actually renovating this city? Who's buying the houses and using their own sweat and funds to restore them and make them liveable? And just how many homes do you think that includes by now? How many thousands? The people who are doing this are doing it out of love for the city. They're renovating not only the physical plant, they're renovating the spirit of the city as well.

The cities will not be saved by the people who feel condemned to live in them, who can hardly wait to move to Marin or San Jose —or Evanston or Westchester. The cities will be saved by the people who like it here. The people who prefer the neighborhood stores to the shopping mall, who go to the plays and eat in the restaurants and go to the discos and worry about the education the kids are getting even if they have no kids of their own.

That's not just the city of the future; it's the city of today. It means new directions, new alliances, new solutions for ancient problems. The typical American family with two cars and 2.2 kids doesn't live here anymore. It hasn't for years. The demographics are different now and we all know it. The city is a city of singles and young marrieds, the city of the retired and the poor, a city of many colors who speak in many tongues.

The city will run itself, it will create its own solutions. District elections was not the end. It was just the beginning. We'll solve our problems—with your help, if we can, without it if we must. We need your help. I don't deny that. But you also need us. We're your customers. We're your future.

I'm riding into that future and frankly I don't know if I'm wearing the fabled helm of Mambrino on my head or if I'm wearing a barber's basin. I guess we wear what we want to wear and we fight what we want to fight. Maybe I see dragons where there are only windmills. But something tells me the dragons are for real and if I shatter a lance or two on a whirling blade, maybe I'll catch a dragon in the bargain.

So I'm asking you to take a chance and ride with me against the windmills—and against the dragons, too. To make the quality of life in San Francisco what it should be, to help our city set an example, to set the style, to show the rest of the country what a city can really be. To prove that Miami's vote was a step backwards and that San Francisco's was two steps forward.

Yesterday, my esteemed colleague on the Board said we cannot live on hope alone. I know that, but I strongly feel the important thing is not that we cannot live on hope alone, but that life is not worth living without it. If the story of Don Quixote means anything, it means that the spirit of life is just as important as its substance. What others may see as a barber's basin, you and I know is that glittering, legendary helmet.

III. The Hope Speech

The following address represents the quintessential stump speech Milk
used as he traveled around both California and the nation as the country's first openly gay city official. This particular speech—the keynote
address at a San Diego dinner of the gay caucus of the California
Democratic Council on March 10, 1978—is perhaps the best example
of Milk's extemporaneous oration included here, since it is not taken
from Milk's prepared notes (like the other speeches in this appendix)
but from an actual tape recording of the event. The standard opening
joke, Milk's characteristic run-on sentences, and his occasional non
sequiturs, therefore, remain intact. The most powerful section of the
speech comes in the final minutes when Milk returned to the theme he
had honed through his 1977 campaign and his year in office—hope.
Milk aides dubbed this routine pitch "The Hope Speech" and it became
the supervisor's political trademark. (The tape was provided by Elmer
Wilhelm, past president of the Minuteman—now the Stonewall—Democratic Club of San Francisco.)

My name is Harvey Milk and I'm here to recruit you.

I've been saving this one for years. It's a political joke. I can't
help it—I've got to tell it. I've never been able to talk to this many
political people before, so if I tell you nothing else you may be able
to go home laughing a bit.

This ocean liner was going across the ocean and it sank. And
there was one little piece of wood floating and three people swam to
it and they realized only one person could hold on to it. So they had
a little debate about which was the person. It so happened the three
people were the Pope, the President, and Mayor Daley. The Pope said
he was titular head of one of the great religions of the world and he
was spiritual adviser to many, many millions and he went on and
pontificated and they thought it was a good argument. Then the
President said he was leader of the largest and most powerful nation
of the world. What takes place in this country affects the whole world

and they thought that was a good argument. And Mayor Daley said he was mayor of the backbone of the United States and what took place in Chicago affected the world, and what took place in the archdiocese of Chicago affected Catholicism. And they thought that was a good argument. So they did it the democratic way and voted. And Daley won, seven to two.

About six months ago, Anita Bryant in her speaking to God said that the drought in California was because of the gay people. On November 9, the day after I got elected, it started to rain. On the day I got sworn in, we walked to City Hall and it was kinda nice, and as soon as I said the word "I do," it started to rain again. It's been raining since then and the people of San Francisco figure the only way to stop it is to do a recall petition. That's a local joke.

So much for that. Why are we here? Why are gay people here? And what's happening? What's happening to me is the antithesis of what you read about in the papers and what you hear about on the radio. You hear about and read about this movement to the right. That we must band together and fight back this movement to the right. And I'm here to go ahead and say that what you hear and read is what they want you to think because it's not happening. The major media in this country has talked about the movement to the right so much that they've got even us thinking that way. Because they want the legislators to think that there is indeed a movement to the right and that the Congress and the legislators and the city councils will start to move to the right the way the major media want them. So they keep on talking about this move to the right.

So let's look at 1977 and see if there was indeed a move to the right. In 1977, gay people had their rights taken away from them in Miami. But you must remember that in the week before Miami and the week after that, the word homosexual or gay appeared in every single newspaper in this nation in articles both pro and con. In every radio station, in every TV station and every household. For the first time in the history of the world, everybody was talking about it, good or bad. Unless you have dialogue, unless you open the walls of dialogue, you can never reach to change people's opinion. In those two weeks, more good and bad, but *more* about the word homosexual and gay was written than probably in the history of mankind. Once you have dialogue starting, you know you can break down the prejudice. In 1977 we saw a dialogue start. In 1977, we saw a gay person elected in San Francisco. In 1977 we saw the state of Mississippi decriminalize marijuana. In 1977, we saw the convention of conventions in Houston. And I want to know where the movement to the right is happening.

What that is is a record of what happened last year. What we must do is make sure that 1978 continues the movement that is really happening that the media don't want you to know about, that is the movement to the left. It's up to CDC to put the pressures on Sacramento—not to just bring flowers to Sacramento—but to break down the walls and the barriers so the movement to the left continues and progress continues in the nation. We have before us coming up several issues we must speak out on. Probably the most important issue outside the Briggs—which we will come to—but we do know what will take place this June. We know there's an issue on the ballot called Jarvis-Gann. We hear the taxpayers talk about it on both sides. But what you don't hear is that it's probably the most racist issue on the ballot in a long time. In the city and county of San Francisco, if it passes and we indeed have to lay off people, who will they be? The last in, not the first in, and who are the last in but the minorities? Jarvis-Gann is a racist issue. We must address that issue. We must not talk away from it. We must not allow them to talk about the money it's going to save, because look at who's going to save the money and who's going to get hurt.

We also have another issue that we've started in some of the north counties and I hope in some of the south counties it continues. In San Francisco elections we're asking—at least we hope to ask—that the U.S. government put pressure on the closing of the South African consulate. That must happen. There is a major difference between an embassy in Washington which is a diplomatic bureau, and a consulate in major cities. A consulate is there for one reason only —to promote business, economic gains, tourism, investment. And every time you have business going to South Africa, you're promoting a regime that's offensive.

In the city of San Francisco, if everyone of 51 percent of that city were to go to South Africa, they would be treated as second-class citizens. That is an offense to the people of San Francisco and I hope all my colleagues up there will take every step we can to close down that consulate and hope that people in other parts of the state follow us in that lead. The battles must be started some place and CDC is the greatest place to start the battles.

I know we are pressed for time so I'm going to cover just one more little point. That is to understand why it is important that gay people run for office and that gay people get elected. I know there are many people in this room who are running for central committee who are gay. I encourage you. There's a major reason why. If my non-gay friends and supporters in this room understand it, they'll probably understand why I've run so often before I finally made it. Y'see right now, there's a controversy going on in this convention about the governor. Is he speaking out enough? Is he strong enough for gay rights? And there is a controversy and for us to say it is not would be foolish. Some people are satisfied and some people are not.

You see there is a major difference—and it remains a vital difference—between a friend and a gay person, a friend in office and a gay person in office. Gay people have been slandered nationwide. We've been tarred and we've been brushed with the picture of pornography. In Dade County, we were accused of child molestation. It's not enough anymore just to have friends represent us. No matter how good that friend may be.

The black community made up its mind to that a long time ago. That the myths against blacks can only be dispelled by electing black leaders, so the black community could be judged by the leaders and not by the myths or black criminals. The Spanish community must not be judged by Latin criminals or myths. The Asian community must not be judged by Asian criminals or myths. The Italian community should not be judged by the mafia, myths. And the time has come when the gay community must not be judged by our criminals and myths.

Like every other group, we must be judged by our leaders and by those who are themselves gay, those who are visible. For invisible, we remain in limbo—a myth, a person with no parents, no brothers, no sisters, no friends who are straight, no important positions in employment. A tenth of a nation supposedly composed of stereotypes and would-be seducers of children—and no offense meant to the stereotypes. But today, the black community is not judged by its friends, but by its black legislators and leaders. And we must give people the chance to judge us by our leaders and legislators. A gay person in office can set a tone, can command respect not only from the larger community, but from the young people in our own community who need both examples and hope.

The first gay people we elect must be strong. They must not be content to sit in the back of the bus. They must not be content to accept pablum. They must be above wheeling and dealing. They must be—for the good of all of us—independent, unbought. The anger and the frustrations that some of us feel is because we are misunderstood, and friends can't feel that anger and frustration. They can sense it in us, but they can't feel it. Because a friend has never gone through what is known as coming out. I will never forget what it was like coming out and having nobody to look up toward. I remember the lack of hope—and our friends can't fulfill that.

I can't forget the looks on faces of people who've lost hope. Be they gay, be they seniors, be they blacks looking for an almost-impossible job, be they Latins trying to explain their problems and aspirations in a tongue that's foreign to them. I personally will never forget that people are more important than buildings. I use the word "I" because I'm proud. I stand here tonight in front of my gay sisters, brothers and friends because I'm proud of you. I think it's time that we have many legislators who are gay and proud of that fact and do not have to remain in the closet. I think that a gay person, up-front, will not walk away from a responsibility and be afraid of being tossed out of office. After Dade County, I walked among the angry and the frustrated night after night and I looked at their faces. And in San Francisco, three days before Gay Pride Day, a person was killed just because he was gay. And that night, I walked among the sad and the frustrated at City Hall in San Francisco and later that night as they lit candles on Castro Street and stood in silence, reaching out for some symbolic thing that would give them hope. These were strong people, people whose faces I knew from the shop, the streets, meetings and people who I never saw before but I knew. They were strong, but even they needed hope.

And the young gay people in the Altoona, Pennsylvanias and the Richmond, Minnesotas who are coming out and hear Anita Bryant on television and her story. The only thing they have to look forward to is hope. And you have to give them hope. Hope for a better world, hope for a better tomorrow, hope for a better place to come to if the pressures at home are too great. Hope that all will be all right. Without hope, not only gays, but the blacks, the seniors, the handicapped, the us'es, the us'es will give up. And if you help elect to the central committee and other offices, more gay people, that gives a green light to all who feel disenfranchised, a green light to move forward. It means hope to a nation that has given up, because if a gay person makes it, the doors are open to everyone.

So if there is a message I have to give, it is that if I've found one overriding thing about my personal election, it's the fact that if a gay person can be elected, it's a green light. And you and you and you, you have to give people hope. Thank you very much.

IV. "That's What America Is."

The Gay Freedom Day Parade of June 25, 1978 was the signal event of the gay emergence in San Francisco during the late 1970s. Estimates of crowd size ranged from a quarter million to 375,000 as confident throngs marched against the imminent threat of the Briggs Initiative. No other single political event of the decade drew such a crowd in San Francisco, if not the nation. Though hounded by an onslaught of assassination threats, Harvey Milk saw the rally at City Hall as one of the most important opportunities to spell out his anger against the coalescing New Right which had so effectively begun to take up the anti-homosexual crusade. What follows is a rendering of the notes from which he read his speech. (Notes provided by the Estate of Harvey Milk.)

MY NAME IS HARVEY MILK—AND I WANT TO RECRUIT YOU. I WANT TO RECRUIT YOU FOR THE FIGHT TO PRESERVE YOUR DEMOCRACY FROM THE JOHN BRIGGS AND THE ANITA BRYANTS WHO ARE TRYING TO CONSTITUTIONALIZE BIGOTRY.

WE ARE NOT GOING TO ALLOW THAT TO HAPPEN. WE ARE NOT GOING TO SIT BACK IN SILENCE AS 300,000 OF OUR GAY BROTHERS AND SISTERS DID IN NAZI GERMANY. WE ARE NOT GOING TO ALLOW OUR RIGHTS TO BE TAKEN AWAY AND THEN MARCH WITH BOWED HEADS INTO THE GAS CHAMBERS. ON THIS ANNIVERSARY OF STONEWALL I ASK MY GAY SISTERS AND BROTHERS TO MAKE THE COMMITMENT TO FIGHT. FOR THEMSELVES. FOR THEIR FREEDOM. FOR THEIR COUNTRY.

HERE, IN SAN FRANCISCO, WE RECENTLY HELD AN ELECTION FOR A JUDGESHIP. AN ANTI-GAY SMEAR CAMPAIGN WAS WAGED AGAINST A PRESIDING JUDGE

BECAUSE SHE WAS SUPPORTED BY LESBIANS AND GAY MEN. HERE, IN SO-CALLED LIBERAL SAN FRANCISCO, AN ANTI-GAY SMEAR CAMPAIGN WAS WAGED BY SO-CALLED LIBERALS.

AND HERE, IN SO-CALLED LIBERAL SAN FRANCISCO, WE HAVE A COLUMNIST FOR THE SAN FRANCISCO EXAMINER, A COLUMNIST NAMED KEVIN STARR, WHO HAS PRINTED A NUMBER OF COLUMNS CONTAINING DISTORTIONS AND LIES ABOUT GAYS. HE'S GETTING AWAY WITH IT.

THESE ANTI-GAY SMEAR CAMPAIGNS, THESE ANTI-GAY COLUMNS, ARE LAYING THE GROUNDWORK FOR THE BRIGGS INITIATIVE. WE HAD BETTER BE PREPARED FOR IT.

IN THE EXAMINER, KEVIN STARR DEFAMES AND LIBELS GAYS. IN THE SAN FRANCISCO CHRONICLE, CHARLES McCABE WARNS US TO BE QUIET, THAT TALKING ABOUT GAY RIGHTS IS COUNTER-PRODUCTIVE. TO MR. McCABE I SAY THAT THE DAY HE STOPS TALKING ABOUT FREEDOM OF THE PRESS IS THE DAY HE NO LONGER HAS IT.

THE BLACKS DID NOT WIN THEIR RIGHTS BY SITTING QUIETLY IN THE BACK OF THE BUS. THEY GOT OFF!

GAY PEOPLE, WE WILL NOT WIN THEIR RIGHTS BY STAYING QUIETLY IN OUR CLOSETS. . . . WE ARE COMING OUT! WE ARE COMING OUT TO FIGHT THE LIES, THE MYTHS, THE DISTORTIONS! WE ARE COMING OUT TO TELL THE TRUTH ABOUT GAYS!

FOR I'M TIRED OF THE CONSPIRACY OF SILENCE.
I'M TIRED OF LISTENING TO THE ANITA BRYANTS TWIST THE LANGUAGE AND THE MEANING OF THE BIBLE TO FIT THEIR OWN DISTORTED OUTLOOK. BUT I'M EVEN MORE TIRED OF THE SILENCE FROM THE RELIGIOUS LEADERS OF THIS NATION WHO KNOW THAT SHE IS PLAYING FAST AND LOOSE WITH THE TRUE MEANING OF THE BIBLE. I'M TIRED OF THEIR SILENCE MORE THAN OF HER BIBLICAL GYMNASTICS!

AND I'M TIRED OF JOHN BRIGGS TALKING ABOUT FALSE ROLE MODELS. HE'S LYING IN HIS TEETH AND HE KNOWS IT. BUT I'M EVEN MORE TIRED OF THE SILENCE FROM EDUCATORS AND PSYCHOLOGISTS WHO KNOW THAT BRIGGS IS LYING AND YET SAY NOTHING. I'M TIRED OF THEIR SILENCE MORE THAN OF BRIGGS' LIES!

I'M TIRED OF THE SILENCE. SO I'M GOING TO TALK ABOUT IT. AND I WANT YOU TO TALK ABOUT IT.

GAY PEOPLE, WE ARE PAINTED AS CHILD MOLEST-ERS. I WANT TO TALK ABOUT THAT. I WANT TO TALK ABOUT THE MYTH OF CHILD MOLESTATIONS BY GAYS. I WANT TO TALK ABOUT THE FACT THAT IN THIS STATE SOME 95 PERCENT OF CHILD MOLESTATIONS ARE HETEROSEXUAL AND USUALLY THE PARENT. . . .

I WANT TO TALK ABOUT THE FACT THAT ALL CHILD ABANDONMENTS ARE HETEROSEXUAL.

I WANT TO TALK ABOUT THE FACT THAT ALL ABUSE OF CHILDREN IS BY THEIR HETEROSEXUAL PARENTS.

I WANT TO TALK ABOUT THE FACT THAT SOME 98 PERCENT OF THE SIX MILLION RAPES COMMITTED AN-NUALLY ARE HETEROSEXUAL.

I WANT TO TALK ABOUT THE FACT THAT ONE OUT OF EVERY THREE WOMEN WHO WILL BE MURDERED IN THIS STATE THIS YEAR WILL BE MURDERED BY THEIR HUSBANDS.

I WANT TO TALK ABOUT THE FACT THAT SOME 30 PERCENT OF ALL MARRIAGES CONTAIN DOMESTIC VIO-LENCE.

AND FINALLY, I WANT TO TELL THE JOHN BRIGGS AND THE ANITA BRYANTS THAT YOU TALK ABOUT THE MYTHS OF GAYS BUT TODAY I'M TALKING ABOUT THE FACTS OF HETEROSEXUAL VIOLENCE AND WHAT THE HELL ARE YOU GOING TO DO ABOUT THAT?????

CLEAN UP YOUR OWN HOUSE BEFORE YOU START
TELLING LIES ABOUT GAYS. DON'T DISTORT THE BIBLE
TO HIDE YOUR OWN SINS. DON'T CHANGE FACTS TO
LIES. DON'T LOOK FOR CHEAP POLITICAL ADVANTAGE
IN PLAYING UPON PEOPLE'S FEARS! JUDGING BY THE
LATEST POLLS, EVEN THE YOUTH CAN TELL YOU'RE
LYING!

[calmer] ANITA BRYANT, JOHN BRIGGS: YOUR UN-
WILLINGNESS TO TALK ABOUT YOUR OWN HOUSE,
YOUR DELIBERATE LIES AND DISTORTIONS, YOUR UN-
WILLINGNESS TO FACE THE TRUTH, CHILLS MY BLOOD
—IT REEKS OF MADNESS!

AND LIKE THE REST OF YOU, I'M TIRED OF OUR SO-
CALLED FRIENDS WHO TELL US THAT WE MUST SET
STANDARDS.

WHAT STANDARDS?

THE STANDARDS OF THE RAPISTS? THE WIFE BEAT-
ERS? THE CHILD ABUSERS? THE PEOPLE WHO ORDERED
THE BOMB TO BE BUILT? THE PEOPLE WHO ORDERED IT
TO BE DROPPED? THE PEOPLE WHO PULLED THE TRIG-
GER? THE PEOPLE WHO GAVE US VIETNAM? THE PEOPLE
WHO BUILT THE GAS CHAMBERS? THE PEOPLE WHO
BUILT THE CONCENTRATION CAMPS——RIGHT HERE,
IN CALIFORNIA, AND THEN HERDED ALL THE JAPA-
NESE-AMERICANS INTO THEM DURING WORLD WAR II.
. . . THE JEW BAITERS? THE NIGGER KNOCKERS? THE
CORPORATE THIEFS? THE NIXONS? THE HITLERS?

WHAT STANDARDS DO YOU WANT US TO SET?
CLEAN UP YOUR ACT, CLEAN UP YOUR VIOLENCE BE-
FORE YOU CRITICIZE LESBIANS AND GAY MEN BECAUSE
OF THEIR SEXUALITY. . . . IT IS MADNESS TO GLORIFY
KILLING AND VIOLENCE ON ONE HAND AND BE
ASHAMED OF THE SEXUAL ACT, THE ACT THAT CON-
CEIVED YOU, ON THE OTHER . . .

THERE IS A DIFFERENCE BETWEEN MORALITY AND
MURDER. THE FACT IS THAT MORE PEOPLE HAVE BEEN
SLAUGHTERED IN THE NAME OF RELIGION THAN FOR

ANY OTHER SINGLE REASON. THAT, THAT, MY FRIENDS, THAT IS TRUE PERVERSION! FOR THE STANDARDS THAT WE SHOULD SET, SHOULD WE READ YOUR NEXT WEEK'S HEADLINES? . . .

WELL, I'M TIRED OF THE LIES OF THE ANITA BRYANTS AND THE JOHN BRIGGS.
I'M TIRED OF THEIR MYTHS.
I'M TIRED OF THEIR DISTORTIONS.
I'M SPEAKING OUT ABOUT IT.

GAY BROTHERS AND SISTERS, WHAT ARE YOU GOING TO DO ABOUT IT? YOU MUST COME OUT. COME OUT . . . TO YOUR PARENTS . . . I KNOW THAT IT IS HARD AND WILL HURT THEM BUT THINK ABOUT HOW THEY WILL HURT YOU IN THE VOTING BOOTH! COME OUT . . . TO YOUR RELATIVES. I KNOW THAT IS HARD AND WILL UPSET THEM BUT THINK OF HOW THEY WILL UPSET YOU IN THE VOTING BOOTH. COME OUT TO YOUR FRIENDS . . . IF THEY INDEED THEY ARE YOUR FRIENDS. COME OUT TO YOUR NEIGHBORS . . . TO YOUR FELLOW WORKERS . . . TO THE PEOPLE WHO WORK WHERE YOU EAT AND SHOP. . . . COME OUT ONLY TO THE PEOPLE YOU KNOW, AND WHO KNOW YOU. NOT TO ANYONE ELSE. BUT ONCE AND FOR ALL, BREAK DOWN THE MYTHS, DESTROY THE LIES AND DISTORTIONS.
FOR YOUR SAKE.
FOR THEIR SAKE.
FOR THE SAKE OF THE YOUNGSTERS WHO ARE BECOMING SCARED BY THE VOTES FROM DADE TO EUGENE.

IF BRIGGS WINS HE WILL NOT STOP. THEY NEVER DO. LIKE ALL MAD PEOPLE, THEY ARE FORCED TO GO ON, TO PROVE THEY WERE RIGHT!

THERE WILL BE NO SAFE "CLOSET" FOR ANY GAY PERSON.
SO BREAK OUT OF YOURS TODAY—TEAR THE DAMN THING DOWN ONCE AND FOR ALL!

AND FINALLY
MOST OF ALL

I'M TIRED OF THE SILENCE FROM THE WHITE HOUSE.

JIMMY CARTER: YOU TALKED ABOUT HUMAN RIGHTS A LOT . . . IN FACT, YOU WANT TO BE THE WORLD'S LEADER FOR HUMAN RIGHTS. WELL, DAMN IT, LEAD!!! THERE ARE SOME FIFTEEN TO TWENTY MILLION LESBIANS AND GAY MEN IN THIS NATION LISTENING AND LISTENING VERY CAREFULLY.

JIMMY CARTER: WHEN ARE YOU GOING TO TALK ABOUT THEIR RIGHTS?

YOU TALK A LOT ABOUT THE BIBLE. . . . BUT WHEN ARE YOU GOING TO TALK ABOUT THAT MOST IMPORTANT PART: "LOVE THY NEIGHBOR?" AFTER ALL, SHE MAY BE GAY.

JIMMY CARTER: THE TIME HAS COME FOR LESBIANS AND GAY MEN TO COME OUT—AND THEY ARE. NOW THE TIME HAS COME FOR YOU TO SPEAK OUT. WHEN ARE YOU?

UNTIL YOU SPEAK OUT AGAINST HATRED, BIGOTRY, MADNESS, YOU ARE JUST JIMMY CARTER. WHEN YOU DO, THEN AND ONLY THEN, WILL SOME TWENTY MILLION LESBIANS AND GAY MEN BE ABLE TO SAY JIMMY CARTER IS OUR PRESIDENT, TOO!

JIMMY CARTER, YOU HAVE THE CHOICE: HOW MANY MORE YEARS?

HOW MUCH MORE DAMAGE?
HOW MUCH MORE VIOLENCE?
HOW MANY MORE LIVES?

HISTORY SAYS THAT, LIKE ALL GROUPS SEEKING THEIR RIGHTS, SOONER OR LATER WE WILL WIN.

THE QUESTION IS: WHEN?

JIMMY CARTER, YOU HAVE TO MAKE THE CHOICE— IT'S IN YOUR HANDS: EITHER YEARS OF VIOLENCE . . . OR

YOU CAN HELP TURN THE PAGES OF HISTORY THAT MUCH FASTER.

IT IS UP TO YOU. AND NOW, BEFORE IT BECOMES TOO LATE, COME TO CALIFORNIA AND SPEAK OUT AGAINST BRIGGS. . . .
IF YOU DON'T—THEN WE WILL COME TO YOU!!!
IF YOU DO NOT SPEAK OUT, IF YOU REMAIN SILENT, IF YOU DO NOT LIFT YOUR VOICE AGAINST BRIGGS, THEN I CALL UPON LESBIANS AND GAY MEN FROM ALL OVER THE NATION . . . YOUR NATION . . . TO GATHER IN WASHINGTON . . . ONE YEAR FROM NOW . . . ON THAT NATIONAL DAY OF FREEDOM, THE FOURTH OF JULY . . . THE FOURTH OF JULY, 1979 . . . TO GATHER IN WASHINGTON ON THAT VERY SAME SPOT WHERE OVER A DECADE AGO DR. MARTIN LUTHER KING SPOKE TO A NATION OF HIS DREAMS . . . DREAMS THAT ARE FAST FADING, DREAMS THAT TO MANY MILLIONS IN THIS NATION HAVE BECOME NIGHTMARES RATHER THAN DREAMS. . . .

I CALL UPON ALL MINORITIES AND ESPECIALLY THE MILLIONS OF LESBIANS AND GAY MEN TO WAKE UP FROM THEIR DREAMS. . . . TO GATHER ON WASHINGTON AND TELL JIMMY CARTER AND THEIR NATION: "WAKE UP . . . WAKE UP, AMERICA . . . NO MORE RACISM, NO MORE SEXISM, NO MORE AGEISM, NO MORE HATRED . . . NO MORE!"

IT'S UP TO YOU, JIMMY CARTER. . . . DO YOU WANT TO GO DOWN IN HISTORY AS A PERSON WHO WOULD NOT LISTEN . . . OR DO YOU WANT TO GO DOWN IN HISTORY AS A LEADER, AS A PRESIDENT?

JIMMY CARTER: LISTEN TO US TODAY . . . OR YOU WILL HAVE TO LISTEN TO LESBIANS AND GAY MEN FROM ALL OVER THIS NATION AS THEY GATHER IN WASHINGTON NEXT YEAR. . . .

FOR WE WILL GATHER THERE AND WE WILL TELL YOU ABOUT AMERICA AND WHAT IT REALLY STANDS FOR. . . .

AND TO THE BIGOTS . . . TO THE JOHN BRIGGS . . . TO THE ANITA BRYANTS . . . TO THE KEVIN STARRS AND ALL THEIR ILK. . . . LET ME REMIND YOU WHAT AMERICA IS . . . LISTEN CAREFULLY:

ON THE STATUE OF LIBERTY IT SAYS: "GIVE ME YOUR TIRED, YOUR POOR, YOUR HUDDLED MASSES YEARNING TO BE FREE. . . ." IN THE DECLARATION OF INDEPENDENCE IT IS WRITTEN: "ALL MEN ARE CREATED EQUAL AND THEY ARE ENDOWED WITH CERTAIN INALIENABLE RIGHTS. . . ." AND IN OUR NATIONAL ANTHEM IT SAYS: "OH, SAY DOES THAT STAR-SPANGLED BANNER YET WAVE O'ER THE LAND OF THE FREE."

FOR MR. BRIGGS AND MRS. BRYANT AND MR. STARR AND ALL THE BIGOTS OUT THERE: THAT'S WHAT AMERICA IS. NO MATTER HOW HARD YOU TRY, YOU CANNOT ERASE THOSE WORDS FROM THE DECLARATION OF INDEPENDENCE. NO MATTER HOW HARD YOU TRY, YOU CANNOT CHIP THOSE WORDS FROM OFF THE BASE OF THE STATUE OF LIBERTY. AND NO MATTER HOW HARD YOU CANNOT SING THE "STAR SPANGLED BANNER" WITHOUT THOSE WORDS.

THAT'S WHAT AMERICA IS.

LOVE IT OR LEAVE IT.

V. Harvey Milk's Political Will

Haunted for years by forebodings that he would fall victim to political assassination, Harvey Milk recorded three tapes to serve as his political will. One was left with his personal attorney John Wahl, one with his close friend Frank Robinson, and another with his friend and political associate, Walter Caplan. Milk spoke only from a bare-bones outline when he recorded the tapes, so all three have variations in specifics. Only Frank Robinson's tape has the passage which was widely quoted after Milk's assassination: "If a bullet should enter my brain, let that bullet destroy every closet door." Only on Walter Caplan's tape is a fifth name, that of former SIR President Doug DeYoung, added to the so-called enemies list of people Milk considered unsuitable to succeed him. Those who have heard all three tapes generally consider Caplan's to be the best-worded of the testaments. This is a complete transcript of that tape:

This is Harvey Milk speaking on Friday November 18. This is tape two. This is to be played only in the event of my death by assassination. I've given long and considerable thought to this, not just since the election. I've been thinking about this for some time prior to the election and certainly over the years. I fully realize that a person who stands for what I stand for—a gay activist—becomes the target or potential target for a person who is insecure, terrified, afraid or very disturbed themselves. Knowing that I could be assassinated at any moment or any time, I feel it's important that some people should understand my thoughts. So the following are my thoughts, my wishes, my desires, whatever. I'd like to pass them on and played for the appropriate people. The first and most obvious concern is that if I was to be shot and killed, the mayor has the power, George Moscone's, of appointing my successor to the Board of Supervisors. I know there will be great pressures on him from various factions, so I'd like to let him know what my thoughts are.

I stood for more than just a candidate. I think there was a strong differential between somebody like Rick Stokes and myself. I have never considered myself a candidate. I have always considered myself part of a movement, part of a candidacy. I've considered the movement the candidate. I think there's a delineation between those who use the movement and those are who part of the movement. I think I was always part of the movement. And I think that. I wish I had time to explain almost everything I did. Almost everything that was done was done with an eye on the gay movement.

I would suggest and urge and hope that the mayor would understand that distinction and that he would appoint somebody to my position who also came from the movement rather than used the movement or never understood the movement. I think those people who actively opposed me—the Jim Fosters, Rick Stokes, Jo Dalys, Doug DeYoungs—those people never understood the movement. I'm not saying they're against it. They just never understood it. They used it. Maybe willingly, maybe unwillingly, but they never understood what it was about. I think those who remained in silence—the Frank Fitches, not wishing to play sides—never understood the movement, that silence is sometimes worse than speaking out. I would hope that the mayor would understand that appointing somebody who actively opposed me or subtly opposed me or kept quiet, stuck their head in the sand, would be an insult to everything I stood for, would be an affront to the campaigns and the people who worked.

I would hope he would give consideration, strong consideration, only to people who came from the movement. I've talked to several people and they know my thoughts, so I put them on tape so there's no doubt in anybody's mind about my thoughts. There are some people I definitely have in mind who I would like the mayor to consider.

The first person I would have is a gentleman by the name of Frank Robinson who is quite an author in his own right. Frank even more so knows my thought processes. Not only has he read everything I've written and helped re-write the major pieces, but Frank is the one who almost daily we had conversations on various points of thinking and philosophies. So he knows my thoughts as well. He understands how I arrived at the decisions and he played devil's advocate time and time again. So if there's anyone who knows me from the depth of the intellect and the emotions, it's Frank Robinson and I think being who he is, he has that incredible ability to express himself clearly and concisely and if there were any problems, he would be able to carry on the philosophy and idea of what I stood for.

If there's some reason Frank is not the choice, the next consideration I would hope the mayor would give would be to Bob Ross. Bob has read everything I've written in the past four years and also has carried on extensive dealings with me and also has the ability to get along with a lot more people than I can, which is also going to be needed. And Bob is a strong person that will not bend and that's vital. You cannot have a weak person—the Rick Stokes types, the professional lawyers. The first few gay people must be strong. That doesn't mean obstinate or uncompromising, but they must be strong.

The third choice would be Harry Britt, who most people don't know. But I've watched Harry and Harry's been involved with three campaigns. He knows where I am. I've watched Harry grow and grow and grow and become more articulate. Some people may find him wrong because he is somewhat emotional, but by God, what fabulous emotions! And he's a very, very dedicated and strong person and will not be pushed around. One that understands what the movement is and where it must go. Some day it will be there anyhow.

A fourth possibility is a person who is younger, newer and learning every day. It's the woman who put my campaign together. Anne Kronenberg who is strong. Who understands and learns fast and thinks fast. And would add a spirit, being a gay woman, that the others cannot add. And I think that would be an outstanding choice.

And I hope the mayor would understand that in cases like this, the tradition has been to replace a person who has been assassinated with someone who is close to the candidate in thought, rather than somebody who actively or quietly opposed the candidate. And it's important that it happens. I cannot urge the mayor strongly enough to hear what I'm saying. I think that if he did that, he would be gaining a tremendous amount of support.

The other aspect of the tapes is the obvious of what would happen should there be an assassination. I cannot prevent some people from feeling angry and frustrated and mad, but I hope they will take that frustration and that madness instead of demonstrating or anything of that type, I would hope that they would take the power and I would hope that five, ten, one hundred, a thousand would rise. I would like to see every gay lawyer, every gay architect come out, stand up and let the world know. That would do more to end prejudice overnight than anybody could imagine. I urge them to do that, urge them to come out. Only that way will we start to achieve our rights.

I hope there are no religious services. I would hope there are no services of any type, but I know some people are into that and you can't prevent it from happening, but, my God, nothing religious. Until the churches speak out against the Anita Bryants who have been playing gymnastics with the Bible, the churches which remain so quiet have the guts to speak out in the name of Judaism or Christianity or whatever they profess to be for in words but not actions and deeds. God—and that's the irony. God—churches don't even know what it's about. I would turn over in my grave if there was any kind of religious ceremony. And it's not a disbelief in God—it's a disbelief and disgust of what most churches are about. How many leaders got up in their pulpits and went to Miami and said, "Anita, you're playing gymnastics with the Bible—you're desecrating the Bible"? How many of them said it? How many of them hid and walked away? Ducked their heads in the name of Christianity and talked about love and brotherhood.

No services whatsoever. If anything, play that tape of Briggs and I, which is somewhere in the cabinet in the back—the file cabinet. Just play that tape of Briggs and I over and over again so people can know what an evil man he is. So people know what our Hitler is like. So people know that where the ideas of hate come from. So they know what the future will bring if they're not careful.

And that's all I ask. That's all. I ask for the movement to continue, for the movement to grow because last week, I got the phone call from Altoona, Pennsylvania and my election gave somebody else, one more person, hope. And after all it's what this is all about. It's not about personal gain, not about ego, not about power—it's about giving those young people out there in the Altoona, Pennsylvania's hope. You gotta give them hope.

Notes on Sources

The following institutions helped in various aspects of the research: Woodmere Public Library, Bayshore High School, California Historical Society, San Francisco History Room of the San Francisco Public Library, Bache & Company, the alumni office of the State University of New York–Albany and the Harvey Milk Archives.

Harvey Milk's Early Years (1930–1956): Much of the information about Harvey's childhood came from memories he shared with his lovers Scott Smith, Doug Franks, and Joe Campbell, as well as from a taped discussion he conducted at Napa State University in June 1974. Robert Milk discussed his parents shortly after Harvey Milk's assassination, but later declined a detailed interview unless he was compensated, a condition that violates standard journalistic ethics and was therefore unacceptable. The information about the German gay movement came from *The Early Homosexual Rights Movement (1864–1935)* by David Thorstad and John Lauritsen. Eileen Mulcahy, Dick Brown, and Clifton LaPlatney recalled much about Harvey's high school years. The names of Harvey's two classmates, Bob and Willy, were changed for legal reasons; these are the only names in the book, however, that were altered. Harvey Milk's Albany State alumni Chris Lievestro, Paul Buchman, Max Fallek, Arlene Struhmeyer, and Howard and Doris Rosman discussed Harvey's college years.

Harvey Milk's Manhattan Years (1956–1972): Among Harvey's friends who shared their memories about this period in Milk's life were Joe Campbell, Tom O'Horgan, author Eve Merriam, Elmer Kline, Craig Rodwell, Jim Bruton, Ellen Steuart, Tom Eure, Joe Turner, and Scott Smith. Oliver "Billy" Sipple was contacted through his attorney and declined to be interviewed. Jack Galen McKinley had commited suicide by the time primary research began on this book. Bache and Company provided Harvey's personnel file and helped me contact Charles Mor-

376

gan, Monty Gordon, and George McGeough, Milk's colleagues at the firm.

Early San Francisco Gay History: Allan Berube of the San Francisco Gay History Project provided the bulk of the information on the impact of World War II on the San Francisco gay community. Among other people interviewed about San Francisco gay history were the late Terry Mangan of the California Historical Society; Jose Sarria; Del Martin and Phyllis Lyon, founders of the Daughters of Bilitis; Pat Bond; Dorr Jones, Steve Kellogg and Hal Cal, former presidents of the San Francisco Mattachine Society; Bill May and Larry Littlejohn, early leaders of the Society for Individual Rights; Charles Morris, publisher of *The Sentinel;* Bob Ross, publisher of the *Bay Area Reporter.* Much of the information on gay life in the 1930s and 1940s came from *Bay Area Reporter* columns written by the late Lou Rand.

Harvey Milk's Navy Career: Determining the truth about Harvey Milk's career in the navy proved the most difficult aspect of this book. On one hand, he freely spread the story that he had been dishonorably discharged. No one who knew Milk before his political career, however, could remember Milk commenting about anything to do with a discharge. Finally, Anne Kronenberg recalled a conversation in which Milk offhandedly mentioned he had made up the story to get votes. Tom Randol also remembered coming across an honorable discharge certificate among Milk's effects after the assassination. The particulars of Milk's ranks came from his 1963 job application with Bache.

San Francisco Gay Politics (1973–1978): Jim Foster, Jo Daly, Rick Stokes, and Frank Fitch, all past presidents of the Alice B. Toklas Memorial Democratic Club; Elmer Wilhelm, past president, Stonewall Democratic Club; Bill Kraus, Chris Perry, Harry Britt, and Gwenn Craig, past presidents of the San Francisco Gay—now the Harvey Milk Gay—Democratic Club. Les Morgan, George Raya, Ken Maley, Mark Feldman, and Jack Davis also discussed various aspects of this period with me. David B. Goodstein declined to be interviewed.

San Francisco City Politics: A number of politicians took time to discuss their analyses of the changing San Francisco politics of the 1970s for this book. Among the politicos who agreed to be interviewed on the record were Mayor Dianne Feinstein, District Attorney Arlo Smith,

Assemblyman Art Agnos, State Senator Milton Marks, Board of Supervisors President John Molinari, Supervisors Harry Britt, Carol Ruth Silver, and Richard Hongisto, and former Supervisor Gordon Lau.

Harvey Milk's Campaigns (1973–1977): Michael Wong, Dennis Peron, Tom Randol, Arlo Smith, Rick Nicholls, Medora Payne, John Ryckman, Dick Pabich, Jim Rivaldo, Anne Kronenberg, Wayne Friday, Bob Ross, Walter Caplan, Hank Wilson, Ann Eliaser, and Bill and Tory Hartmann all discussed their roles in Harvey's various campaigns. Among the organized labor leaders interviewed about their support of Milk's campaigns were Stan Smith of the Building and Construction Trades Council, Leon Broschura of the Firefighters Union, George Evankovich of the Laborer's Union, Teamster Allan Baird and Jim Elliot of the Automotive Machinists.

Harvey Milk's Personal Life (1973–1978): Scott Smith provided the bulk of this information with former Castro Camera employees Danny Nicoletta and Ken Denning and Harvey's friends Frank Robinson, Hector Cacares, Carl Carlson, Tom Randol, Rick Nicholls, Dennis Seely, Ric Puglia, Don Amador, Tony Karnes, and Milk's personal lawyer, John Wahl. Jack Lira had committed suicide by the time research on this book began. Doug Franks, Bob Tuttle, and Bill Wiegardt also candidly discussed their relationships with Harvey.

Michael Wong's Diary: Many of the dialogues recreated in the book come from Michael Wong's diary. Virtually all the figures mentioned in Wong's meticulous recording of his experiences with Harvey Milk have corroborated the journal's accuracy.

Castro Street: The information on the history of the Castro neighborhood was drawn from nearly one hundred interviews I have conducted on the area over the years, especially with older Castro residents. Particularly helpful in the primary research for this project, however, were Allan Baird, Rick Slick, Cleve Jones, Steve Lowell, and two past presidents of the Castro Village Association, Ernie Astin and Donn Tatum. The stories about the outbreaks of police brutality in the Castro during 1974 and 1979 came largely from news accounts in the *Bay Area Reporter* and *The Sentinel.*

Fundamentalists: The information and analysis of the fundamentalist movement in the late 1970s is drawn largely from my own travels through Dade County, Wichita, St. Paul, and California during the various gay-rights controversies of that period. All the statements from the ministers and born-again Christians quoted come from this research. The archetypal fundamentalist profiled in Chapter 13, Pat of Central Pomona Baptist Church, was the subject of a television special I produced and anchored in 1978 on the emerging political clout of fundamentalists for KQED-TV. Because the interview was granted for purposes of the television documentary and since she would object to having her name in a book about a major gay figure, I did not use Pat's full name in this account.

Harvey Milk, The Clown: The paragraphs from *Letting Their Clowns Out* by Ira Kamin, which appeared in the August 20, 1978 issue of *California Living Magazine* of the *San Francisco Sunday Examiner and Chronicle,* copyright © 1978 by the *San Francisco Examiner,* are excerpted with permission.

The Hillsborough Murder: The background information on John Cordova, murderer of Robert Hillsborough, came in part from a team investigation conducted for *New West* magazine by Francis Moriarty, Nora Gallagher and Randy Shilts.

Background Information on Dan White: The information concerning Dan White's life was drawn largely from the trial transcript, the probation report drawn up by the California Adult Authority for use in his sentencing, and interviews with *Chronicle* reporters Warren Hinckle and Maitland Zaine. Details of the FBI investigation of White came from files from the Federal Bureau of Investigation obtained under provisions of the Freedom of Information Act.

The Trial: Neither Dan White nor his attorney Doug Schmidt responded to interview requests. Prosecuting attorney Tom Norman initially indicated he would be interviewed for this book. He never made himself available for an interview, however, despite repeated attempts to contact him. Many of the details are drawn from contemporary news accounts.

The Assassinations: The killings were reconstructed from information contained in the Dan White trial transcript and photographs presented as exhibits at the trial. The anatomical aspects of the assassination were verified with a forensic pathologist. The account did not include the sketchy details offered by Dan White during his taped confession, since that statement contains various contradictions which make its truthfulness doubtful.

City Hall: Bill Roddy, former director of the Mayor's Visitors Assistance Bureau, and Gladys Hanson of the library's San Francisco History Room helped in my research on City Hall.

Journalists: A number of reporters shared their experiences and memories with me, providing a wealth of background material that made this account much richer. They included *Chronicle* staffers Jerry Burns, Jerry Roberts, Maitland Zane, and Warren Hinckle, *Examiner* reporter Jim Wood, *Bay Area Reporter* editor Paul Lorch and free-lance journalists Francis Moriarty, David Israels, and Mike Weiss.

The following people and news organizations gave me access to video- and audiotapes of Harvey Milk: KQED-TV, KTVU-TV, Jack Davis, Paul Bentley, Tom Randol, Elmer Wilhelm, George Osterkamp, Walter Caplan, and N.A. Diaman of the Queer Blue Light Collective.

Index